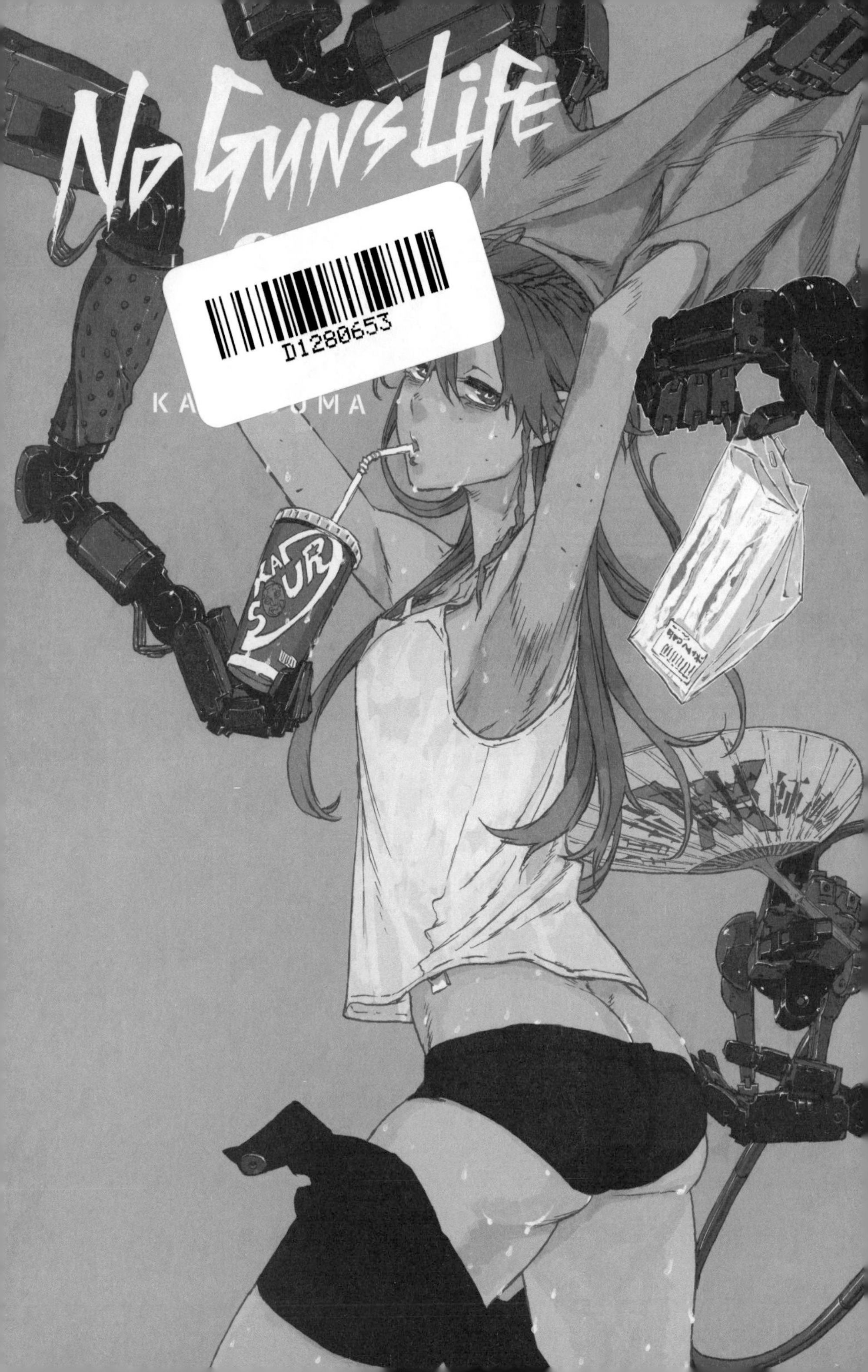
No Guns Life

CONTENTS

NO GUNS LIFE

... FUNNN!
CHNNG

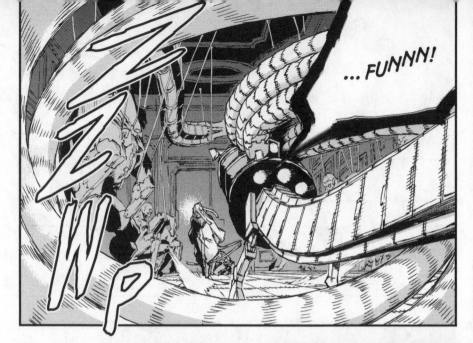

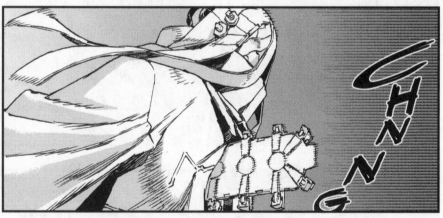

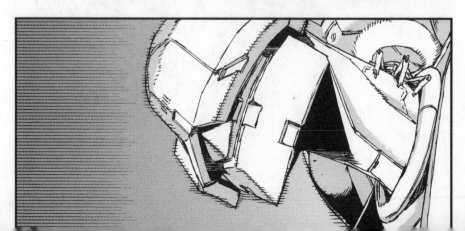

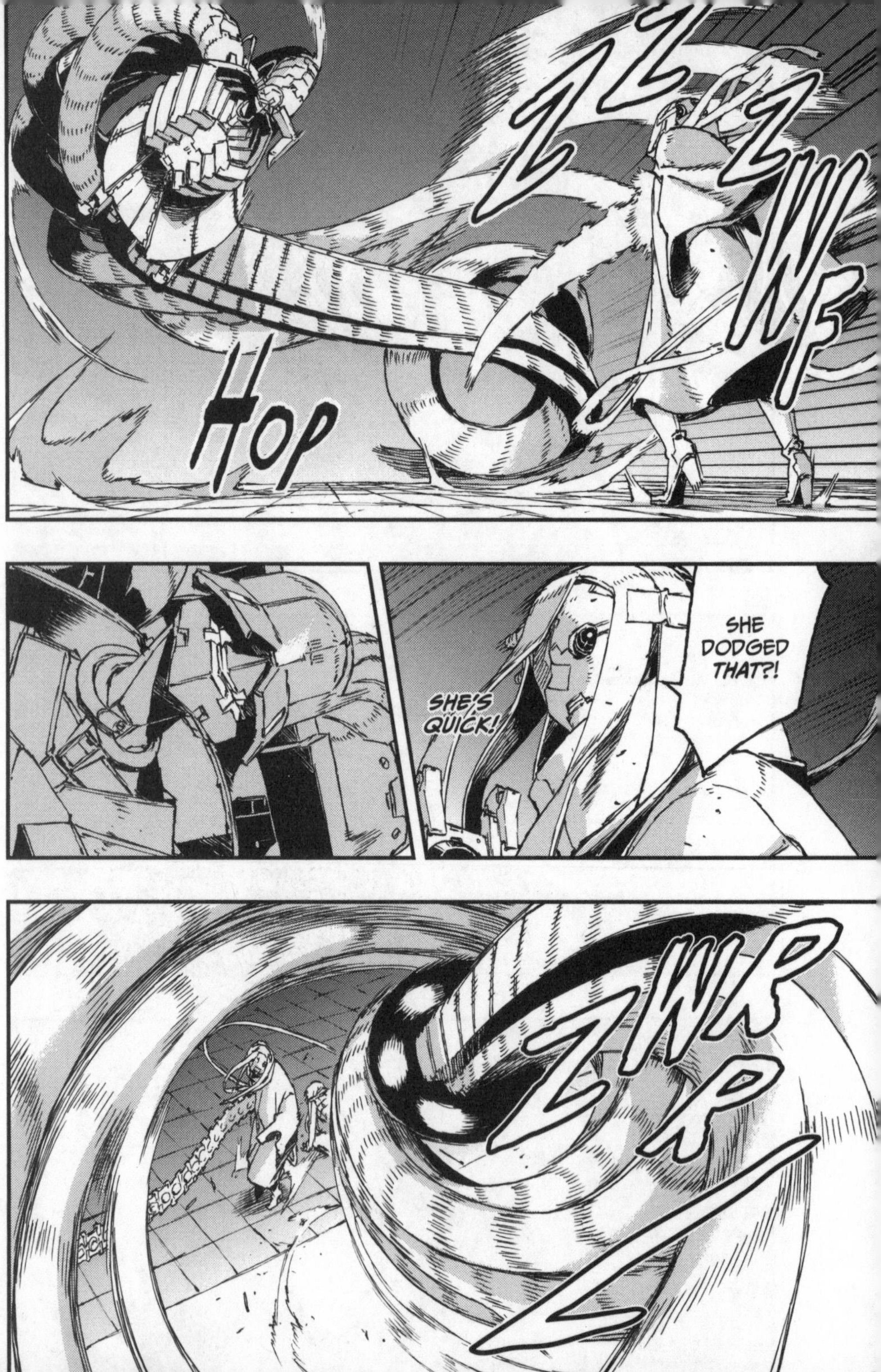
ZZZWF
HOP
SHE DODGED THAT?!
SHE'S QUICK!
ZWIP
ZIP

Chapter 51
Engineer

SKWK KCH
PTOK

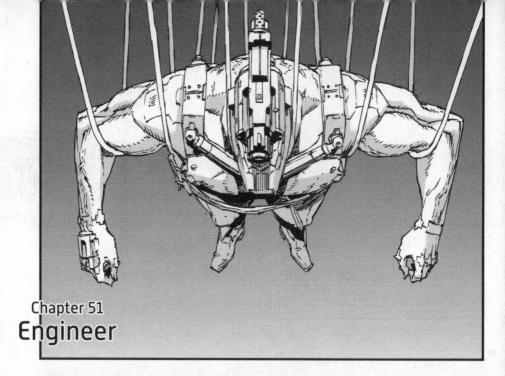

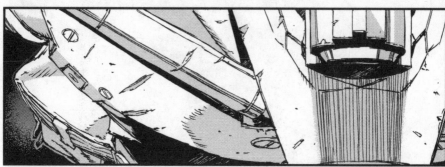

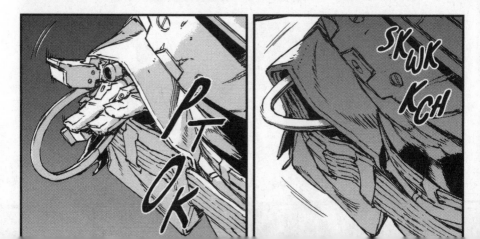

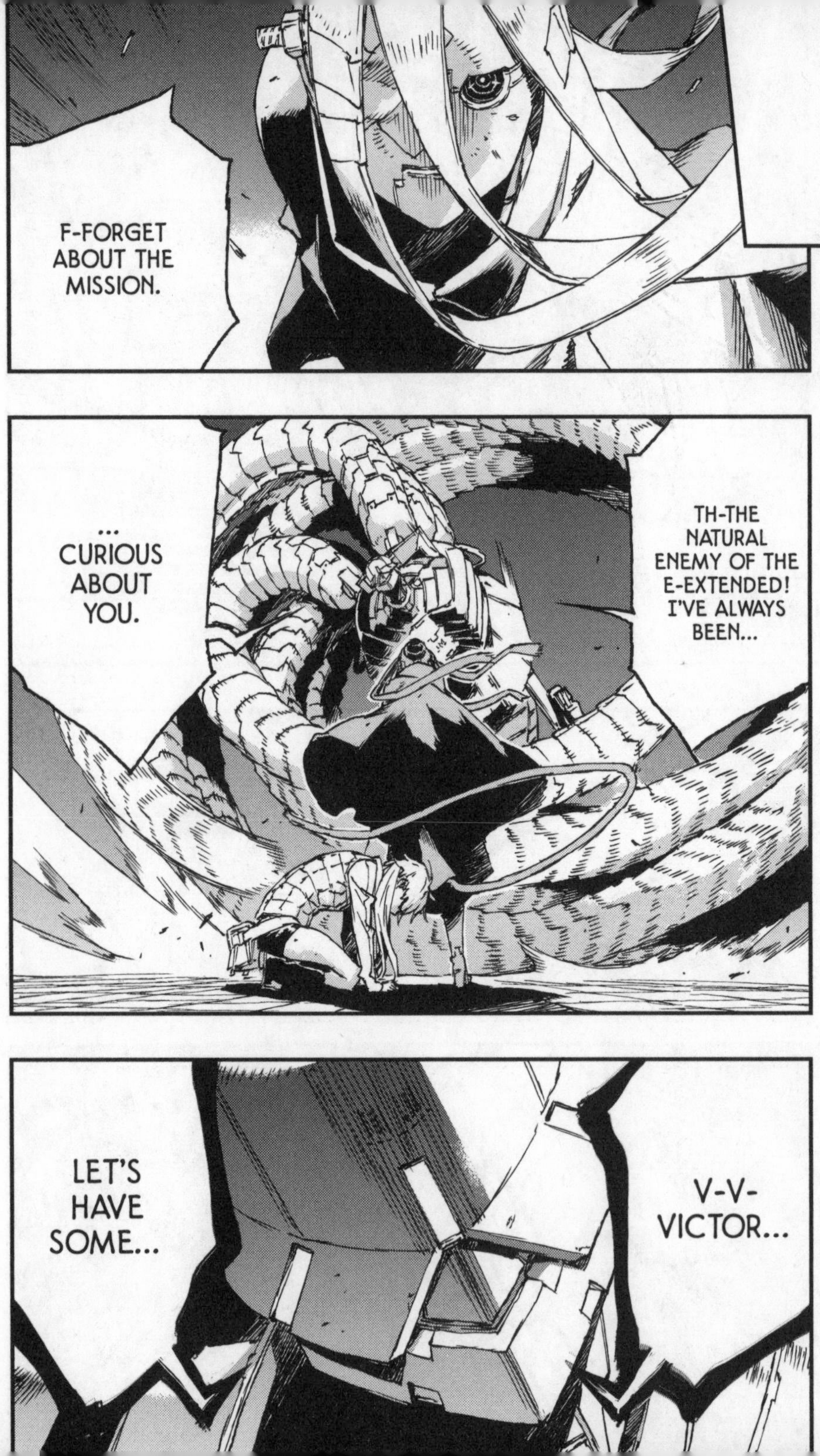
F-FORGET ABOUT THE MISSION.
TH-THE NATURAL ENEMY OF THE E-EXTENDED! I'VE ALWAYS BEEN...
...CURIOUS ABOUT YOU.
V-V-VICTOR...
LET'S HAVE SOME...

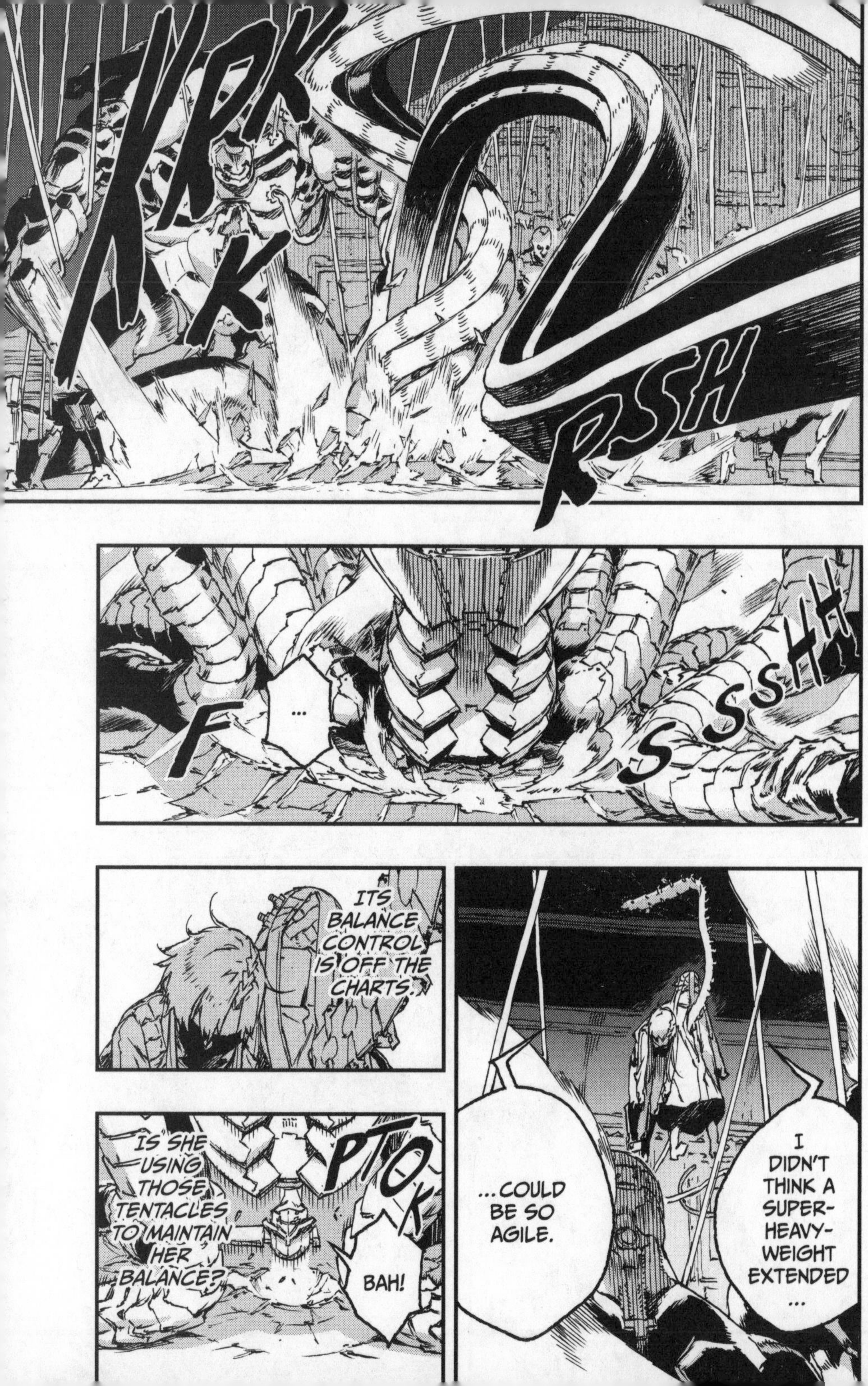

RSH
...
FSSSHH
I DIDN'T THINK A SUPER-HEAVYWEIGHT EXTENDED ...
...COULD BE SO AGILE.
ITS BALANCE CONTROL IS OFF THE CHARTS.
PTOK
IS SHE USING THOSE TENTACLES TO MAINTAIN HER BALANCE?
BAH!

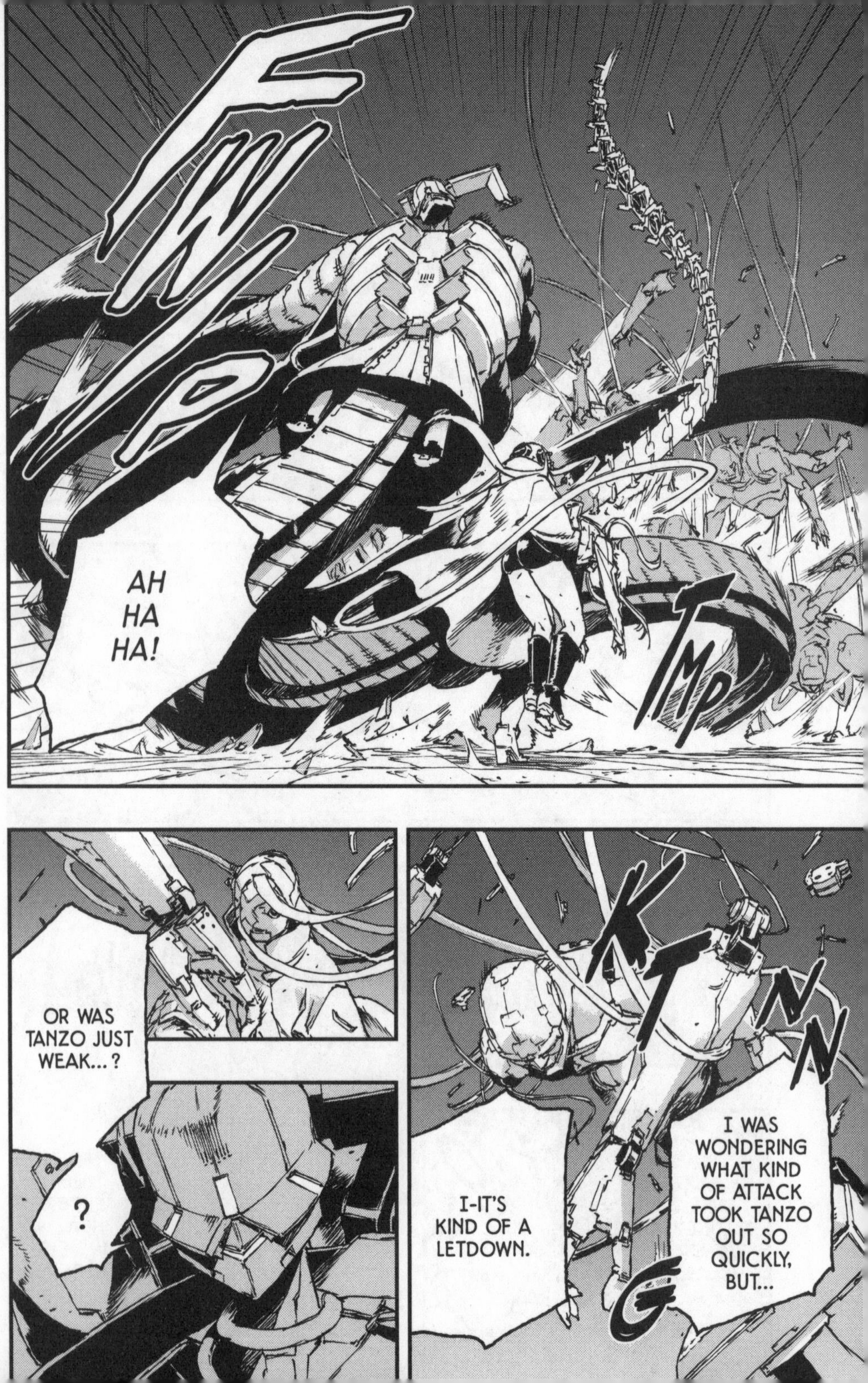
FWIP
AH HA HA!
TMP
KTNNN
I WAS WONDERING WHAT KIND OF ATTACK TOOK TANZO OUT SO QUICKLY, BUT...
I-IT'S KIND OF A LETDOWN.
G
OR WAS TANZO JUST WEAK...?
?

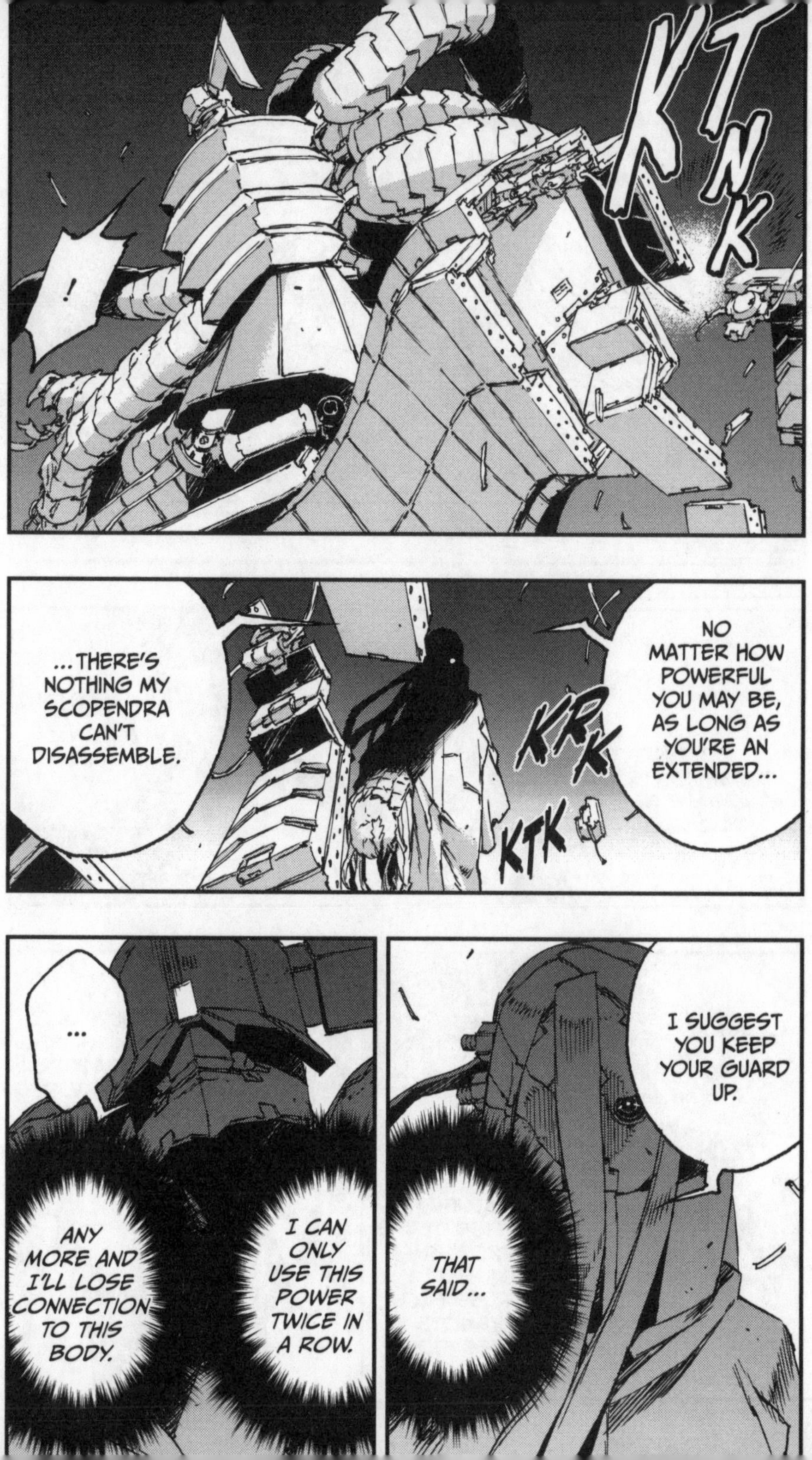
KTNK
...!
NO MATTER HOW POWERFUL YOU MAY BE, AS LONG AS YOU'RE AN EXTENDED...
KRK
KTK
...THERE'S NOTHING MY SCOPENDRA CAN'T DISASSEMBLE.
I SUGGEST YOU KEEP YOUR GUARD UP.
THAT SAID...
...
I CAN ONLY USE THIS POWER TWICE IN A ROW.
ANY MORE AND I'LL LOSE CONNECTION TO THIS BODY.

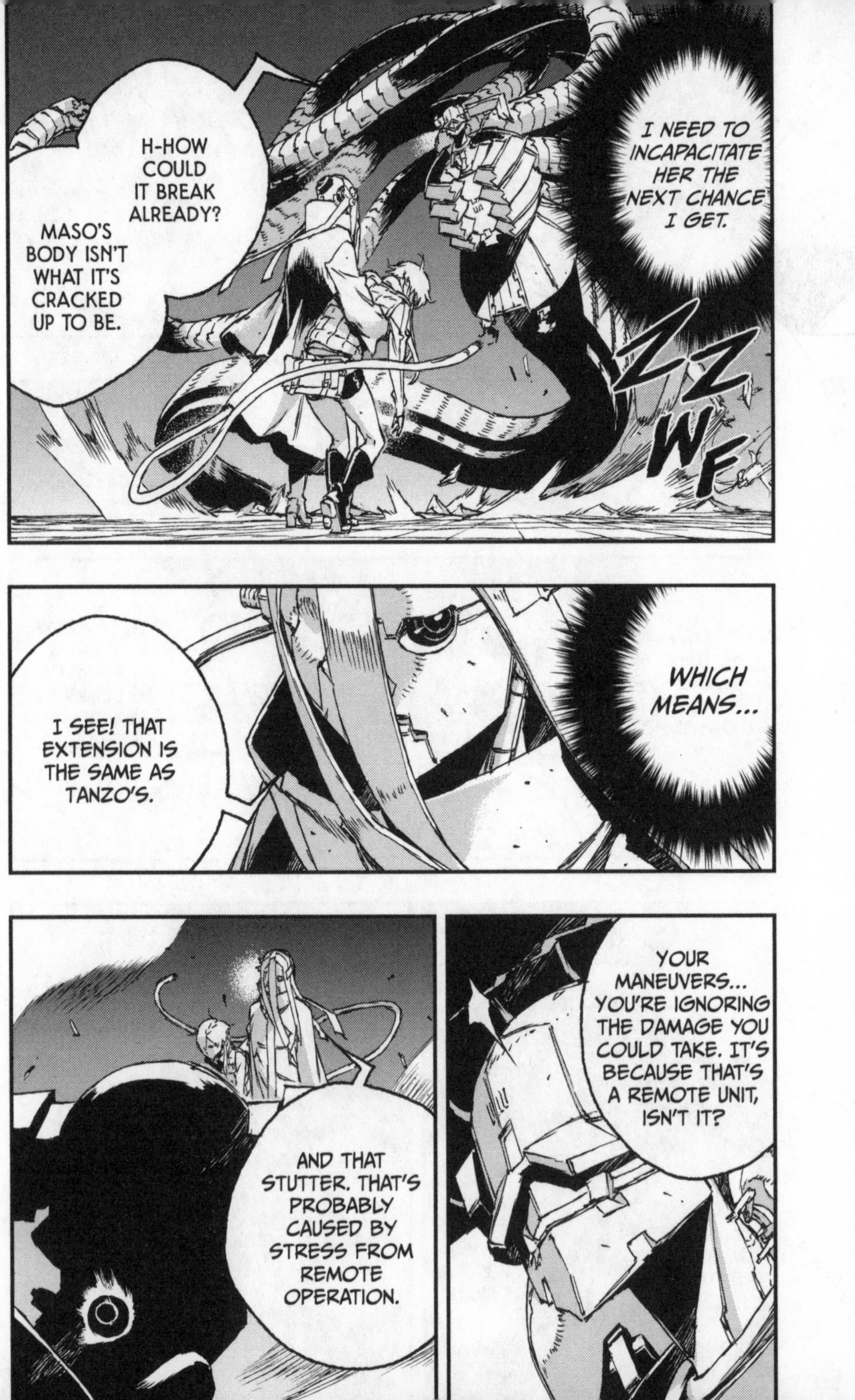
I NEED TO INCAPACITATE HER THE NEXT CHANCE I GET.
ZZWF
H-HOW COULD IT BREAK ALREADY?
MASO'S BODY ISN'T WHAT IT'S CRACKED UP TO BE.
WHICH MEANS...
I SEE! THAT EXTENSION IS THE SAME AS TANZO'S.
YOUR MANEUVERS... YOU'RE IGNORING THE DAMAGE YOU COULD TAKE. IT'S BECAUSE THAT'S A REMOTE UNIT, ISN'T IT?
AND THAT STUTTER. THAT'S PROBABLY CAUSED BY STRESS FROM REMOTE OPERATION.

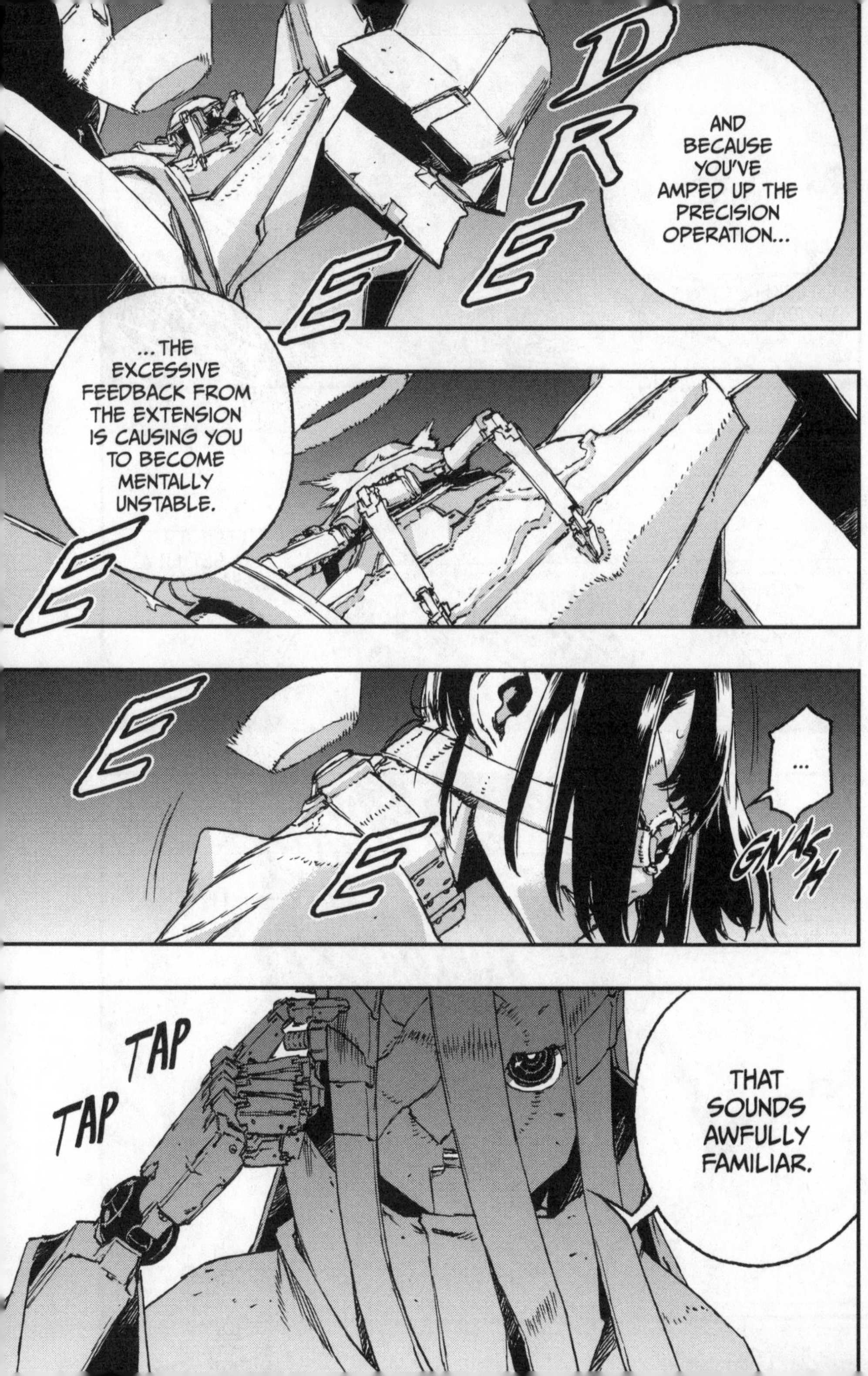
AND BECAUSE YOU'VE AMPED UP THE PRECISION OPERATION...
DREE
...THE EXCESSIVE FEEDBACK FROM THE EXTENSION IS CAUSING YOU TO BECOME MENTALLY UNSTABLE.
E
...
GNASH
EE
THAT SOUNDS AWFULLY FAMILIAR.
TAP
TAP

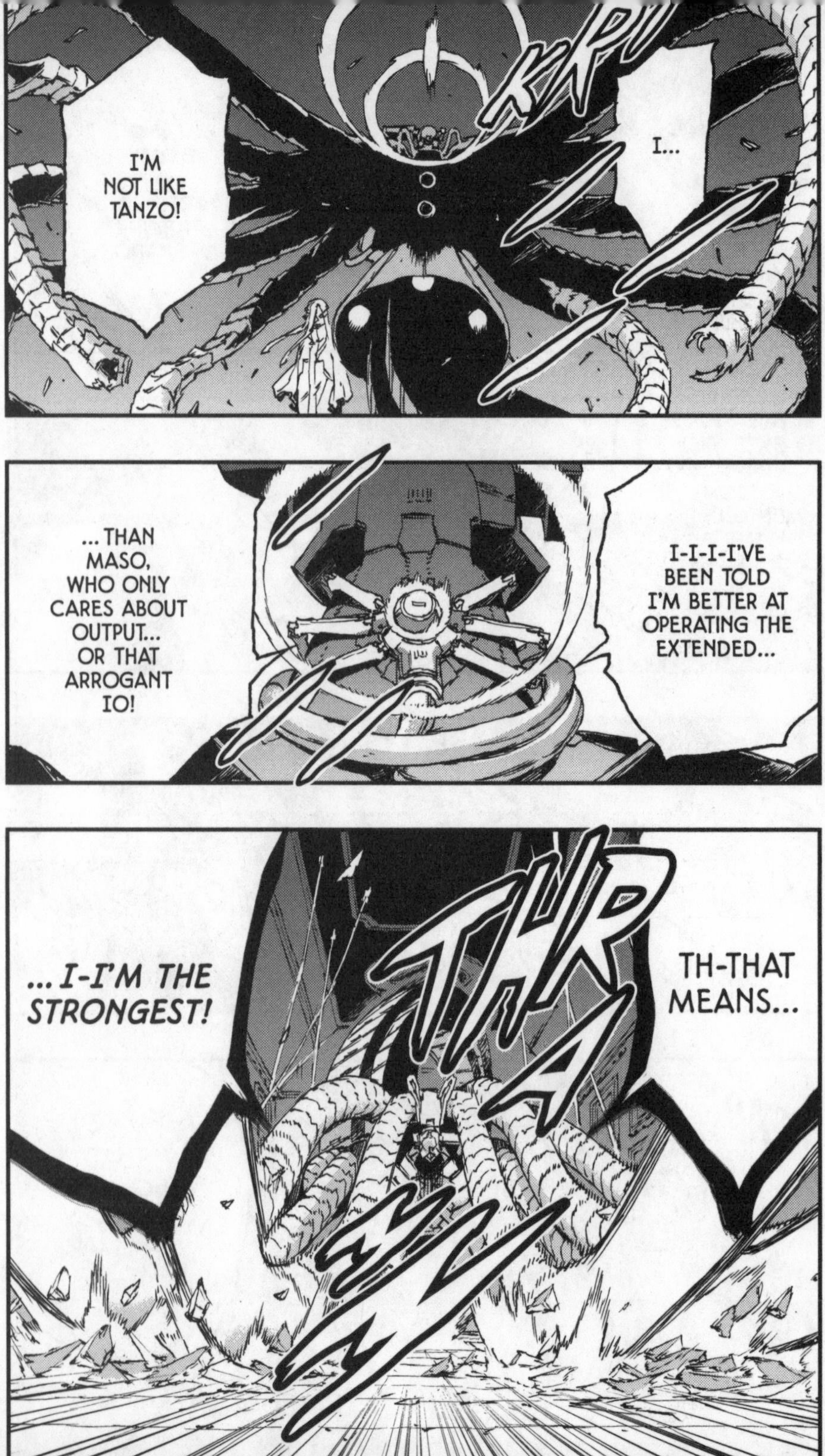
I...
I'M NOT LIKE TANZO!
I-I-I-I'VE BEEN TOLD I'M BETTER AT OPERATING THE EXTENDED...
...THAN MASO, WHO ONLY CARES ABOUT OUTPUT... OR THAT ARROGANT IO!
TH-THAT MEANS...
...*I-I'M THE STRONGEST!*

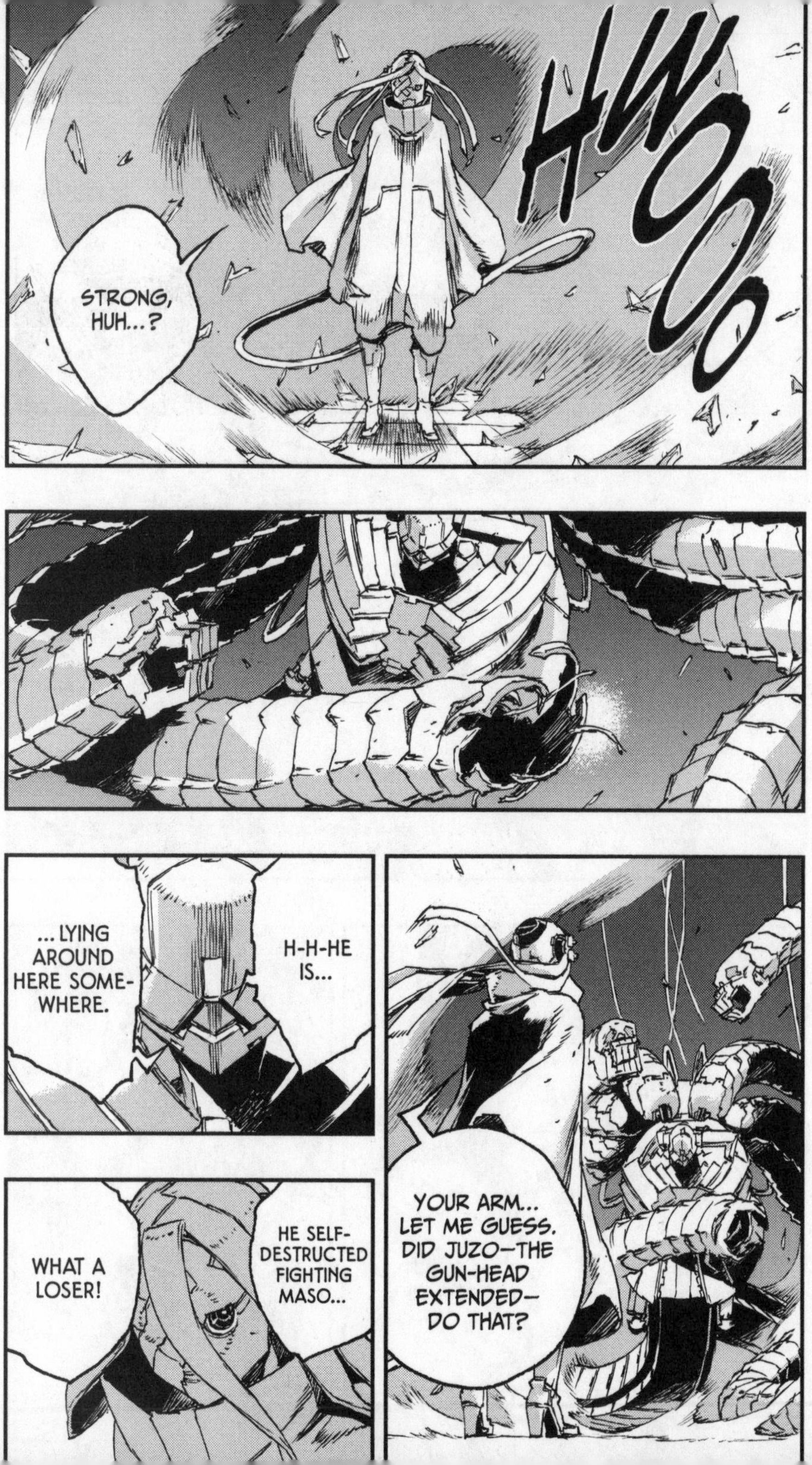
HWOOO
STRONG, HUH...?
YOUR ARM... LET ME GUESS. DID JUZO—THE GUN-HEAD EXTENDED—DO THAT?
H-H-HE IS...
...LYING AROUND HERE SOME-WHERE.
HE SELF-DESTRUCTED FIGHTING MASO...
WHAT A LOSER!

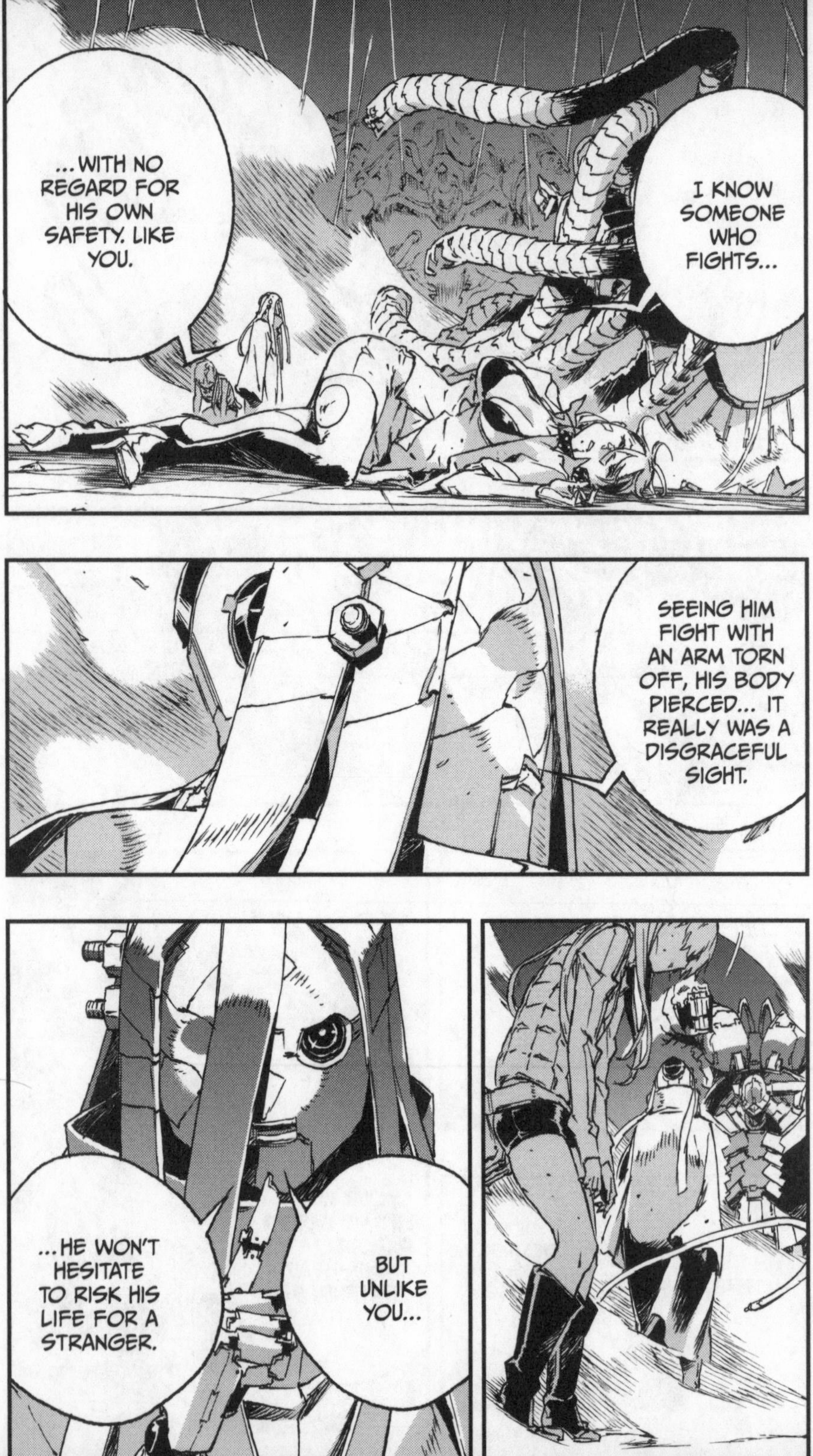
I KNOW SOMEONE WHO FIGHTS...
...WITH NO REGARD FOR HIS OWN SAFETY. LIKE YOU.
SEEING HIM FIGHT WITH AN ARM TORN OFF, HIS BODY PIERCED... IT REALLY WAS A DISGRACEFUL SIGHT.
BUT UNLIKE YOU...
...HE WON'T HESITATE TO RISK HIS LIFE FOR A STRANGER.

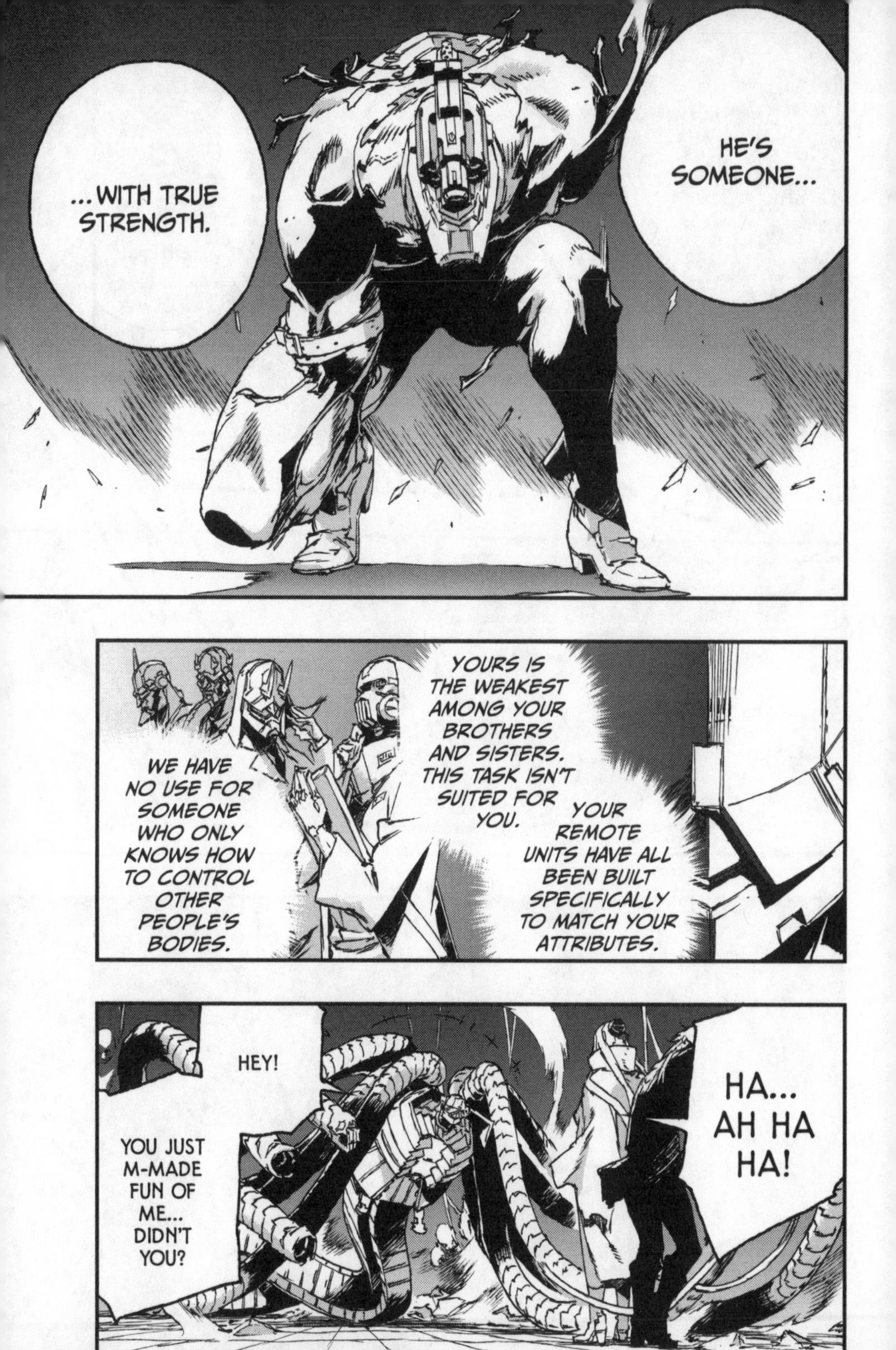
HE'S SOMEONE...
...WITH TRUE STRENGTH.
YOUR REMOTE UNITS HAVE ALL BEEN BUILT SPECIFICALLY TO MATCH YOUR ATTRIBUTES.
YOURS IS THE WEAKEST AMONG YOUR BROTHERS AND SISTERS. THIS TASK ISN'T SUITED FOR YOU.
WE HAVE NO USE FOR SOMEONE WHO ONLY KNOWS HOW TO CONTROL OTHER PEOPLE'S BODIES.
HA... AH HA HA!
HEY!
YOU JUST M-MADE FUN OF ME... DIDN'T YOU?

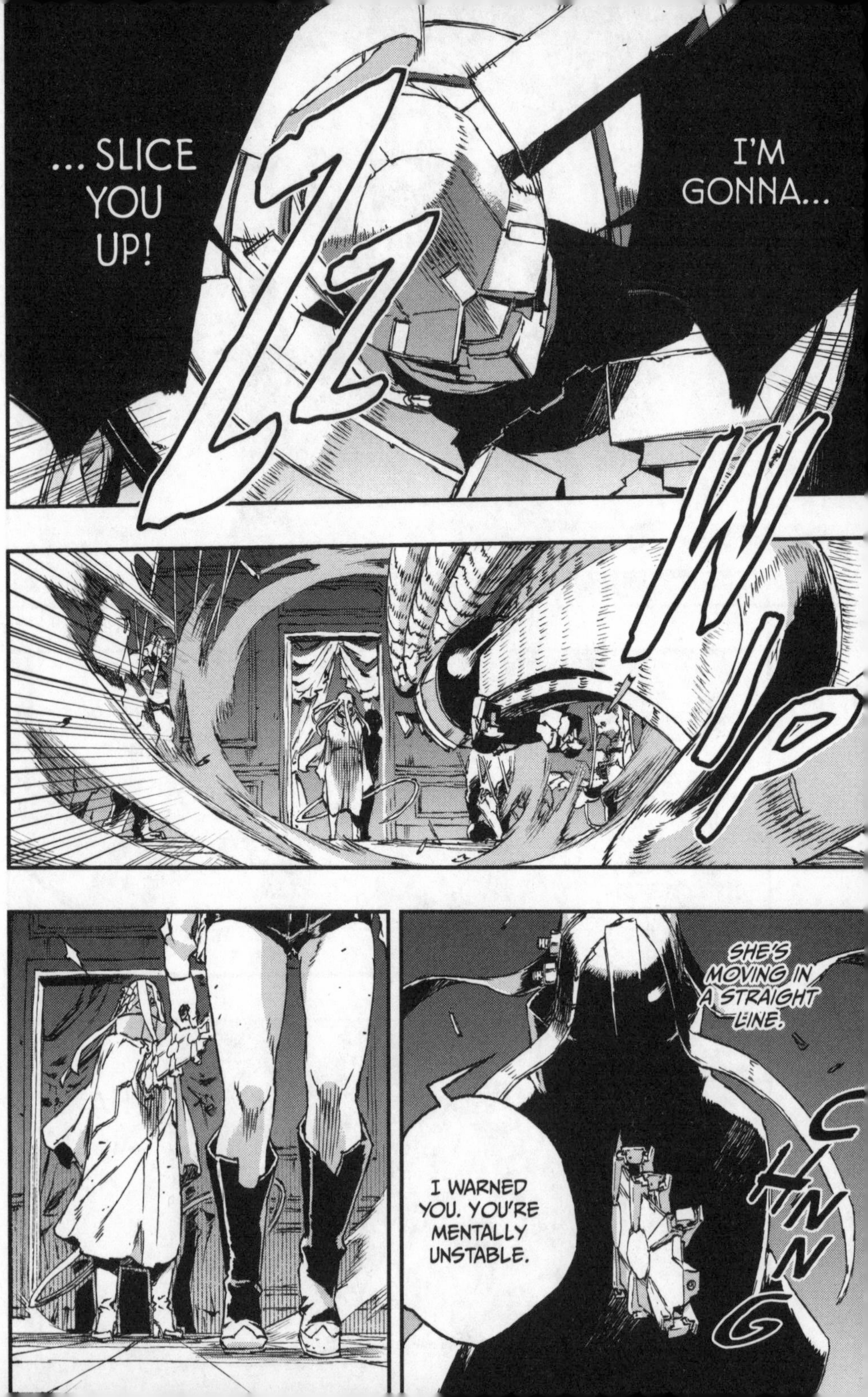
I'M GONNA...
...SLICE YOU UP!
WHIP
SHE'S MOVING IN A STRAIGHT LINE.
I WARNED YOU. YOU'RE MENTALLY UNSTABLE.
CHNNG

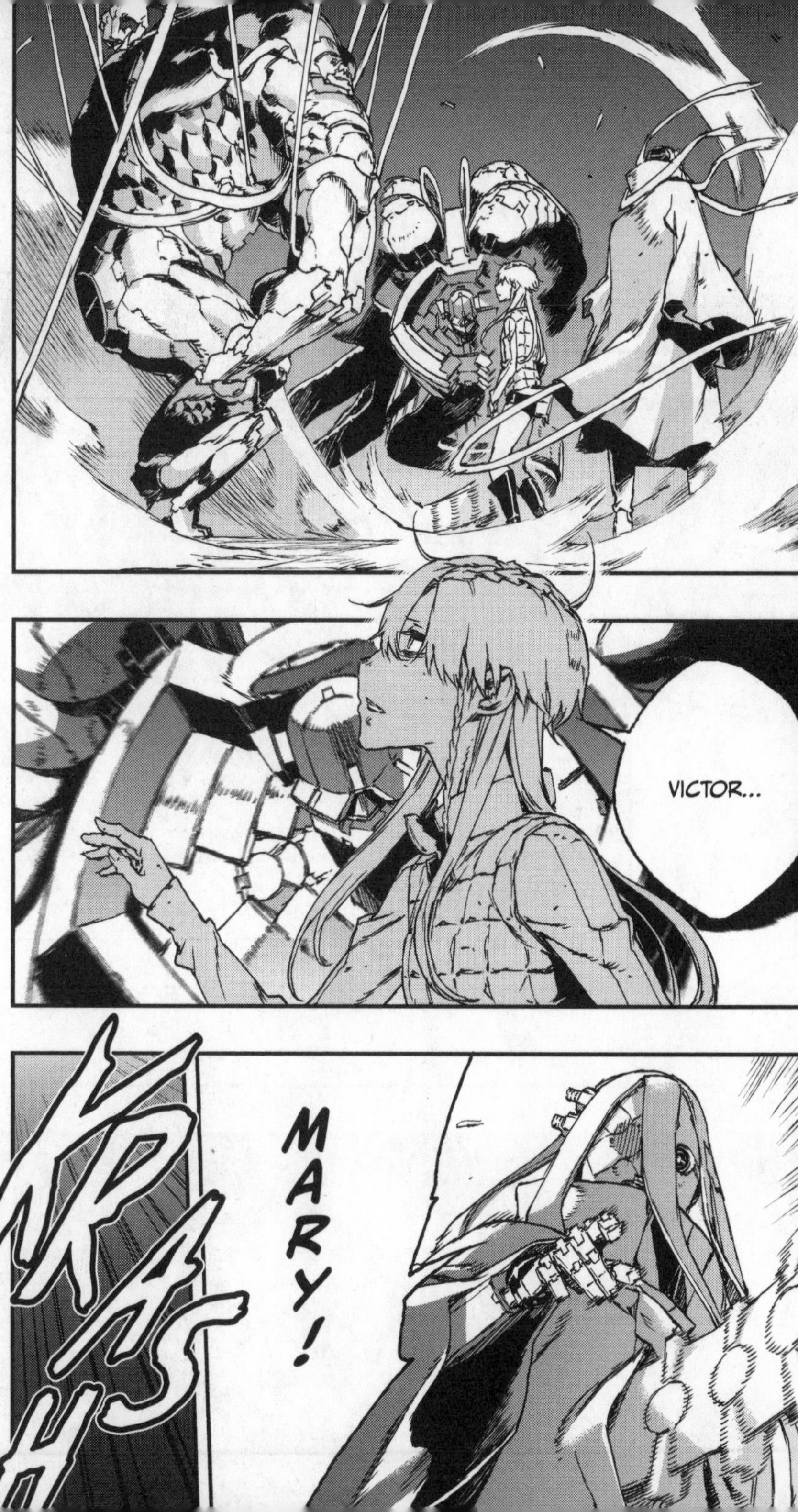
VICTOR...
MARY!
KRASH

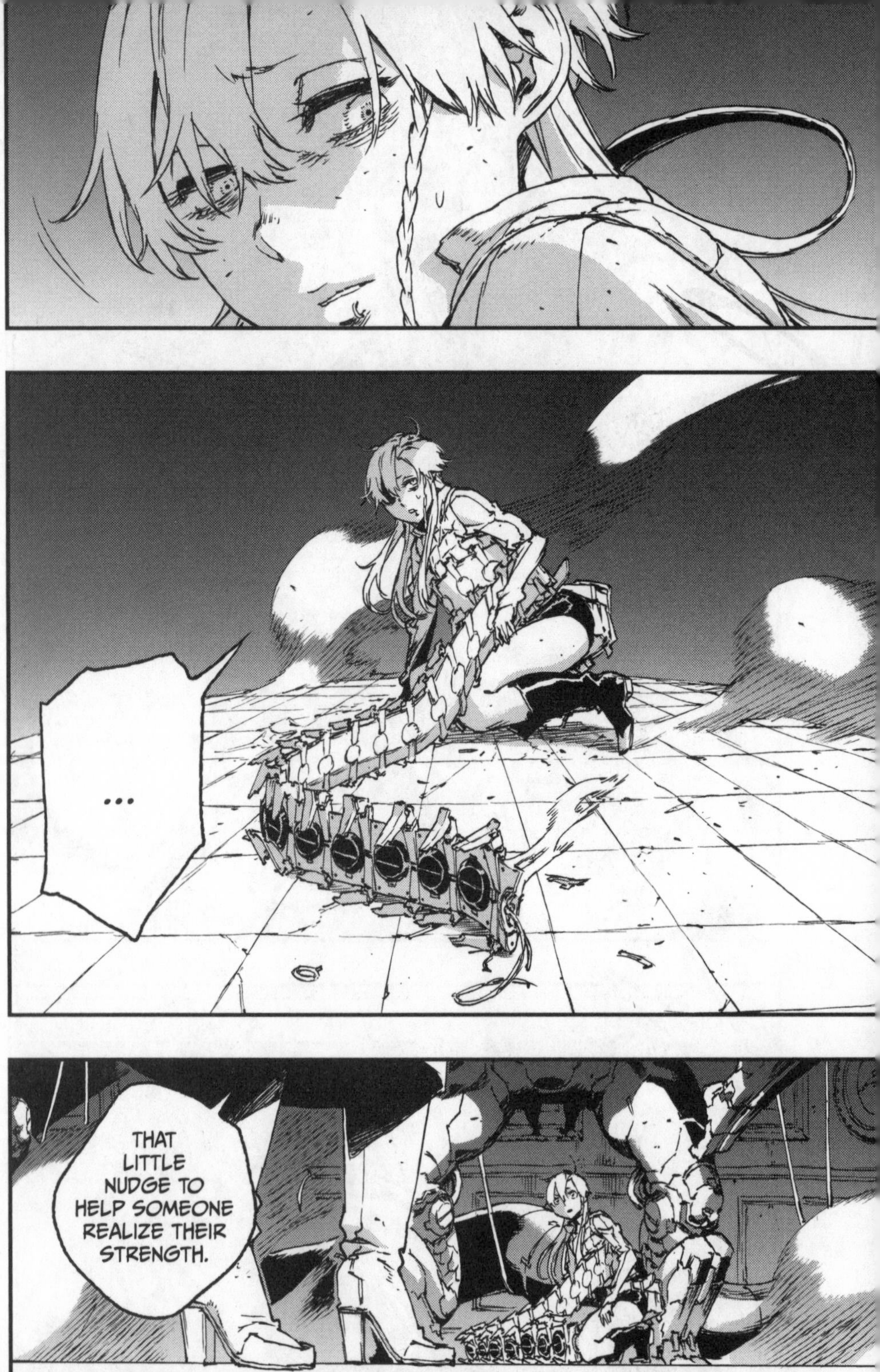
...
THAT LITTLE NUDGE TO HELP SOMEONE REALIZE THEIR STRENGTH.

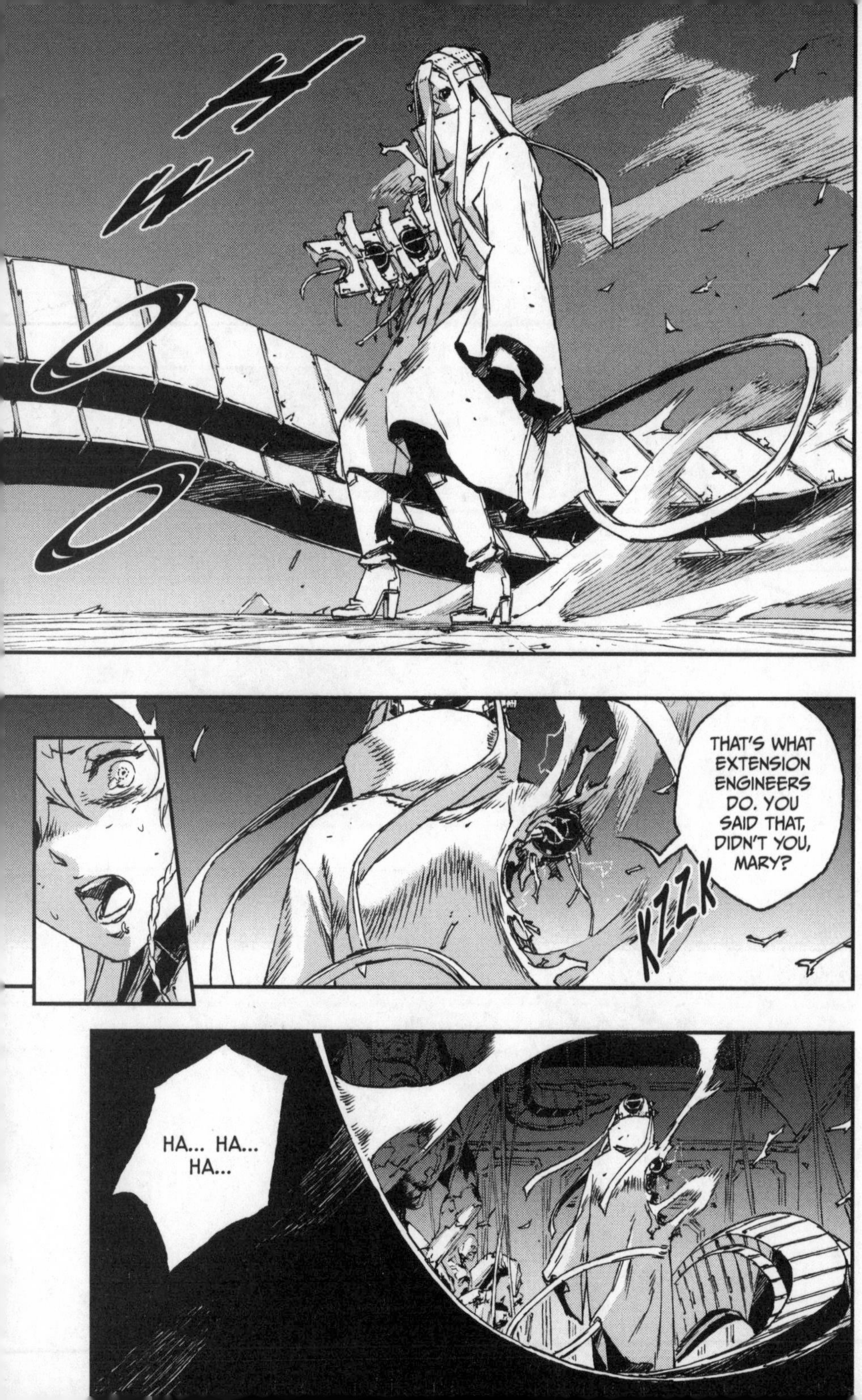
THAT'S WHAT EXTENSION ENGINEERS DO. YOU SAID THAT, DIDN'T YOU, MARY?
KZZK
HA... HA... HA...

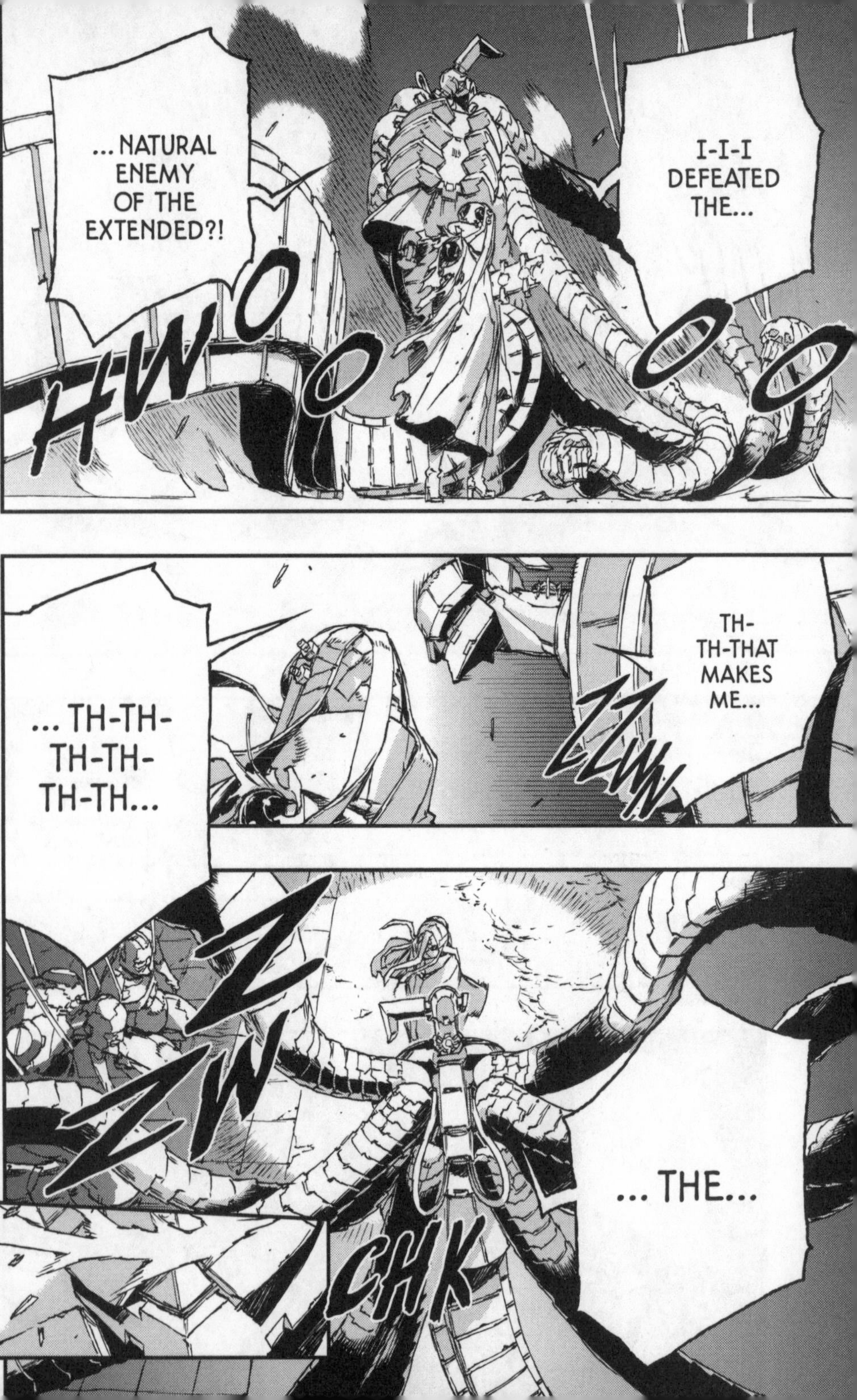

I-I-I DEFEATED THE...
...NATURAL ENEMY OF THE EXTENDED?!
HWOOOOO
TH- TH-THAT MAKES ME...
ZZUWN
... TH-TH- TH-TH- TH-TH...
... THE...
ZZW
CHK

...THE STRONGEST OF ALL!

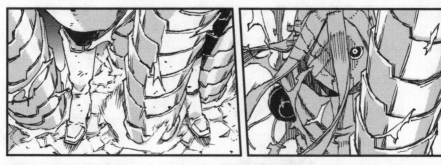

I ALMOST FORGOT...

?!

?

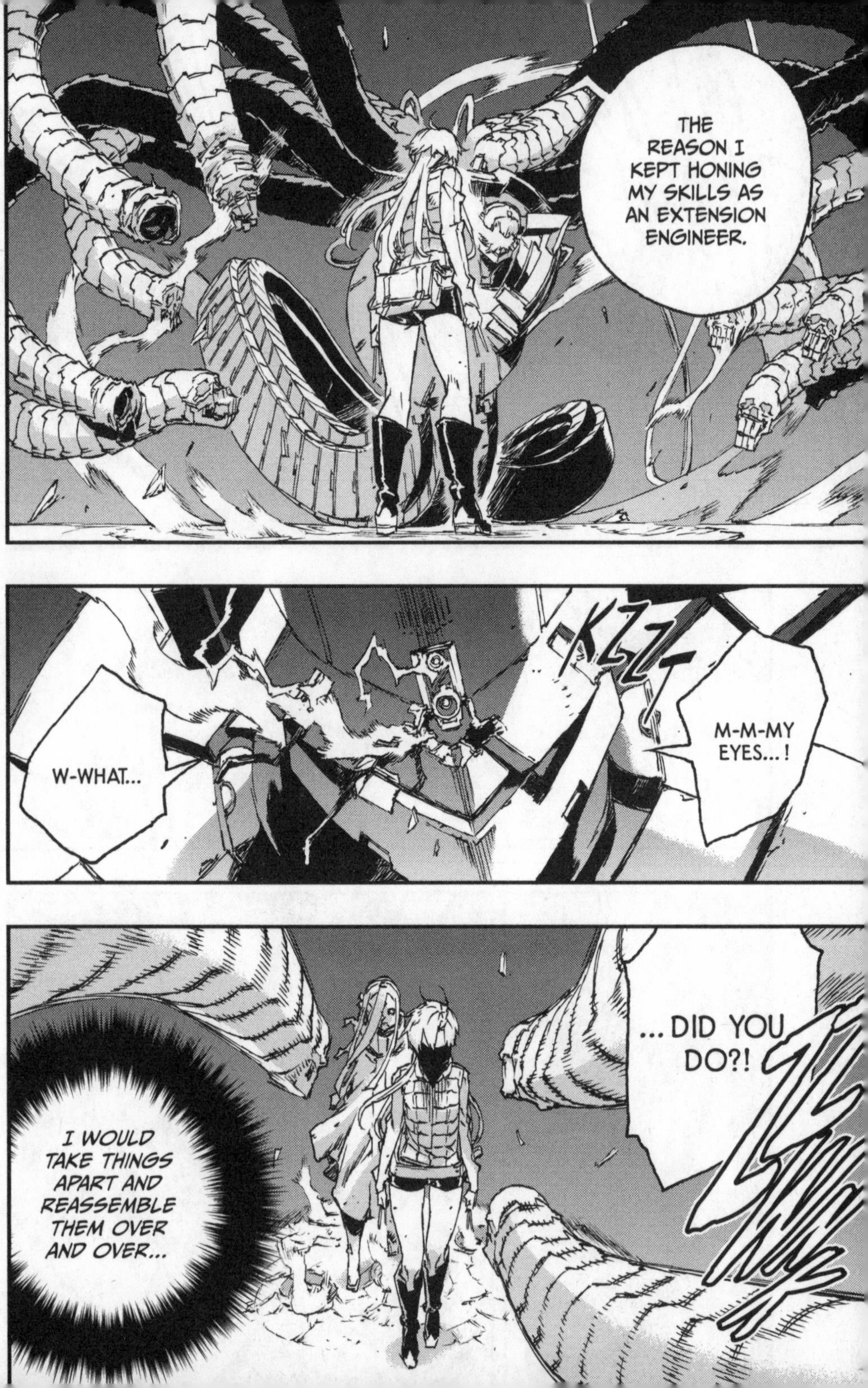
THE REASON I KEPT HONING MY SKILLS AS AN EXTENSION ENGINEER.
KZZT
M-M-MY EYES...!
W-WHAT...
... DID YOU DO?!
I WOULD TAKE THINGS APART AND REASSEMBLE THEM OVER AND OVER...

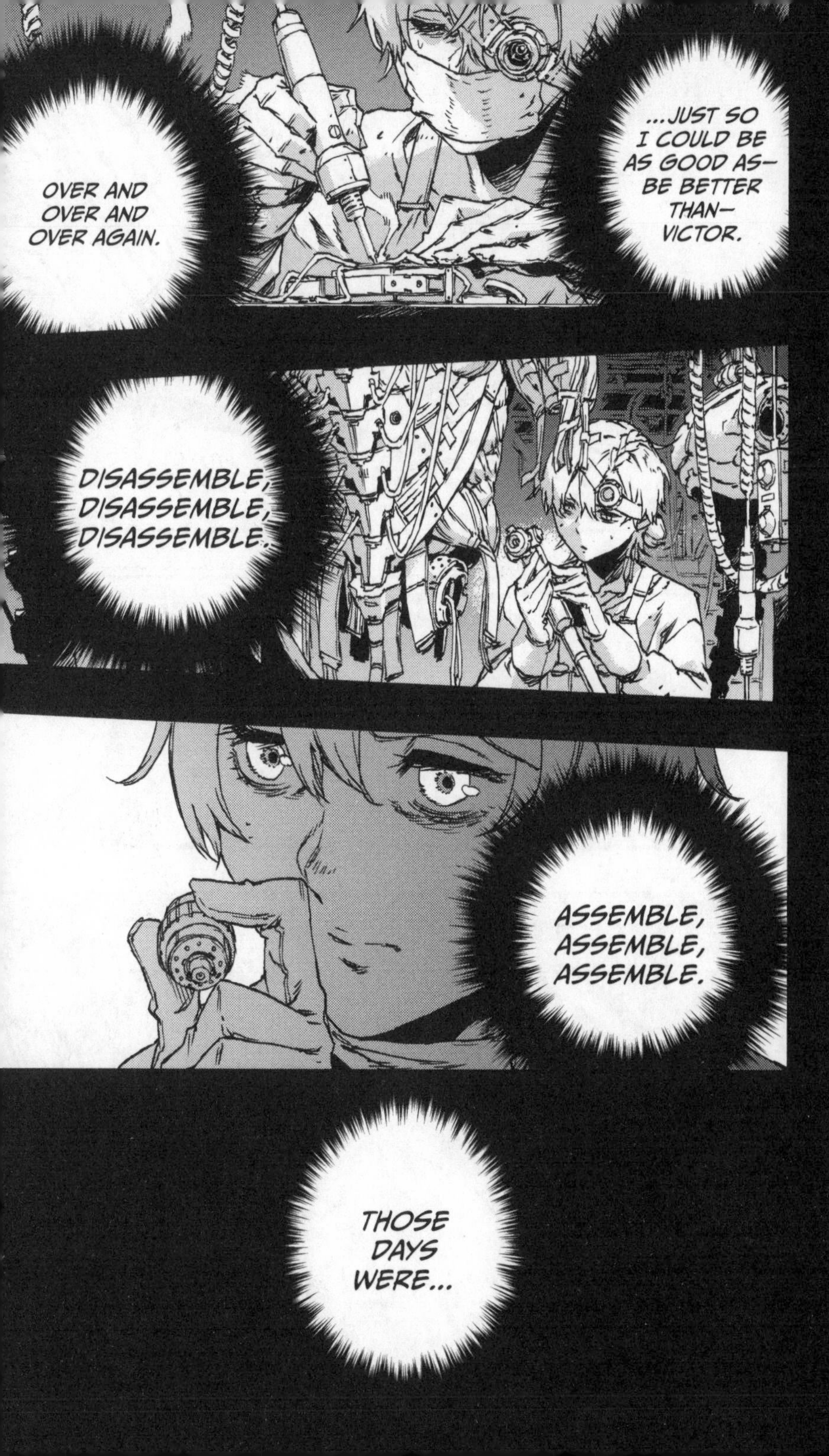
...JUST SO I COULD BE AS GOOD AS— BE BETTER THAN— VICTOR.
OVER AND OVER AND OVER AGAIN.
DISASSEMBLE, DISASSEMBLE, DISASSEMBLE.
ASSEMBLE, ASSEMBLE, ASSEMBLE.
THOSE DAYS WERE...

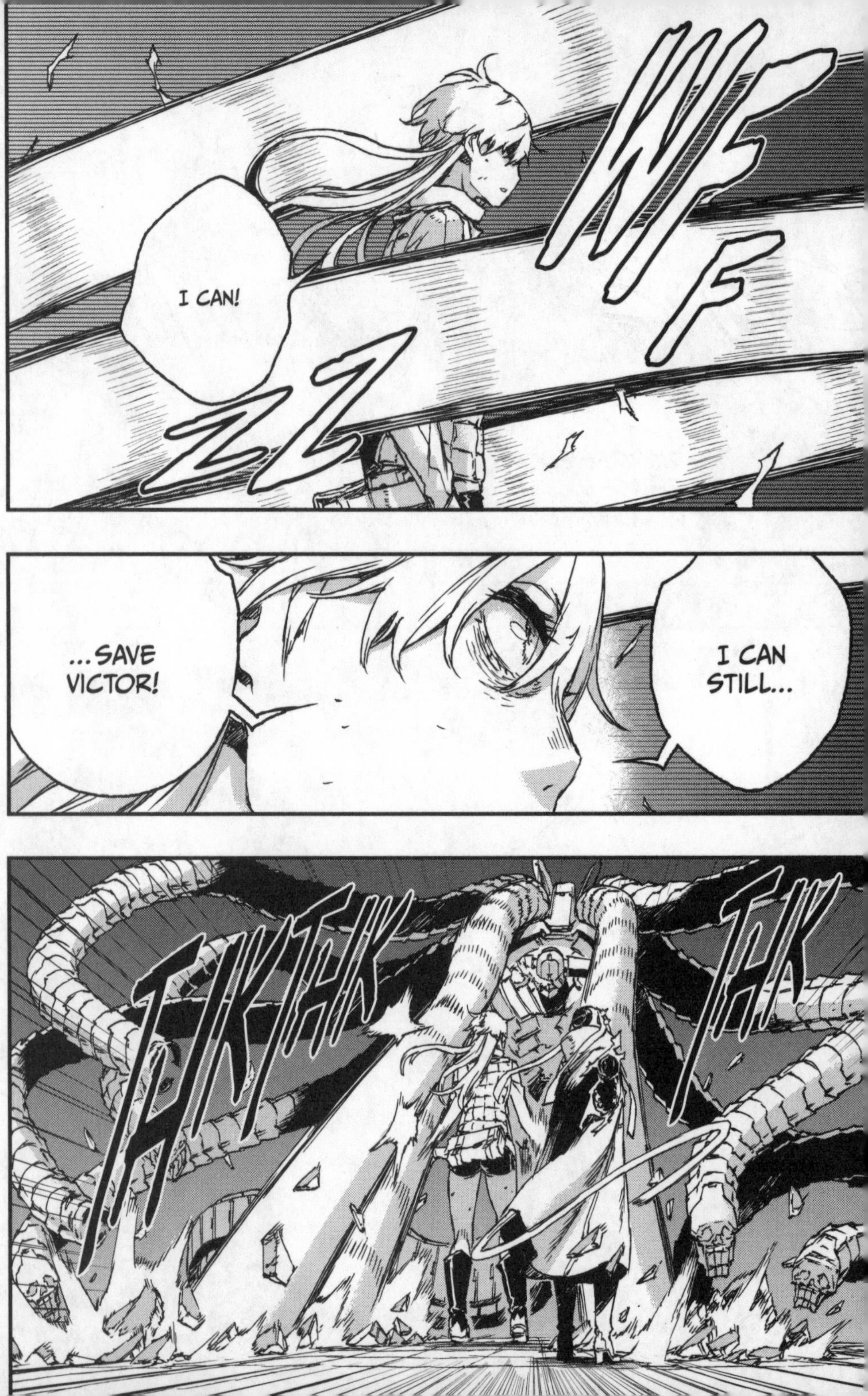

WHF
I CAN!
ZZ
I CAN STILL...
...SAVE VICTOR!
TAK
TAKTAK

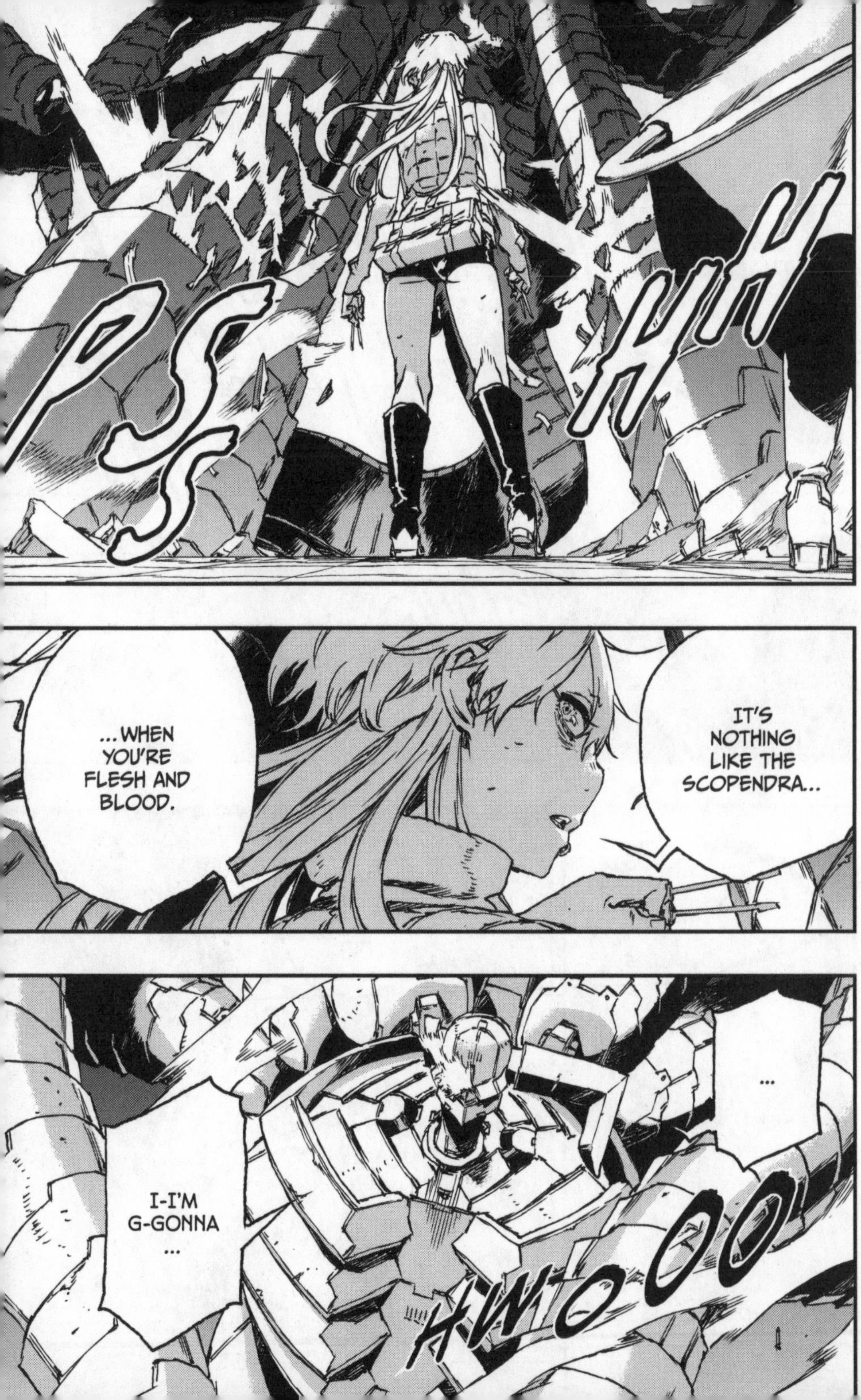
PSSHH
IT'S NOTHING LIKE THE SCOPENDRA...
...WHEN YOU'RE FLESH AND BLOOD.
...
I-I'M G-GONNA ...
HWOOOO

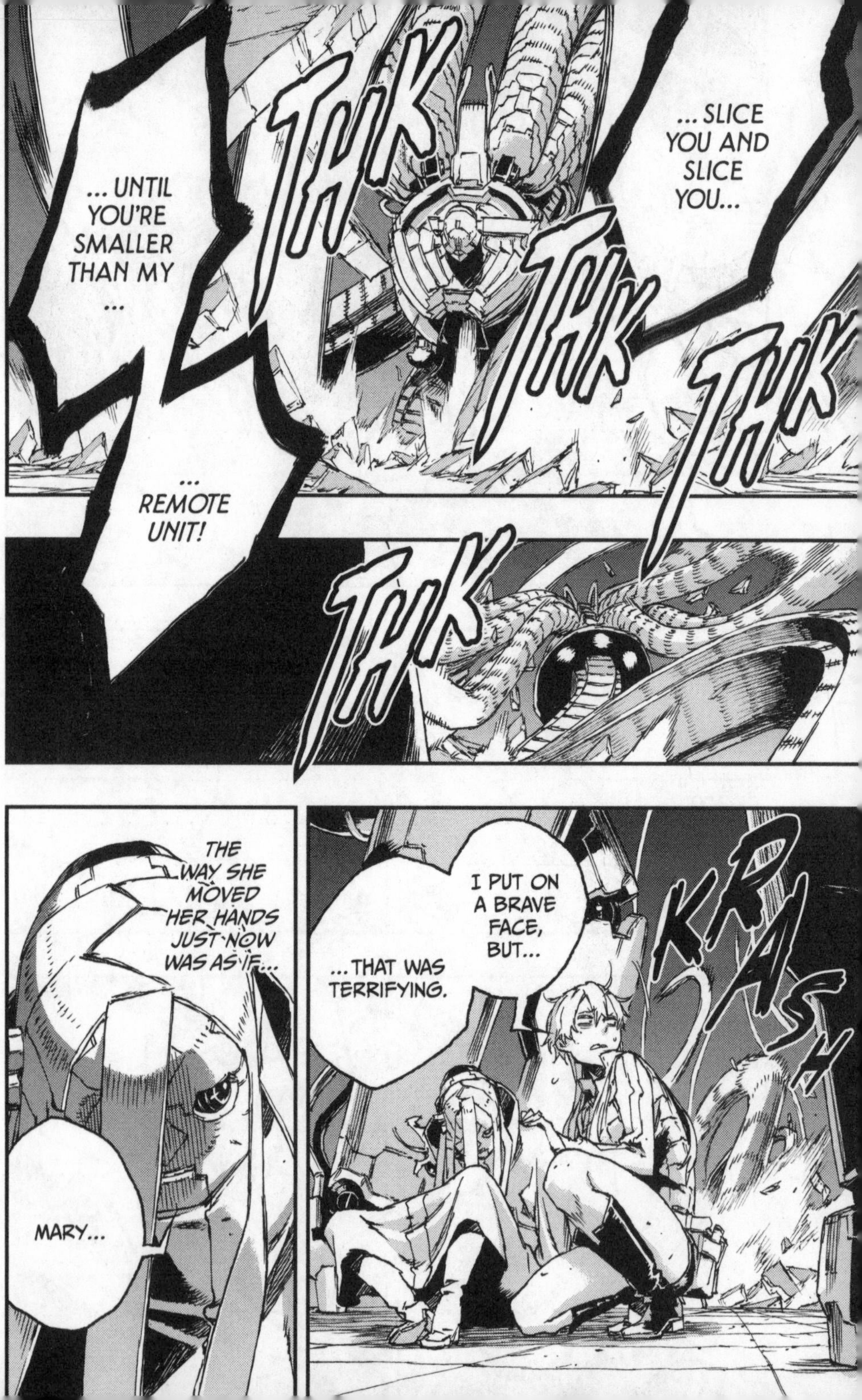
... SLICE YOU AND SLICE YOU...
THK
THK
THK
... UNTIL YOU'RE SMALLER THAN MY ...
... REMOTE UNIT!
THK
KRASH
I PUT ON A BRAVE FACE, BUT...
...THAT WAS TERRIFYING.
THE WAY SHE MOVED HER HANDS JUST NOW WAS AS IF...
MARY...

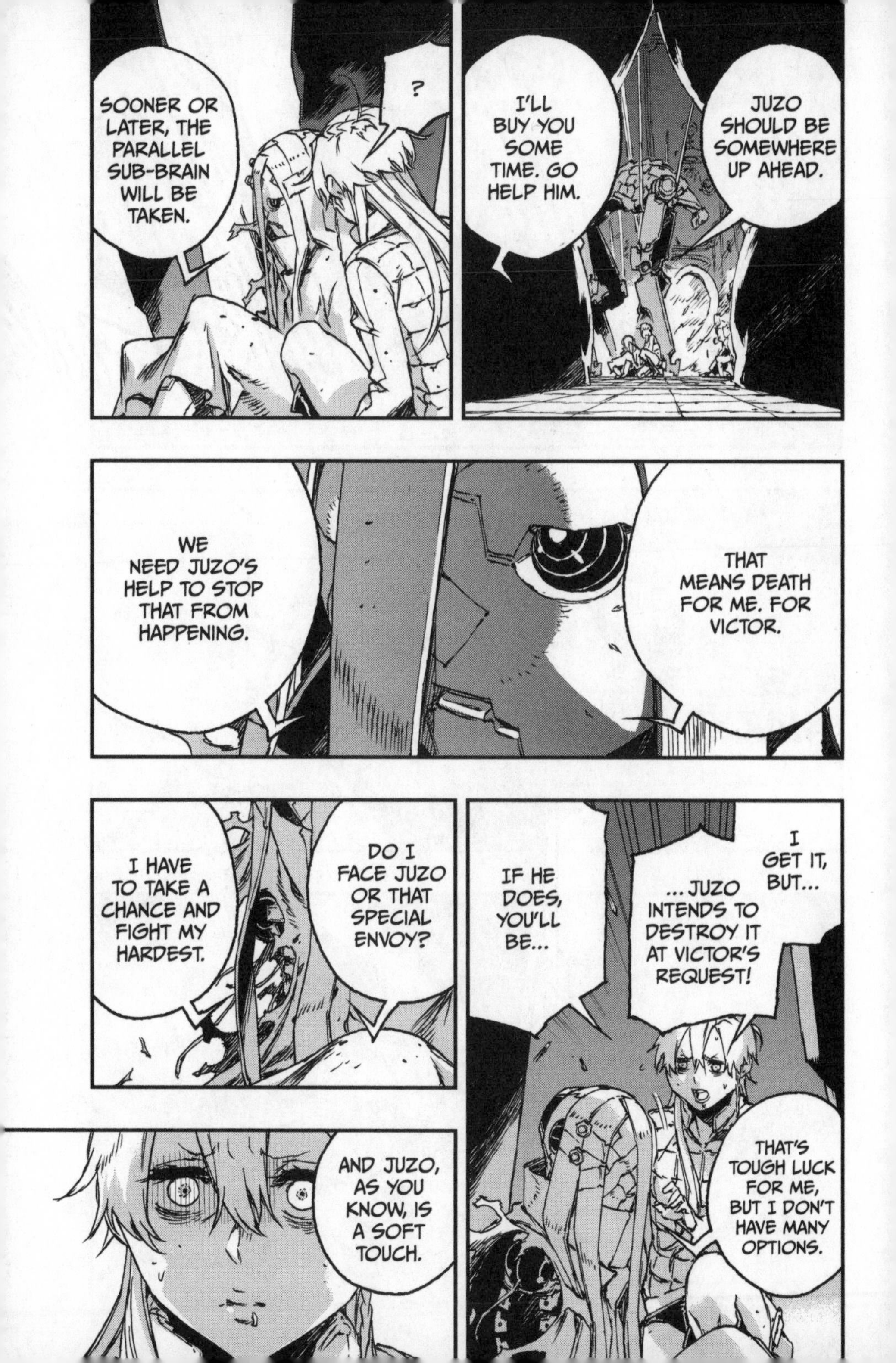
JUZO SHOULD BE SOMEWHERE UP AHEAD.
I'LL BUY YOU SOME TIME. GO HELP HIM.
?
SOONER OR LATER, THE PARALLEL SUB-BRAIN WILL BE TAKEN.
THAT MEANS DEATH FOR ME. FOR VICTOR.
WE NEED JUZO'S HELP TO STOP THAT FROM HAPPENING.
I GET IT, BUT...
...JUZO INTENDS TO DESTROY IT AT VICTOR'S REQUEST!
IF HE DOES, YOU'LL BE...
THAT'S TOUGH LUCK FOR ME, BUT I DON'T HAVE MANY OPTIONS.
DO I FACE JUZO OR THAT SPECIAL ENVOY?
I HAVE TO TAKE A CHANCE AND FIGHT MY HARDEST.
AND JUZO, AS YOU KNOW, IS A SOFT TOUCH.

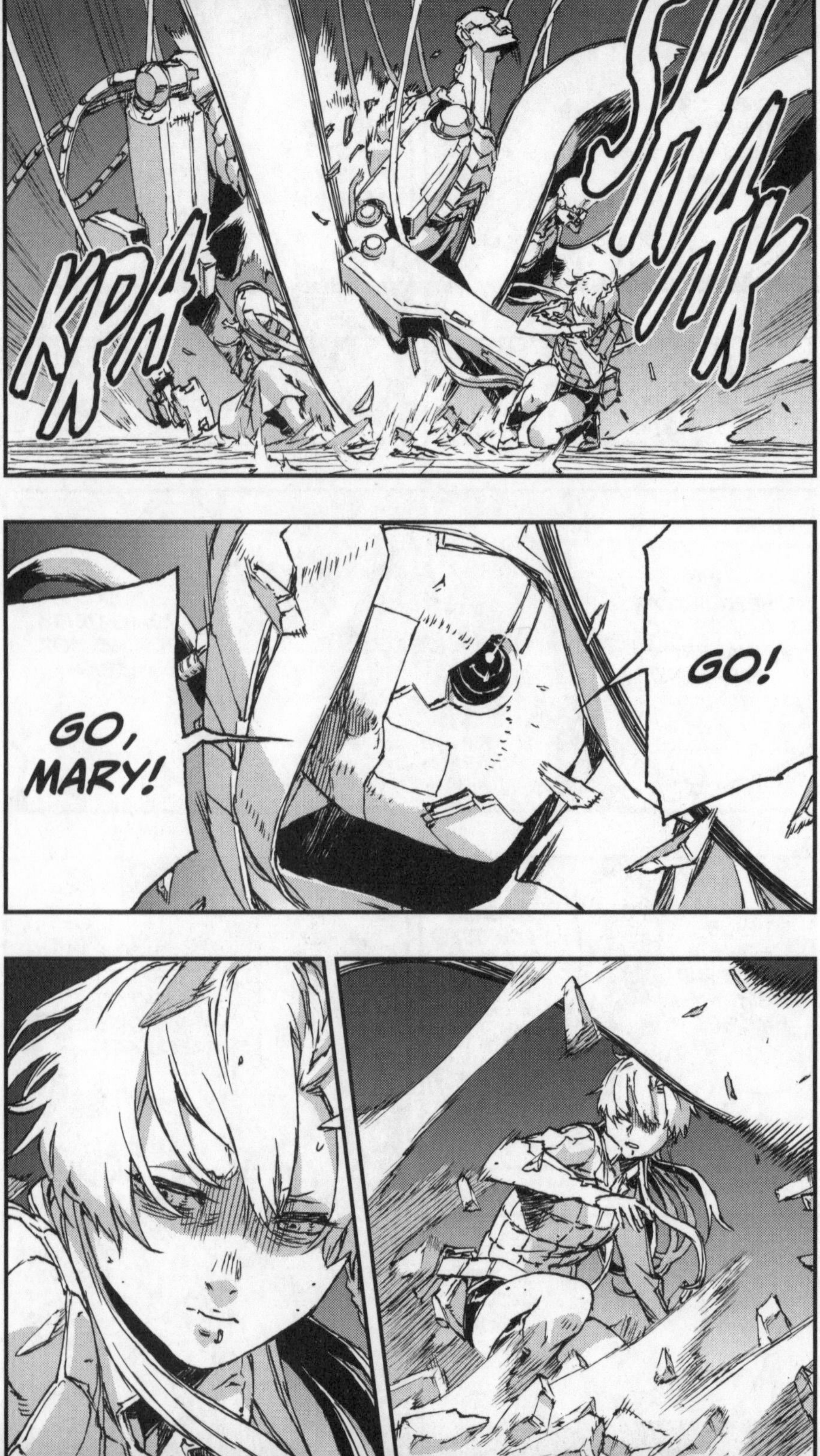
SHAK
KRA
GO!
GO, MARY!

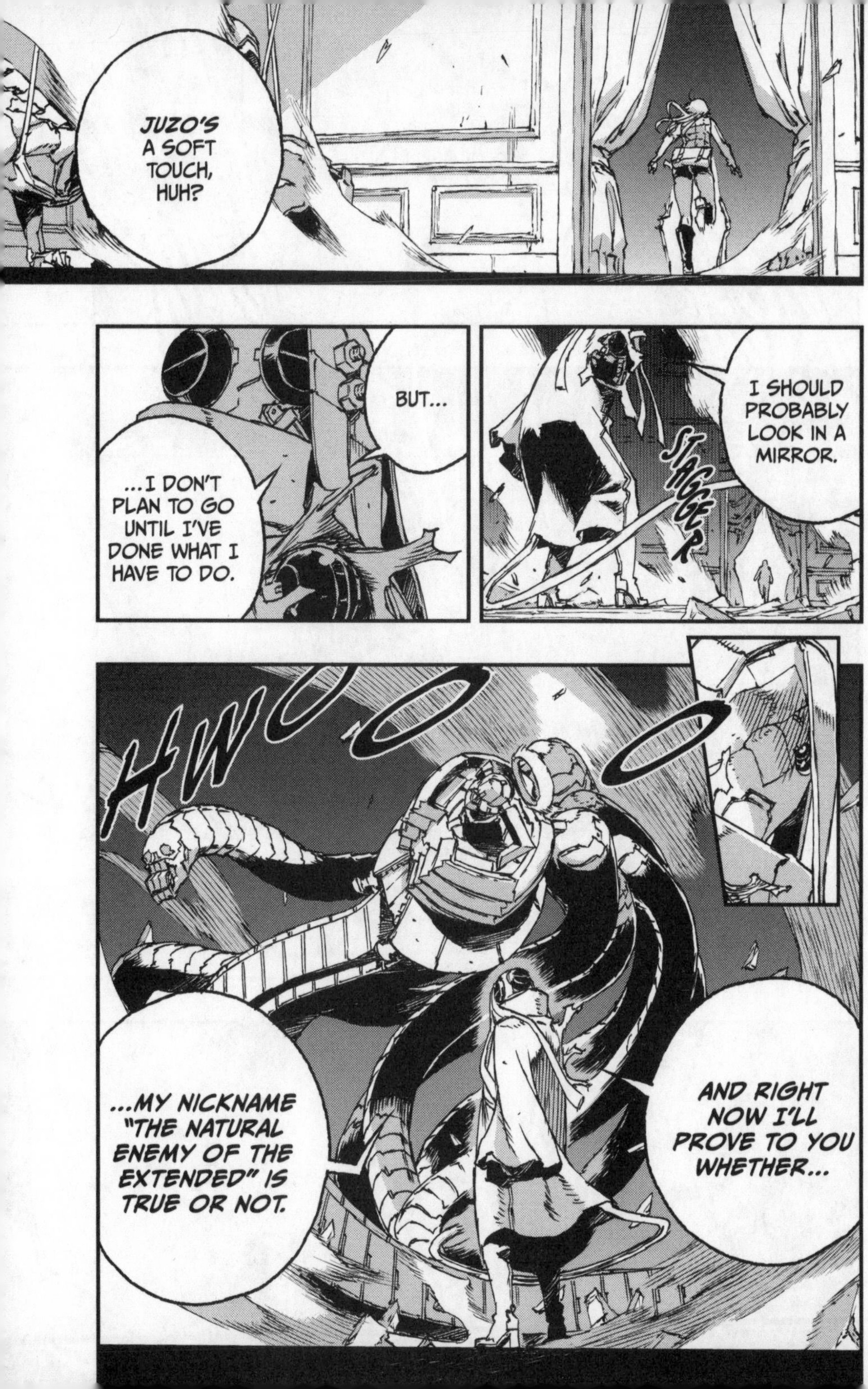
JUZO'S A SOFT TOUCH, HUH?
I SHOULD PROBABLY LOOK IN A MIRROR.
STAGGER
BUT...
...I DON'T PLAN TO GO UNTIL I'VE DONE WHAT I HAVE TO DO.
HWOOO
AND RIGHT NOW I'LL PROVE TO YOU WHETHER...
...MY NICKNAME "THE NATURAL ENEMY OF THE EXTENDED" IS TRUE OR NOT.

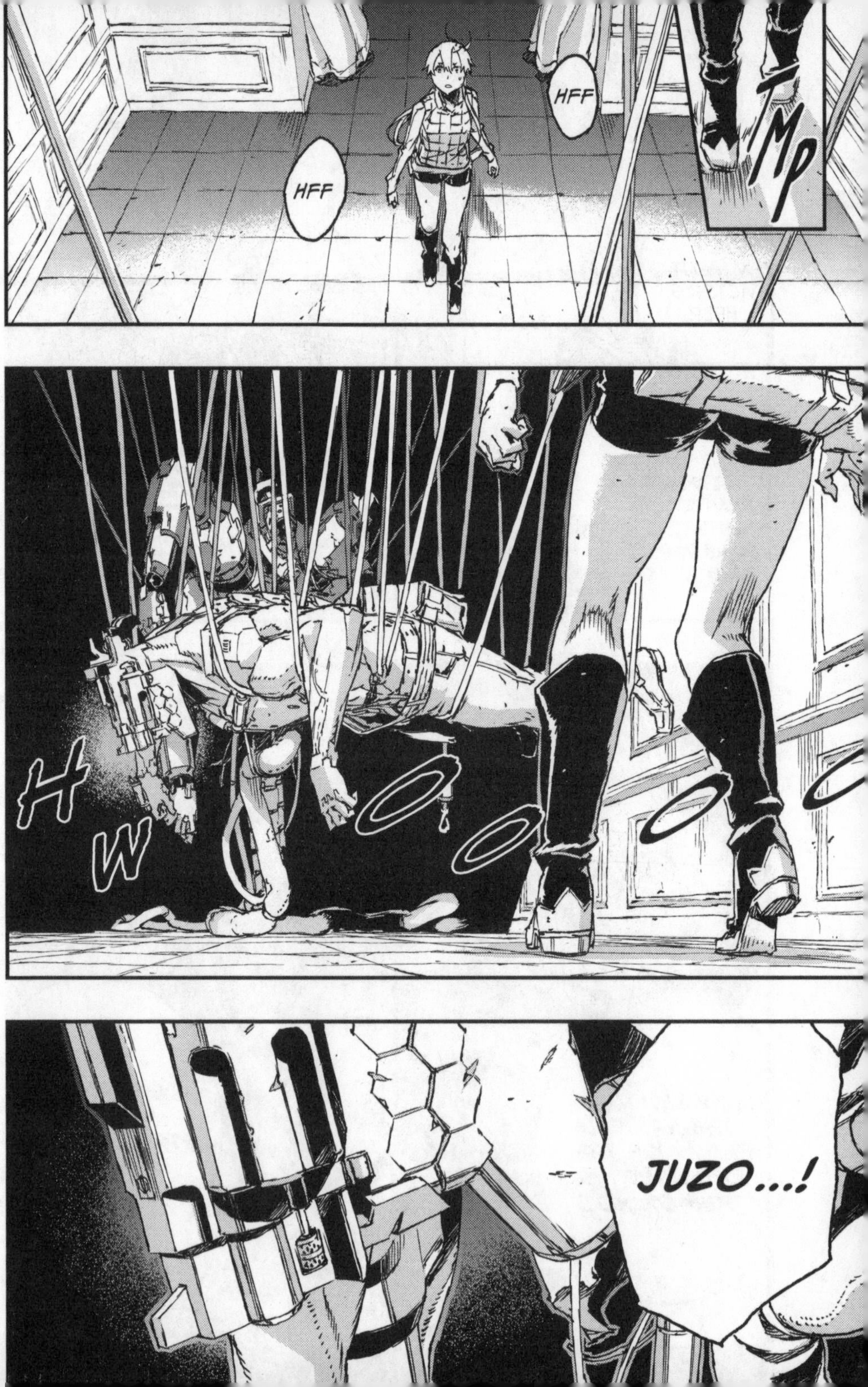
TMP
HFF
HFF
HWOOOO
JUZO...!

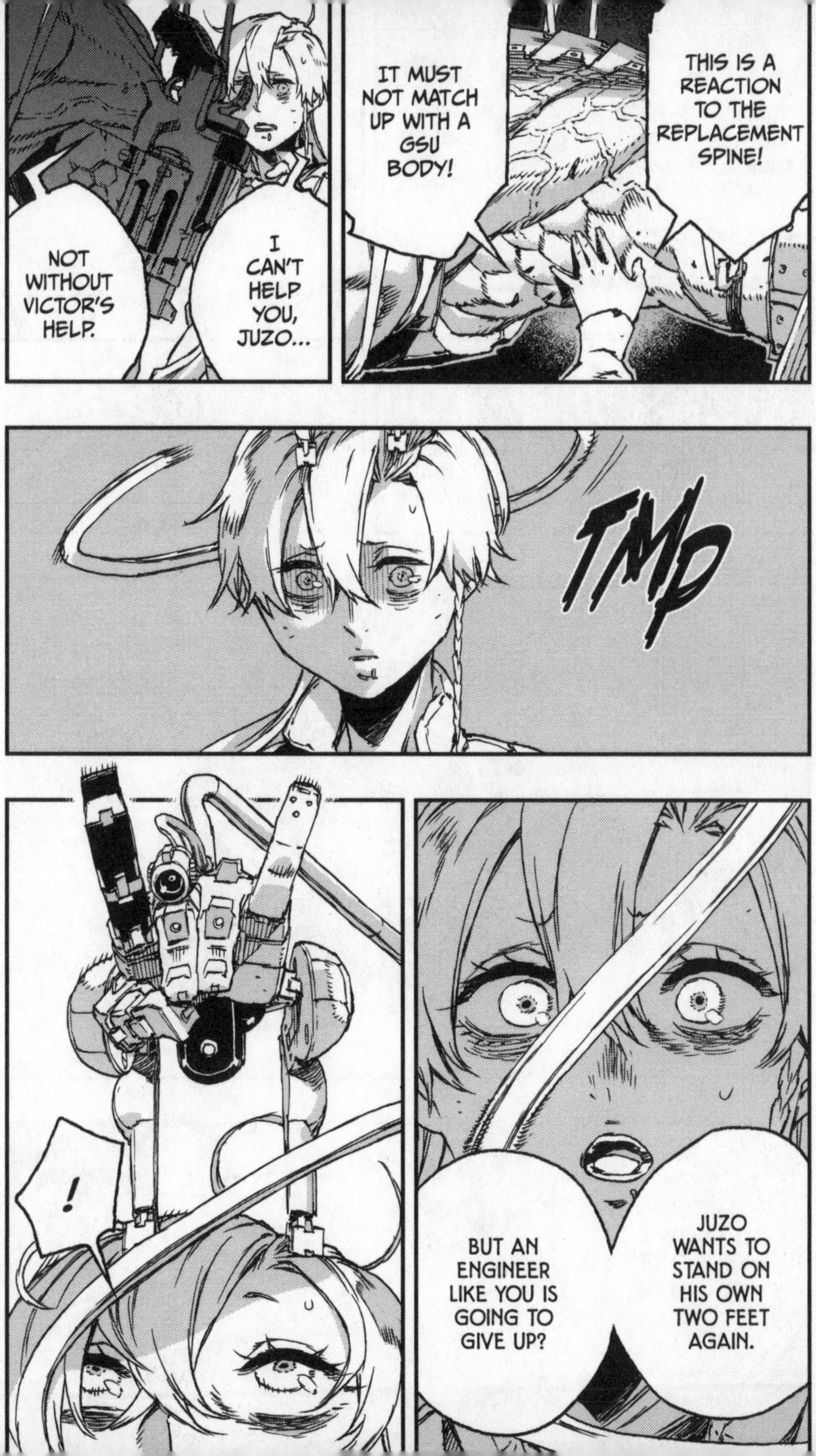
THIS IS A REACTION TO THE REPLACEMENT SPINE!
IT MUST NOT MATCH UP WITH A GSU BODY!
I CAN'T HELP YOU, JUZO...
NOT WITHOUT VICTOR'S HELP.
TMP
JUZO WANTS TO STAND ON HIS OWN TWO FEET AGAIN.
BUT AN ENGINEER LIKE YOU IS GOING TO GIVE UP?
!

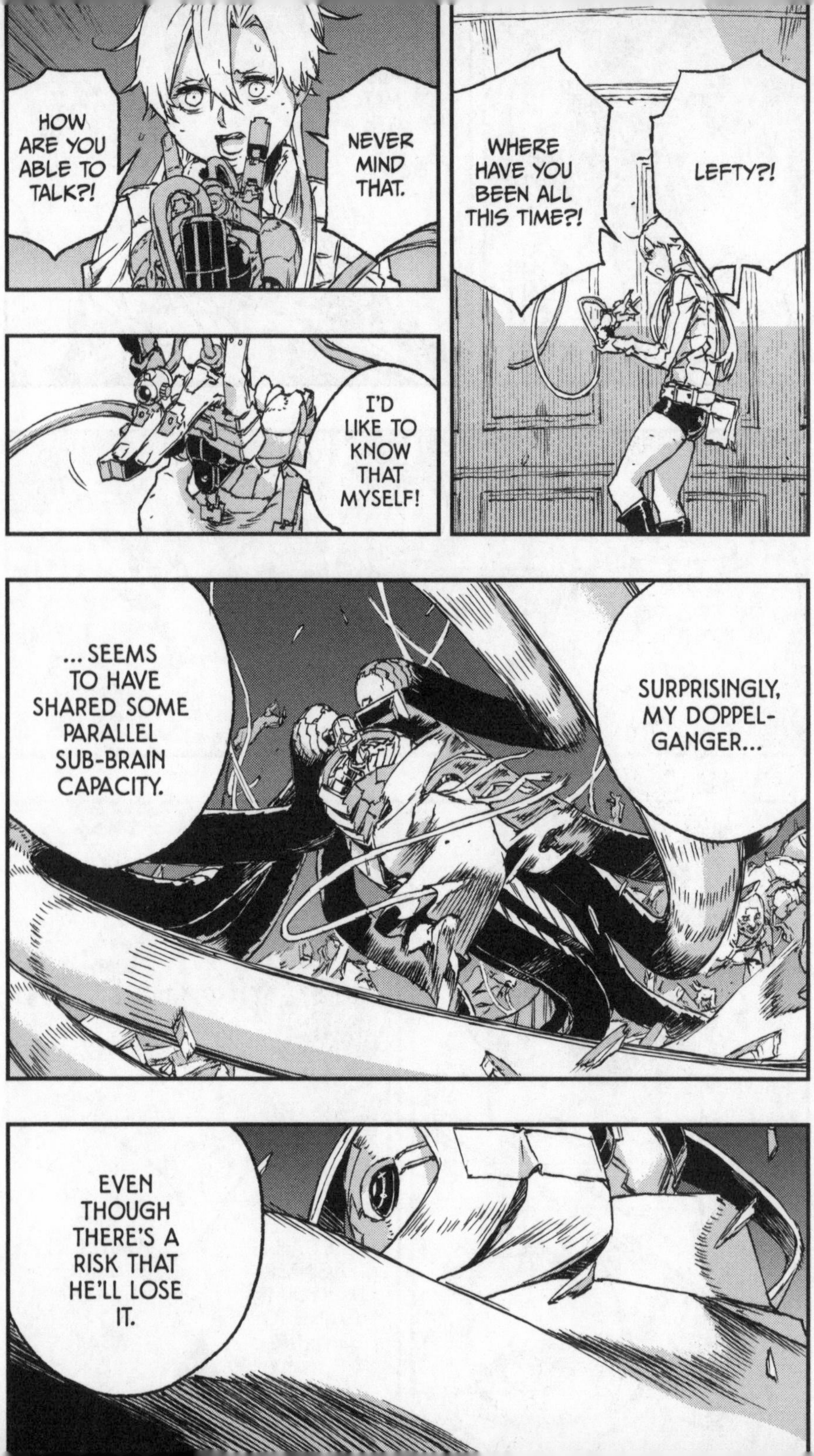
LEFTY?!
WHERE HAVE YOU BEEN ALL THIS TIME?!
NEVER MIND THAT.
HOW ARE YOU ABLE TO TALK?!
I'D LIKE TO KNOW THAT MYSELF!
SURPRISINGLY, MY DOPPEL-GANGER...
...SEEMS TO HAVE SHARED SOME PARALLEL SUB-BRAIN CAPACITY.
EVEN THOUGH THERE'S A RISK THAT HE'LL LOSE IT.

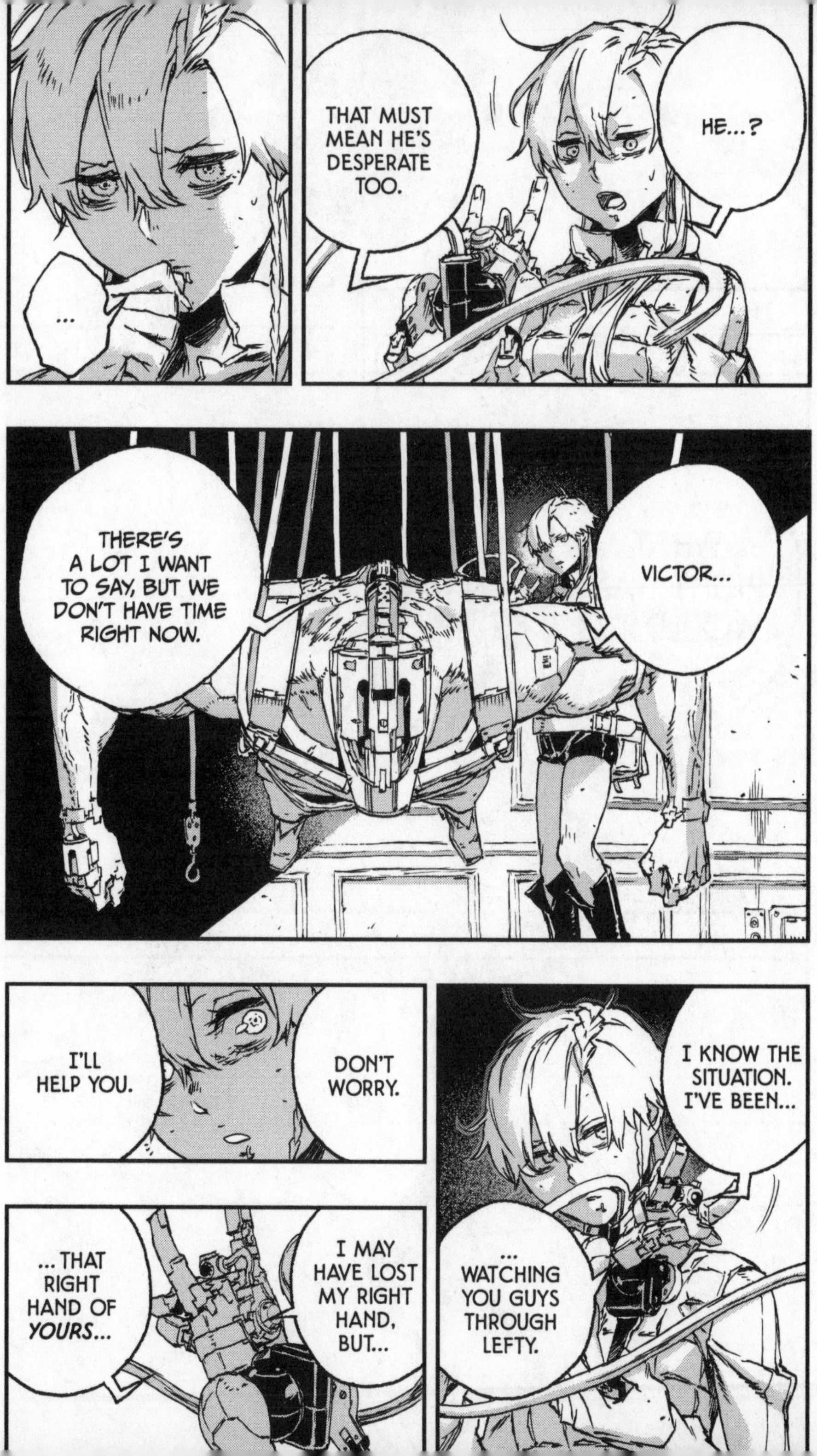
HE...?
THAT MUST MEAN HE'S DESPERATE TOO.
...
VICTOR...
THERE'S A LOT I WANT TO SAY, BUT WE DON'T HAVE TIME RIGHT NOW.
I KNOW THE SITUATION. I'VE BEEN...
...WATCHING YOU GUYS THROUGH LEFTY.
DON'T WORRY.
I'LL HELP YOU.
I MAY HAVE LOST MY RIGHT HAND, BUT...
...THAT RIGHT HAND OF *YOURS*...

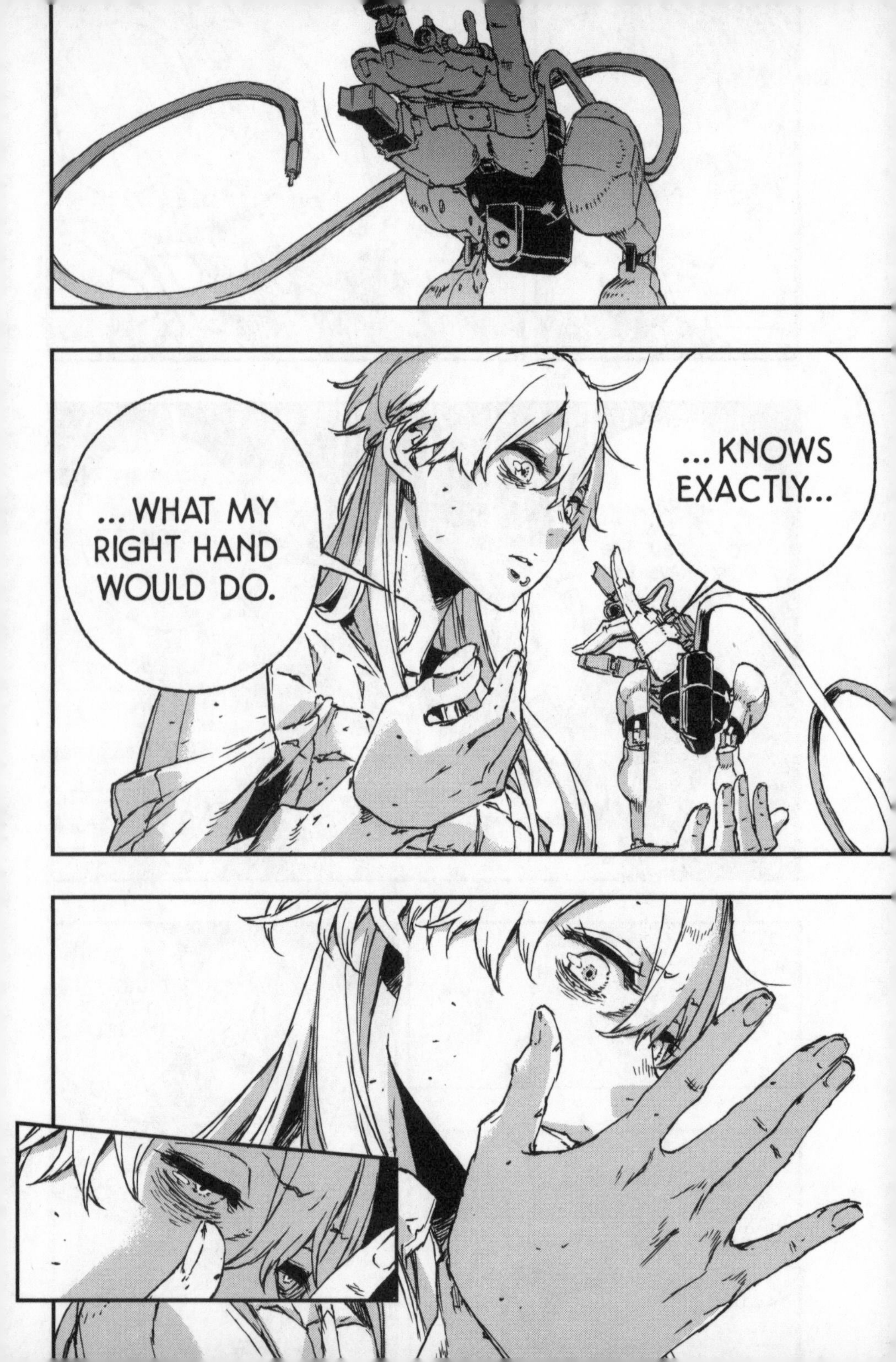
...KNOWS EXACTLY...
...WHAT MY RIGHT HAND WOULD DO.

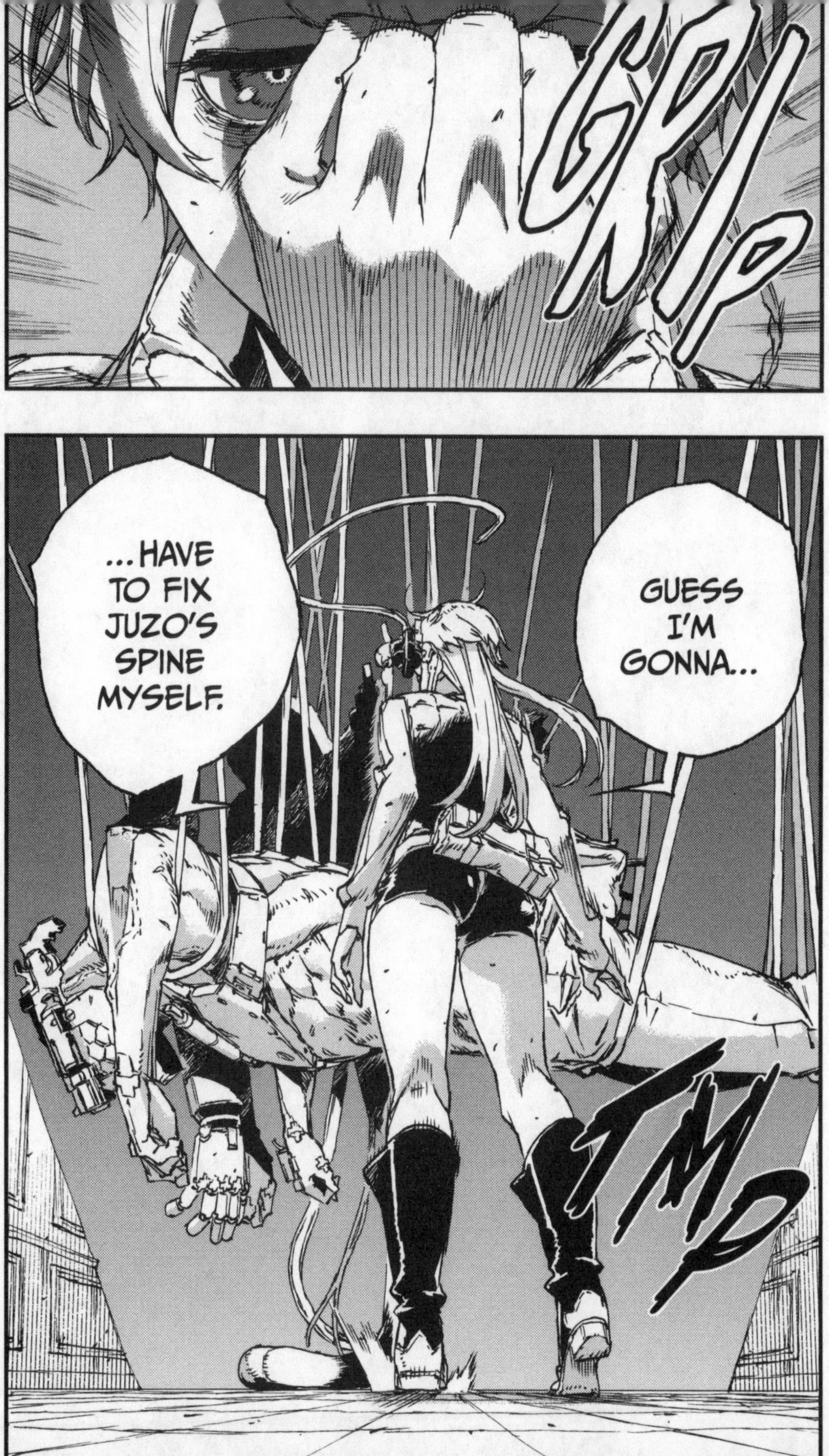
GUESS I'M GONNA...
...HAVE TO FIX JUZO'S SPINE MYSELF.

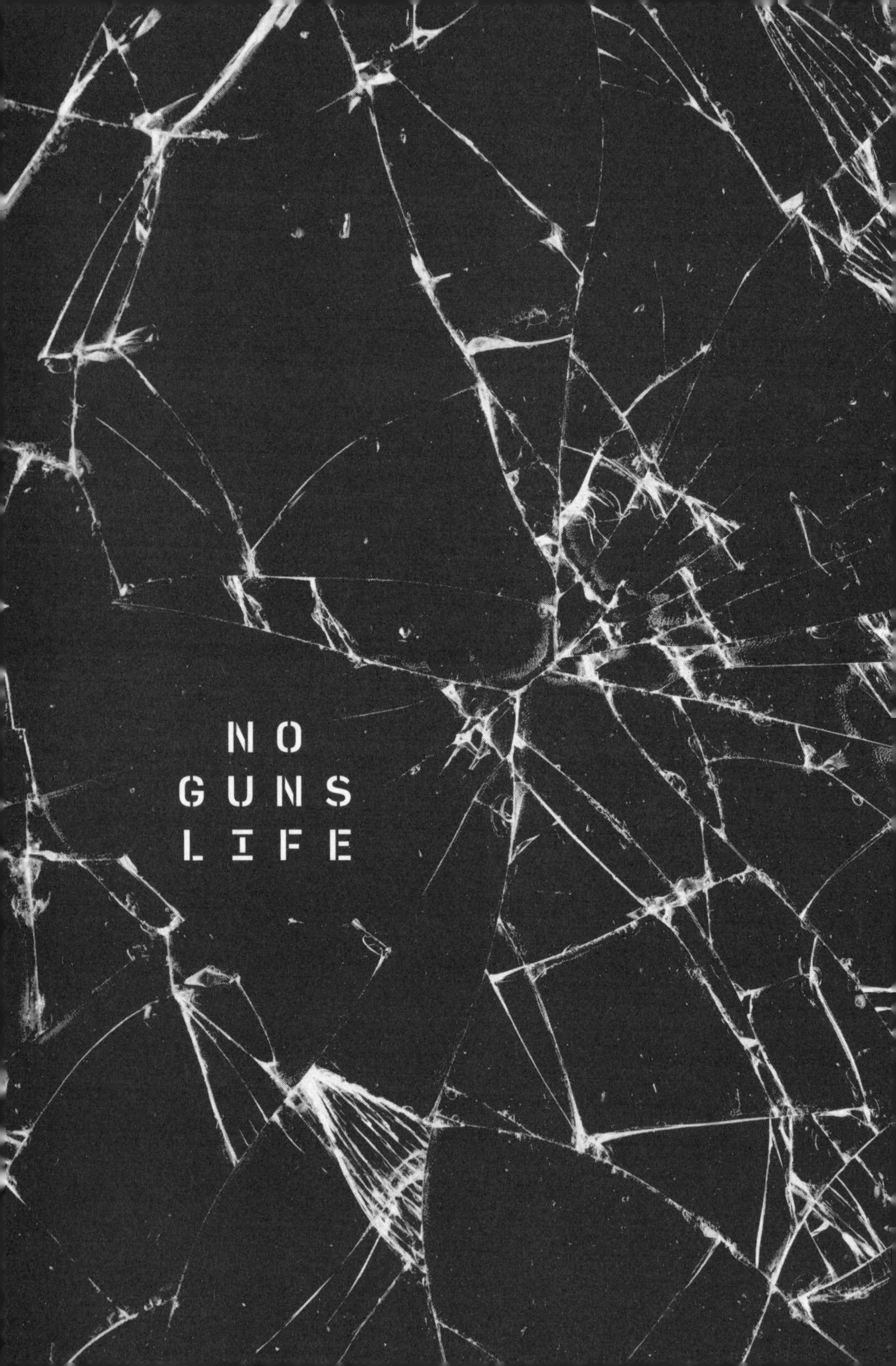
NO
GUNS
LIFE

Chapter 52
Sycophantic

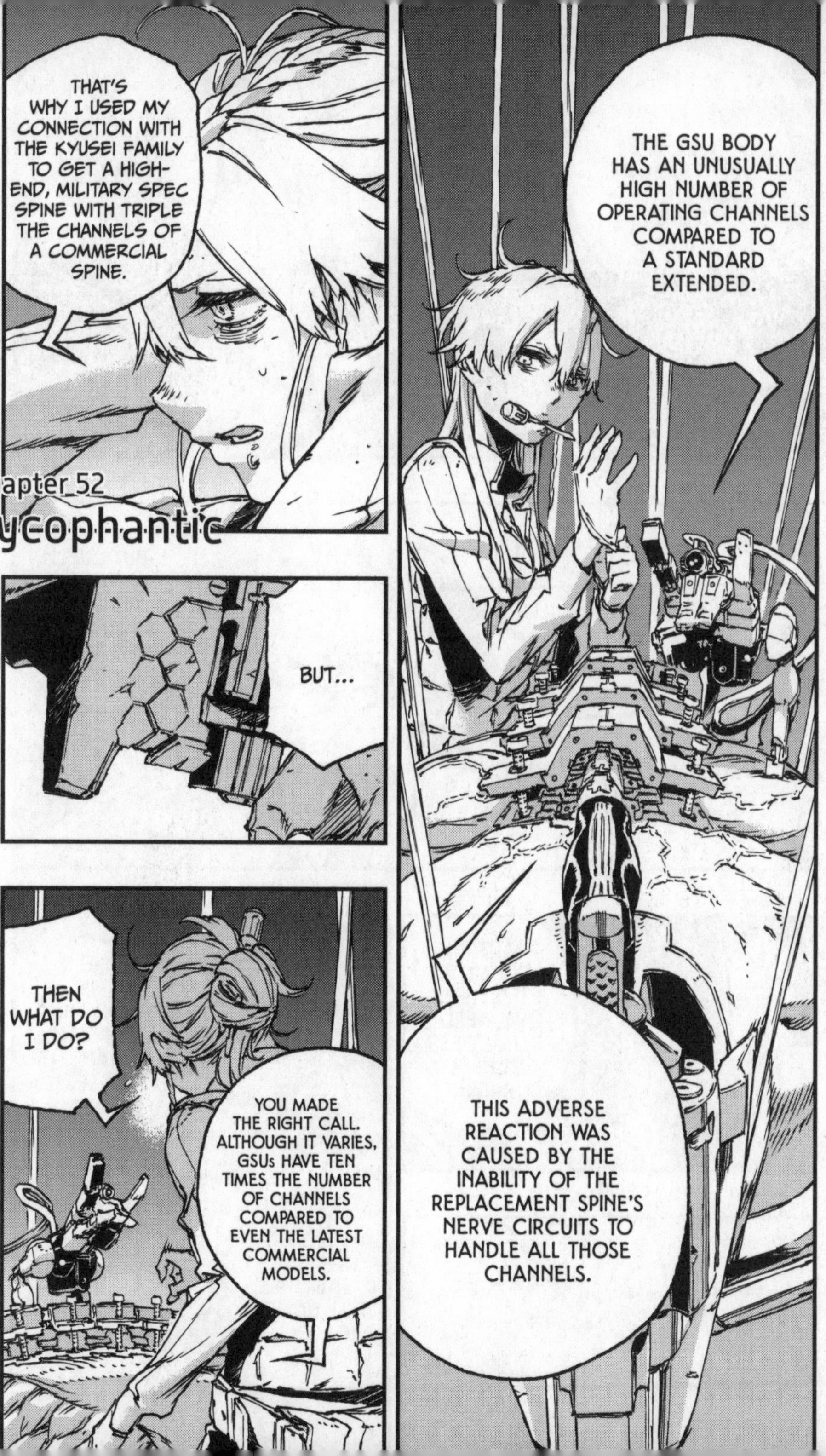
THE GSU BODY HAS AN UNUSUALLY HIGH NUMBER OF OPERATING CHANNELS COMPARED TO A STANDARD EXTENDED.
THIS ADVERSE REACTION WAS CAUSED BY THE INABILITY OF THE REPLACEMENT SPINE'S NERVE CIRCUITS TO HANDLE ALL THOSE CHANNELS.
THAT'S WHY I USED MY CONNECTION WITH THE KYUSEI FAMILY TO GET A HIGH-END, MILITARY SPEC SPINE WITH TRIPLE THE CHANNELS OF A COMMERCIAL SPINE.
BUT...
THEN WHAT DO I DO?
YOU MADE THE RIGHT CALL. ALTHOUGH IT VARIES, GSUs HAVE TEN TIMES THE NUMBER OF CHANNELS COMPARED TO EVEN THE LATEST COMMERCIAL MODELS.

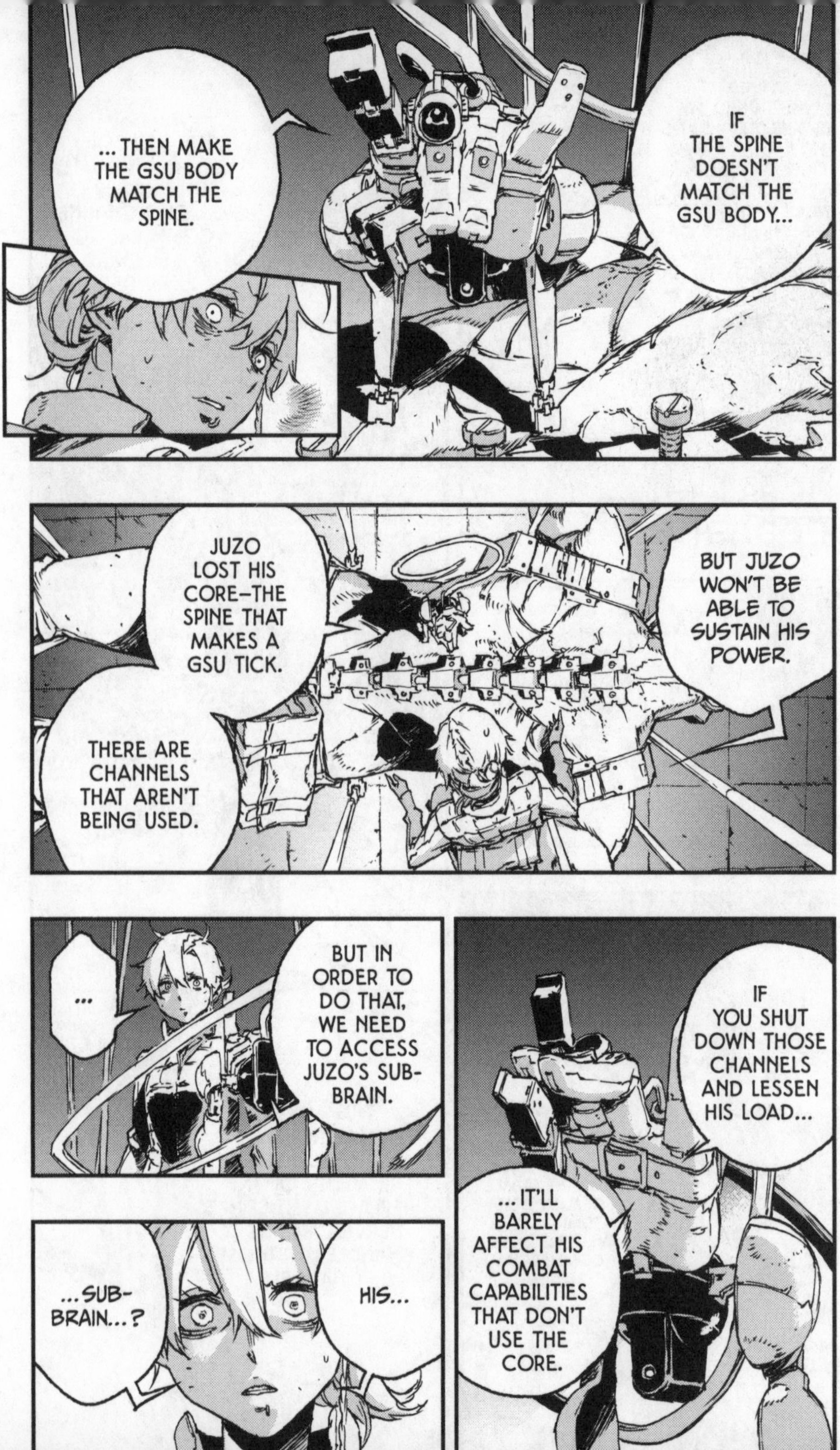
IF THE SPINE DOESN'T MATCH THE GSU BODY...
...THEN MAKE THE GSU BODY MATCH THE SPINE.
BUT JUZO WON'T BE ABLE TO SUSTAIN HIS POWER.
JUZO LOST HIS CORE—THE SPINE THAT MAKES A GSU TICK.
THERE ARE CHANNELS THAT AREN'T BEING USED.
IF YOU SHUT DOWN THOSE CHANNELS AND LESSEN HIS LOAD...
...IT'LL BARELY AFFECT HIS COMBAT CAPABILITIES THAT DON'T USE THE CORE.
BUT IN ORDER TO DO THAT, WE NEED TO ACCESS JUZO'S SUB-BRAIN.
...
HIS...
...SUB-BRAIN...?

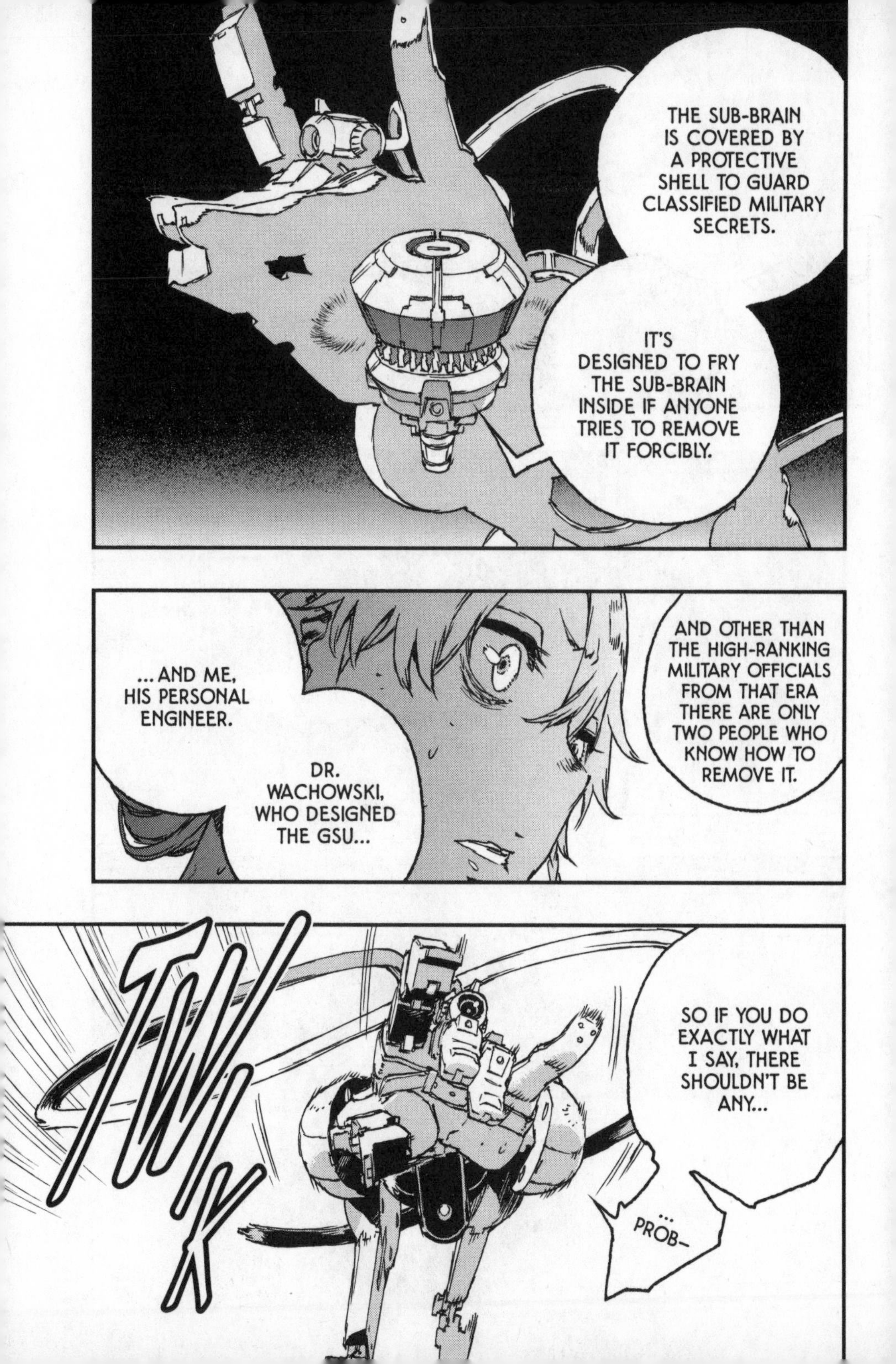
THE SUB-BRAIN IS COVERED BY A PROTECTIVE SHELL TO GUARD CLASSIFIED MILITARY SECRETS.
IT'S DESIGNED TO FRY THE SUB-BRAIN INSIDE IF ANYONE TRIES TO REMOVE IT FORCIBLY.
AND OTHER THAN THE HIGH-RANKING MILITARY OFFICIALS FROM THAT ERA THERE ARE ONLY TWO PEOPLE WHO KNOW HOW TO REMOVE IT.
DR. WACHOWSKI, WHO DESIGNED THE GSU...
...AND ME, HIS PERSONAL ENGINEER.
SO IF YOU DO EXACTLY WHAT I SAY, THERE SHOULDN'T BE ANY...
... PROB-
TWK

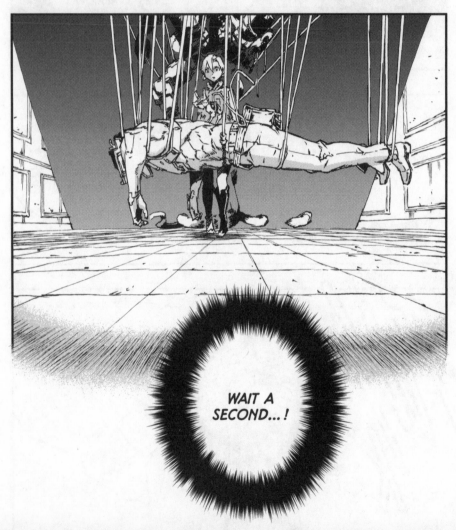

WAIT A
SECOND...!

A few minutes earlier...

ONE LAST QUESTION...

TELL ME WHY BERÜHREN IS DESPERATE TO GET THEIR HANDS ON YOUR PARALLEL SUB-BRAIN.

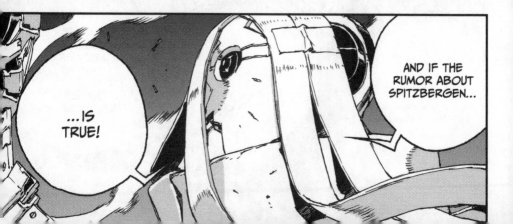

AND IF THE RUMOR ABOUT SPITZBERGEN...

...IS TRUE!

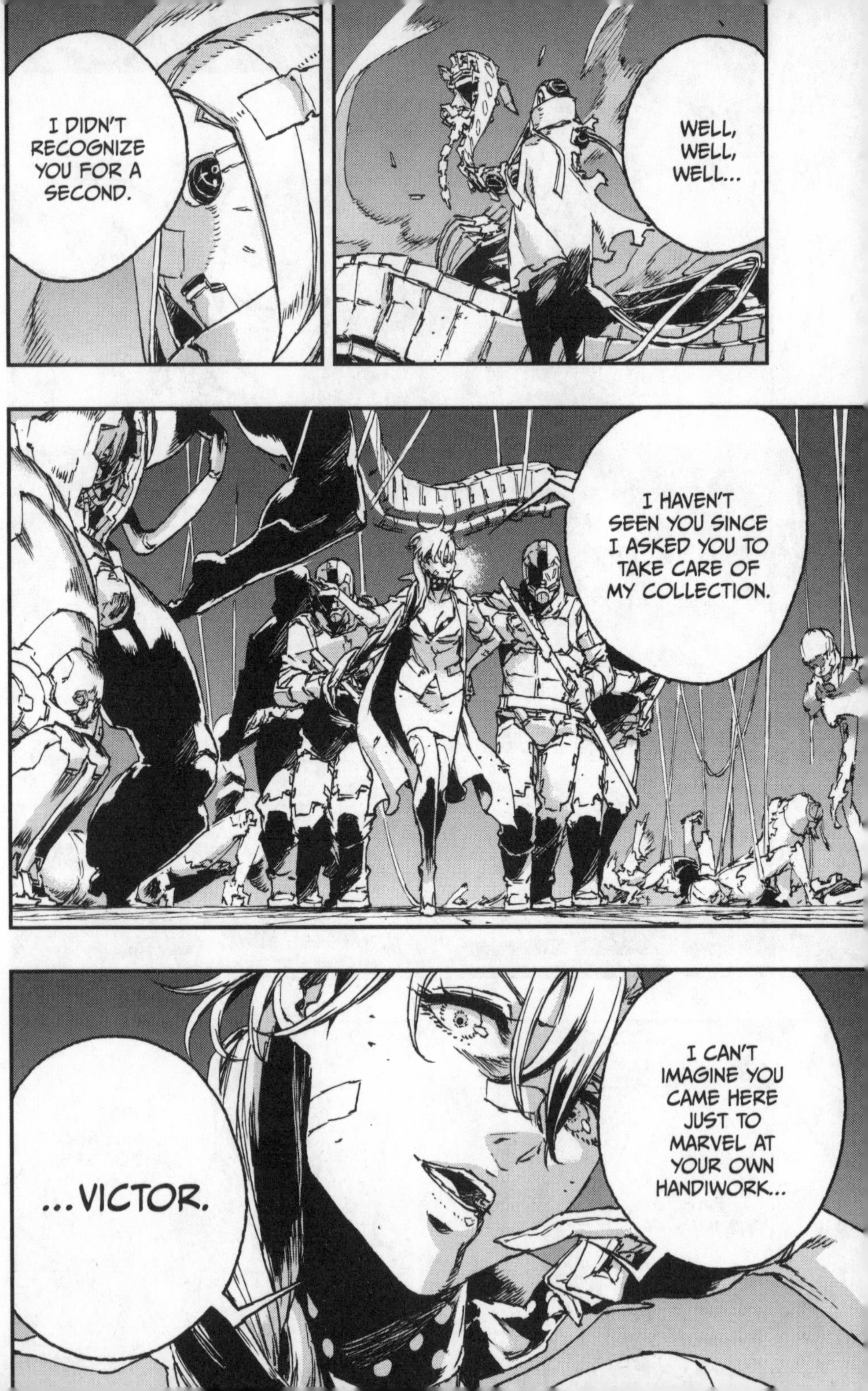
WELL, WELL, WELL...
I DIDN'T RECOGNIZE YOU FOR A SECOND.
I HAVEN'T SEEN YOU SINCE I ASKED YOU TO TAKE CARE OF MY COLLECTION.
I CAN'T IMAGINE YOU CAME HERE JUST TO MARVEL AT YOUR OWN HANDIWORK...
...VICTOR.

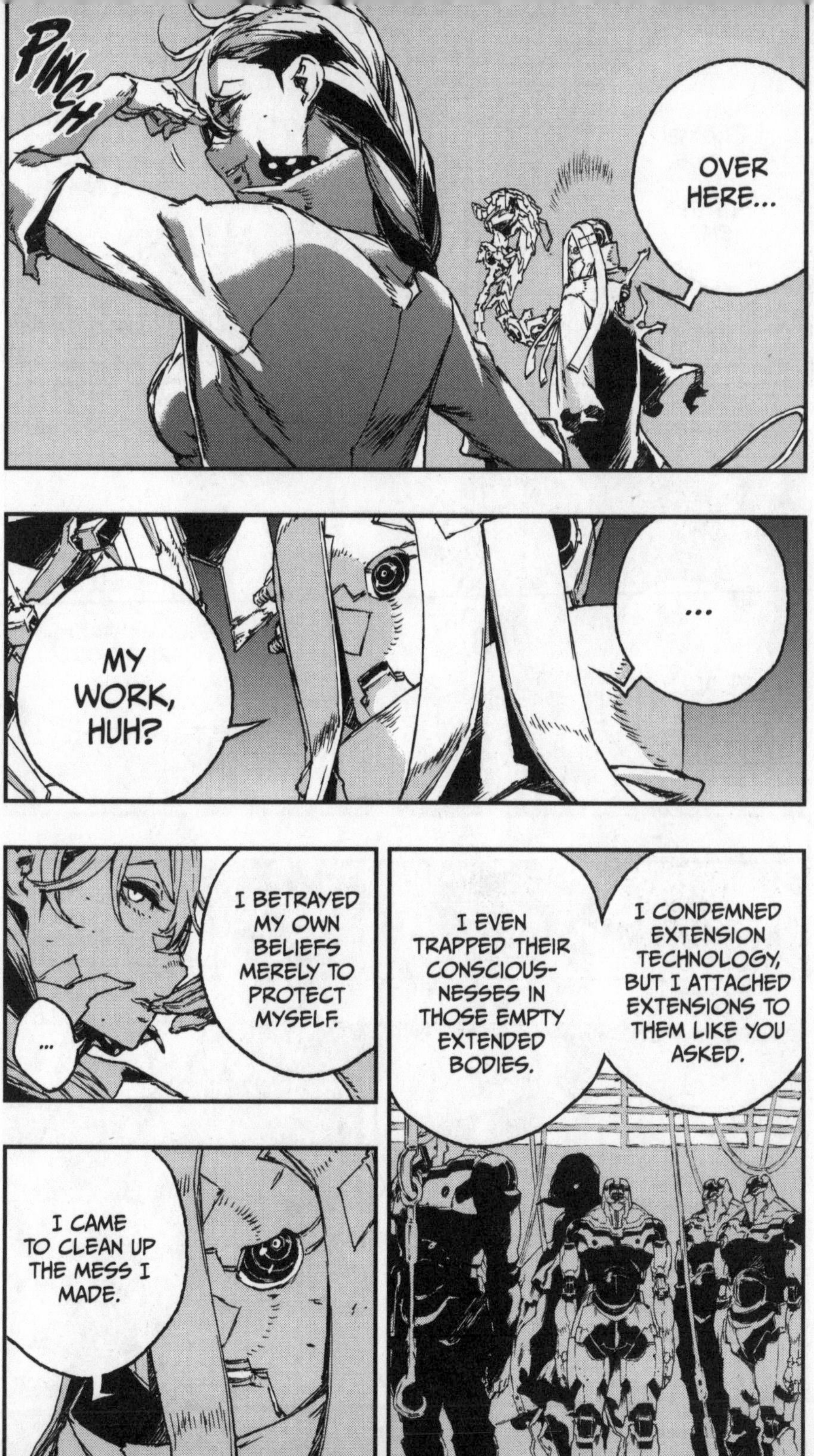
PINCH
OVER HERE...
...
MY WORK, HUH?
I CONDEMNED EXTENSION TECHNOLOGY, BUT I ATTACHED EXTENSIONS TO THEM LIKE YOU ASKED.
I EVEN TRAPPED THEIR CONSCIOUS-NESSES IN THOSE EMPTY EXTENDED BODIES.
I BETRAYED MY OWN BELIEFS MERELY TO PROTECT MYSELF.
...
I CAME TO CLEAN UP THE MESS I MADE.

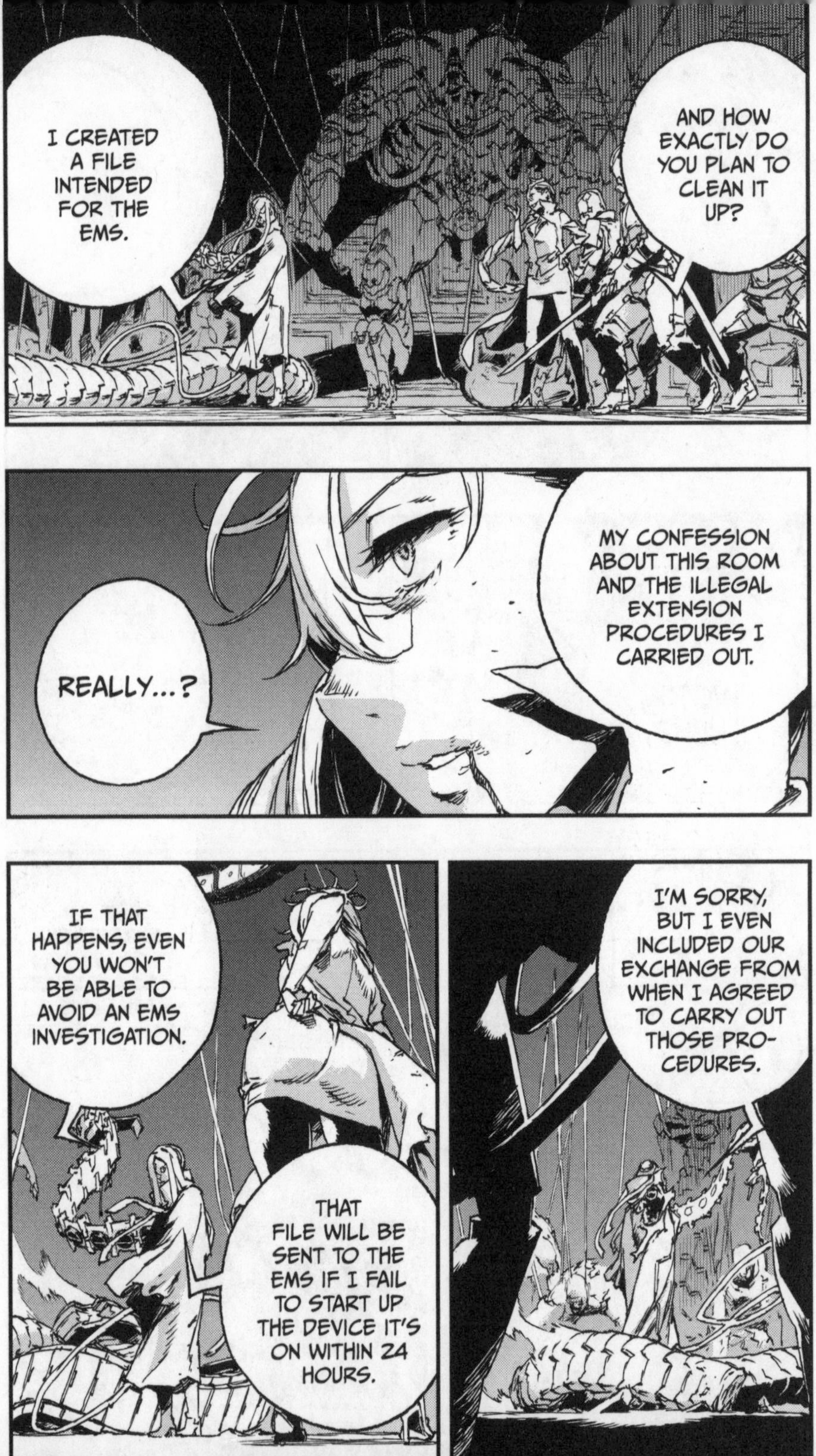
AND HOW EXACTLY DO YOU PLAN TO CLEAN IT UP?
I CREATED A FILE INTENDED FOR THE EMS.
MY CONFESSION ABOUT THIS ROOM AND THE ILLEGAL EXTENSION PROCEDURES I CARRIED OUT.
REALLY...?
I'M SORRY, BUT I EVEN INCLUDED OUR EXCHANGE FROM WHEN I AGREED TO CARRY OUT THOSE PRO-CEDURES.
THAT FILE WILL BE SENT TO THE EMS IF I FAIL TO START UP THE DEVICE IT'S ON WITHIN 24 HOURS.
IF THAT HAPPENS, EVEN YOU WON'T BE ABLE TO AVOID AN EMS INVESTIGATION.

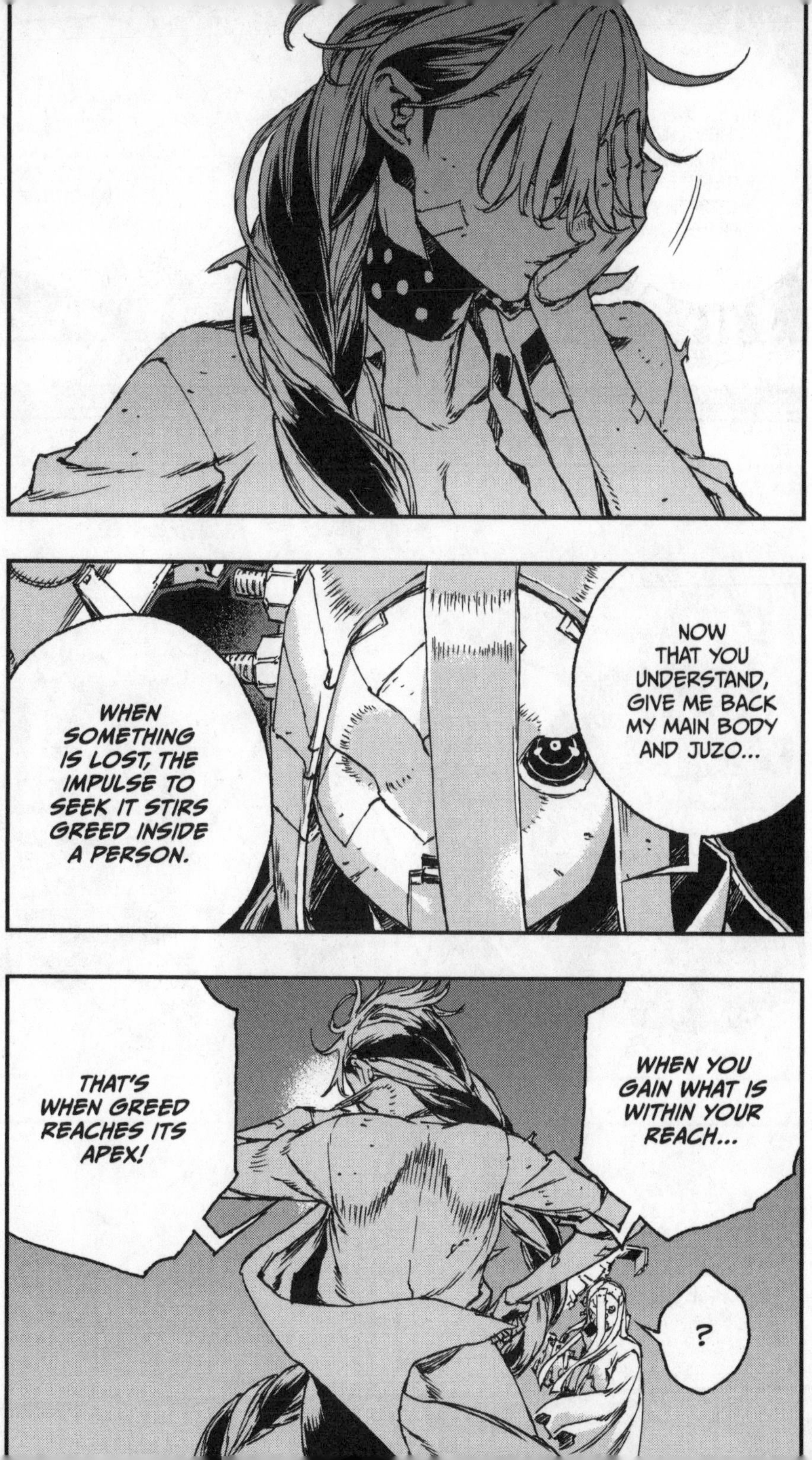
NOW THAT YOU UNDERSTAND, GIVE ME BACK MY MAIN BODY AND JUZO...
WHEN SOMETHING IS LOST, THE IMPULSE TO SEEK IT STIRS GREED INSIDE A PERSON.
WHEN YOU GAIN WHAT IS WITHIN YOUR REACH...
THAT'S WHEN GREED REACHES ITS APEX!
?

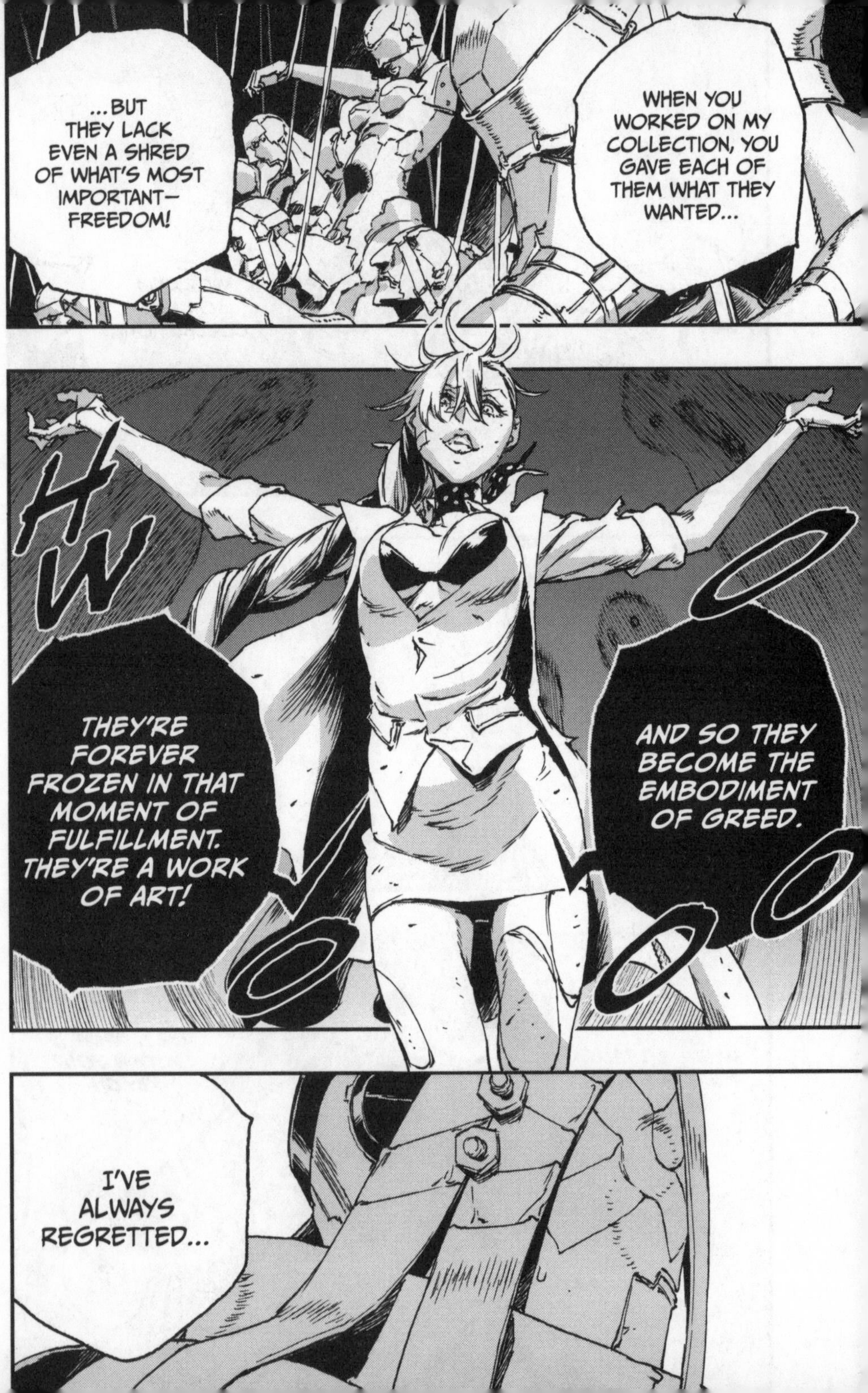
WHEN YOU WORKED ON MY COLLECTION, YOU GAVE EACH OF THEM WHAT THEY WANTED...
...BUT THEY LACK EVEN A SHRED OF WHAT'S MOST IMPORTANT—FREEDOM!
AND SO THEY BECOME THE EMBODIMENT OF GREED.
THEY'RE FOREVER FROZEN IN THAT MOMENT OF FULFILLMENT. THEY'RE A WORK OF ART!
HWOOOOO
I'VE ALWAYS REGRETTED...

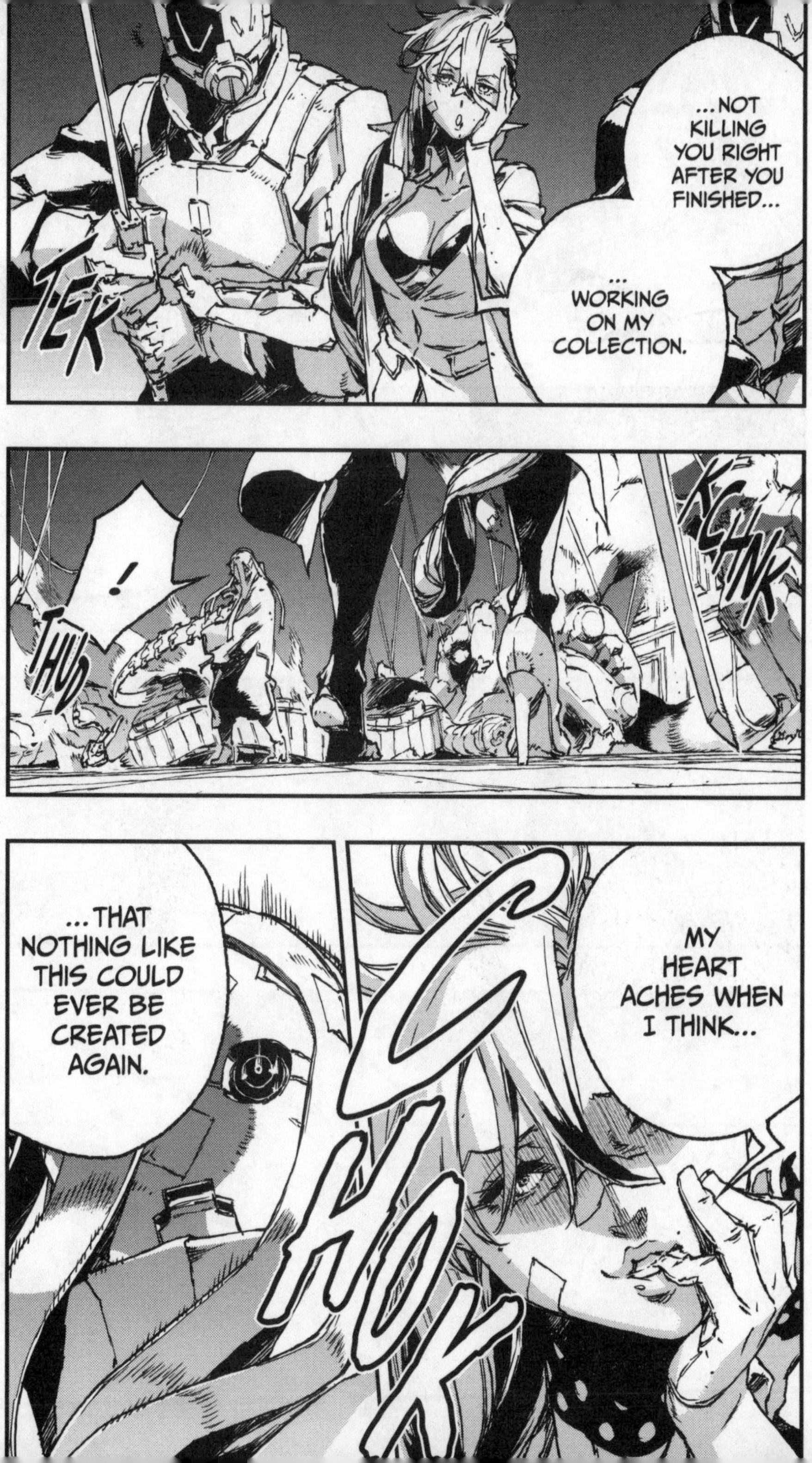
...NOT KILLING YOU RIGHT AFTER YOU FINISHED...
... WORKING ON MY COLLECTION.
TEK
KCHINK
!
THUD
MY HEART ACHES WHEN I THINK...
...THAT NOTHING LIKE THIS COULD EVER BE CREATED AGAIN.
CHOK

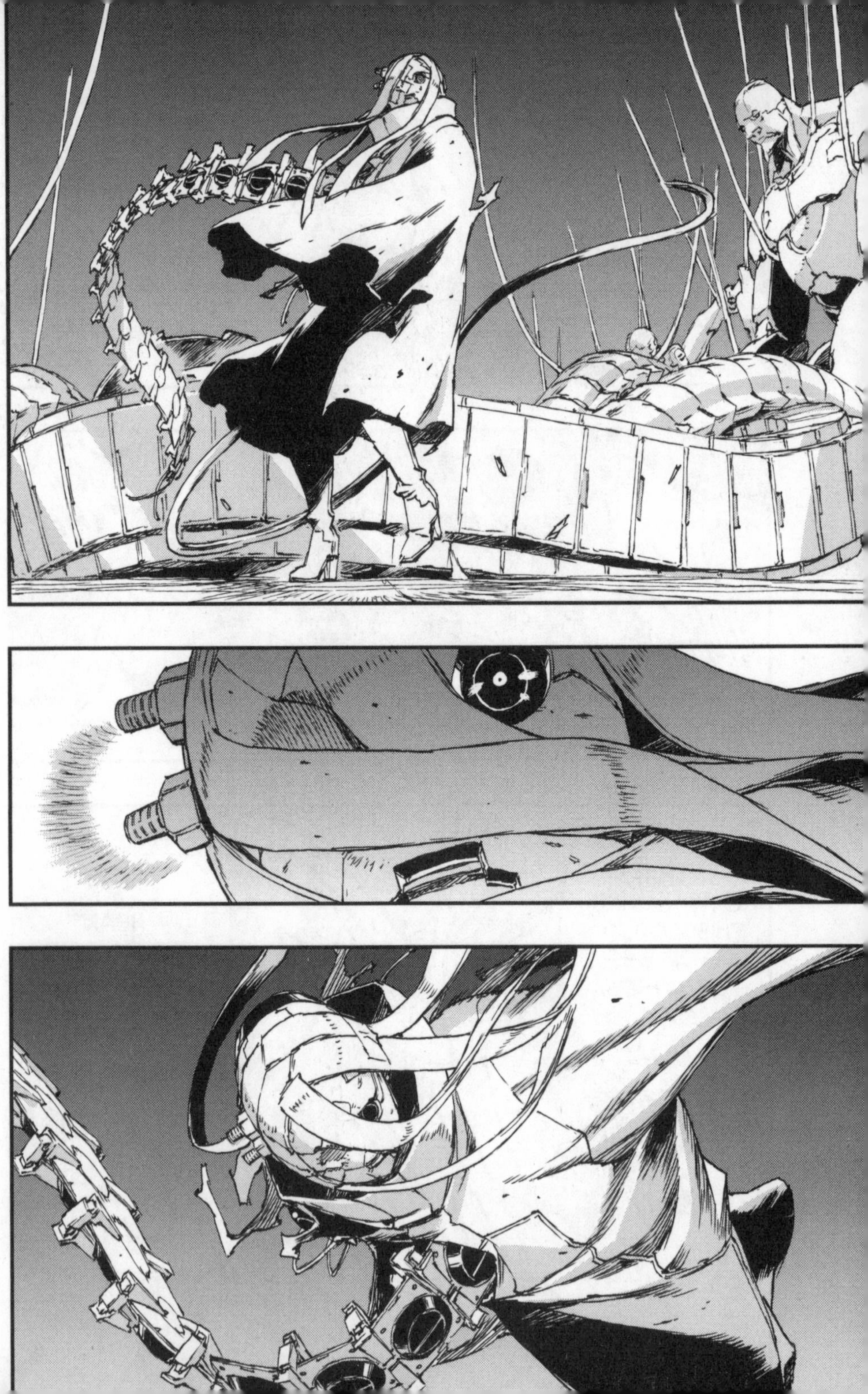

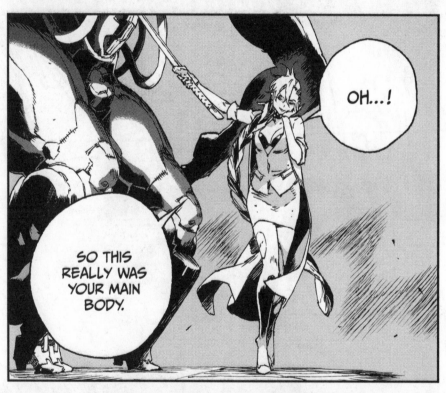

OH...!

SO THIS REALLY WAS YOUR MAIN BODY.

TO BE HONEST, I DIDN'T QUITE BELIEVE IT.

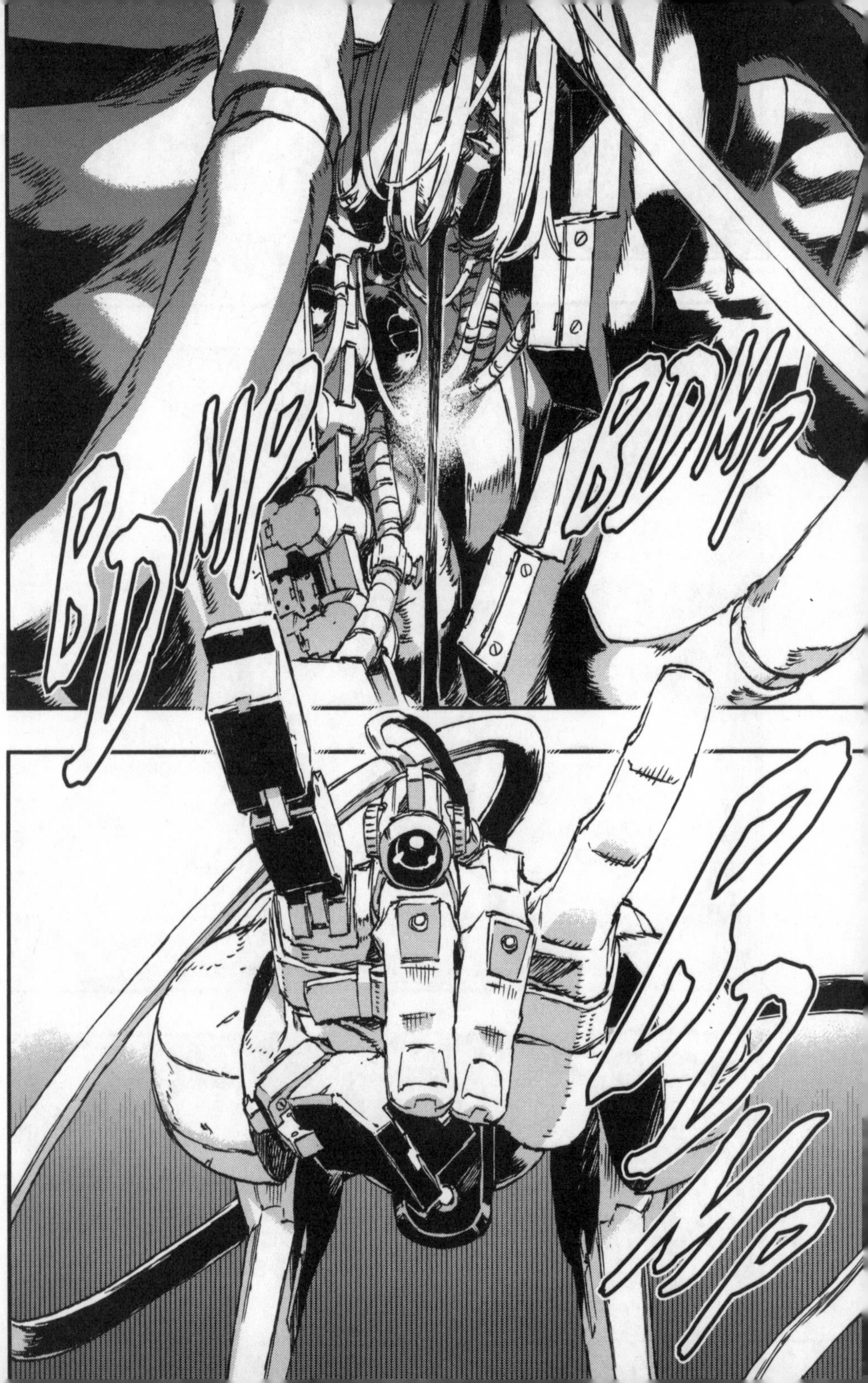
BDMP
BDMP
BDMP

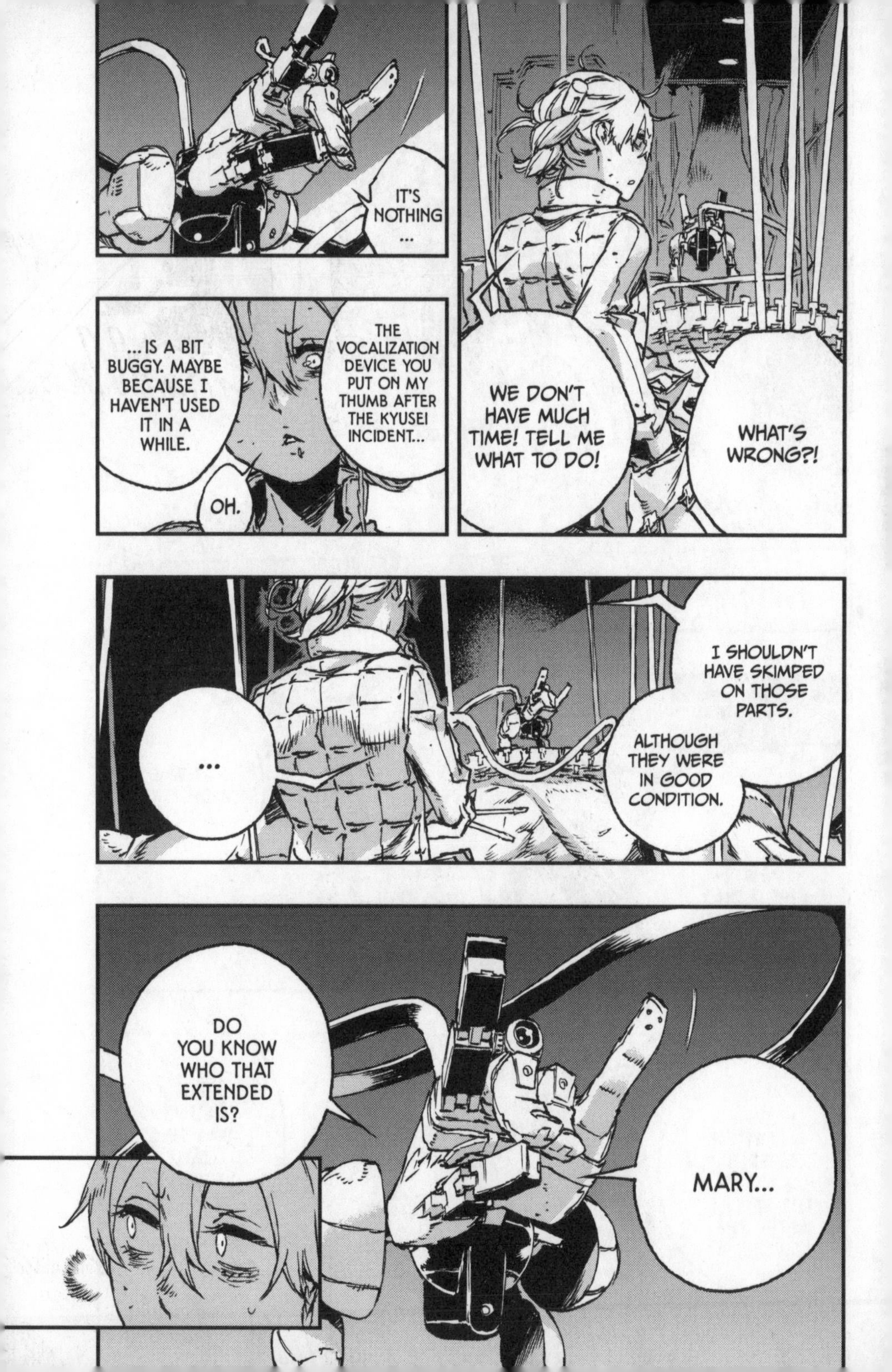
WHAT'S WRONG?!
WE DON'T HAVE MUCH TIME! TELL ME WHAT TO DO!
IT'S NOTHING ...
THE VOCALIZATION DEVICE YOU PUT ON MY THUMB AFTER THE KYUSEI INCIDENT...
...IS A BIT BUGGY. MAYBE BECAUSE I HAVEN'T USED IT IN A WHILE.
OH.
I SHOULDN'T HAVE SKIMPED ON THOSE PARTS.
ALTHOUGH THEY WERE IN GOOD CONDITION.
...
DO YOU KNOW WHO THAT EXTENDED IS?
MARY...

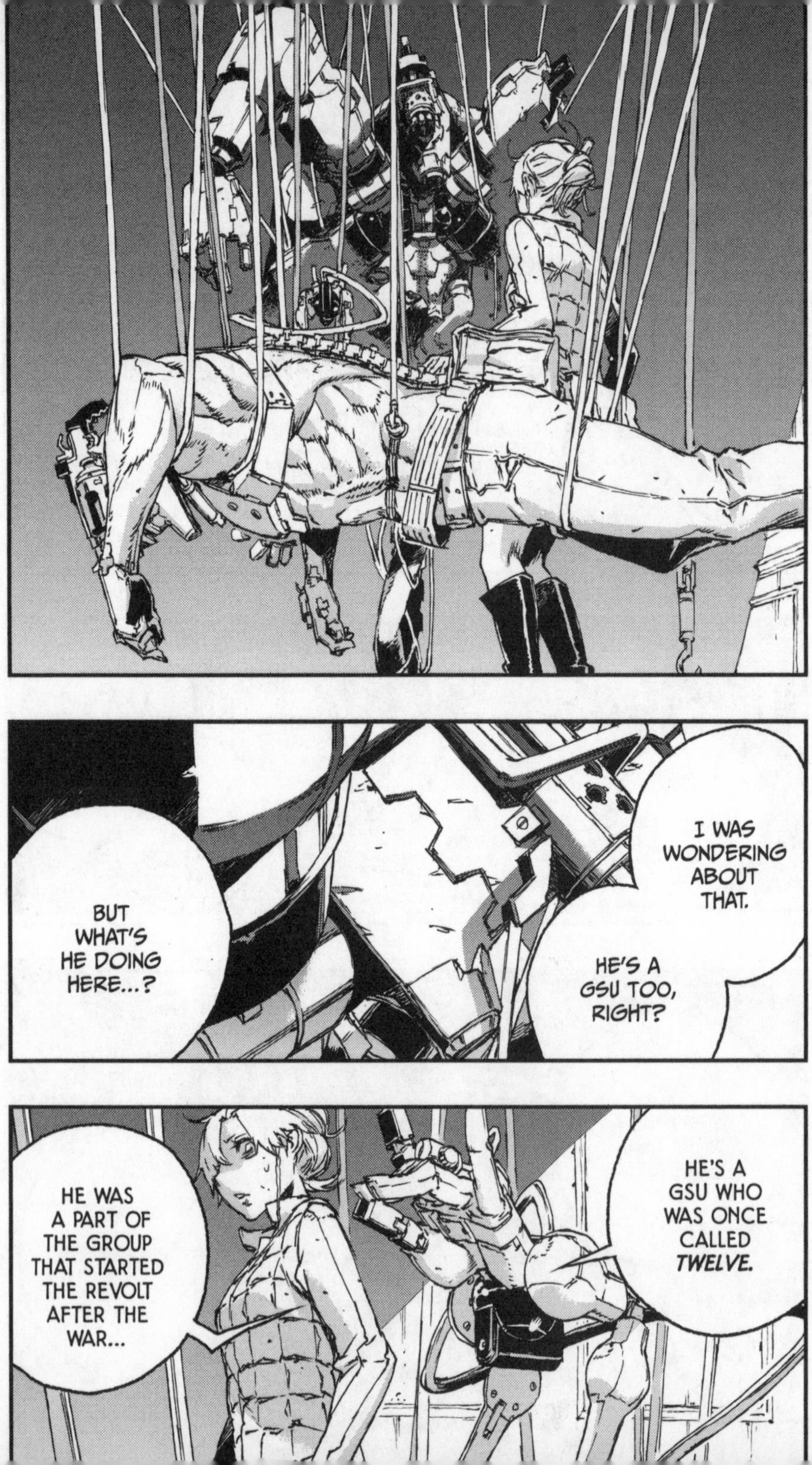
I WAS WONDERING ABOUT THAT.
HE'S A GSU TOO, RIGHT?
BUT WHAT'S HE DOING HERE...?
HE'S A GSU WHO WAS ONCE CALLED *TWELVE.*
HE WAS A PART OF THE GROUP THAT STARTED THE REVOLT AFTER THE WAR...

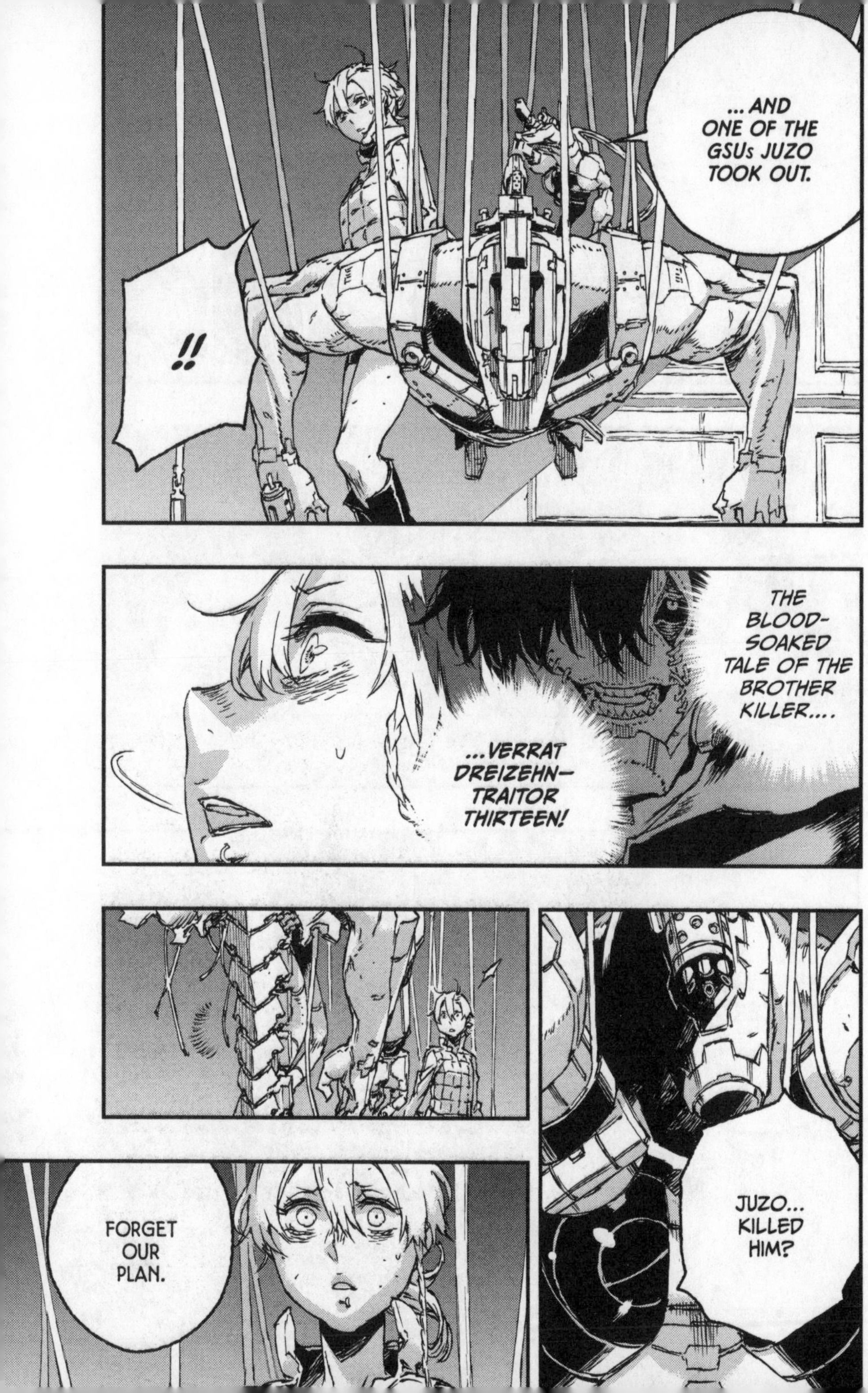
...AND ONE OF THE GSUs JUZO TOOK OUT.
!!
THE BLOOD-SOAKED TALE OF THE BROTHER KILLER....
...VERRAT DREIZEHN—TRAITOR THIRTEEN!
JUZO... KILLED HIM?
FORGET OUR PLAN.

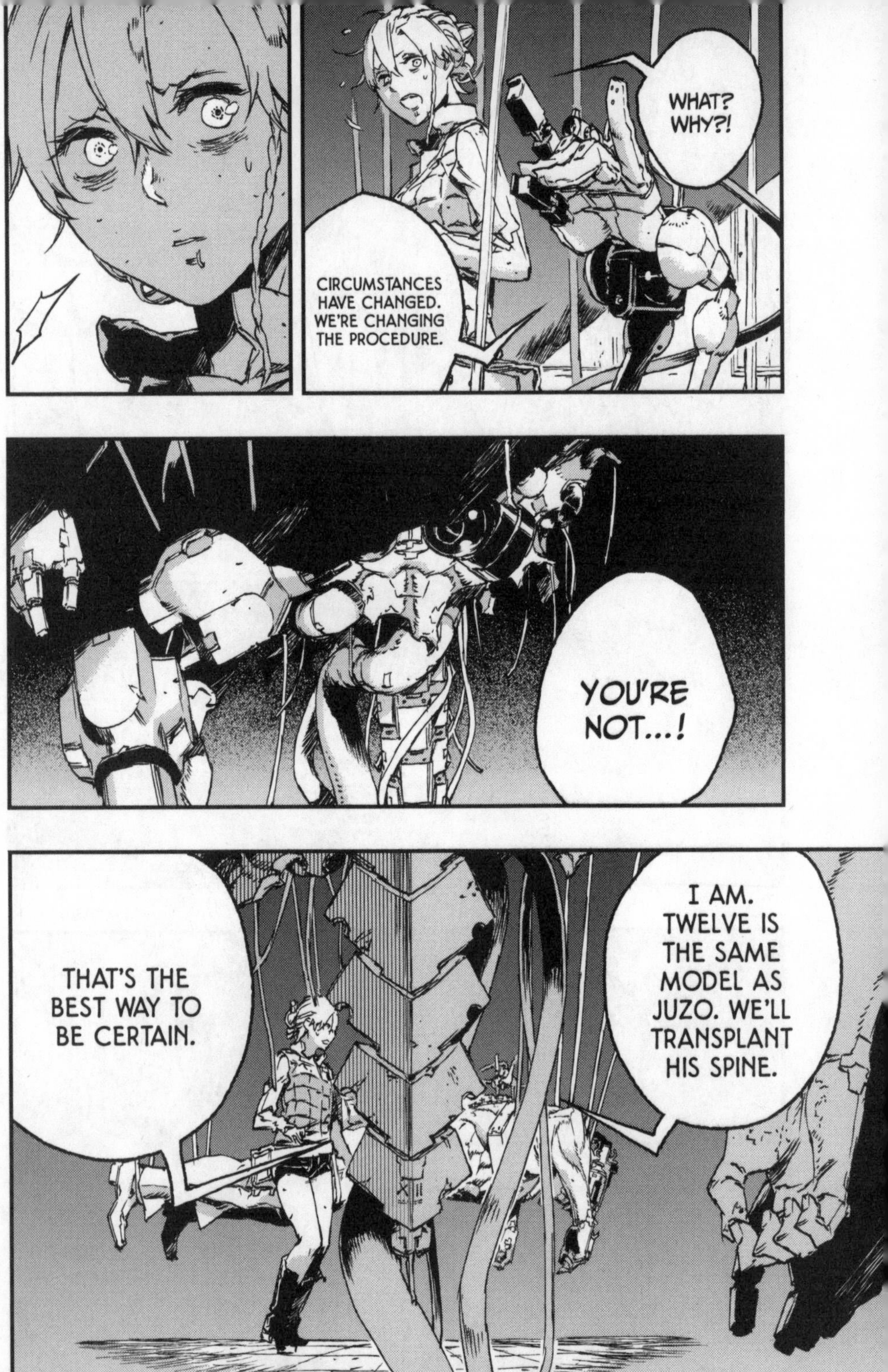
WHAT? WHY?!
CIRCUMSTANCES HAVE CHANGED. WE'RE CHANGING THE PROCEDURE.
YOU'RE NOT...!
I AM. TWELVE IS THE SAME MODEL AS JUZO. WE'LL TRANSPLANT HIS SPINE.
THAT'S THE BEST WAY TO BE CERTAIN.

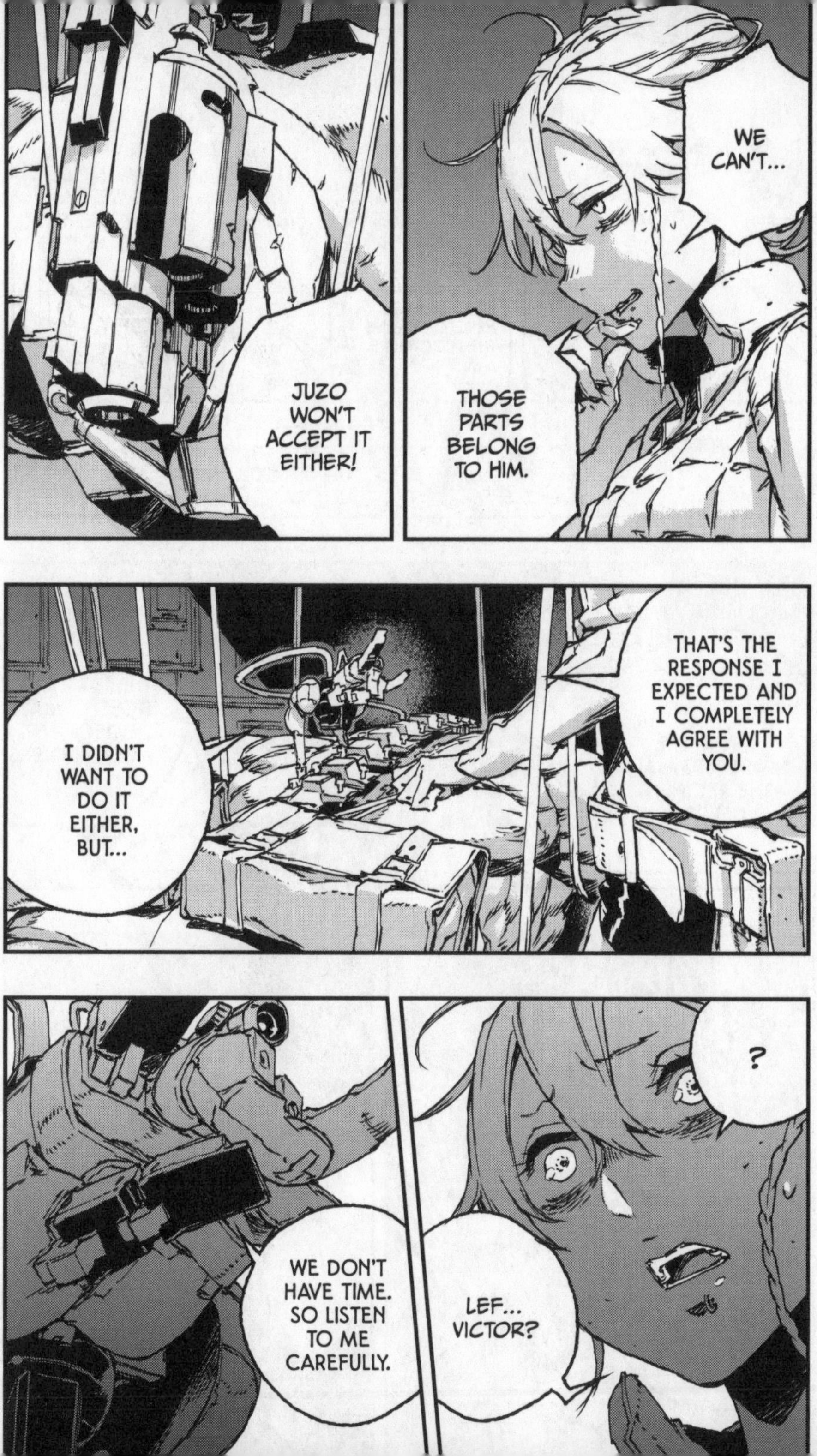
WE CAN'T...
THOSE PARTS BELONG TO HIM.
JUZO WON'T ACCEPT IT EITHER!
THAT'S THE RESPONSE I EXPECTED AND I COMPLETELY AGREE WITH YOU.
I DIDN'T WANT TO DO IT EITHER, BUT...
?
LEF... VICTOR?
WE DON'T HAVE TIME. SO LISTEN TO ME CAREFULLY.

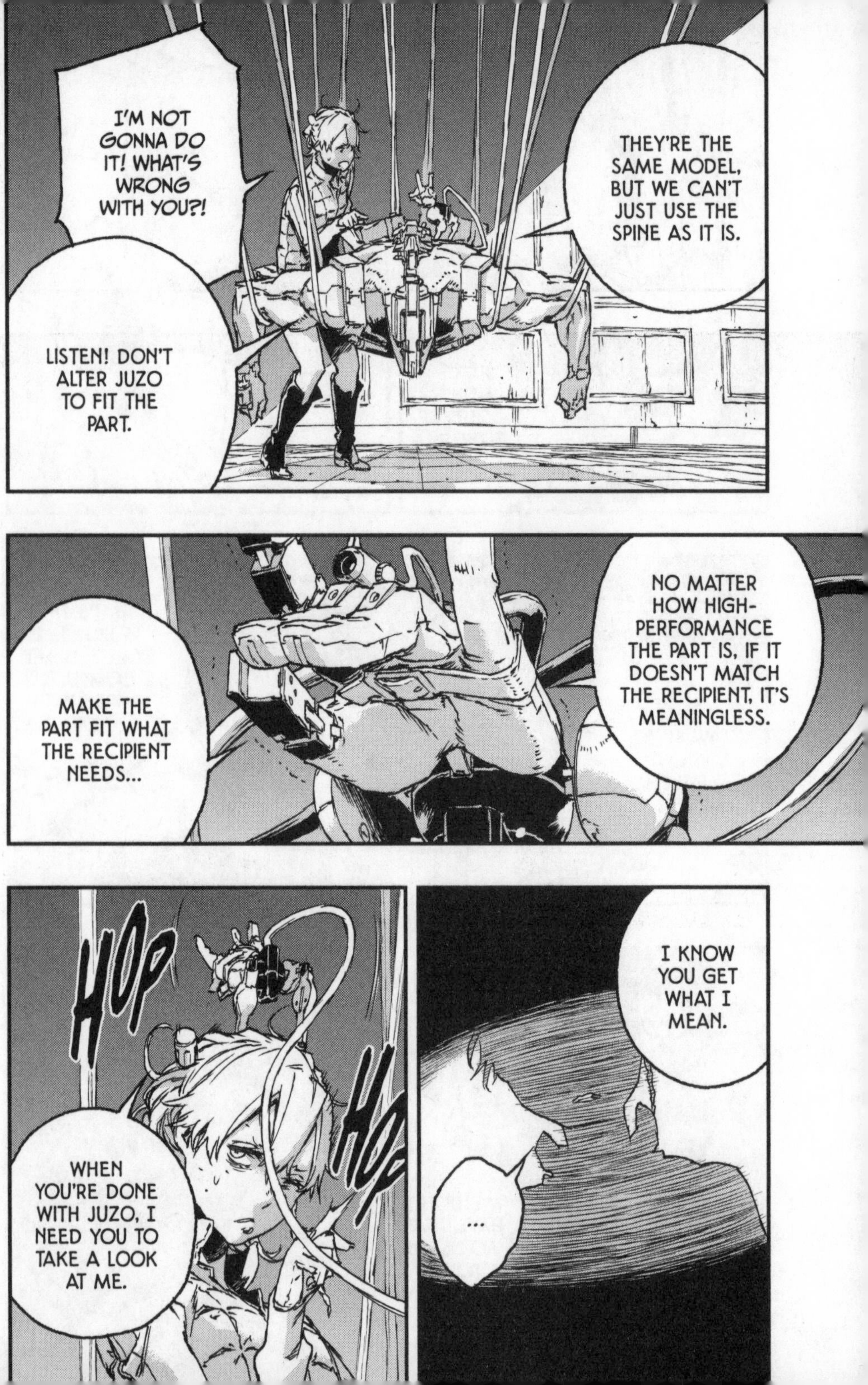
THEY'RE THE SAME MODEL, BUT WE CAN'T JUST USE THE SPINE AS IT IS.
I'M NOT GONNA DO IT! WHAT'S WRONG WITH YOU?!
LISTEN! DON'T ALTER JUZO TO FIT THE PART.
NO MATTER HOW HIGH-PERFORMANCE THE PART IS, IF IT DOESN'T MATCH THE RECIPIENT, IT'S MEANINGLESS.
MAKE THE PART FIT WHAT THE RECIPIENT NEEDS...
I KNOW YOU GET WHAT I MEAN.
...
HOP
HOP
WHEN YOU'RE DONE WITH JUZO, I NEED YOU TO TAKE A LOOK AT ME.

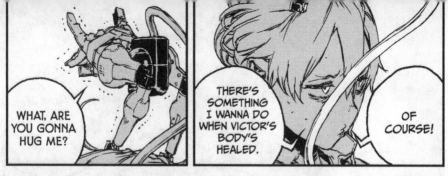

OF COURSE!
THERE'S SOMETHING I WANNA DO WHEN VICTOR'S BODY'S HEALED.
WHAT, ARE YOU GONNA HUG ME?
NO! I'M GOING TO PUNCH YOU!
I RAN OFF TO THE WAR LEAVING YOU BEHIND...
... WHEN YOU WERE JUST A CHILD.
ALL FOR THE SAKE OF MY SO-CALLED DREAM.
HEH...

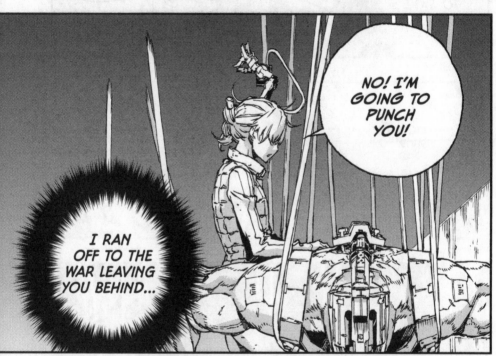

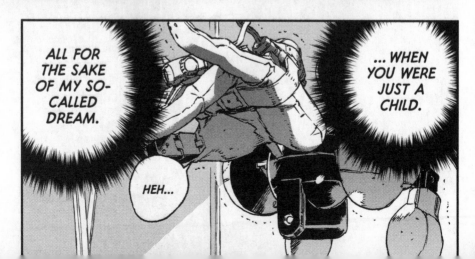

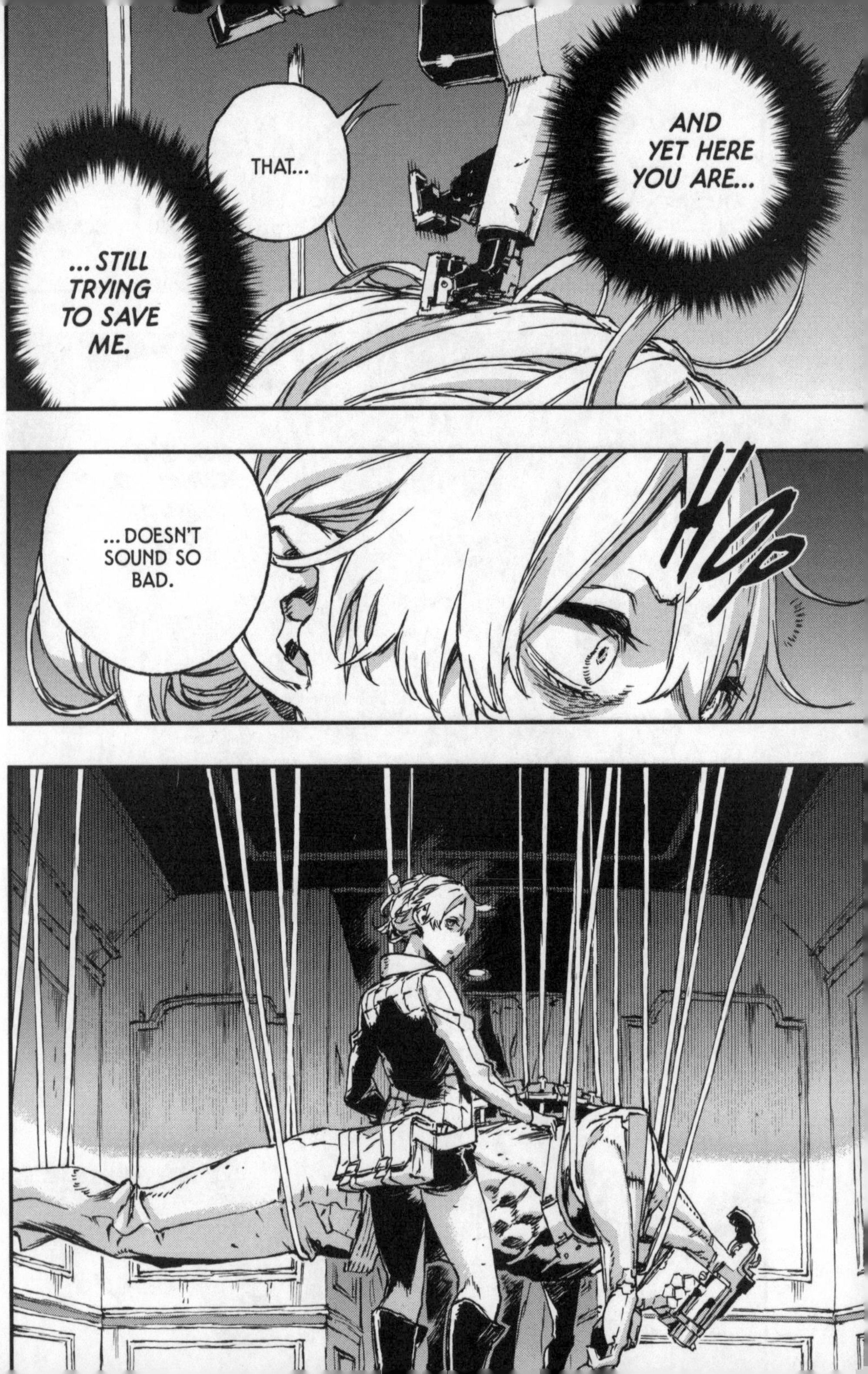
AND YET HERE YOU ARE...
...STILL TRYING TO SAVE ME.
THAT...
...DOESN'T SOUND SO BAD.
HOP

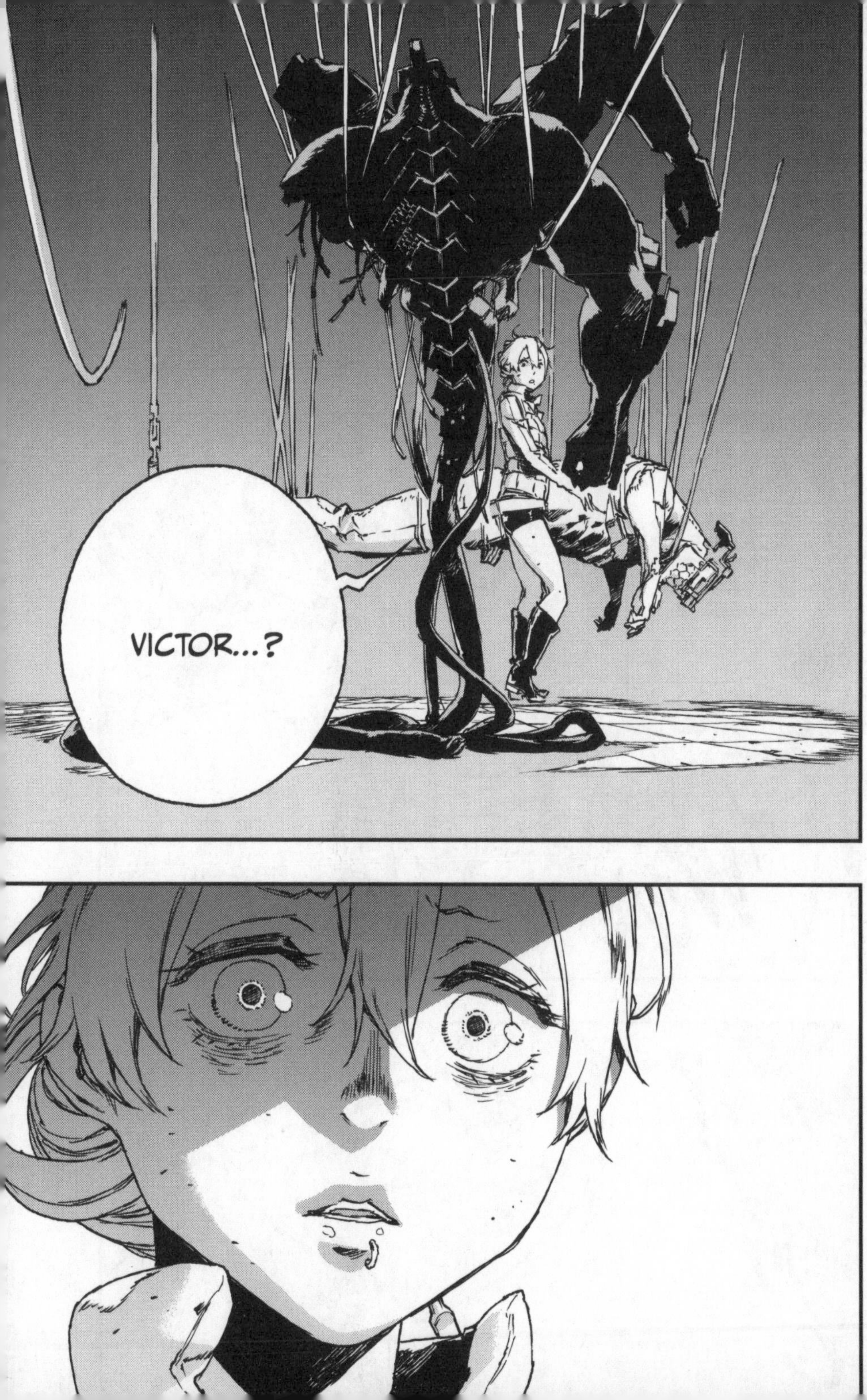
VICTOR...?

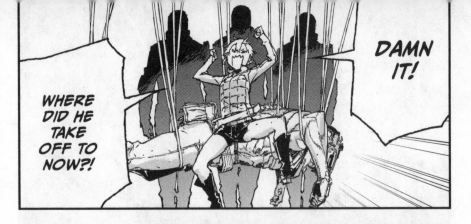

DAMN IT!
WHERE DID HE TAKE OFF TO NOW?!
BY ORDER OF THE DIRECTOR...
WE'RE HERE TO ELIMINATE YOU FOR ABETTING A PRISONER ESCAPE.
HWOOO
...
RRING

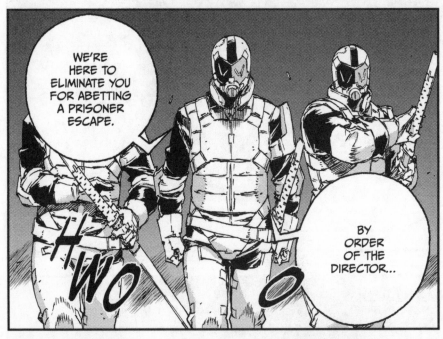

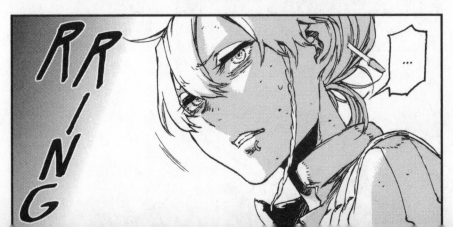

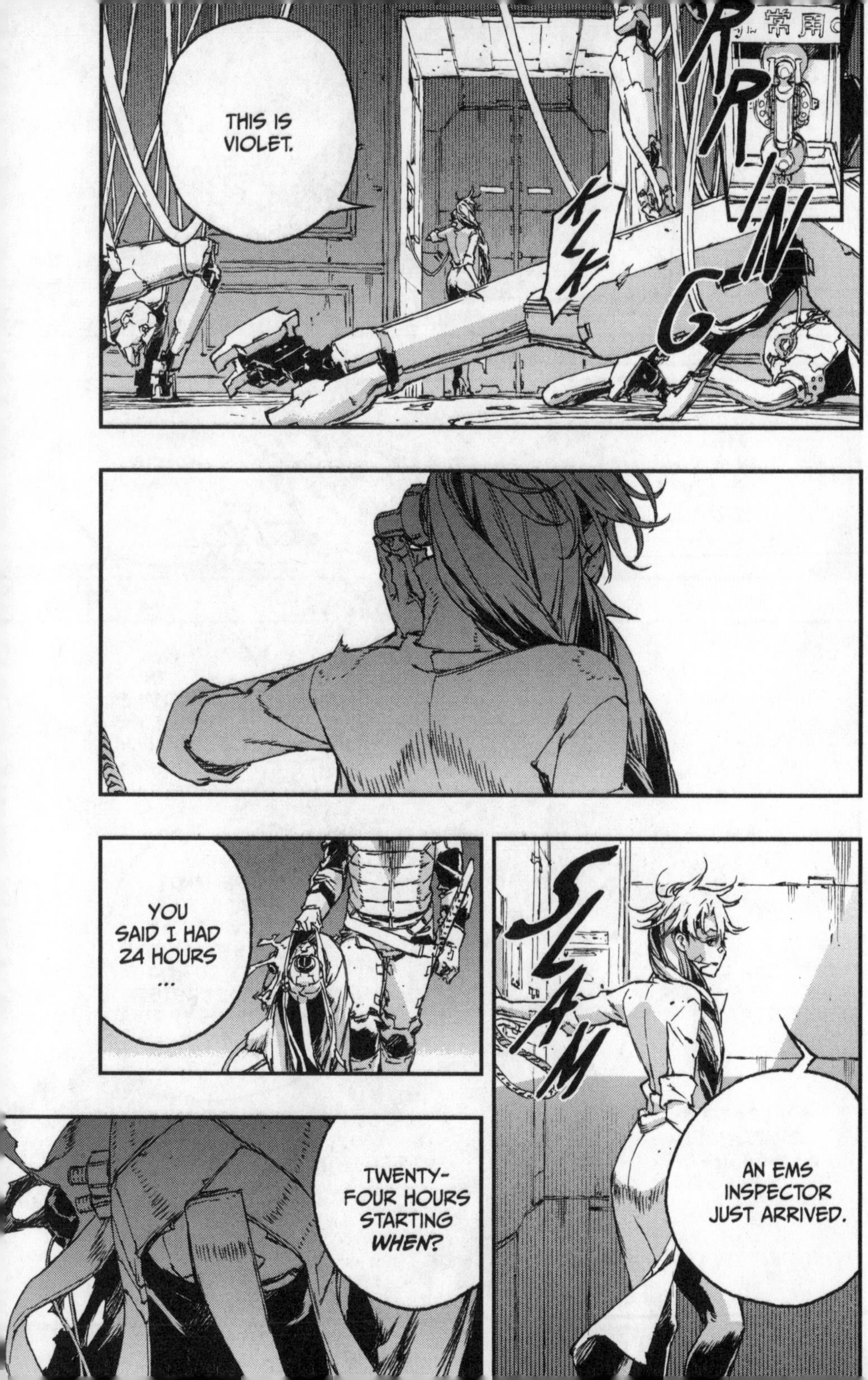
RRING
KLK
THIS IS VIOLET.
SLAM
AN EMS INSPECTOR JUST ARRIVED.
YOU SAID I HAD 24 HOURS ...
TWENTY-FOUR HOURS STARTING *WHEN?*

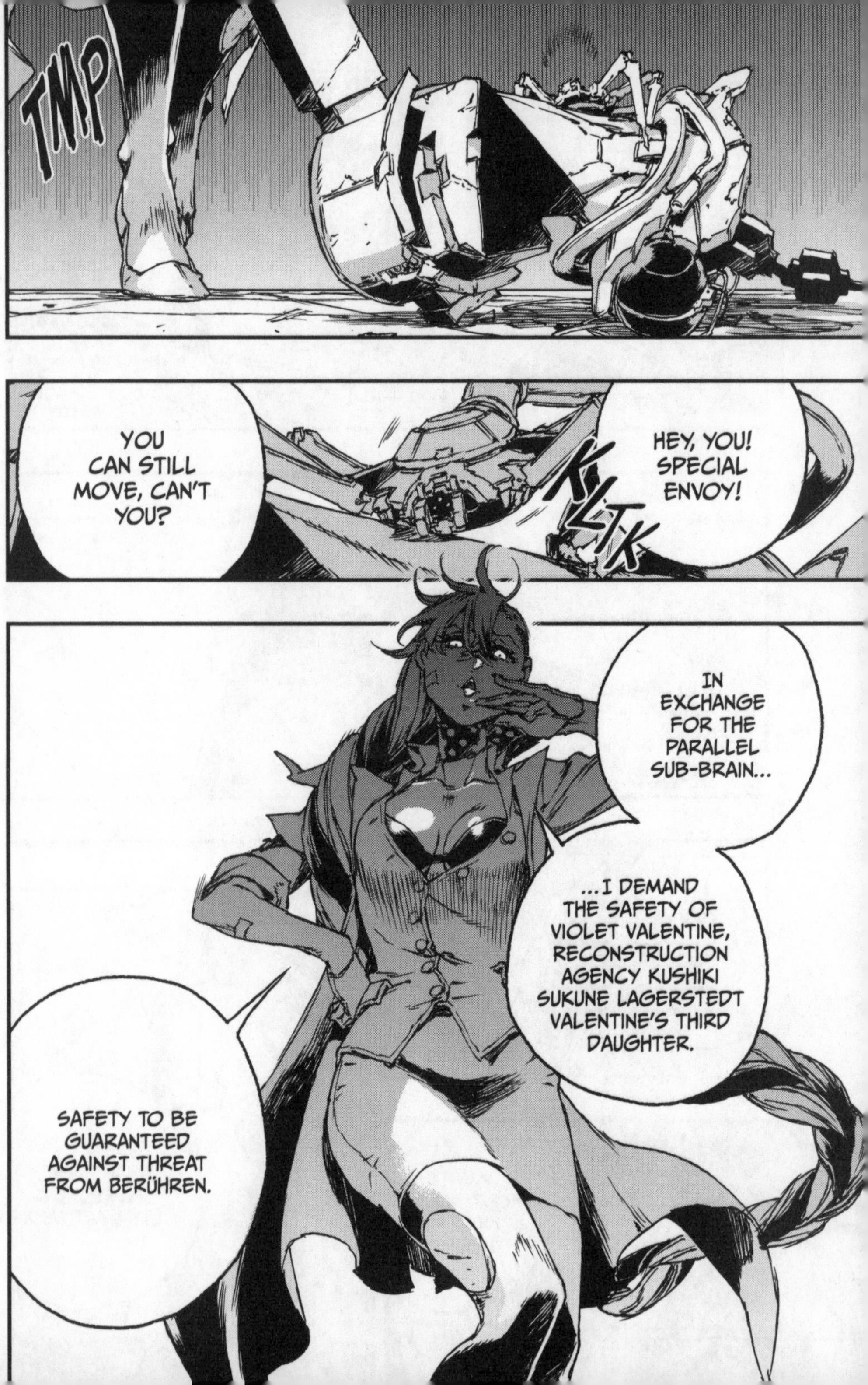
TMP
HEY, YOU! SPECIAL ENVOY!
KLTK
YOU CAN STILL MOVE, CAN'T YOU?
IN EXCHANGE FOR THE PARALLEL SUB-BRAIN...
...I DEMAND THE SAFETY OF VIOLET VALENTINE, RECONSTRUCTION AGENCY KUSHIKI SUKUNE LAGERSTEDT VALENTINE'S THIRD DAUGHTER.
SAFETY TO BE GUARANTEED AGAINST THREAT FROM BERÜHREN.

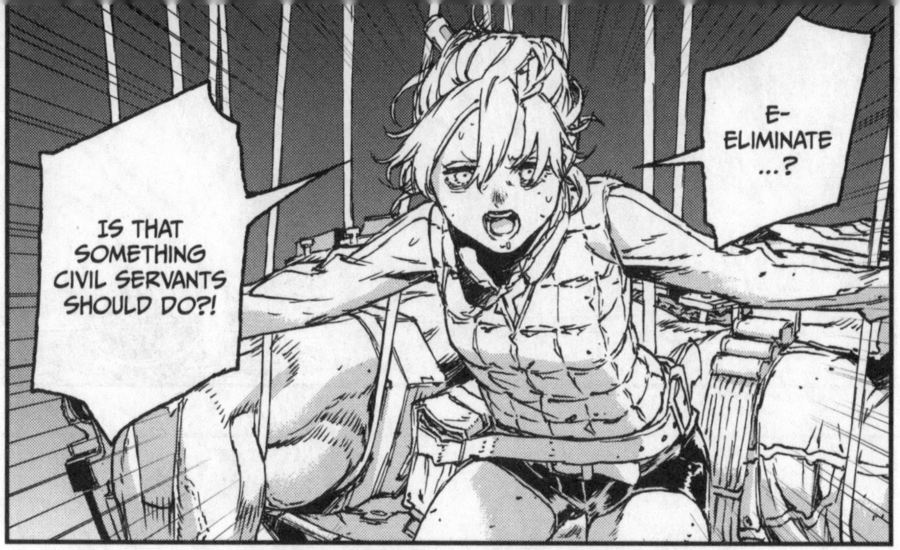
E-
ELIMINATE
...?
IS THAT SOMETHING CIVIL SERVANTS SHOULD DO?!

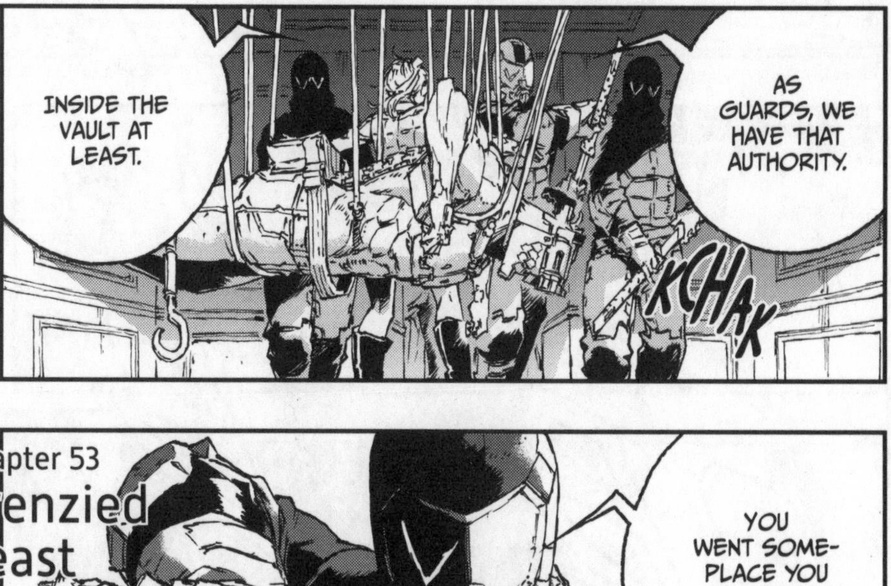
AS GUARDS, WE HAVE THAT AUTHORITY.
INSIDE THE VAULT AT LEAST.
KCHAK

Chapter 53
Frenzied Feast

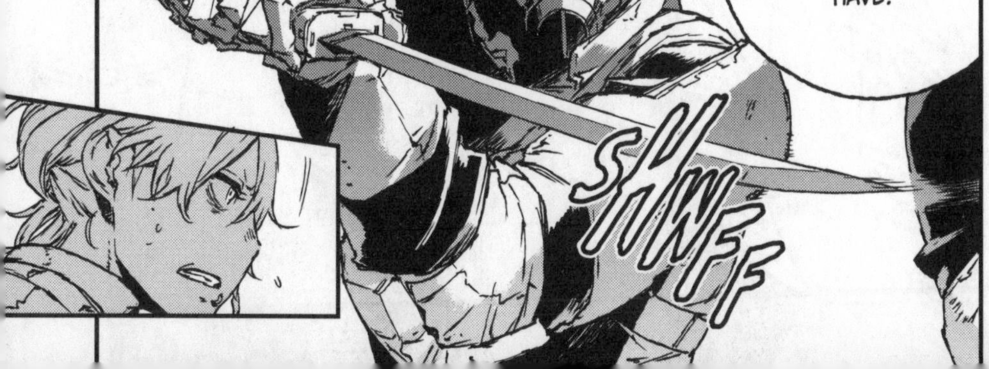
YOU WENT SOME-PLACE YOU SHOULDN'T HAVE.
SHWFF

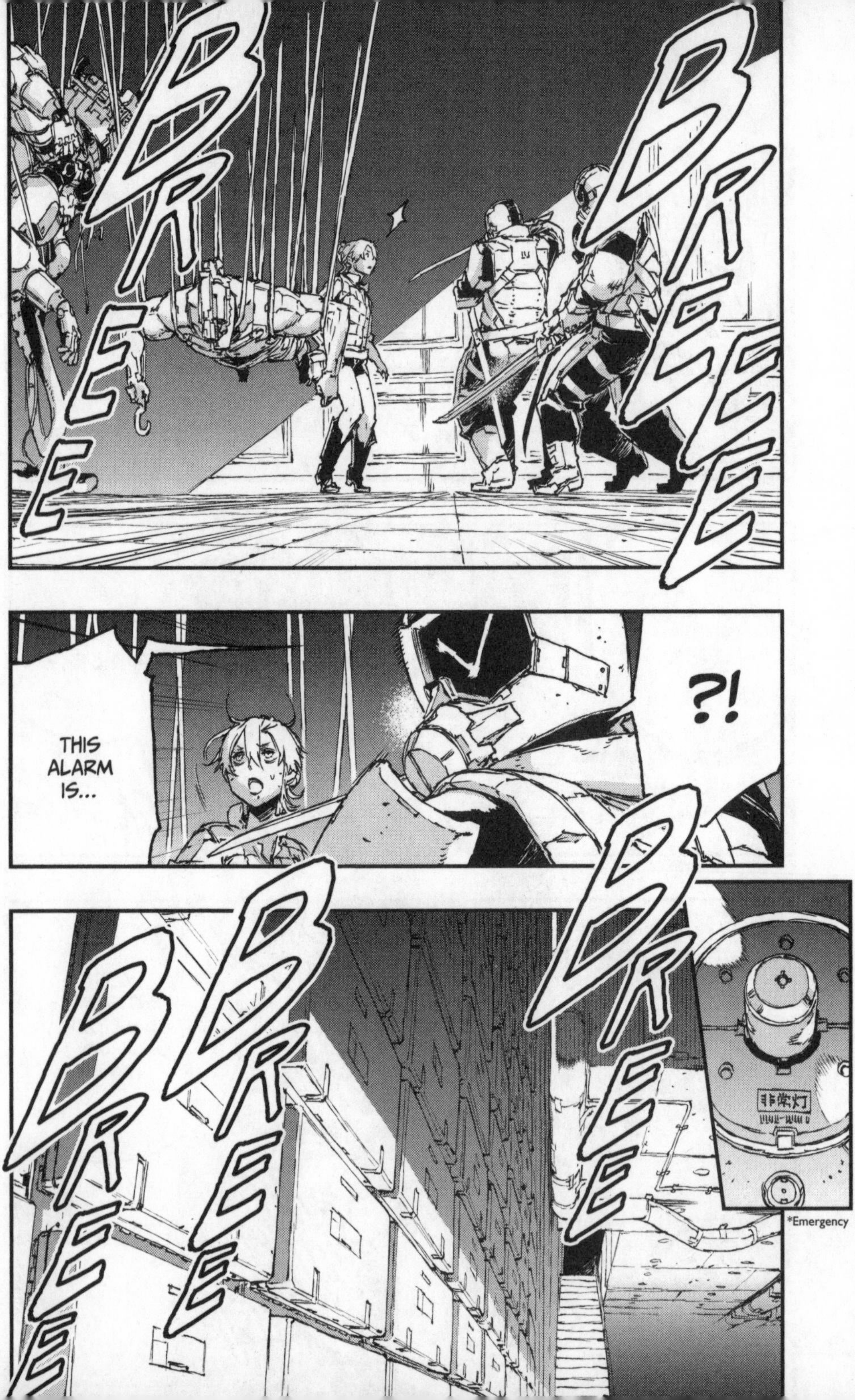
BREEE
BREEEE
THIS ALARM IS...
?!
BREEE
BREEEE
BREEEE
非常灯

*Emergency

CH-CHOK
0137
FWSSHH
KLANG
POK POK POK POK
BREEE
BREEEE

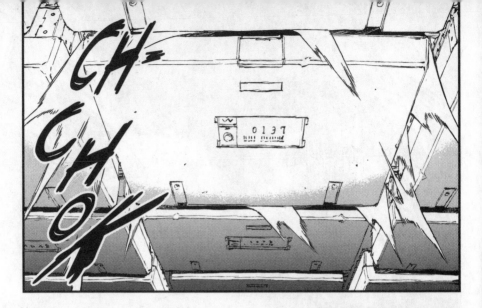

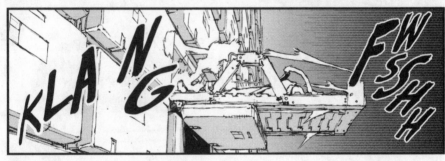

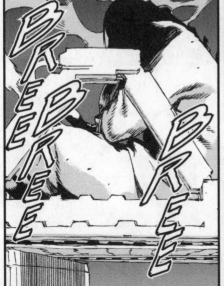

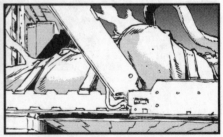

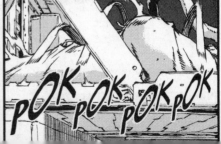

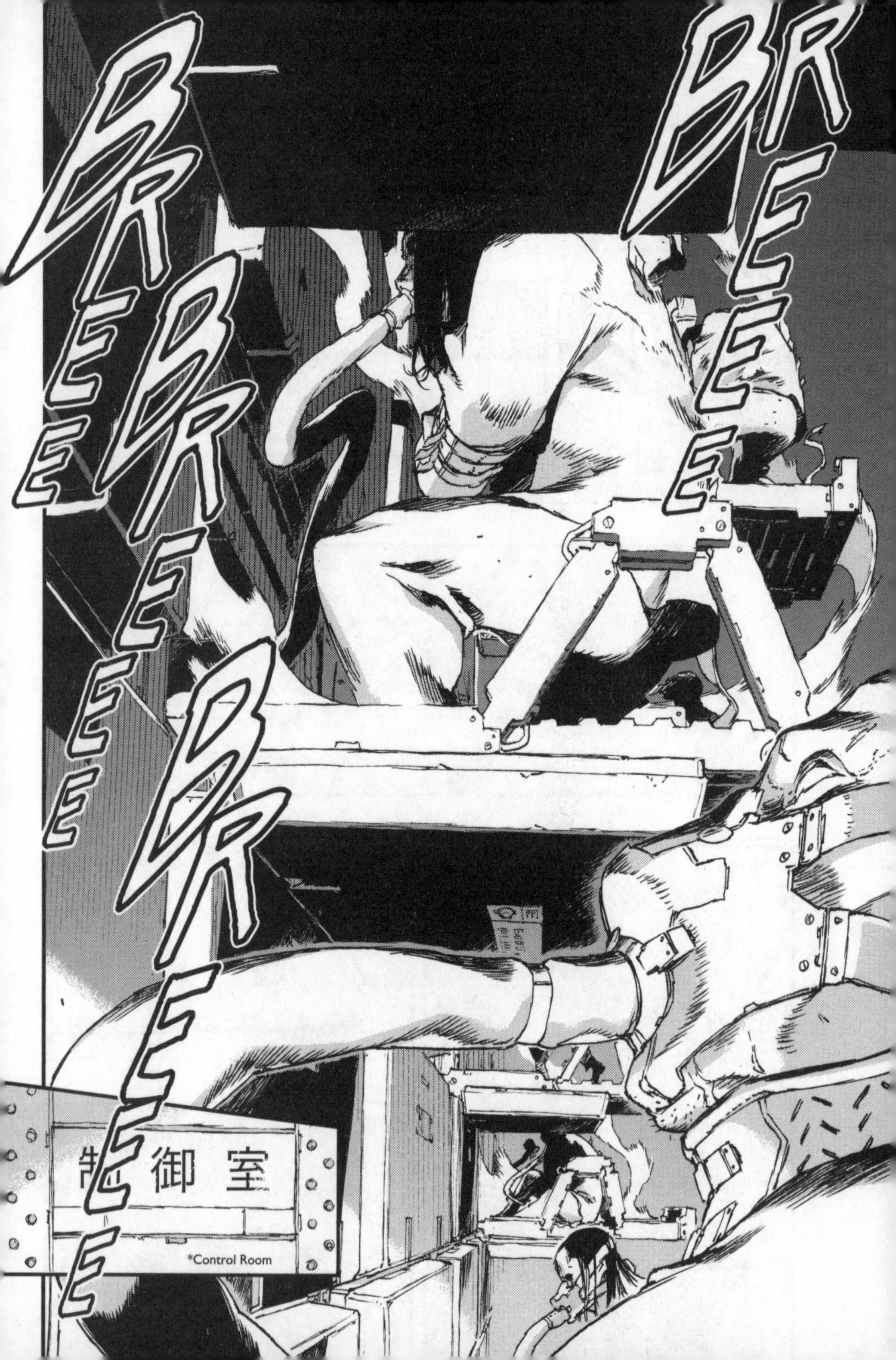
BREEEEE
BREEE
BREEEEE
BREEEEEE
制御室
*Control Room

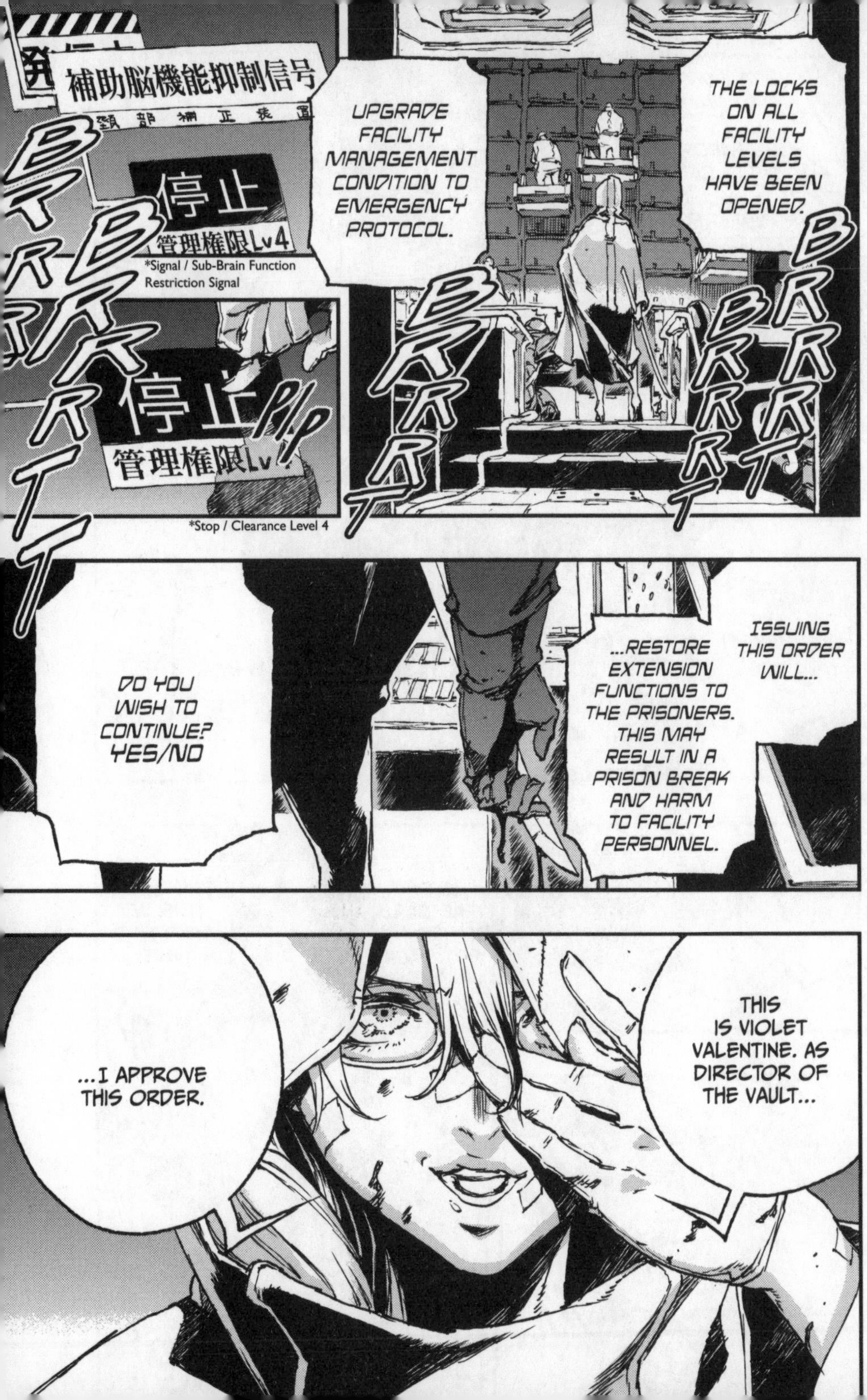
THE LOCKS ON ALL FACILITY LEVELS HAVE BEEN OPENED.
UPGRADE FACILITY MANAGEMENT CONDITION TO EMERGENCY PROTOCOL.
BRRRT
BRRRT
BRRRT
補助脳機能抑制信号
停止
管理権限Lv4
*Signal / Sub-Brain Function Restriction Signal
BRRRT
BRRRT
停止
管理権限Lv
PIP
*Stop / Clearance Level 4
ISSUING THIS ORDER WILL...
...RESTORE EXTENSION FUNCTIONS TO THE PRISONERS. THIS MAY RESULT IN A PRISON BREAK AND HARM TO FACILITY PERSONNEL.
DO YOU WISH TO CONTINUE? YES/NO
THIS IS VIOLET VALENTINE. AS DIRECTOR OF THE VAULT...
...I APPROVE THIS ORDER.

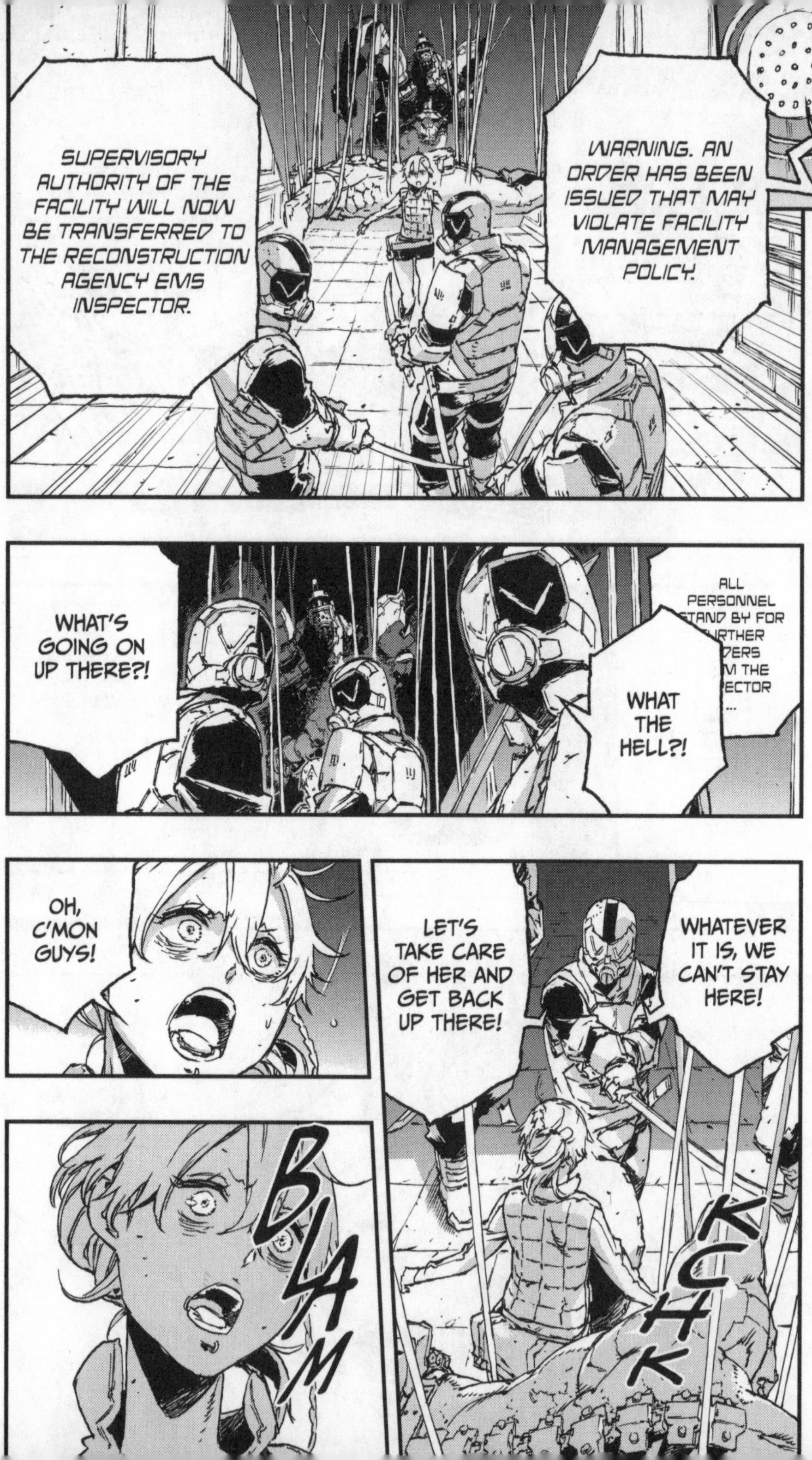

WARNING. AN ORDER HAS BEEN ISSUED THAT MAY VIOLATE FACILITY MANAGEMENT POLICY.
SUPERVISORY AUTHORITY OF THE FACILITY WILL NOW BE TRANSFERRED TO THE RECONSTRUCTION AGENCY EMS INSPECTOR.
ALL PERSONNEL STAND BY FOR
WHAT THE HELL?!
WHAT'S GOING ON UP THERE?!
WHATEVER IT IS, WE CAN'T STAY HERE!
LET'S TAKE CARE OF HER AND GET BACK UP THERE!
OH, C'MON GUYS!
KCHK
BLAM

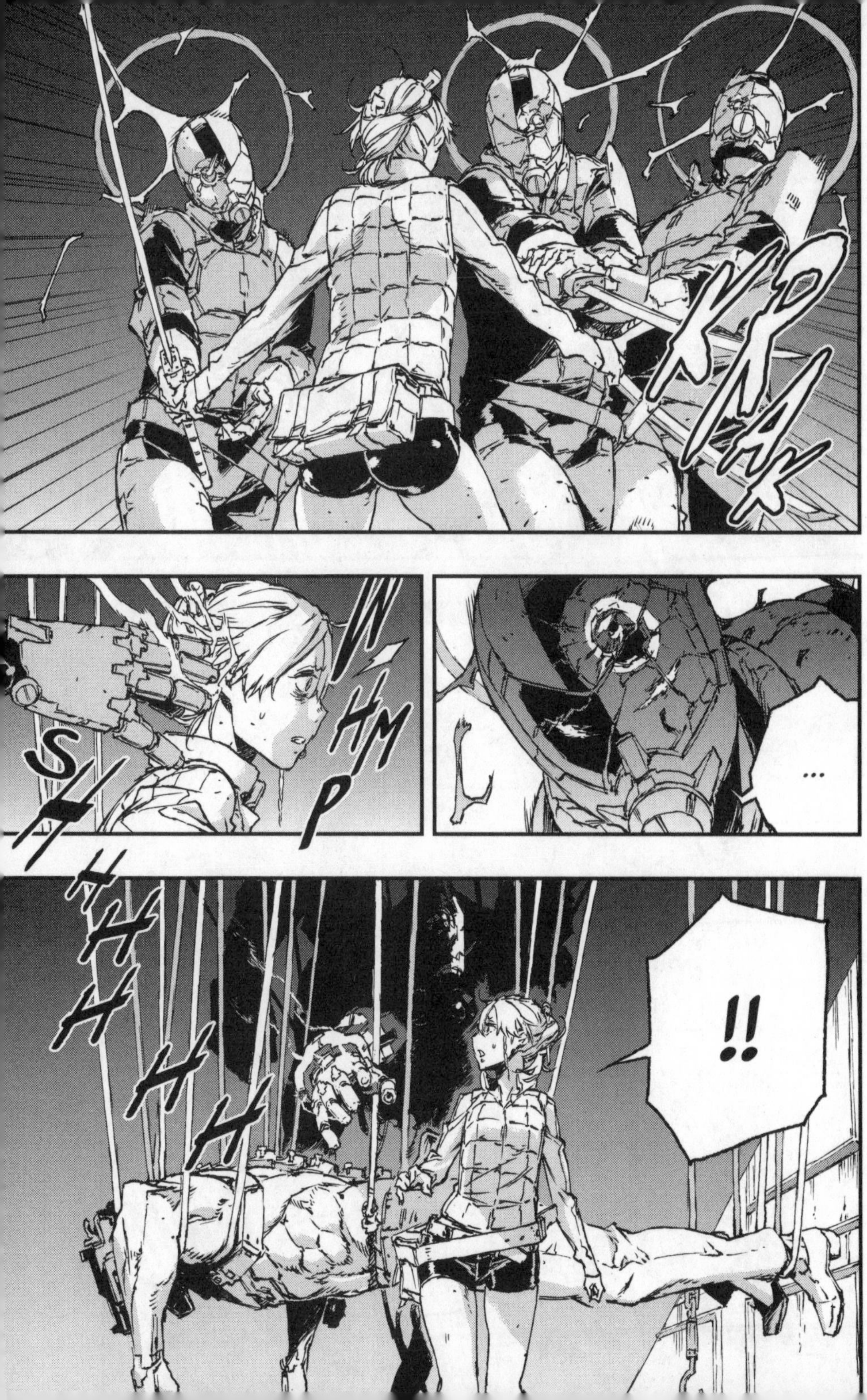
KRAK
...
WHMP
SHHHHHH
!!

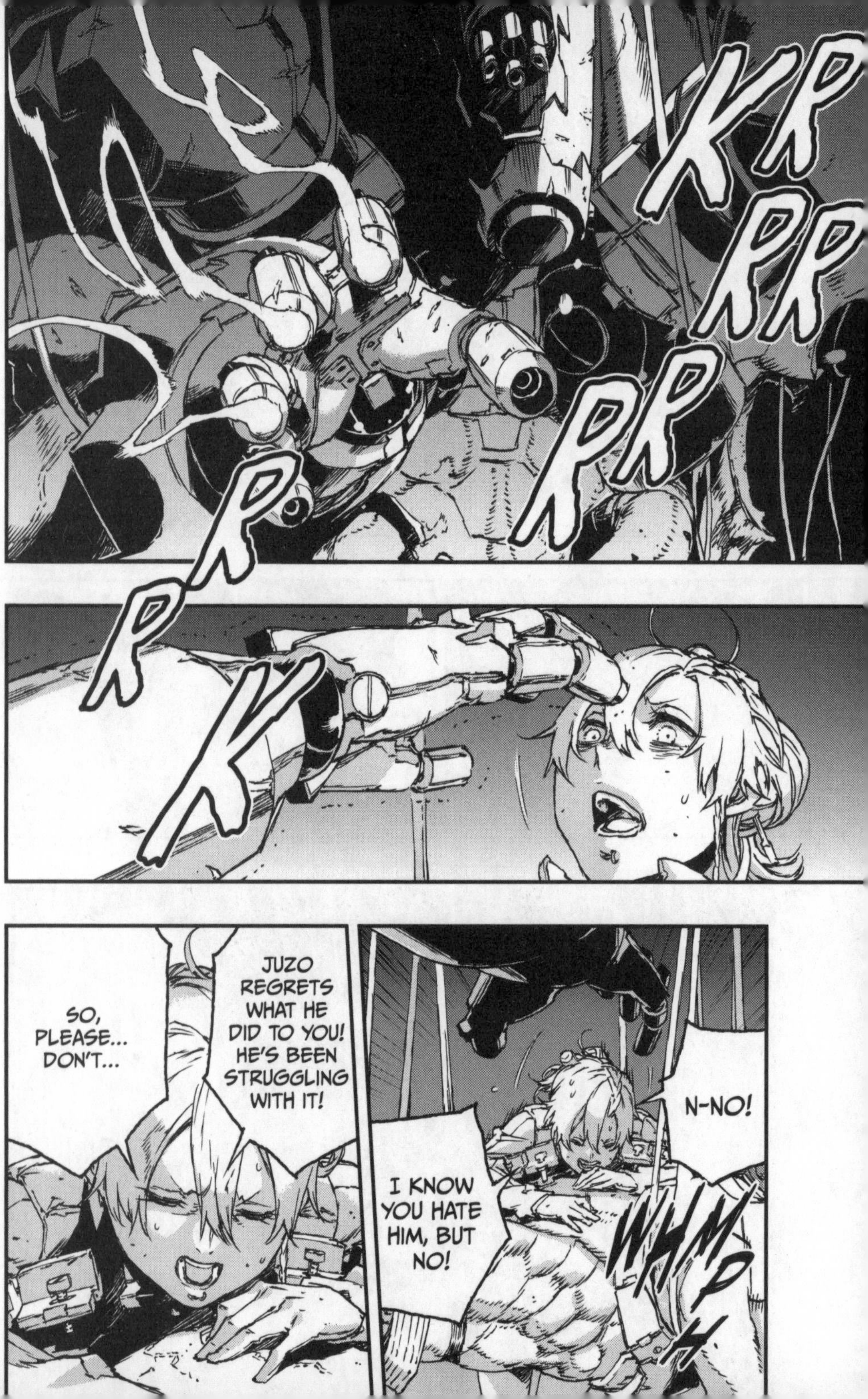
KRRRRRRRK
N-NO!
I KNOW YOU HATE HIM, BUT NO!
WHMPH
JUZO REGRETS WHAT HE DID TO YOU! HE'S BEEN STRUGGLING WITH IT!
SO, PLEASE... DON'T...

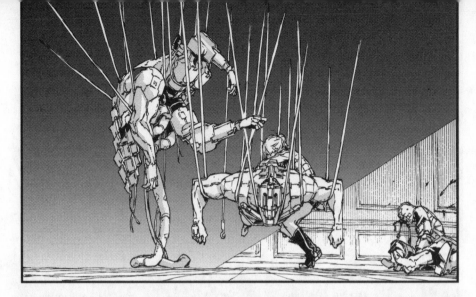

...

HE'S
ALREADY...

WAIT...!
YOU PROTECTED ME!
NO...
I THINK HE...

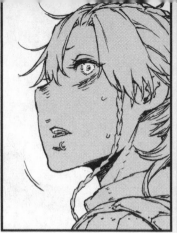

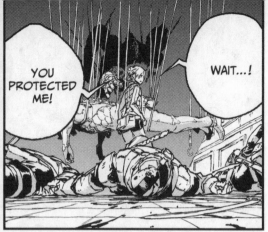

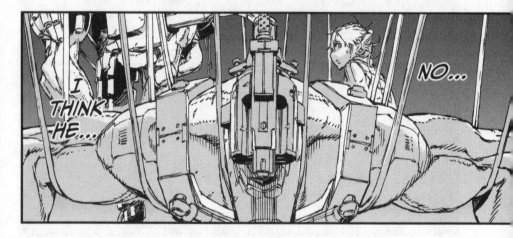

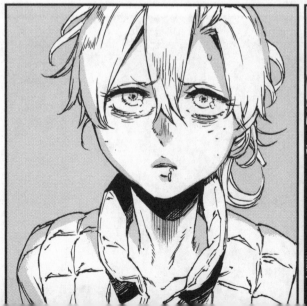

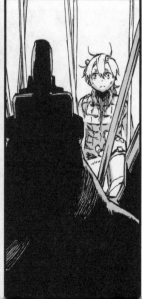

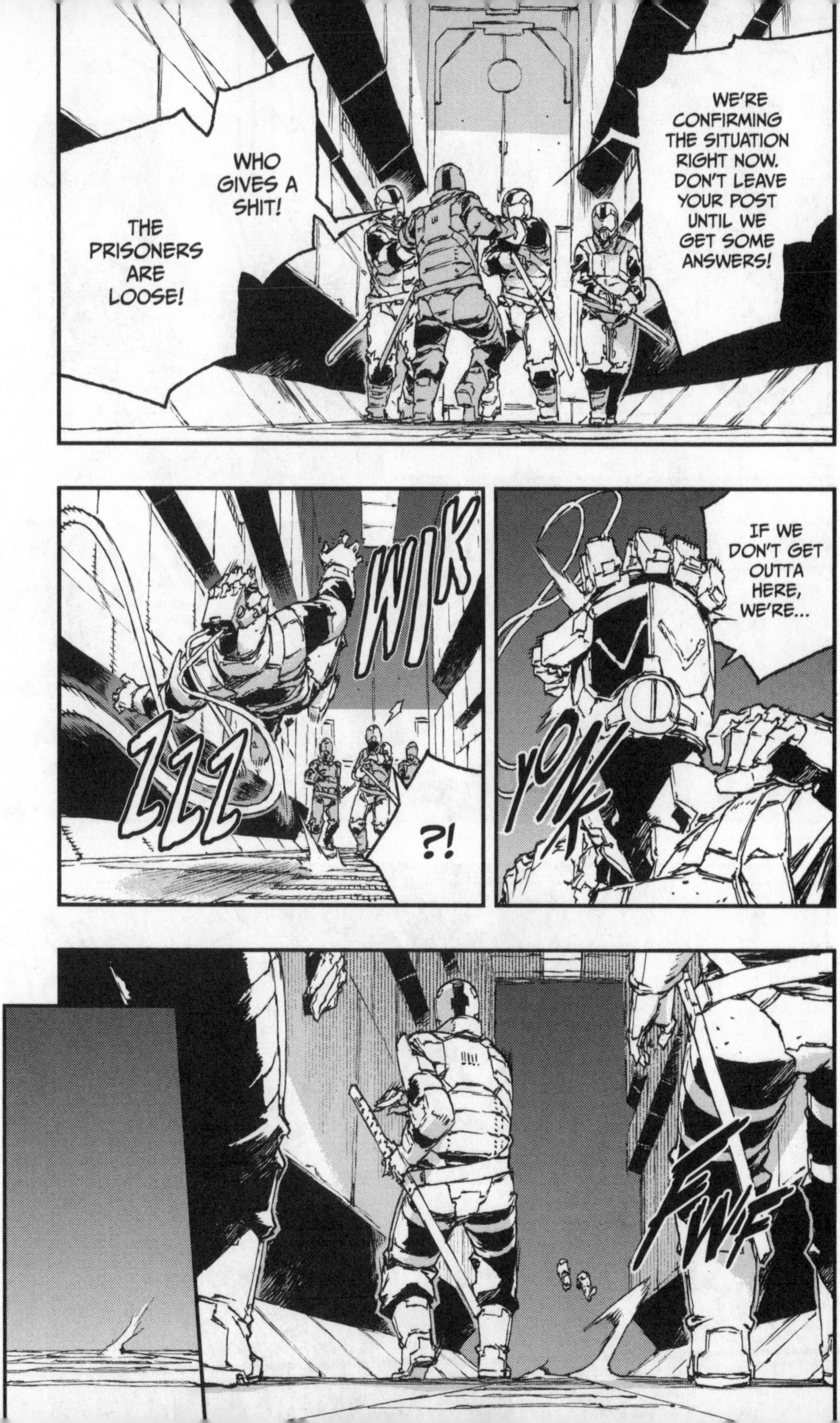
WE'RE CONFIRMING THE SITUATION RIGHT NOW. DON'T LEAVE YOUR POST UNTIL WE GET SOME ANSWERS!
WHO GIVES A SHIT!
THE PRISONERS ARE LOOSE!
IF WE DON'T GET OUTTA HERE, WE'RE...
YOINK
WIK
ZZZ
?!
FWF

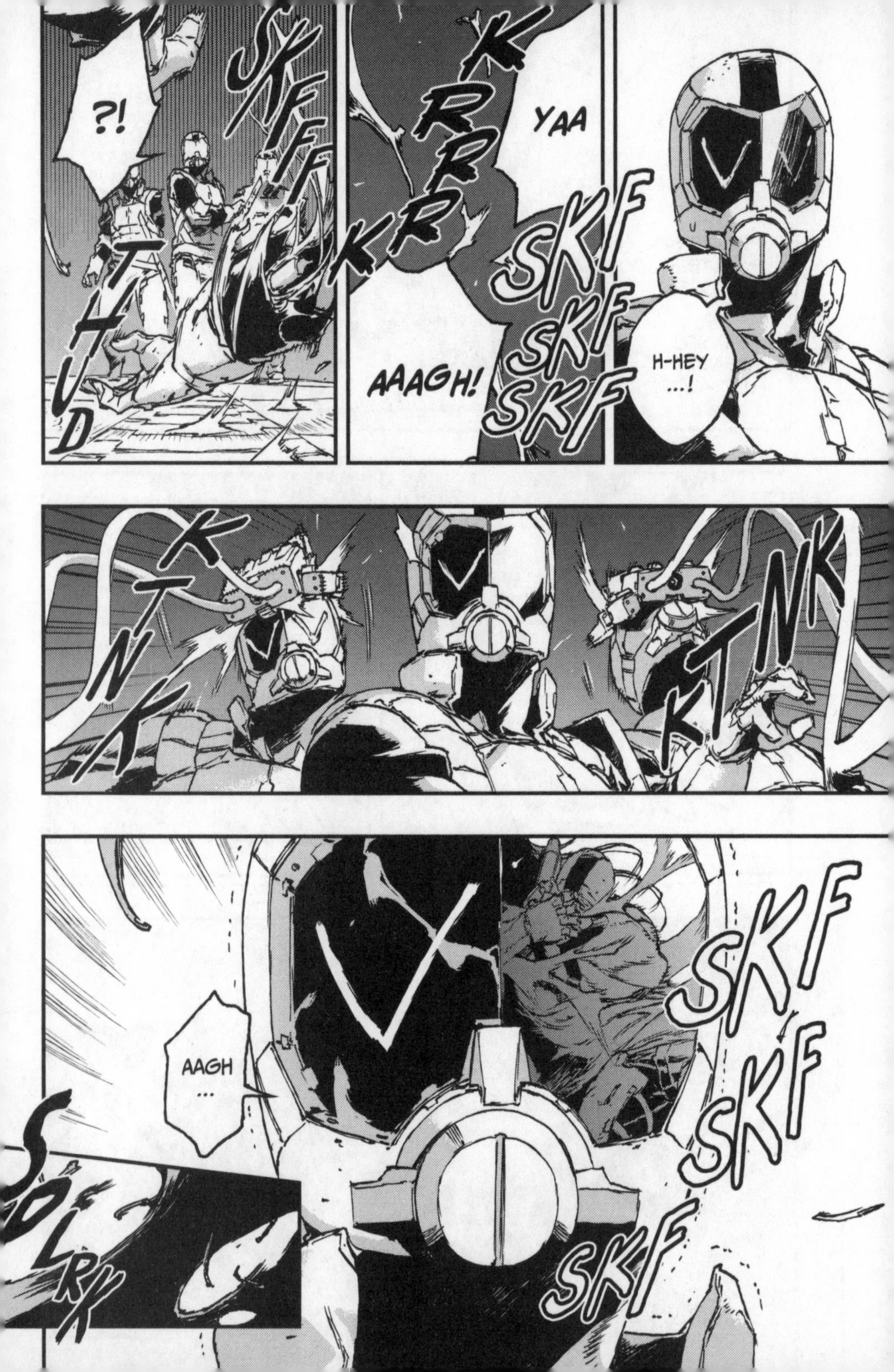
H-HEY ...!
SKF SKF SKF
KRRRKR
YAA
AAAGH!
?!
SKFFF
THUD
KTNK
KTNK
SKF SKF SKF
AAGH ...
SDLRK

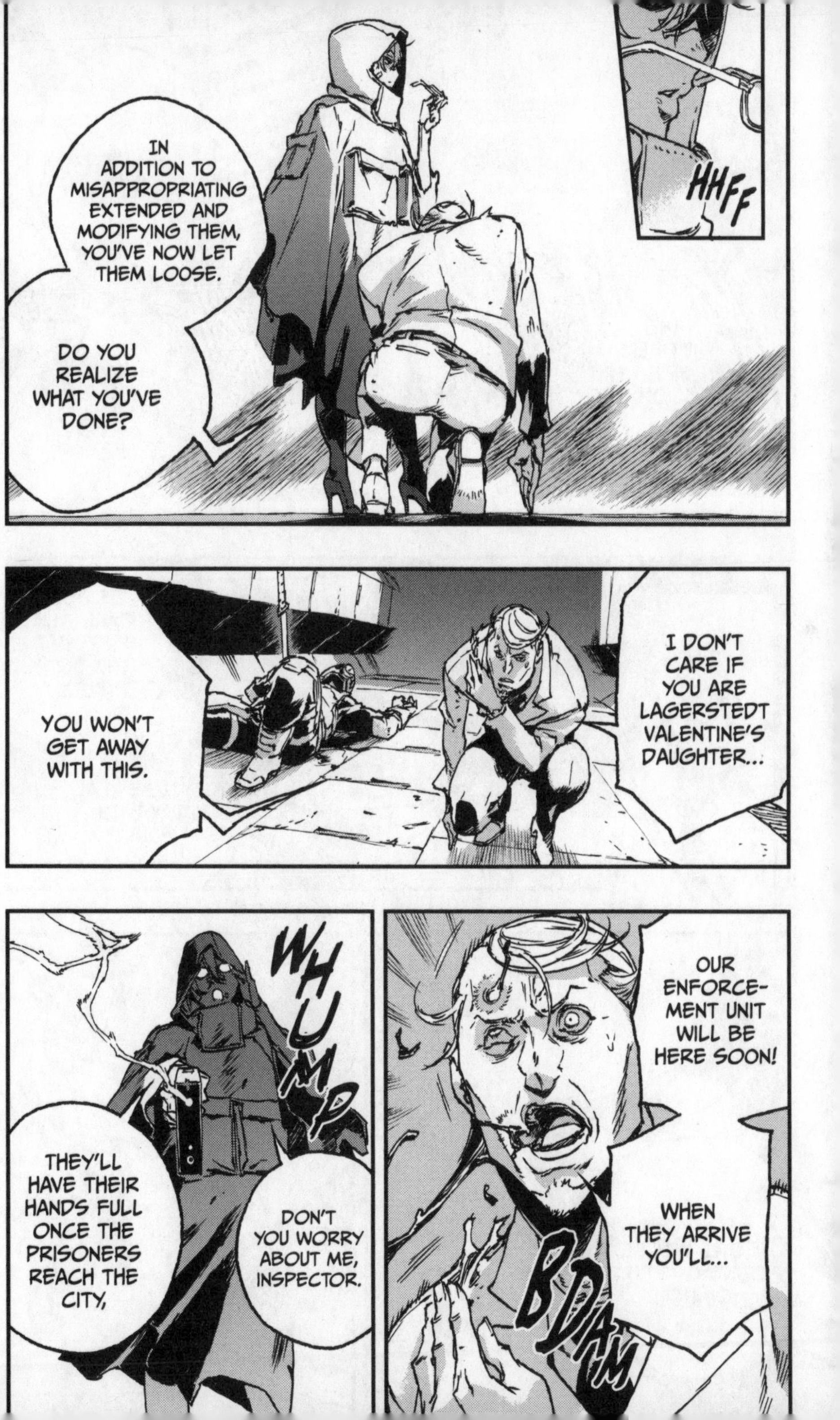
HHFF
IN ADDITION TO MISAPPROPRIATING EXTENDED AND MODIFYING THEM, YOU'VE NOW LET THEM LOOSE.
DO YOU REALIZE WHAT YOU'VE DONE?
I DON'T CARE IF YOU ARE LAGERSTEDT VALENTINE'S DAUGHTER...
YOU WON'T GET AWAY WITH THIS.
OUR ENFORCE-MENT UNIT WILL BE HERE SOON!
WHEN THEY ARRIVE YOU'LL...
BDAM
WHUMP
DON'T YOU WORRY ABOUT ME, INSPECTOR.
THEY'LL HAVE THEIR HANDS FULL ONCE THE PRISONERS REACH THE CITY,

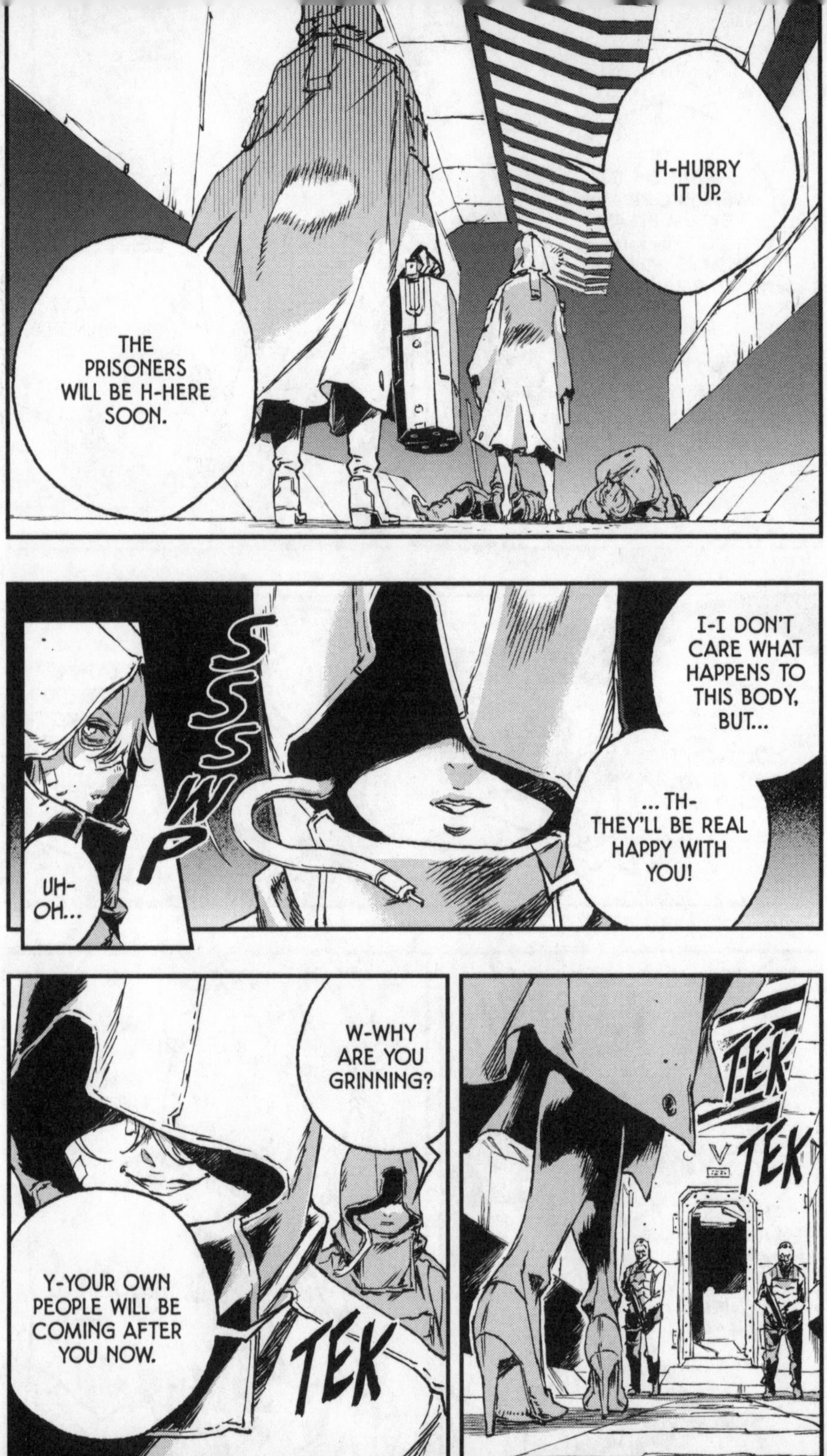
H-HURRY IT UP.
THE PRISONERS WILL BE H-HERE SOON.
I-I DON'T CARE WHAT HAPPENS TO THIS BODY, BUT...
... TH- THEY'LL BE REAL HAPPY WITH YOU!
SSSWP
UH- OH...
TEK TEK
W-WHY ARE YOU GRINNING?
Y-YOUR OWN PEOPLE WILL BE COMING AFTER YOU NOW.
TEK

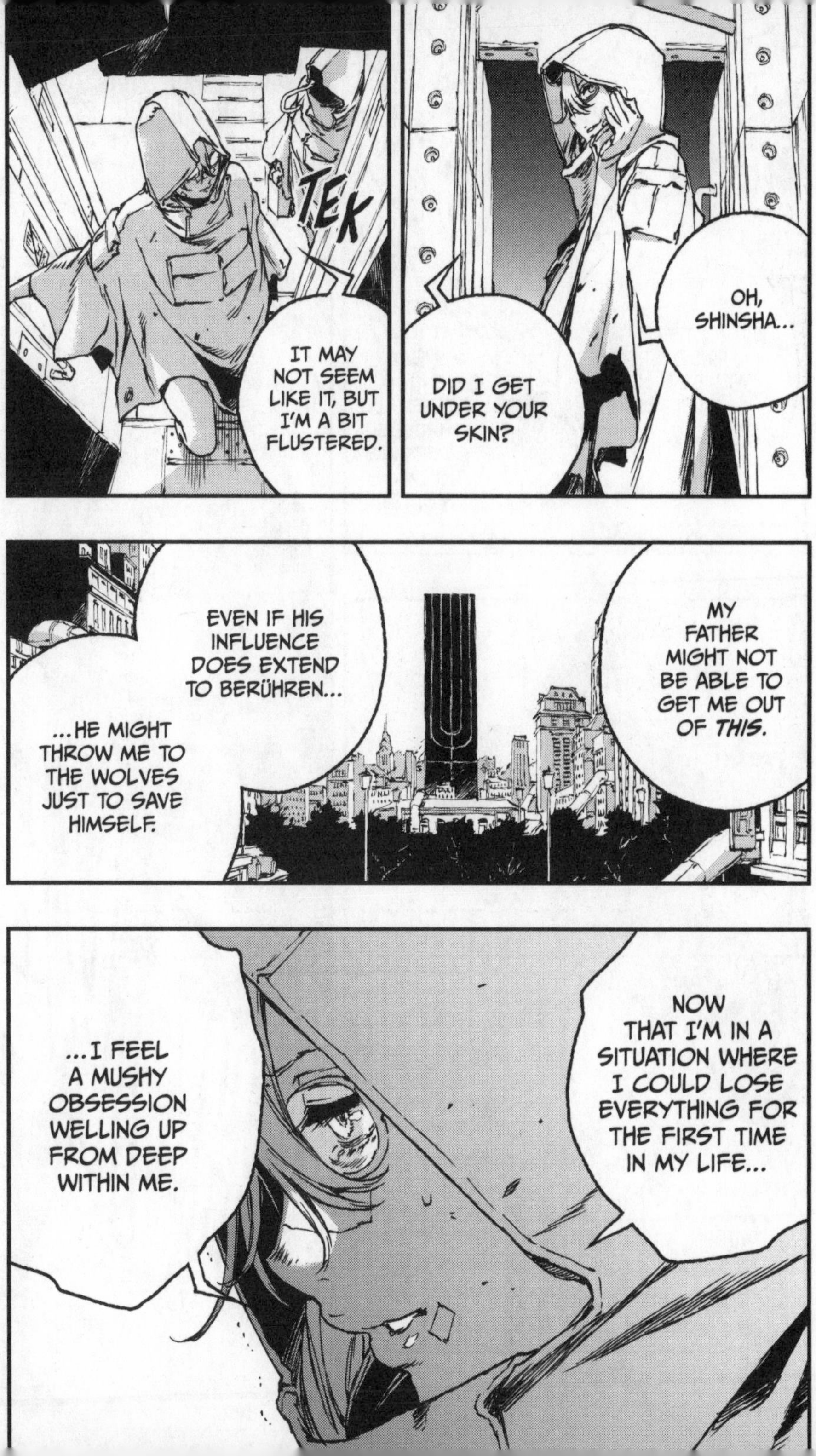
OH, SHINSHA...
DID I GET UNDER YOUR SKIN?
TEK
IT MAY NOT SEEM LIKE IT, BUT I'M A BIT FLUSTERED.
MY FATHER MIGHT NOT BE ABLE TO GET ME OUT OF *THIS*.
EVEN IF HIS INFLUENCE DOES EXTEND TO BERÜHREN...
...HE MIGHT THROW ME TO THE WOLVES JUST TO SAVE HIMSELF.
NOW THAT I'M IN A SITUATION WHERE I COULD LOSE EVERYTHING FOR THE FIRST TIME IN MY LIFE...
...I FEEL A MUSHY OBSESSION WELLING UP FROM DEEP WITHIN ME.

WHAT IS THIS POWERFUL IMPULSE COURSING THROUGH ME...?!

I'M TREMBLING!

TWCH TWCH

Y-YOU'RE...

...A FREAK!

GASP

SHIVER

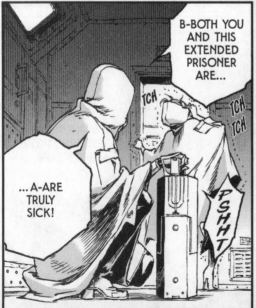

B-BOTH YOU AND THIS EXTENDED PRISONER ARE...

...A-ARE TRULY SICK!

TCH

TCH TCH

PSHHT

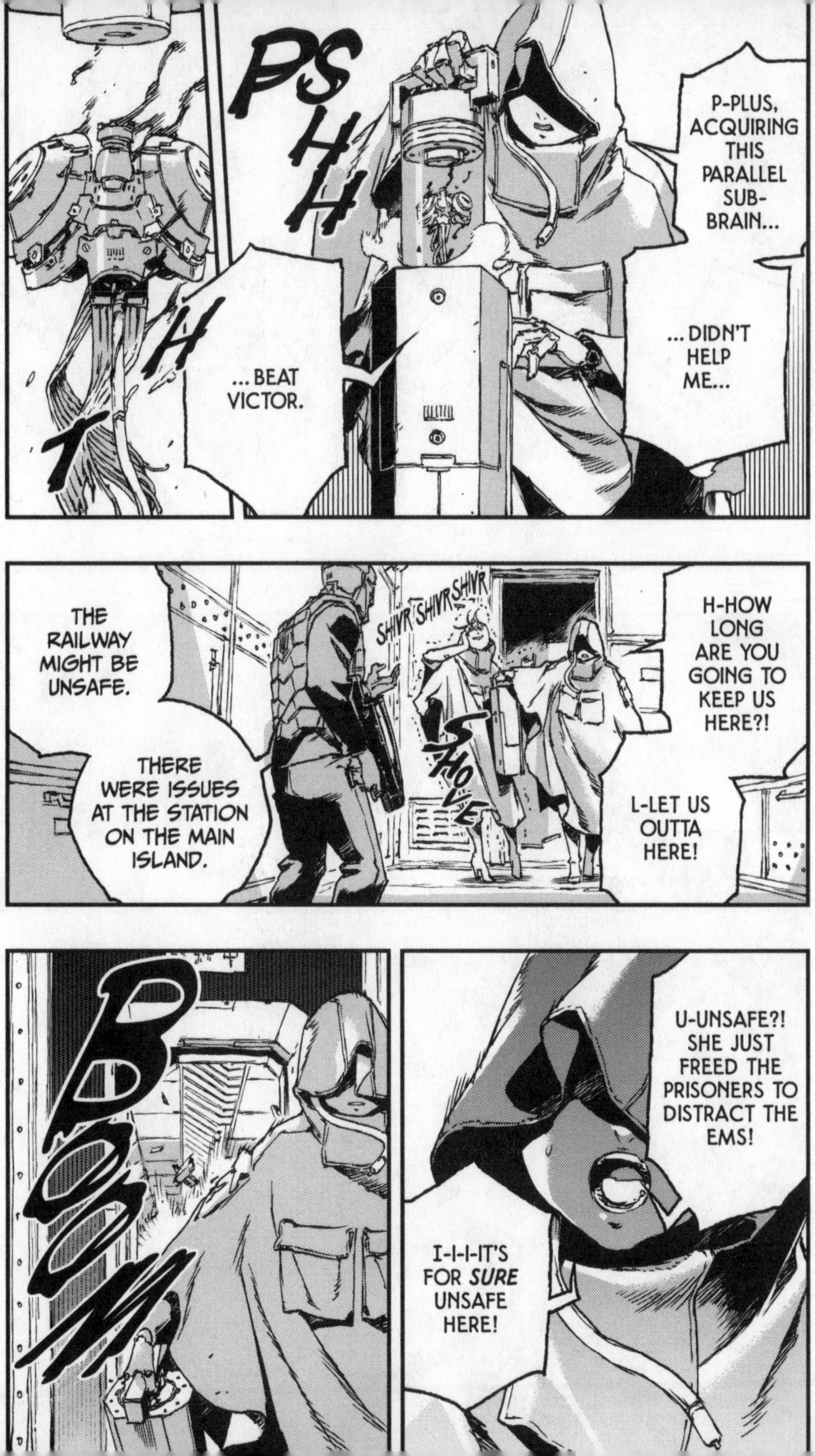
P-PLUS, ACQUIRING THIS PARALLEL SUB-BRAIN...
...DIDN'T HELP ME...
...BEAT VICTOR.
PSHHHT
H-HOW LONG ARE YOU GOING TO KEEP US HERE?!
L-LET US OUTTA HERE!
SHIVR SHIVR SHIVR
SHOVE
THE RAILWAY MIGHT BE UNSAFE.
THERE WERE ISSUES AT THE STATION ON THE MAIN ISLAND.
U-UNSAFE?! SHE JUST FREED THE PRISONERS TO DISTRACT THE EMS!
I-I-I-IT'S FOR *SURE* UNSAFE HERE!
BOOM

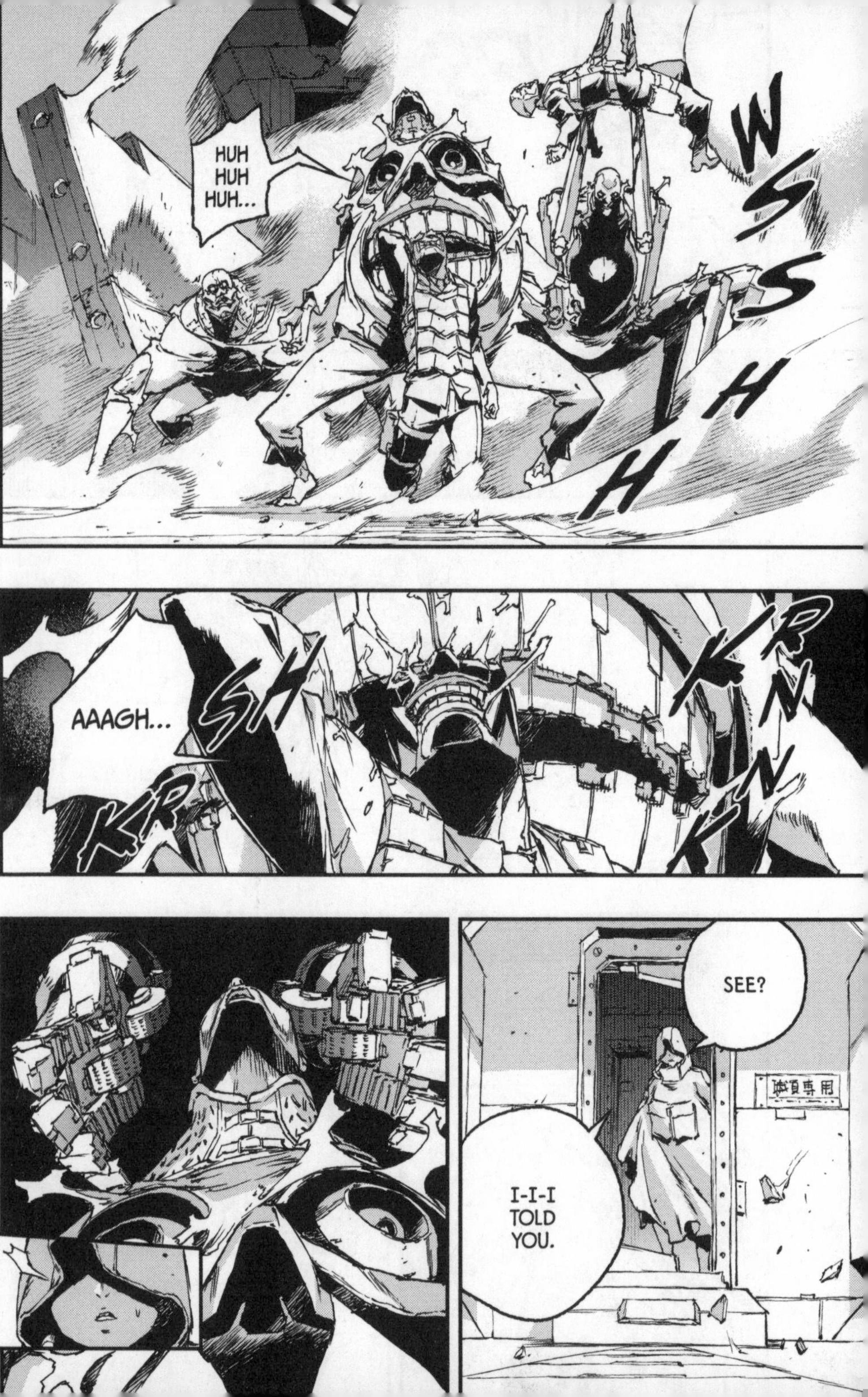
WSSHH
HUH HUH HUH...
KRN
KN
AAAGH...
SH
KR
SEE?
I-I-I TOLD YOU.

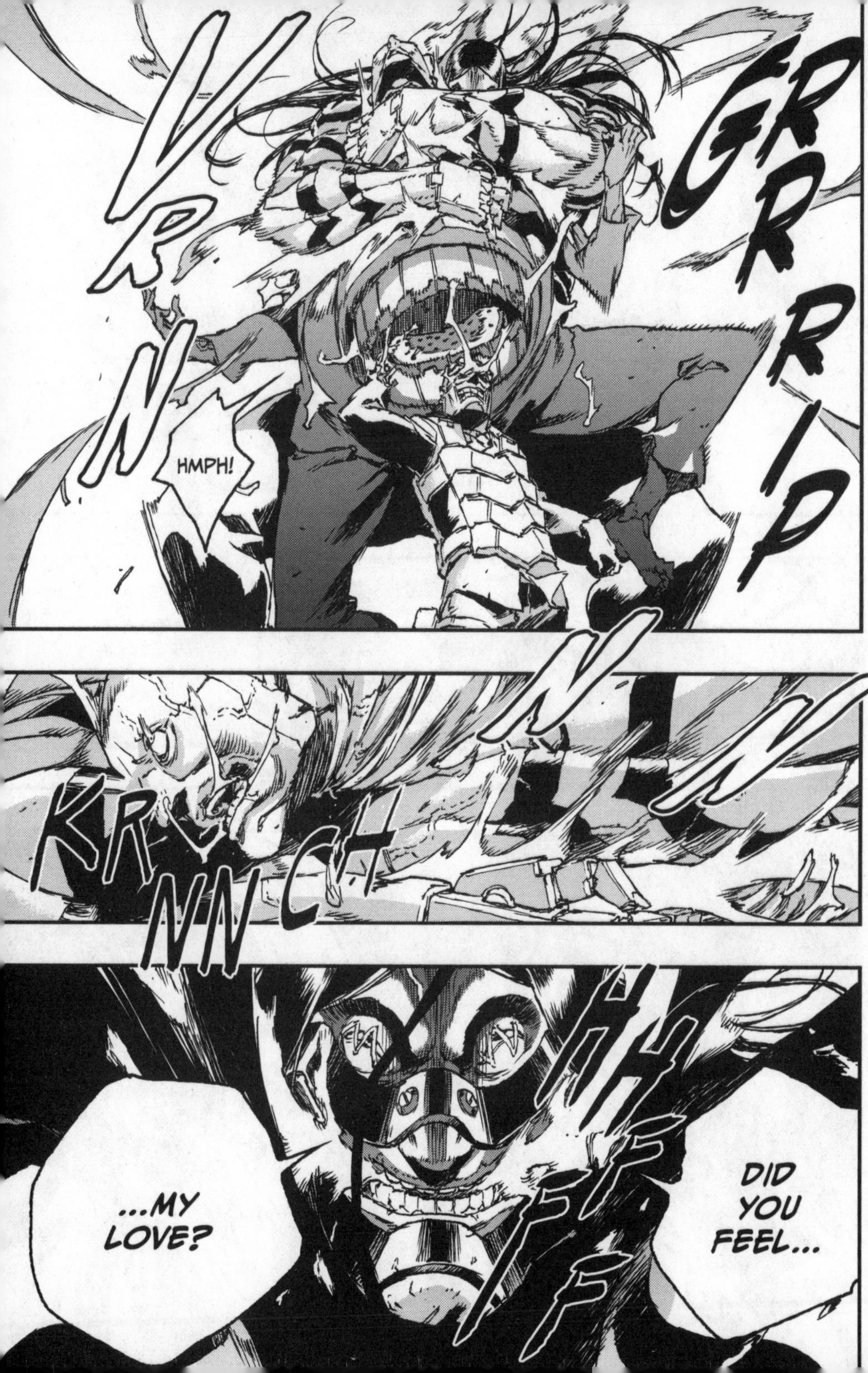
GRRRIP
VRNN
HMPH!
NNN
KRNNCH
HHFFF
DID YOU FEEL...
...MY LOVE?

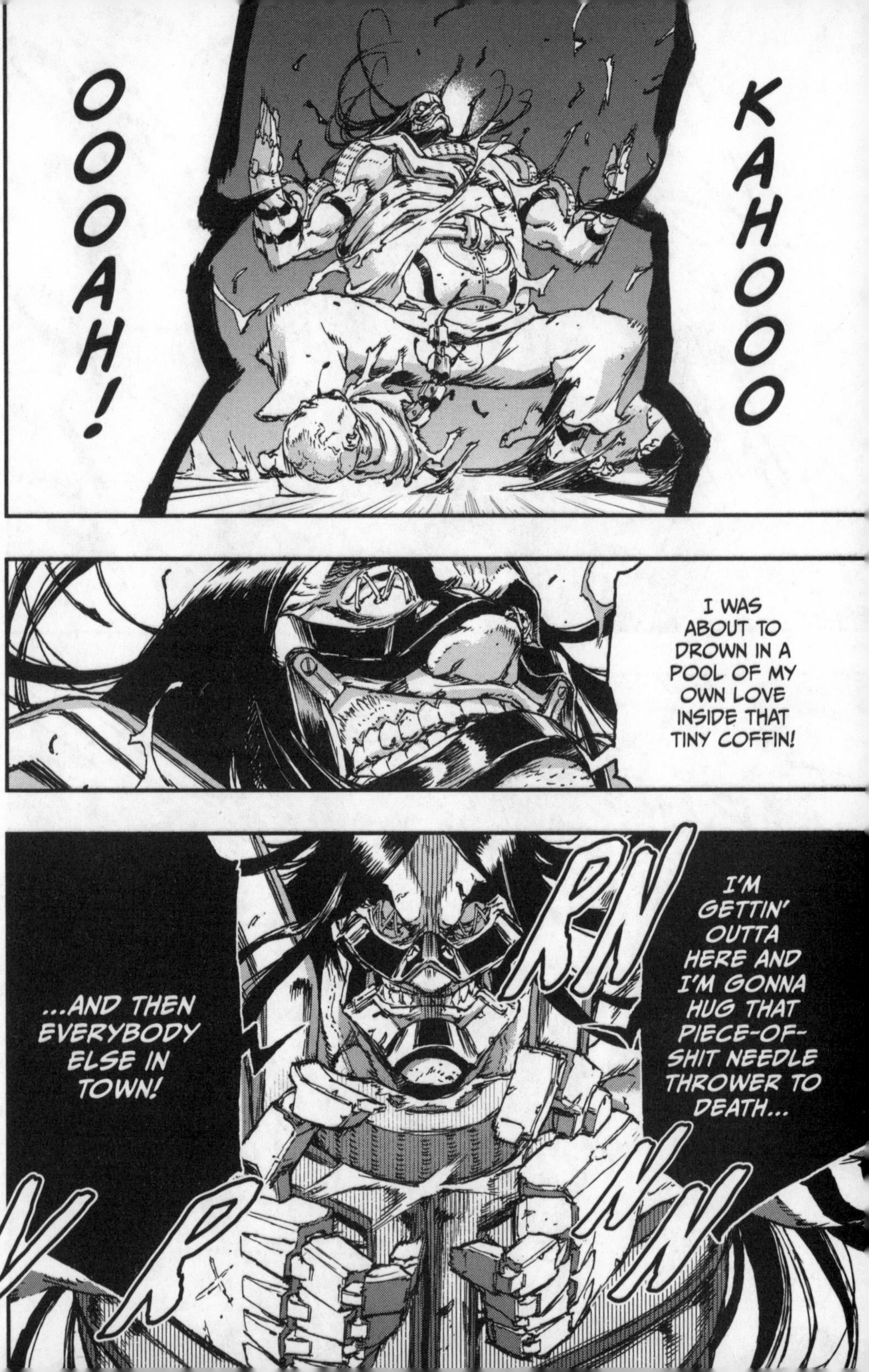
KAHOOOO
OOOAH!
I WAS ABOUT TO DROWN IN A POOL OF MY OWN LOVE INSIDE THAT TINY COFFIN!
RN
I'M GETTIN' OUTTA HERE AND I'M GONNA HUG THAT PIECE-OF-SHIT NEEDLE THROWER TO DEATH...
...AND THEN EVERYBODY ELSE IN TOWN!

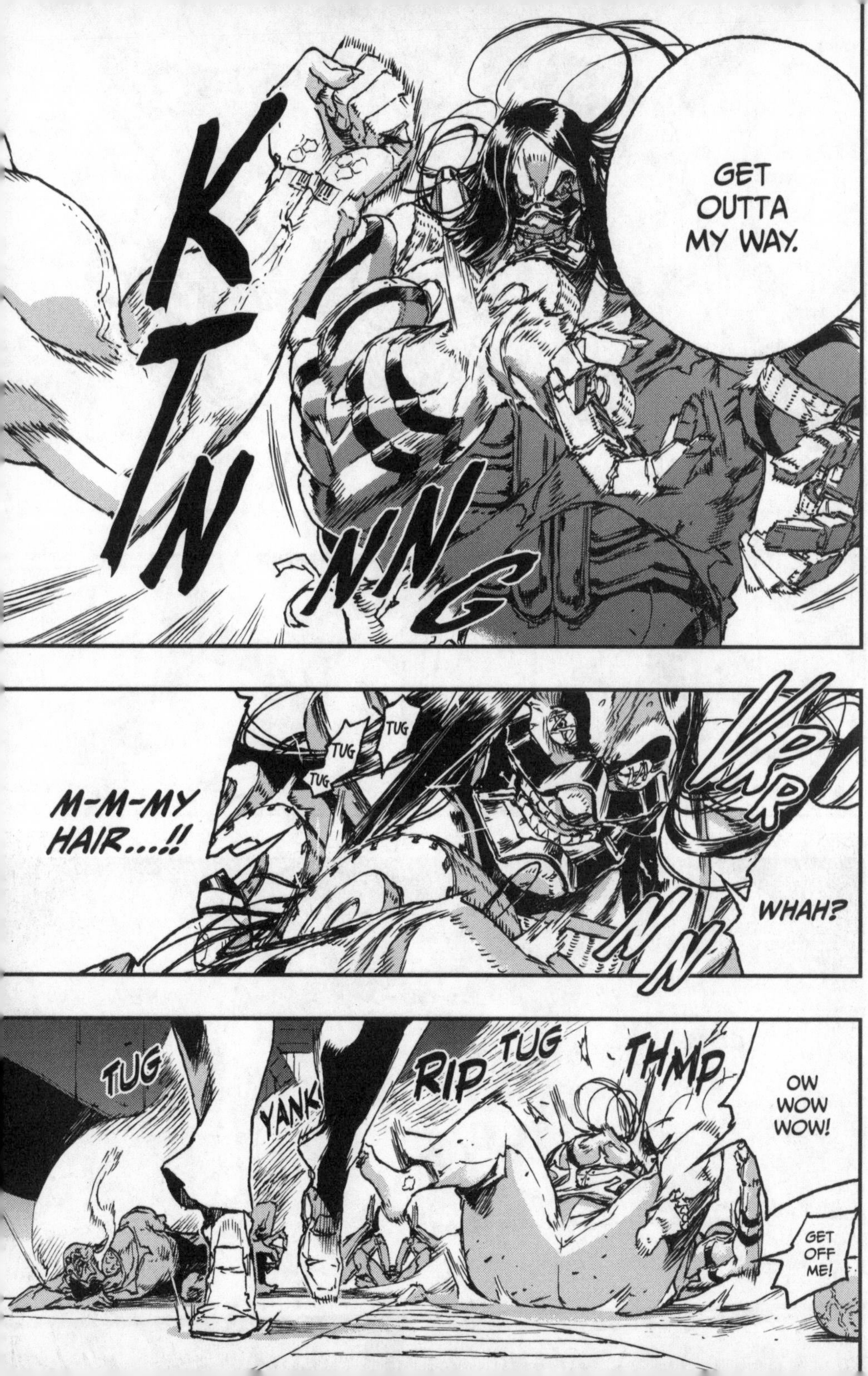
GET OUTTA MY WAY.
KTINNNG
VRRNNN
WHAH?
TUG
TUG
TUG
M-M-MY HAIR...!!
OW WOW WOW!
THMP
TUG
RIP
YANK
TUG
GET OFF ME!

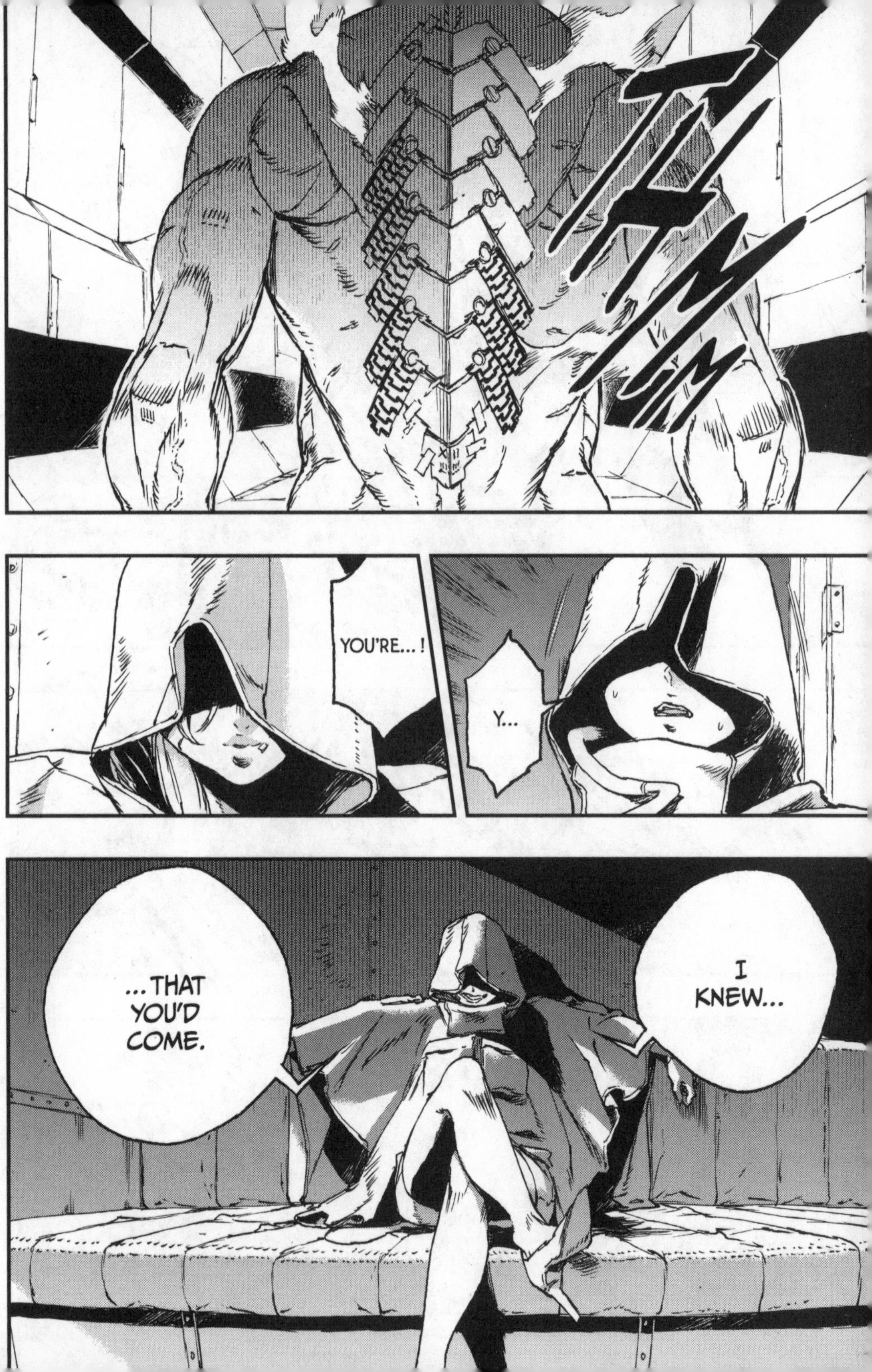
THUM
Y...
YOU'RE...!
I KNEW...
...THAT YOU'D COME.

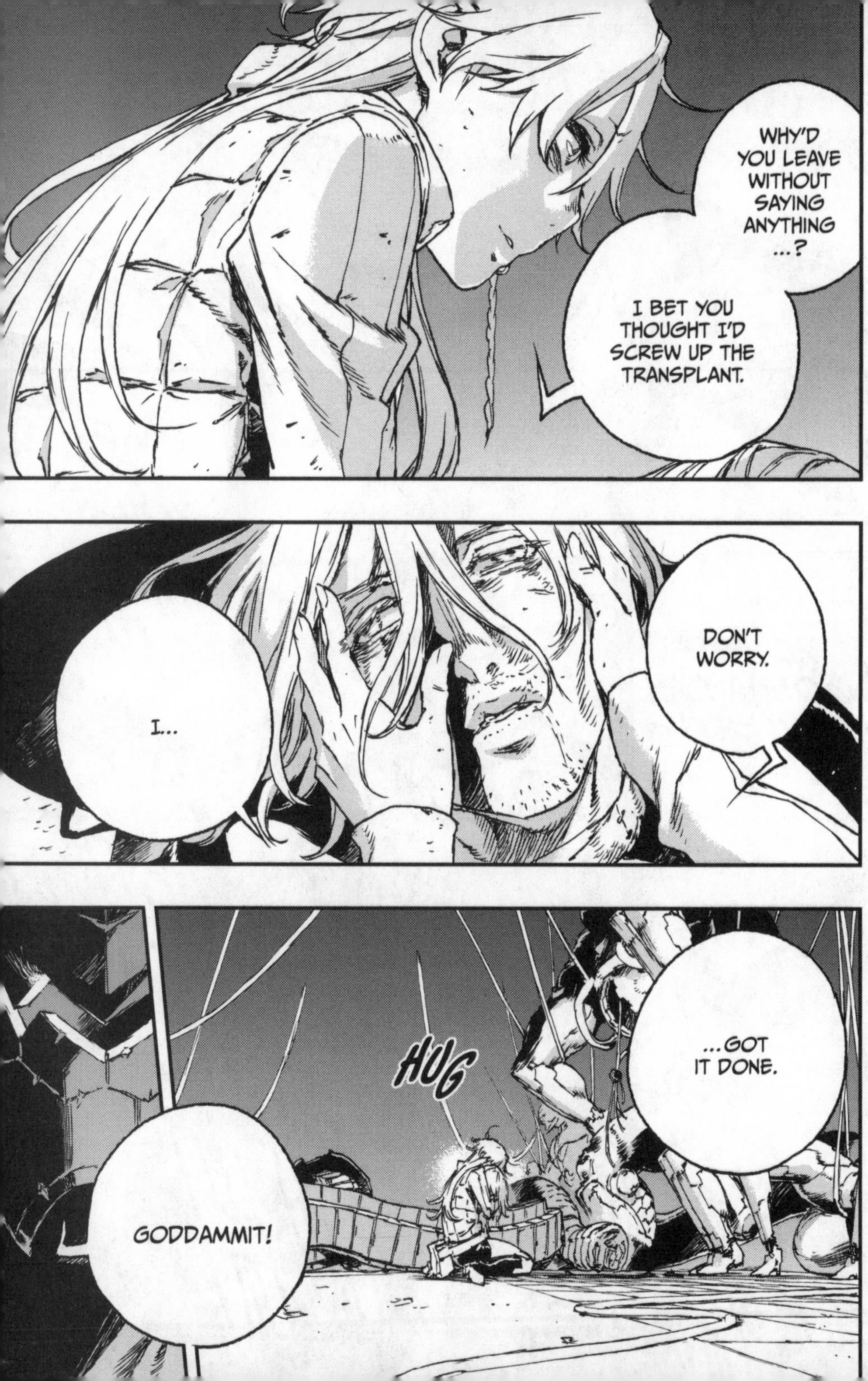
WHY'D YOU LEAVE WITHOUT SAYING ANYTHING ...?
I BET YOU THOUGHT I'D SCREW UP THE TRANSPLANT.
DON'T WORRY.
I...
...GOT IT DONE.
HUG
GODDAMMIT!

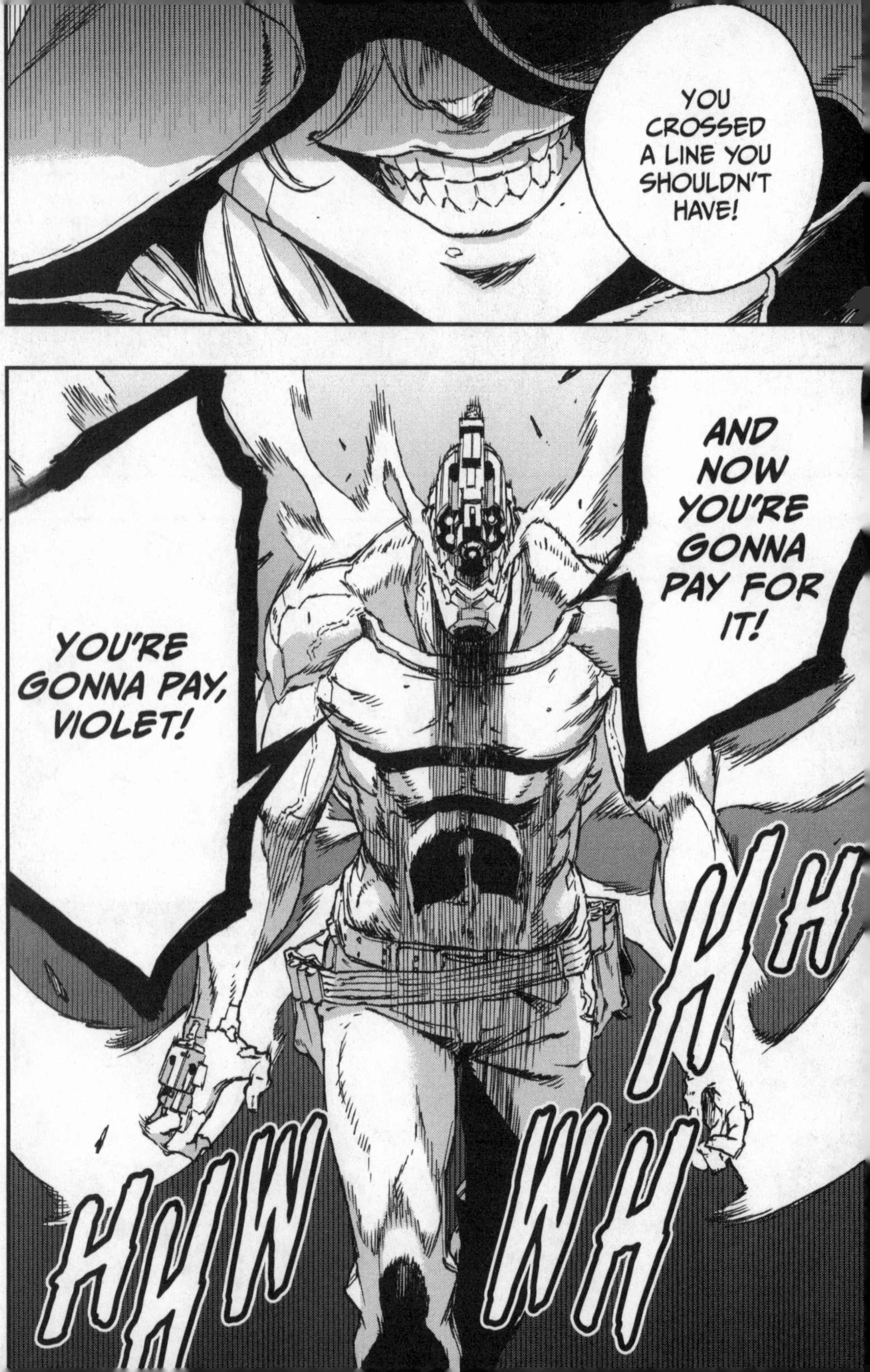
YOU CROSSED A LINE YOU SHOULDN'T HAVE!
AND NOW YOU'RE GONNA PAY FOR IT!
YOU'RE GONNA PAY, VIOLET!
HHWWHHH

NO GUNS LIFE

The gunsmoke drifts, the muzzle talks

NO GUNS LIFE

The gunsmoke drifts, the muzzle talks

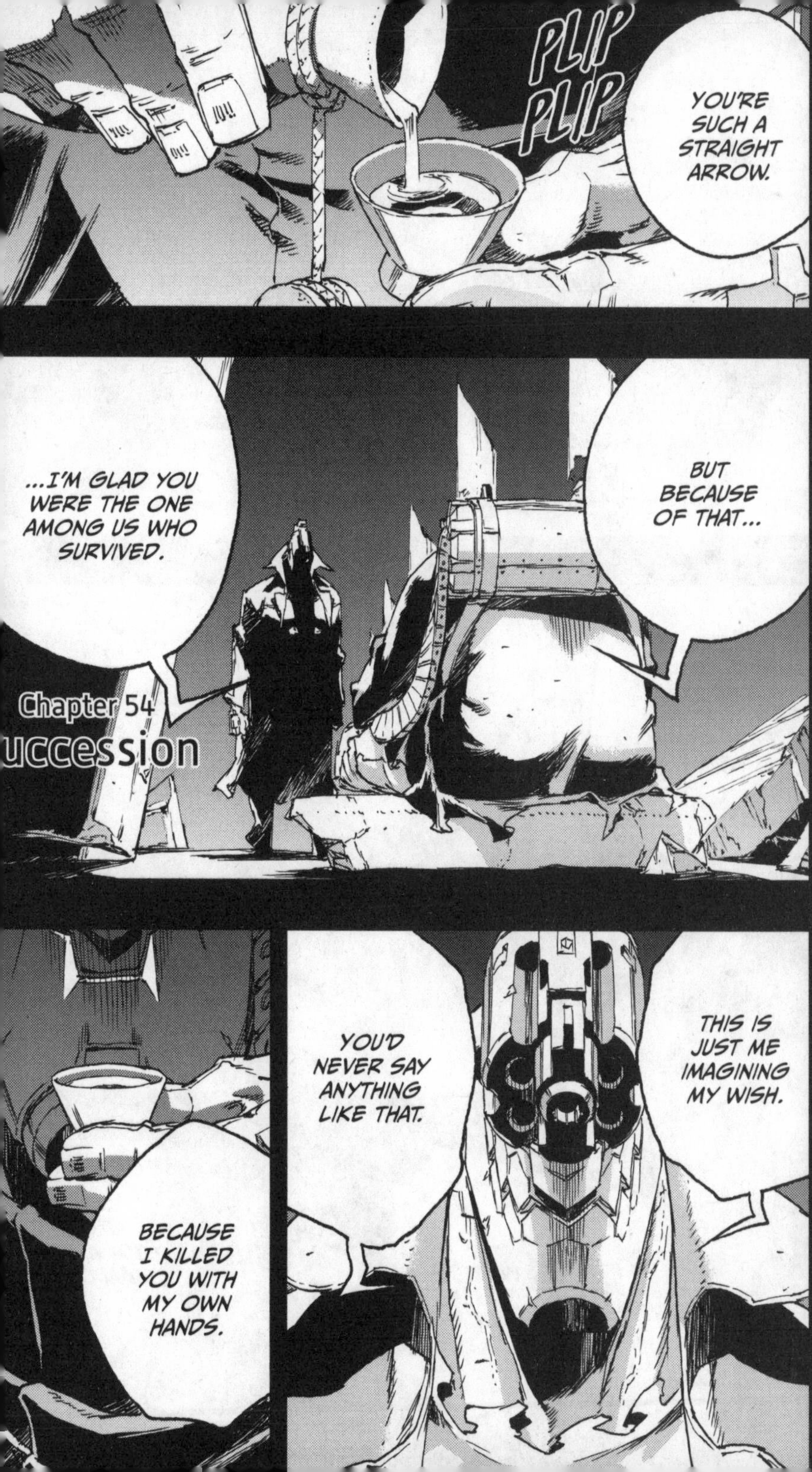
PLIP PLIP
YOU'RE SUCH A STRAIGHT ARROW.
BUT BECAUSE OF THAT...
...I'M GLAD YOU WERE THE ONE AMONG US WHO SURVIVED.
Chapter 54
uccession
THIS IS JUST ME IMAGINING MY WISH.
YOU'D NEVER SAY ANYTHING LIKE THAT.
BECAUSE I KILLED YOU WITH MY OWN HANDS.

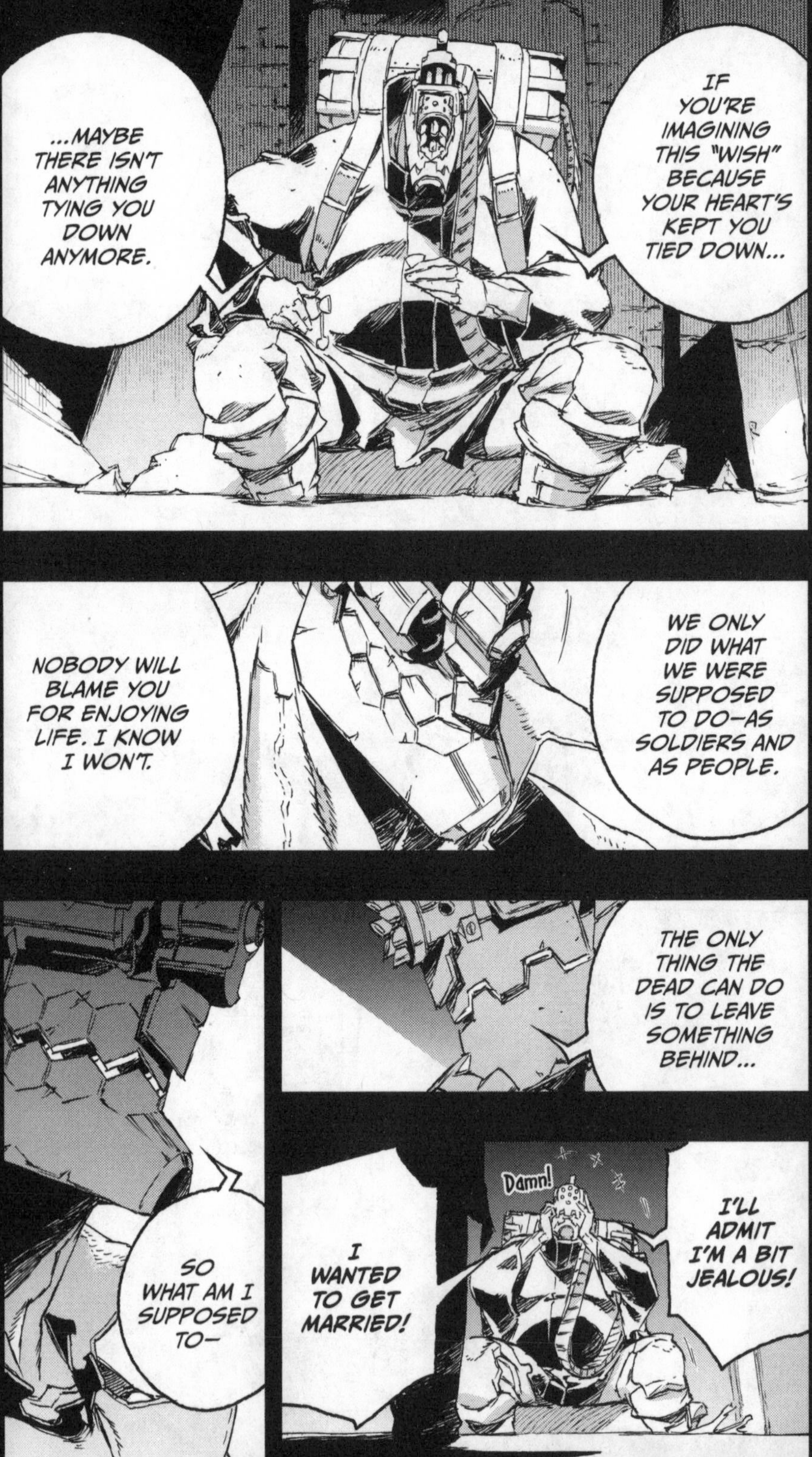
IF YOU'RE IMAGINING THIS "WISH" BECAUSE YOUR HEART'S KEPT YOU TIED DOWN...
...MAYBE THERE ISN'T ANYTHING TYING YOU DOWN ANYMORE.
WE ONLY DID WHAT WE WERE SUPPOSED TO DO—AS SOLDIERS AND AS PEOPLE.
NOBODY WILL BLAME YOU FOR ENJOYING LIFE. I KNOW I WON'T.
THE ONLY THING THE DEAD CAN DO IS TO LEAVE SOMETHING BEHIND...
I'LL ADMIT I'M A BIT JEALOUS!
Damn!
I WANTED TO GET MARRIED!
SO WHAT AM I SUPPOSED TO–

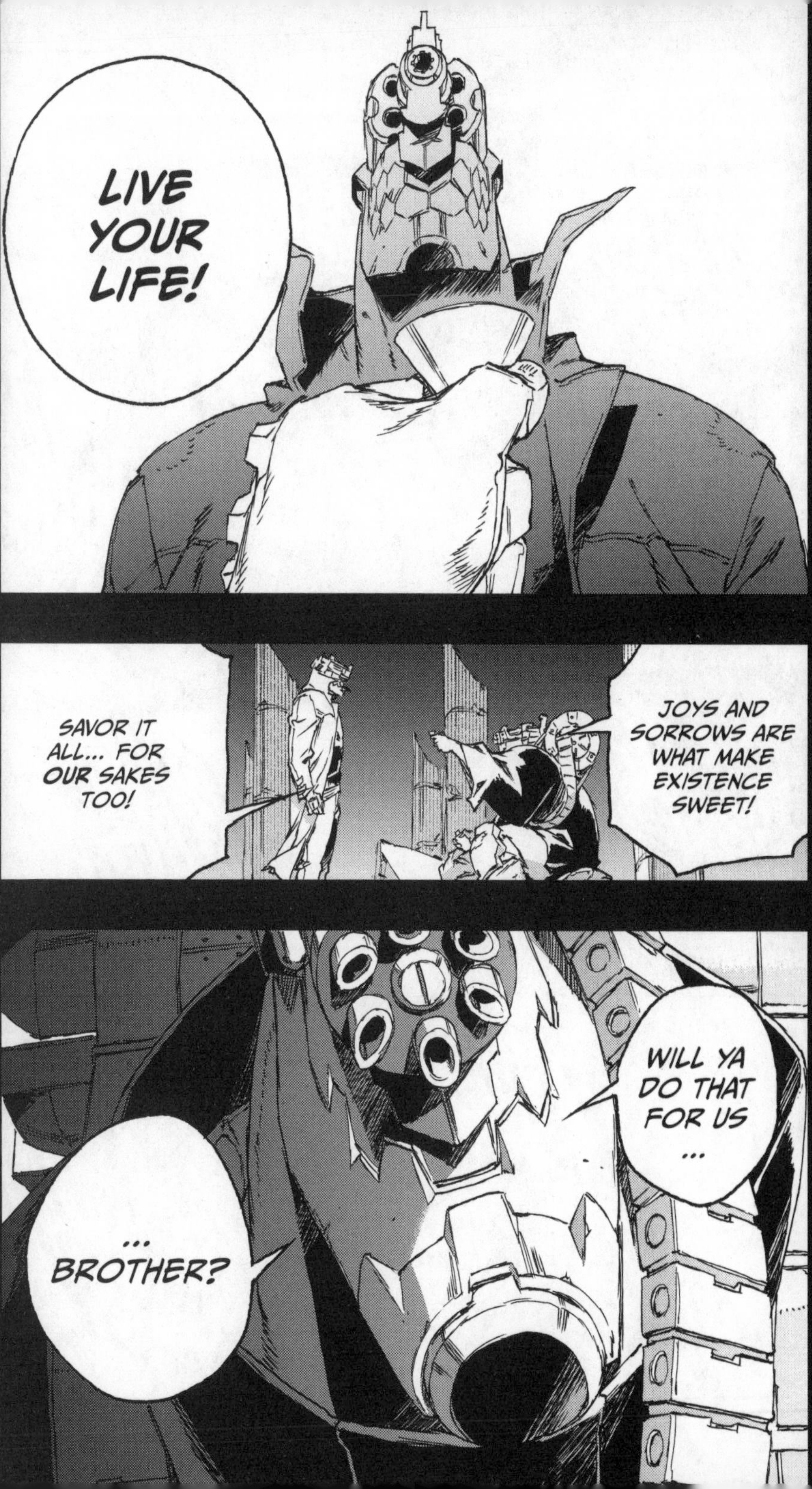
LIVE YOUR LIFE!
JOYS AND SORROWS ARE WHAT MAKE EXISTENCE SWEET!
SAVOR IT ALL... FOR OUR SAKES TOO!
WILL YA DO THAT FOR US ...
... BROTHER?

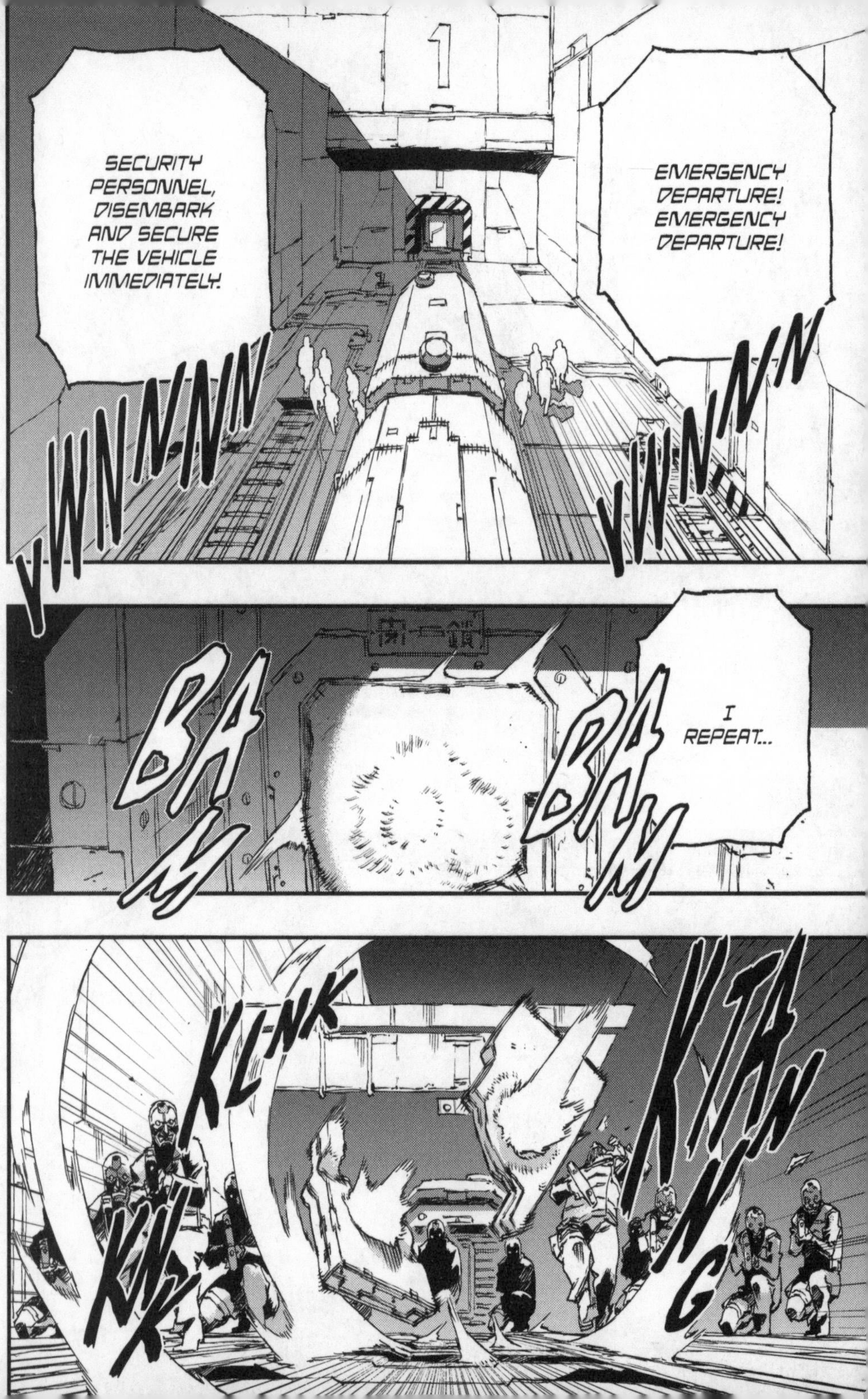
EMERGENCY DEPARTURE! EMERGENCY DEPARTURE!
SECURITY PERSONNEL, DISEMBARK AND SECURE THE VEHICLE IMMEDIATELY.
I REPEAT...
BAM
BAM
KLINK

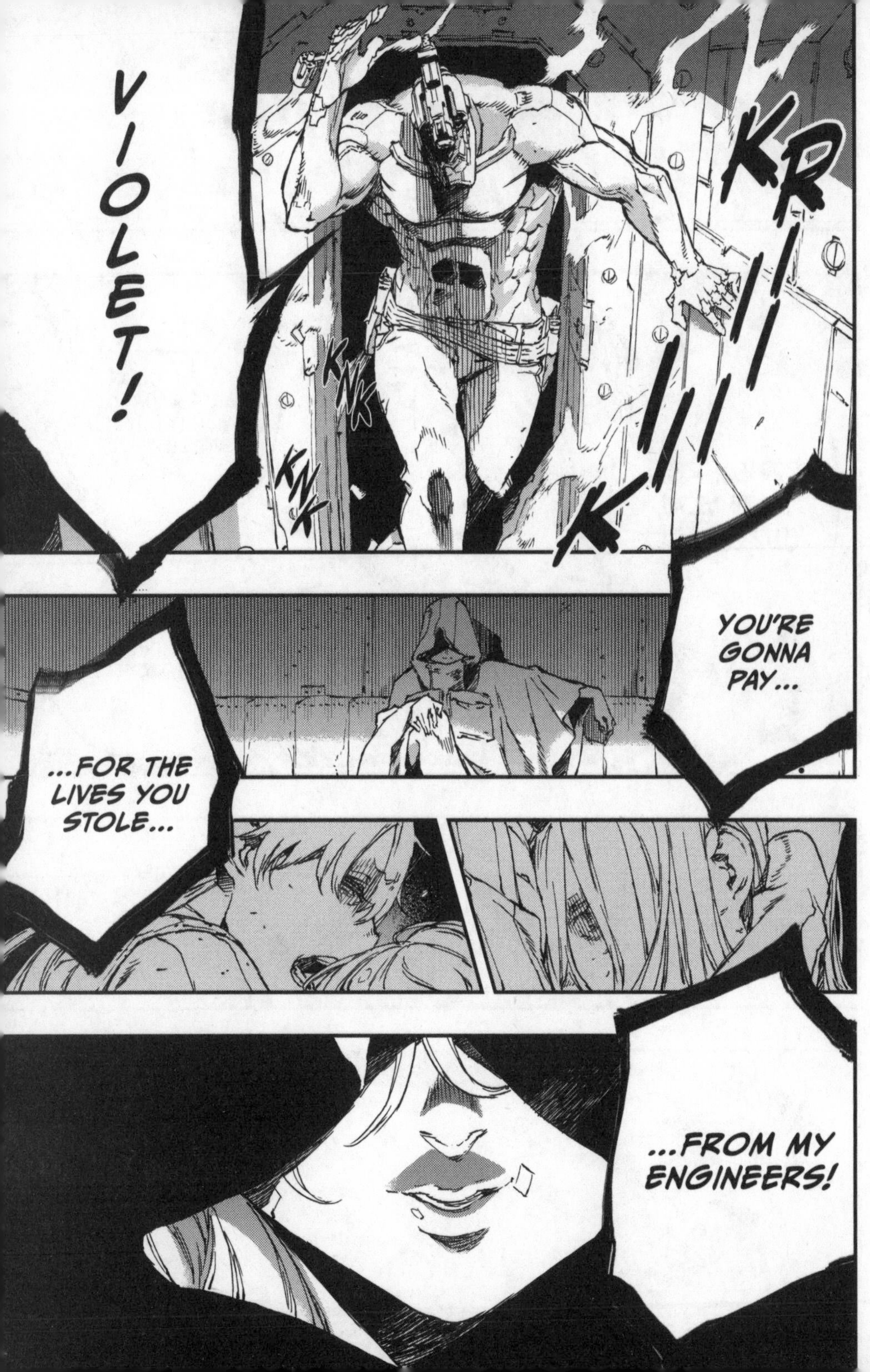
KRIIIIK
VIOLET!
KNK
KNK
YOU'RE GONNA PAY...
...FOR THE LIVES YOU STOLE...
...FROM MY ENGINEERS!

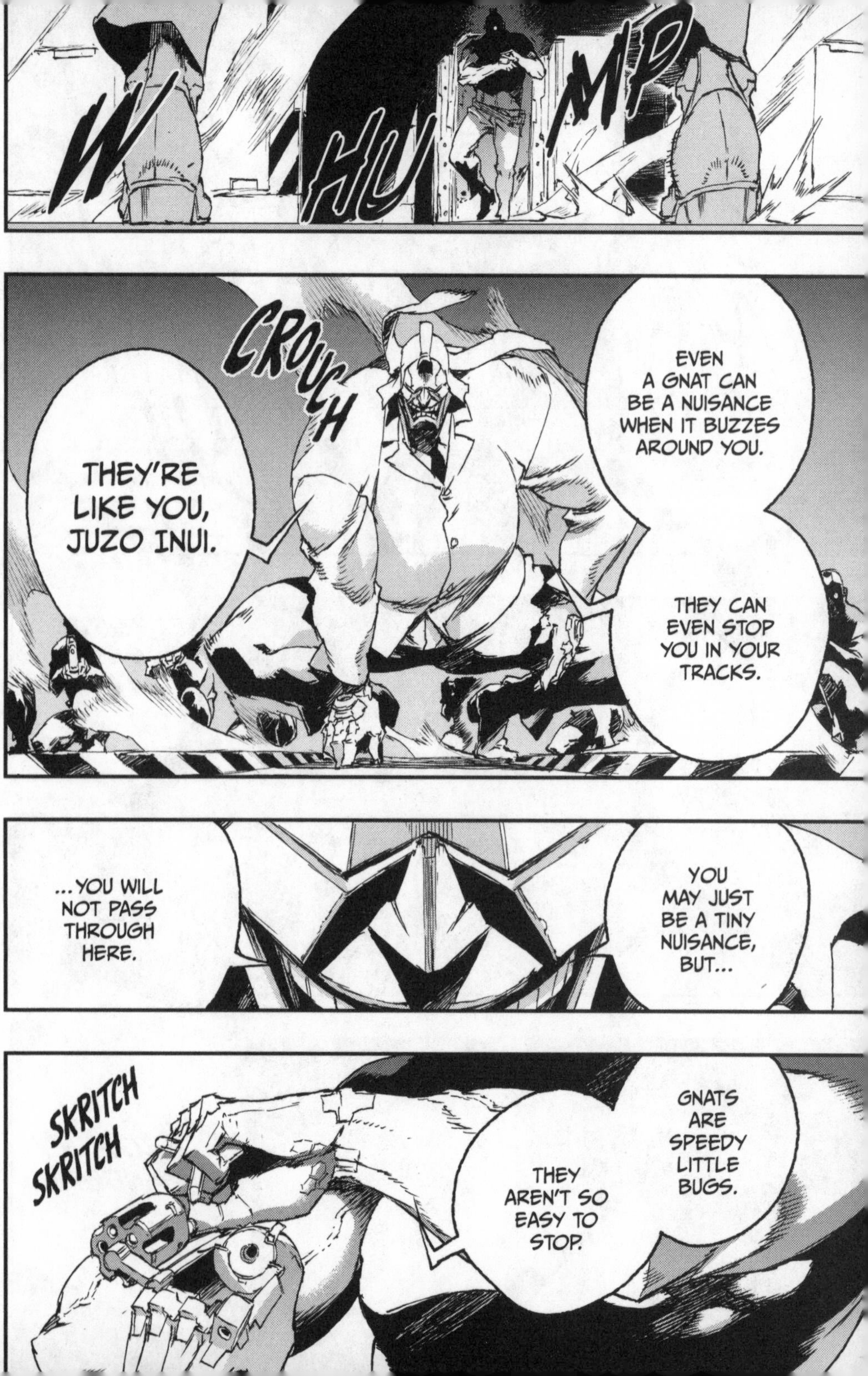
WHUMP
EVEN A GNAT CAN BE A NUISANCE WHEN IT BUZZES AROUND YOU.
CROUCH
THEY CAN EVEN STOP YOU IN YOUR TRACKS.
THEY'RE LIKE YOU, JUZO INUI.
YOU MAY JUST BE A TINY NUISANCE, BUT...
...YOU WILL NOT PASS THROUGH HERE.
GNATS ARE SPEEDY LITTLE BUGS.
THEY AREN'T SO EASY TO STOP.
SKRITCH SKRITCH

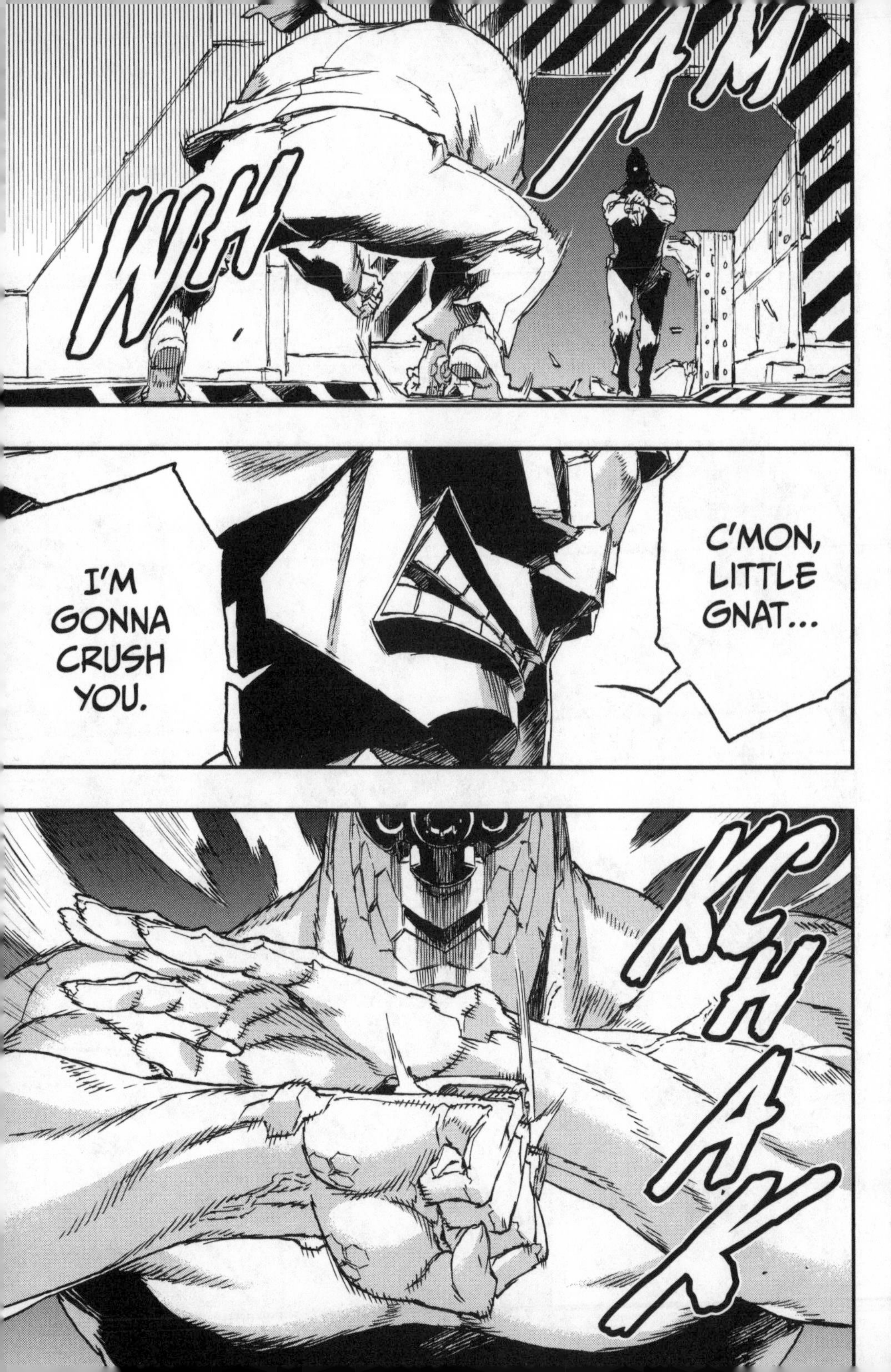
WHAM
C'MON, LITTLE GNAT...
I'M GONNA CRUSH YOU.
KCHAK

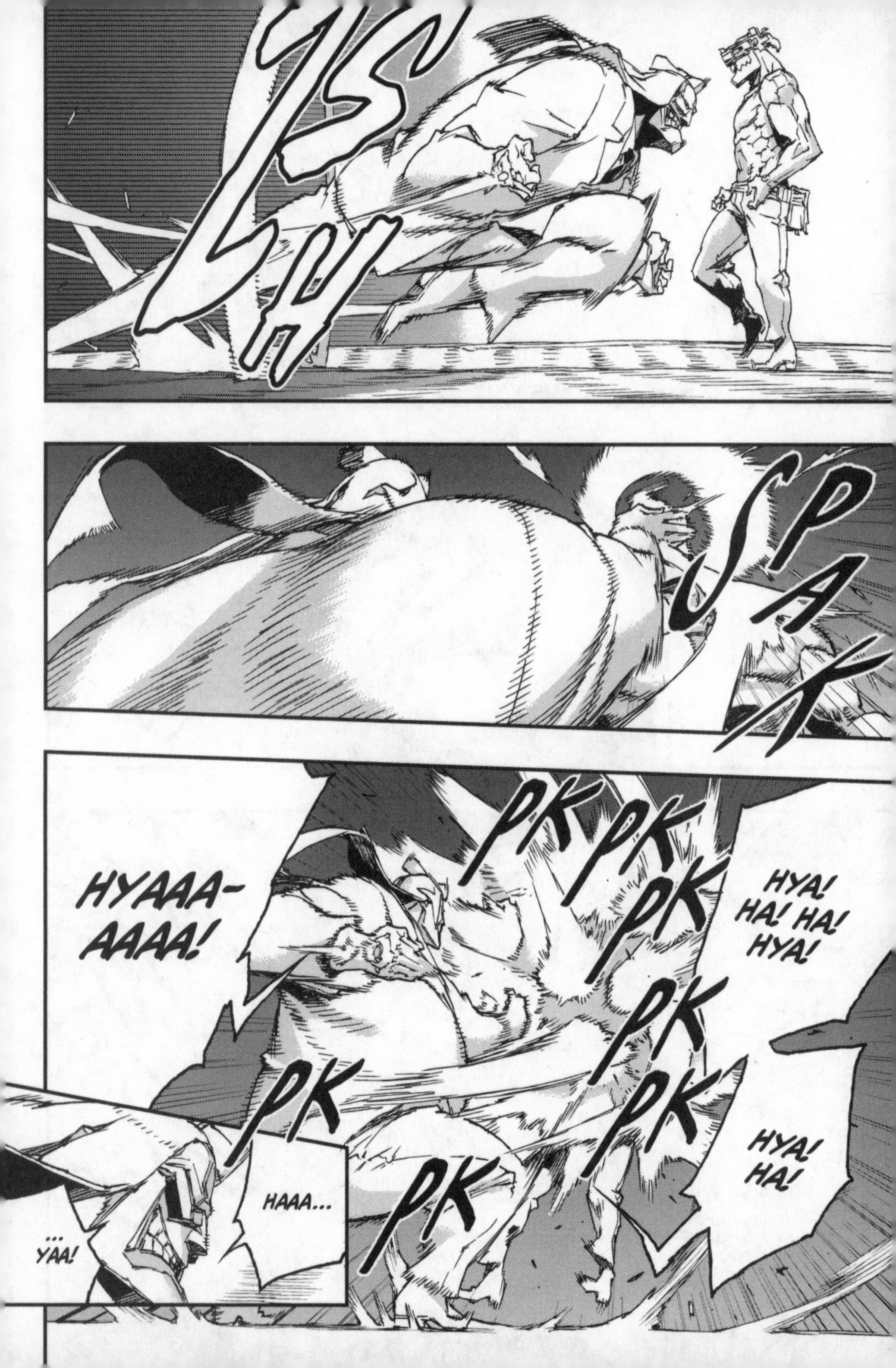
SPAK
HYA! HA! HA! HYA!
PK PK PK PK PK PK
HYAAA-AAAA!
HYA! HA!
PK
PK
HAAA...
...YAA!

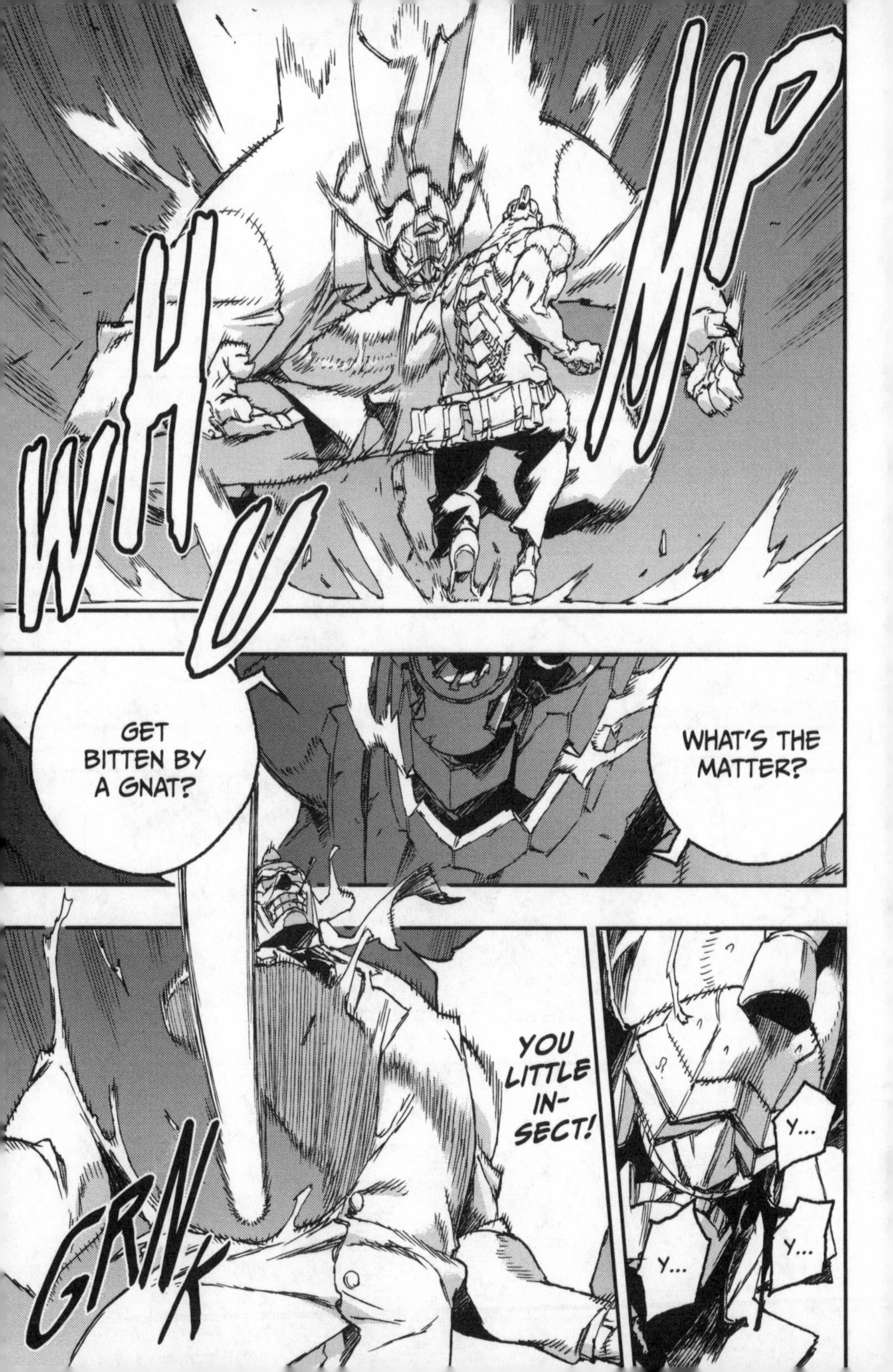
WHUMP
WHAT'S THE MATTER?
GET BITTEN BY A GNAT?
Y...
Y...
Y...
YOU LITTLE IN-SECT!
GRNK

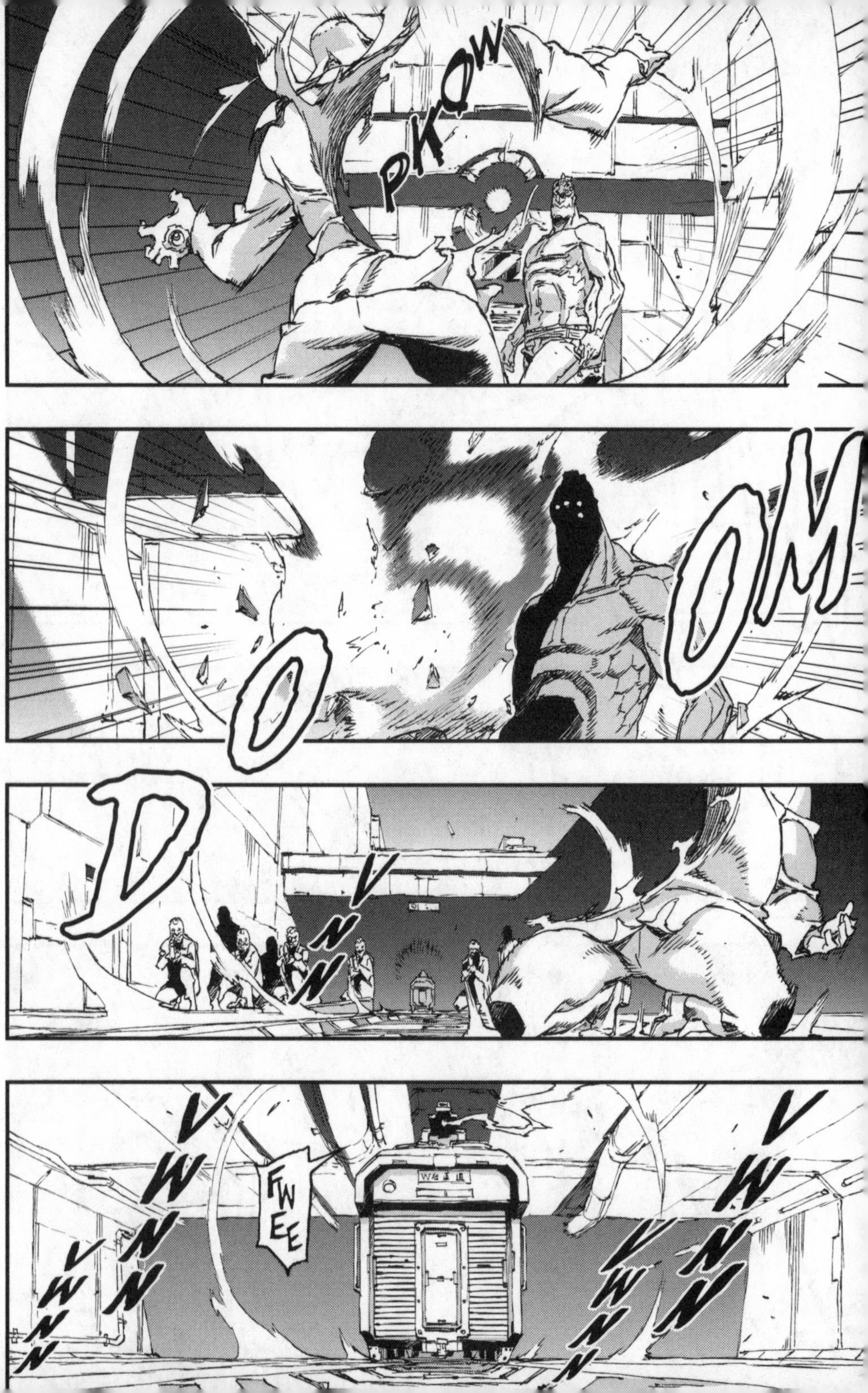

PKOW
DOOM
VNNN
VWNNN
VWNNN
FWEE
VWNNN
VWNNN

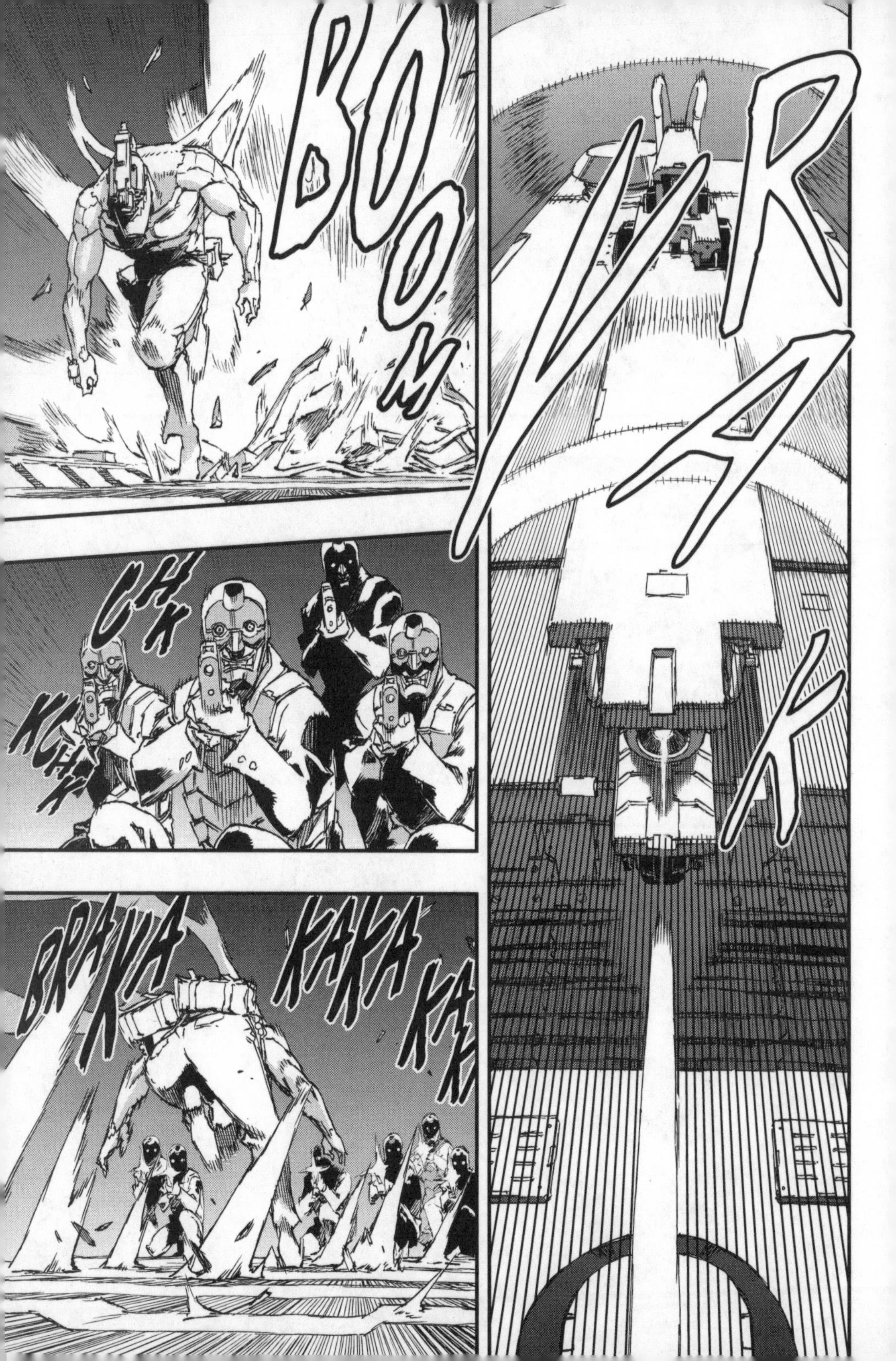
VRAKK
BOOOM
CHK
KCHK
BRAKA
KAKA
KAKA

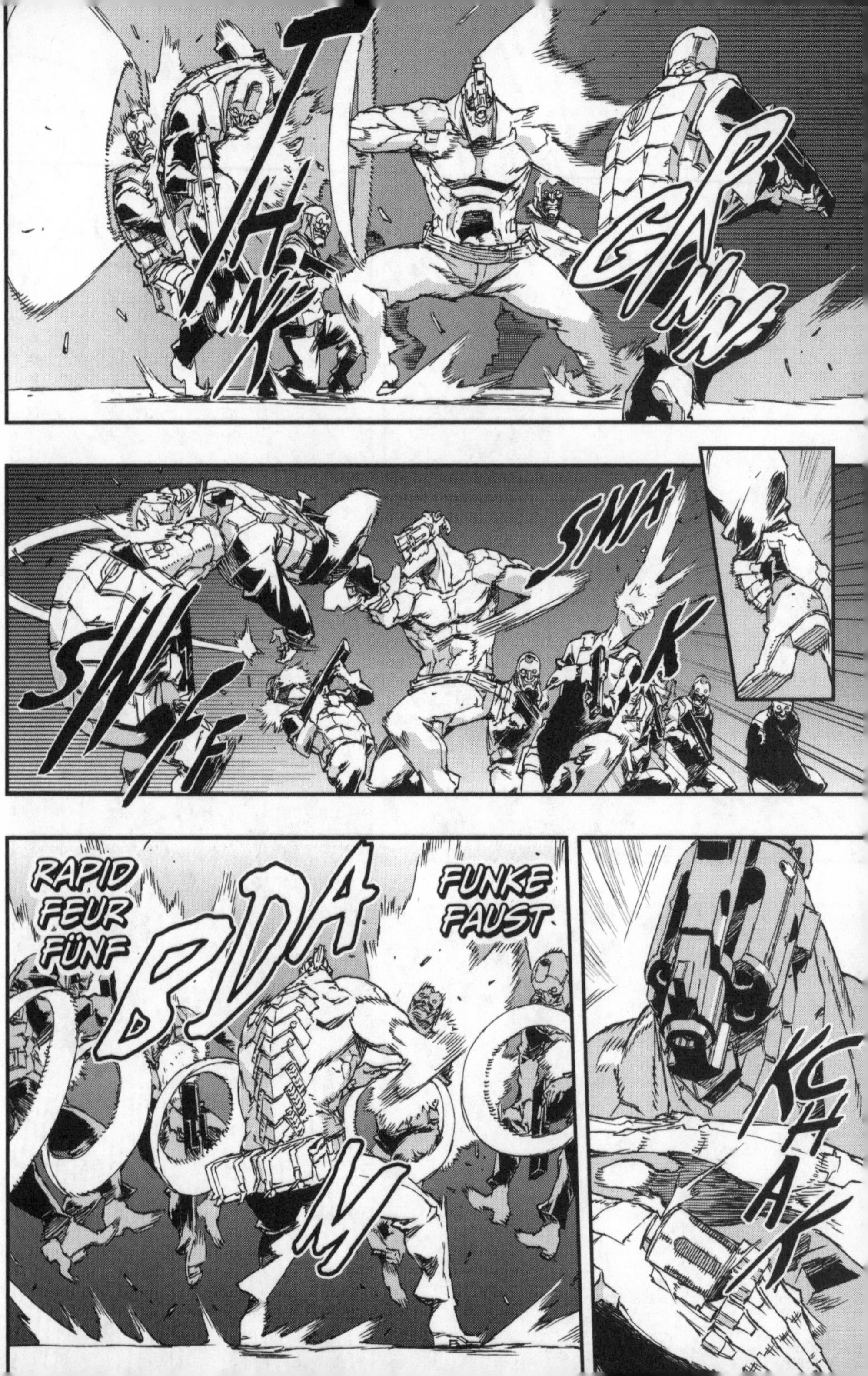
GRGNN
THNK
SMA
K
SWFF
KCHAK
FUNKE
FAUST
RAPID
FEUR
FÜNF
BDA
M

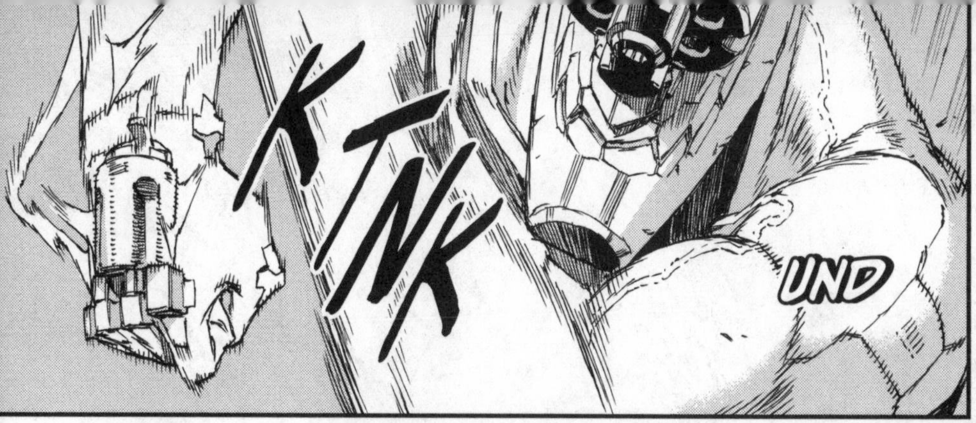
KTINK
UND
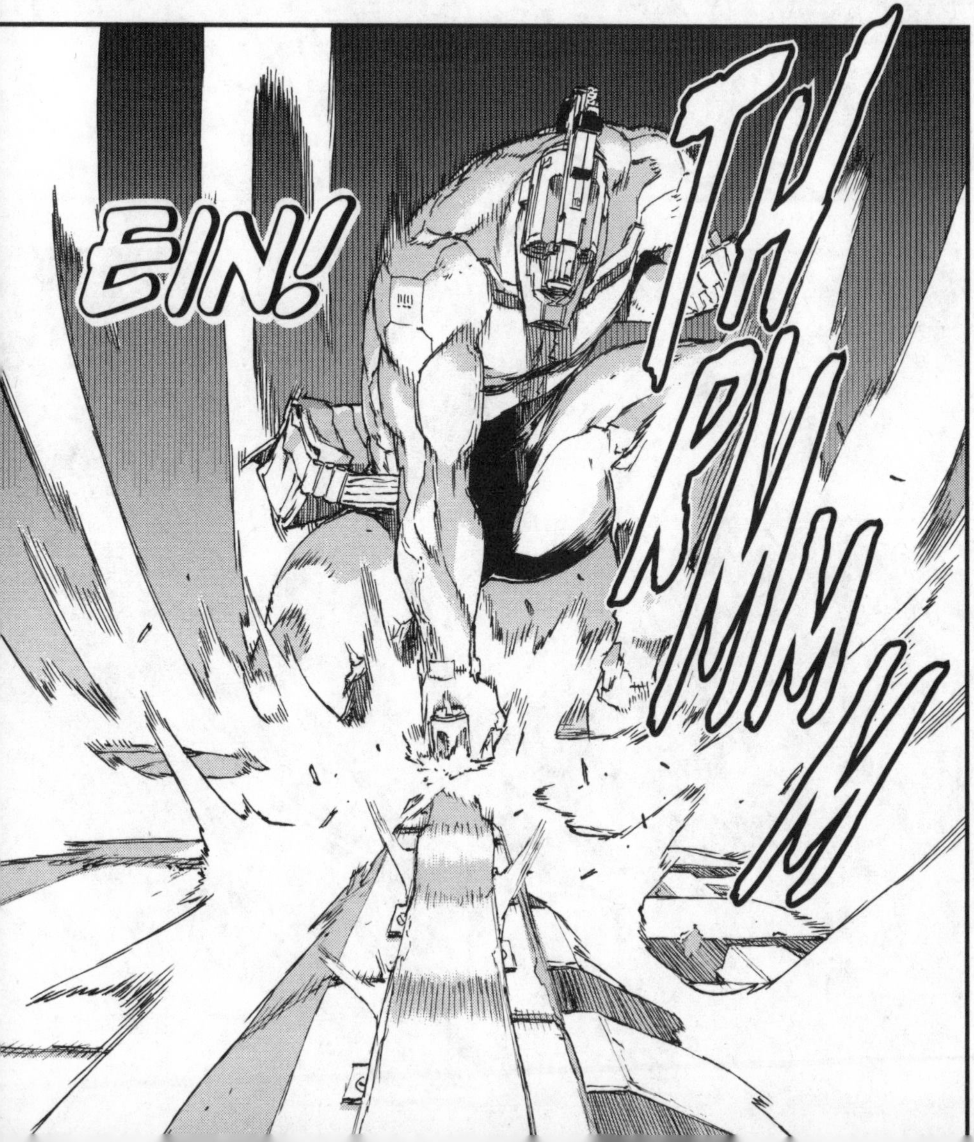
THPMMM
EIN!

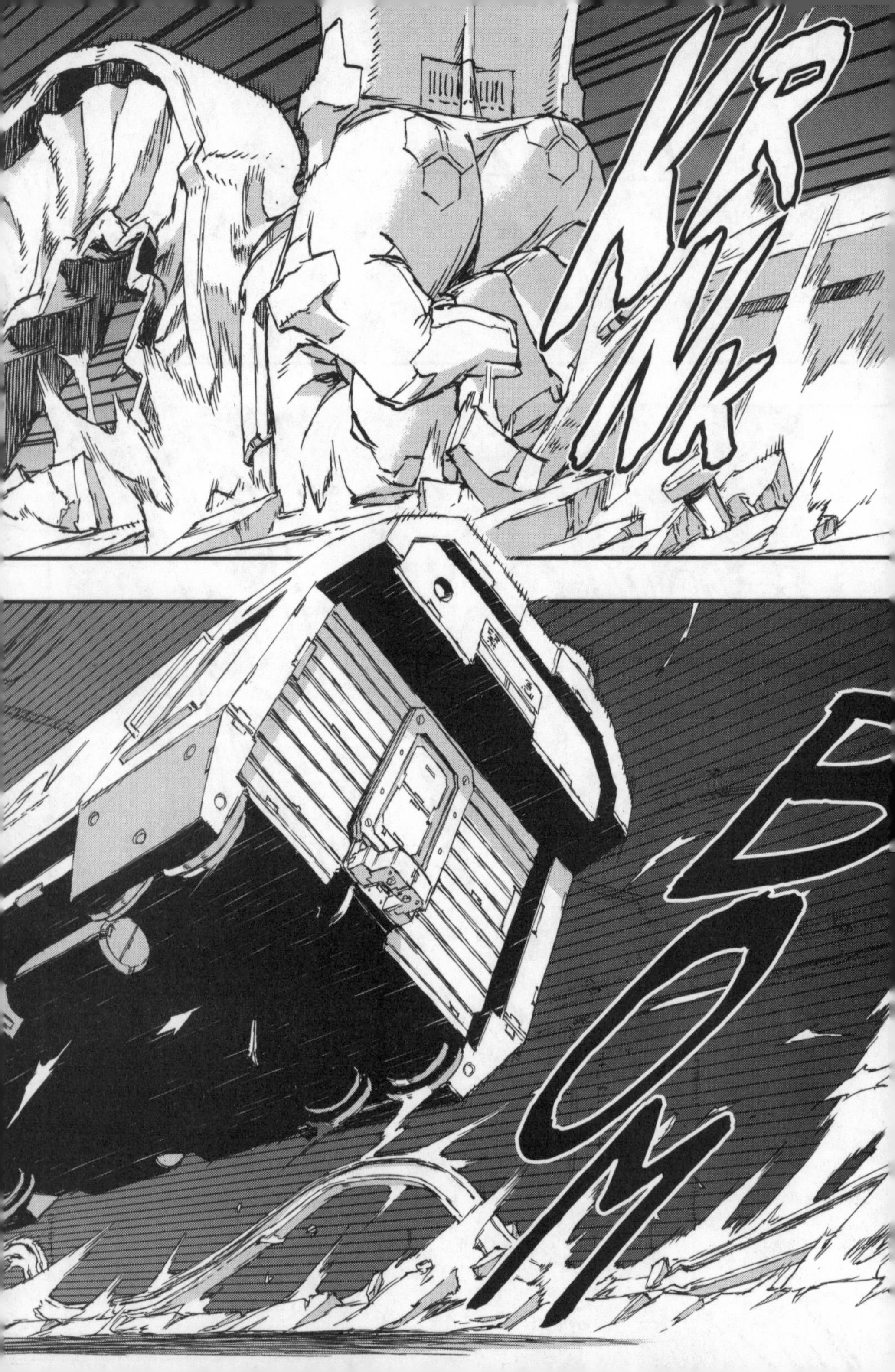

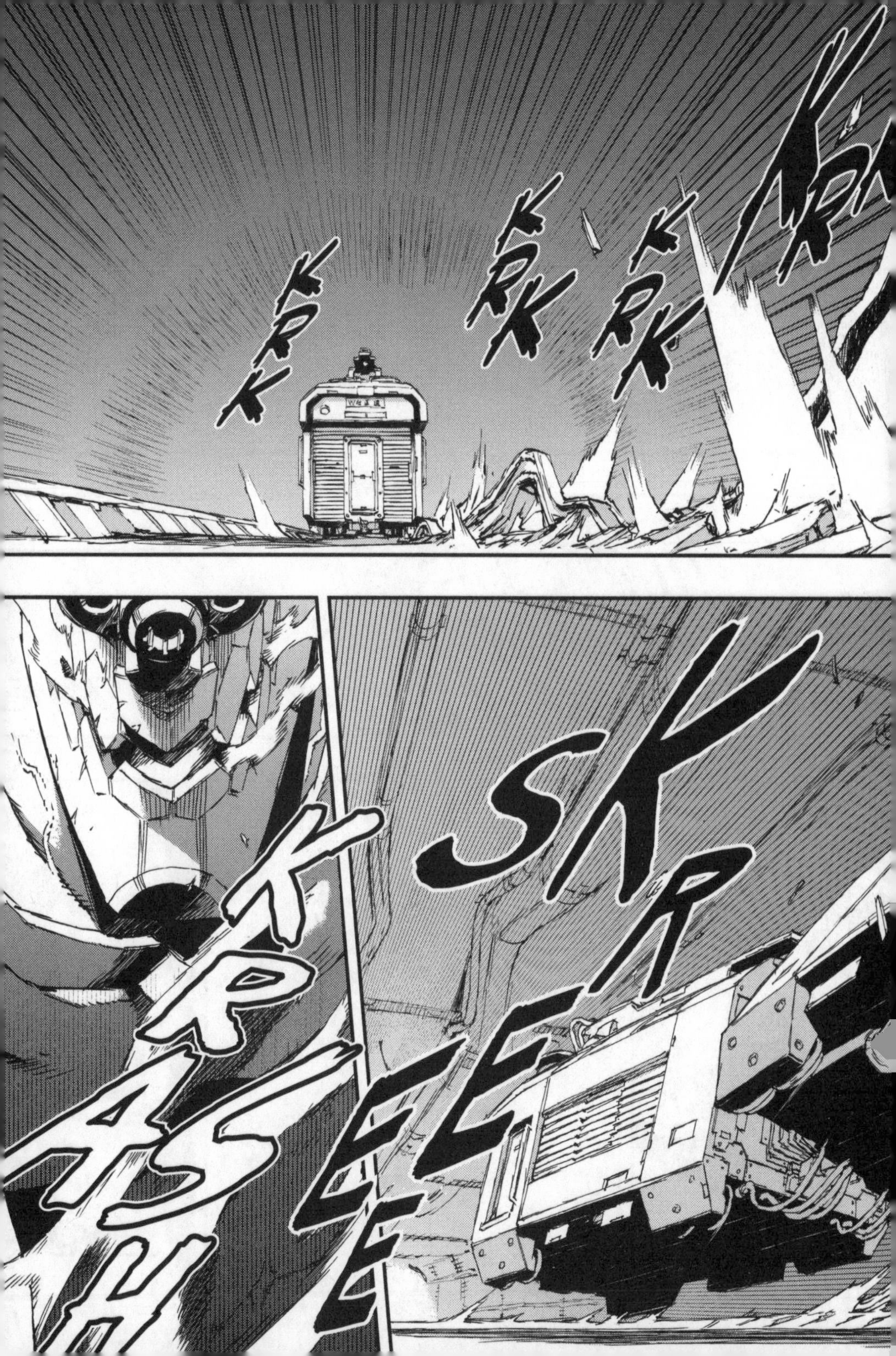
KRK
KRK
KRK
KRK
SKREEEE
KRASH

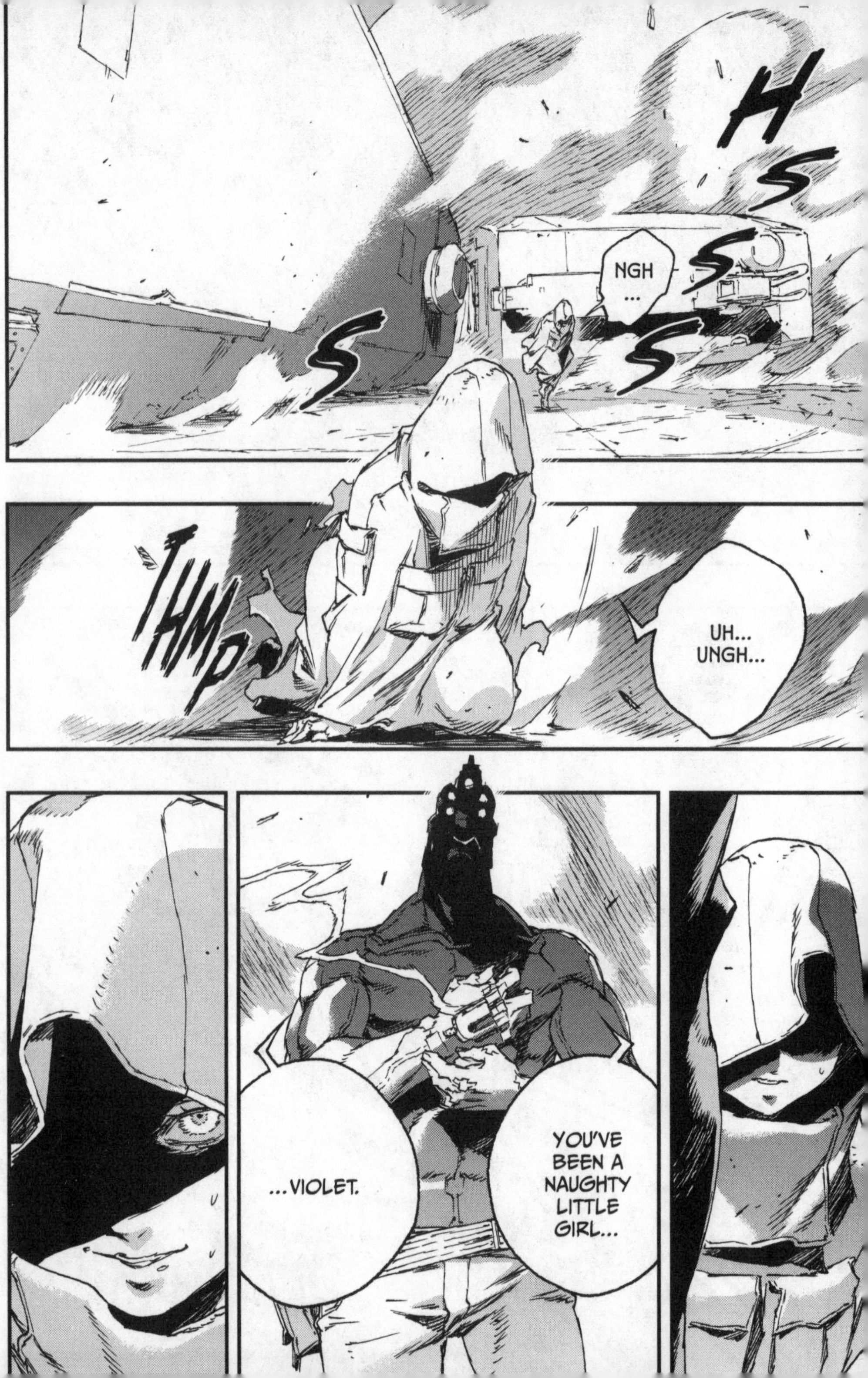
HSSS
NGH...
S
UH... UNGH...
THMP
YOU'VE BEEN A NAUGHTY LITTLE GIRL...
...VIOLET.

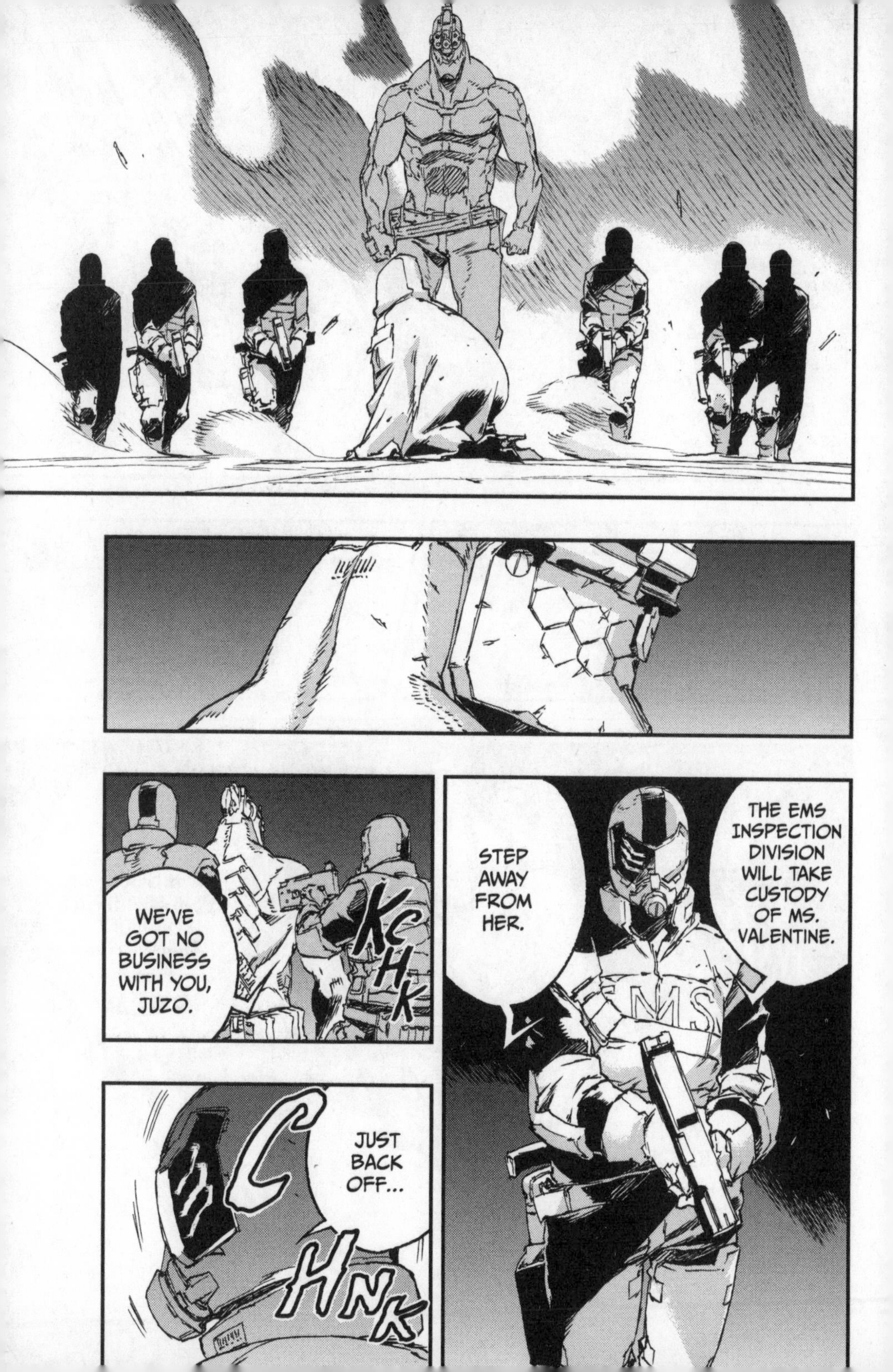
THE EMS INSPECTION DIVISION WILL TAKE CUSTODY OF MS. VALENTINE.
STEP AWAY FROM HER.
EMS
KCHK
WE'VE GOT NO BUSINESS WITH YOU, JUZO.
JUST BACK OFF...
CHNK

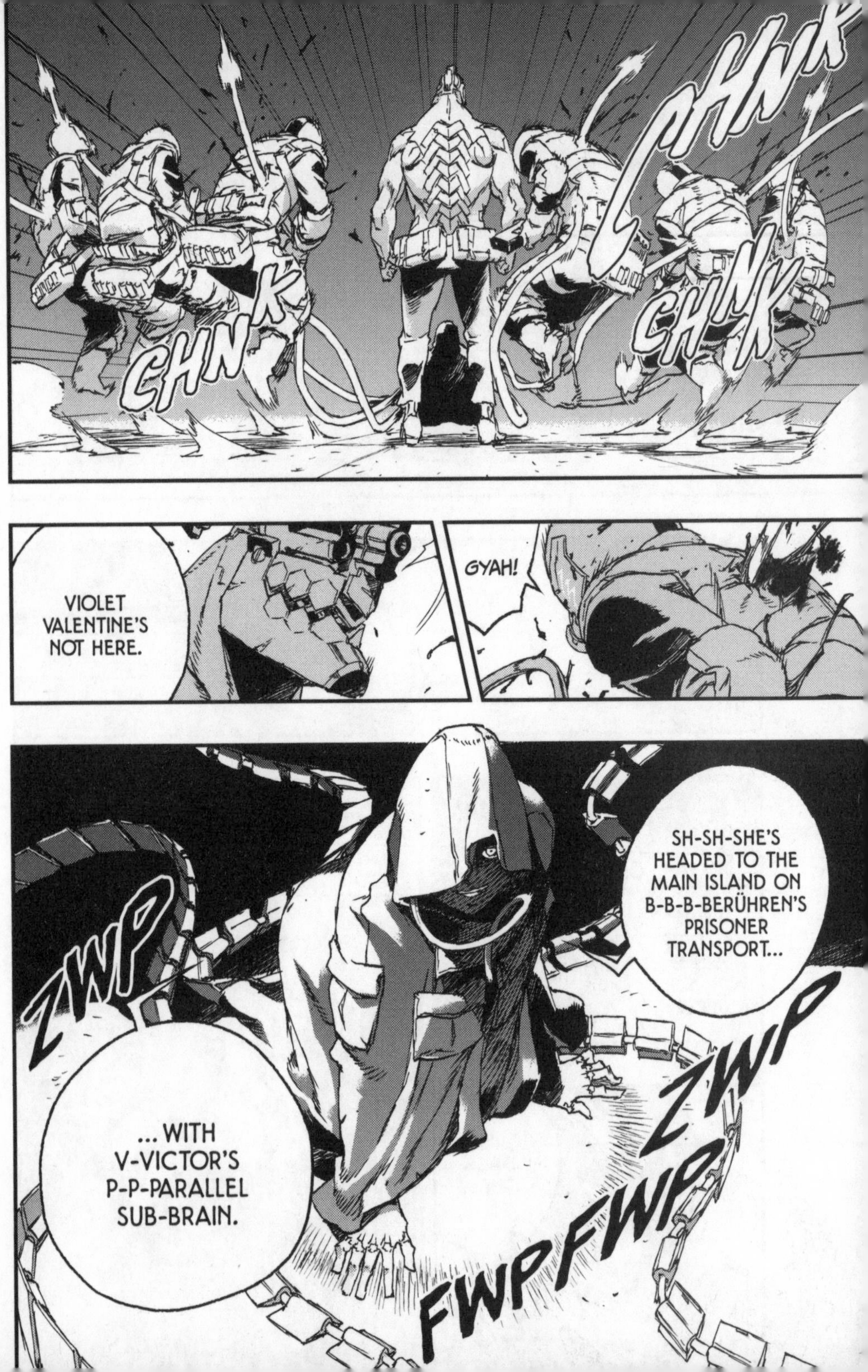

CHNK
CHNK
CHNK
GYAH!
VIOLET VALENTINE'S NOT HERE.
SH-SH-SHE'S HEADED TO THE MAIN ISLAND ON B-B-B-BERÜHREN'S PRISONER TRANSPORT...
ZWP
ZWP
FWP FWP
...WITH V-VICTOR'S P-P-PARALLEL SUB-BRAIN.

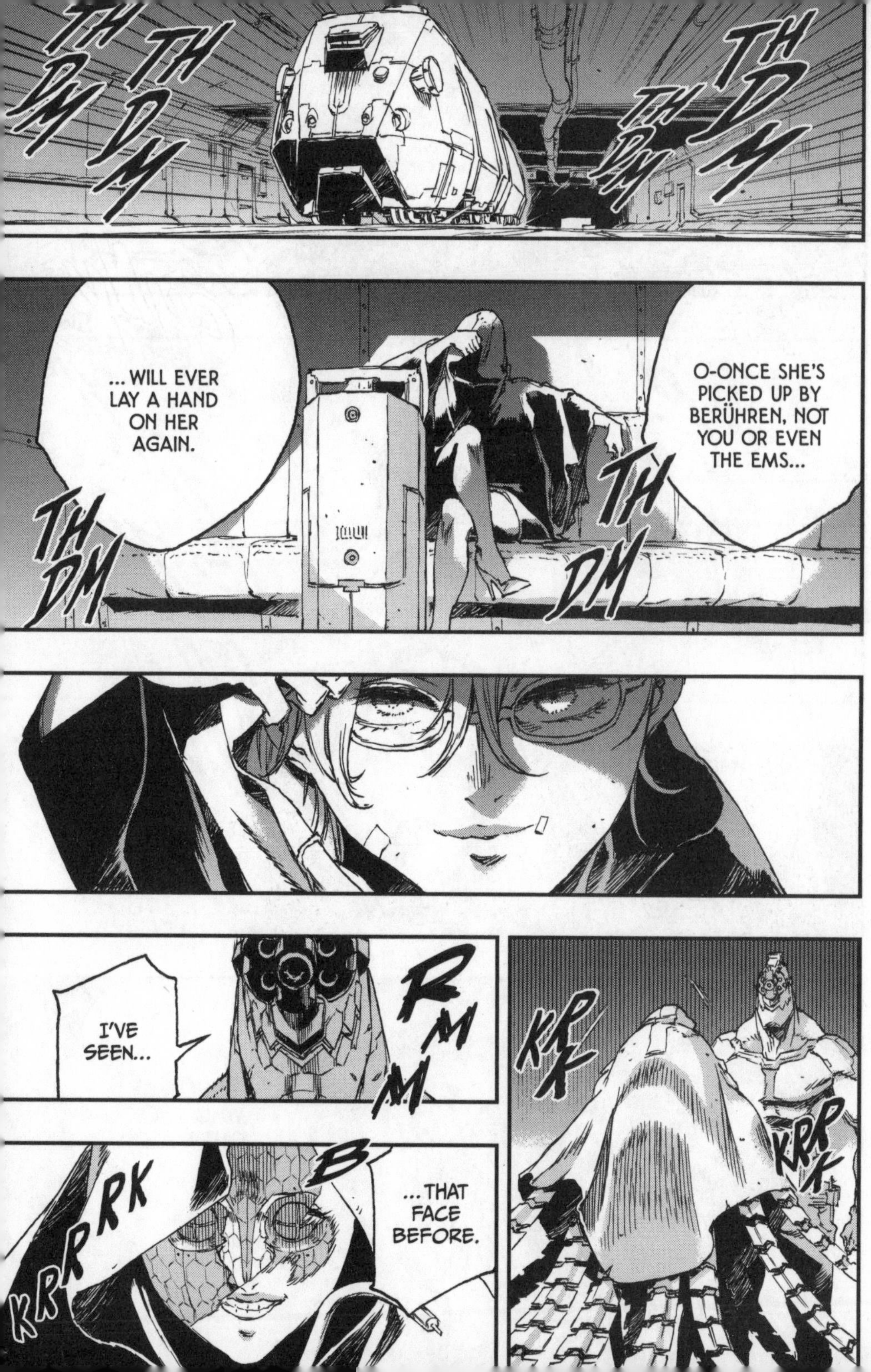
THDM
THDM
THDM
THDM
O-ONCE SHE'S PICKED UP BY BERÜHREN, NOT YOU OR EVEN THE EMS...
THDM
...WILL EVER LAY A HAND ON HER AGAIN.
THDM
KRRK
KRRK
I'VE SEEN...
RMMMB
...THAT FACE BEFORE.
KRRRK
KRRK

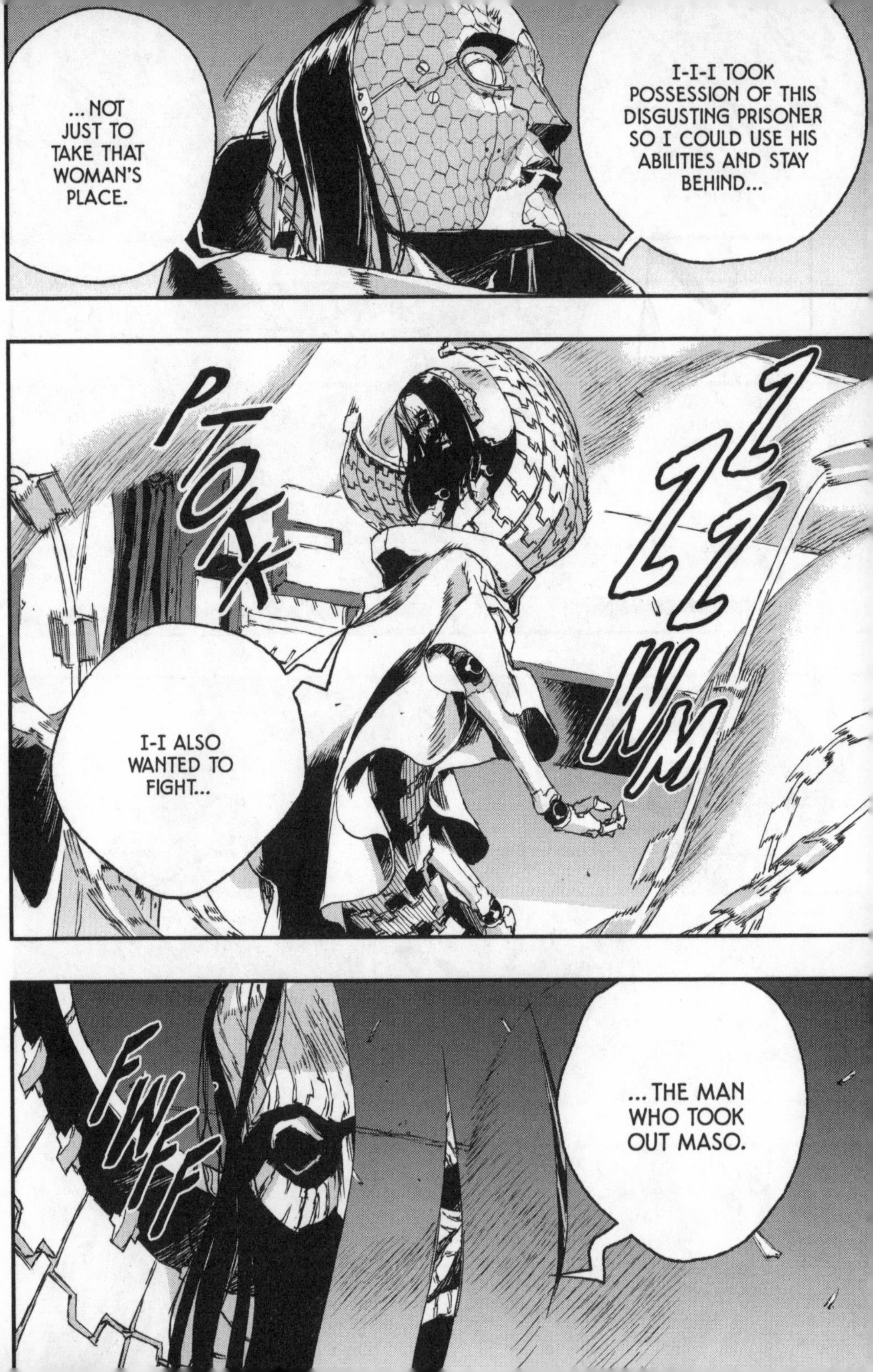
I-I-I TOOK POSSESSION OF THIS DISGUSTING PRISONER SO I COULD USE HIS ABILITIES AND STAY BEHIND...
...NOT JUST TO TAKE THAT WOMAN'S PLACE.
ZZZNM
PTOKK
I-I ALSO WANTED TO FIGHT...
...THE MAN WHO TOOK OUT MASO.
FWFF

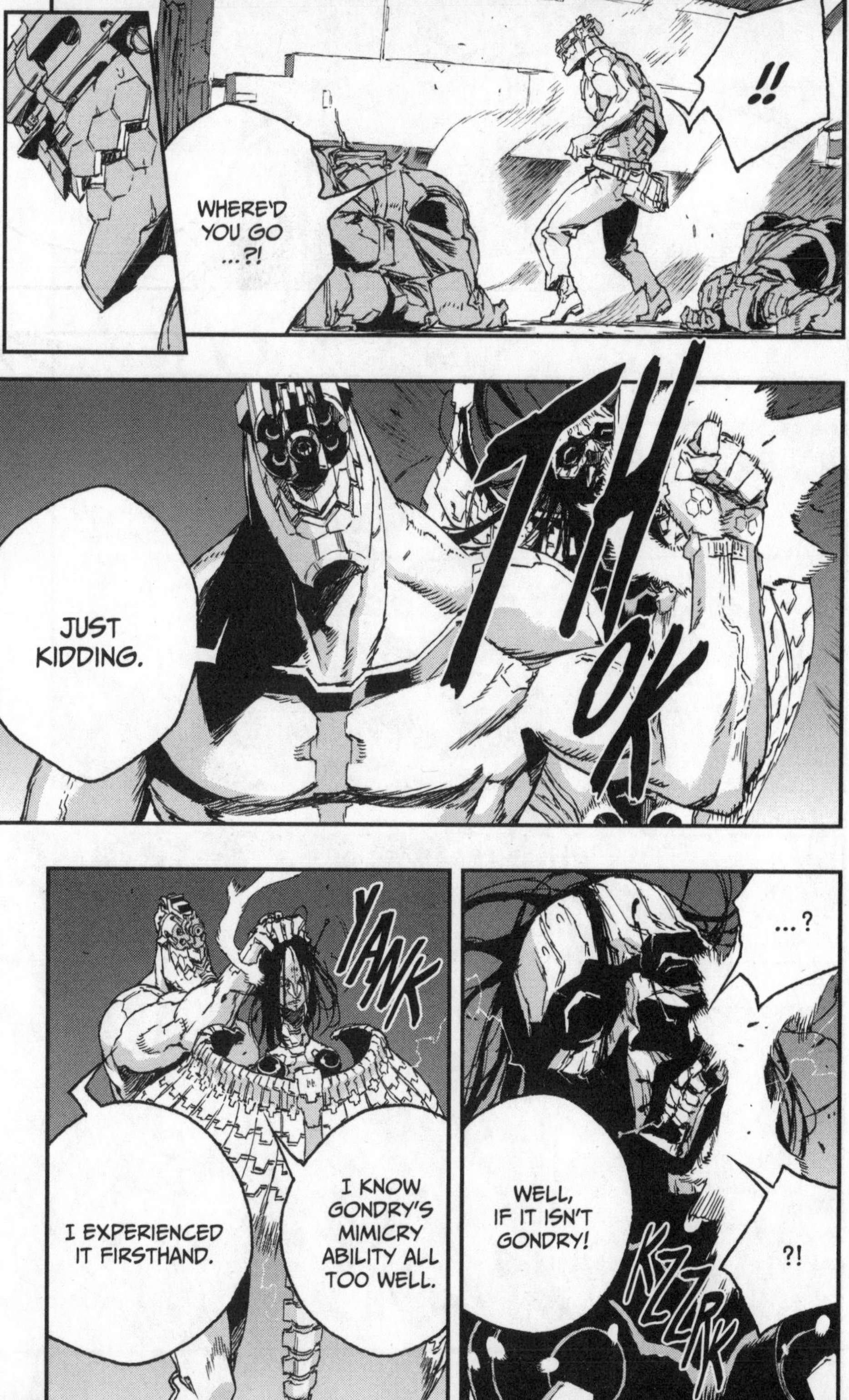
!!
WHERE'D YOU GO ...?!
THOK
JUST KIDDING.
...?
WELL, IF IT ISN'T GONDRY!
?!
KZZRK
YANK
I KNOW GONDRY'S MIMICRY ABILITY ALL TOO WELL.
I EXPERIENCED IT FIRSTHAND.

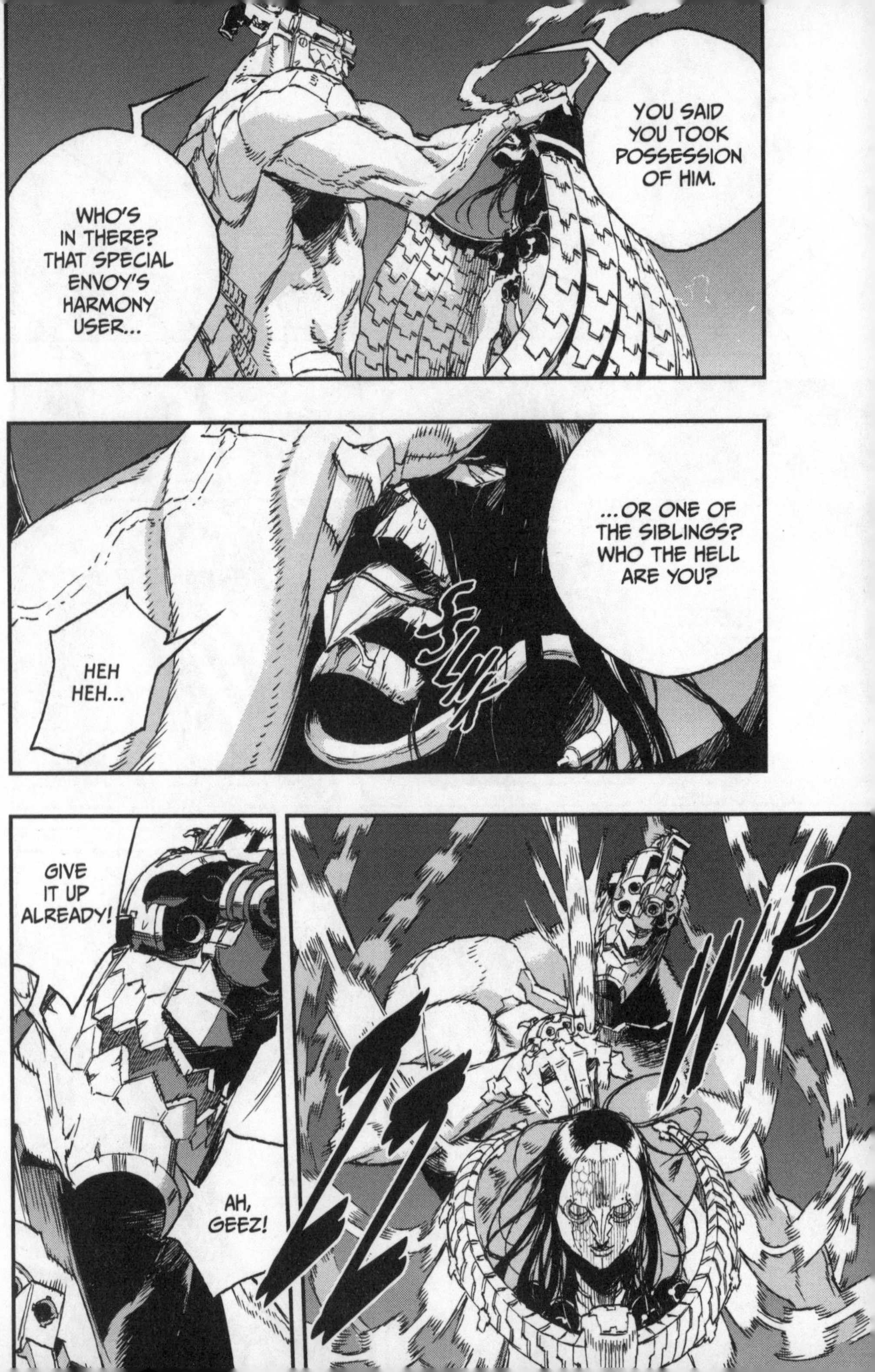
YOU SAID YOU TOOK POSSESSION OF HIM.
WHO'S IN THERE? THAT SPECIAL ENVOY'S HARMONY USER...
...OR ONE OF THE SIBLINGS? WHO THE HELL ARE YOU?
HEH HEH...
GIVE IT UP ALREADY!
AH, GEEZ!

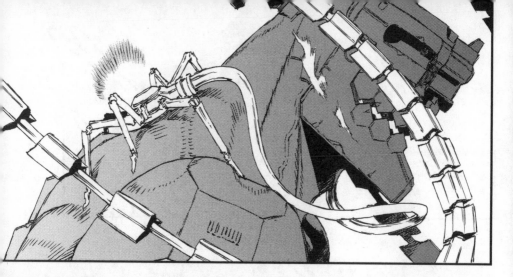

SKITTER

I HAVE POSSESSION OF HIM!

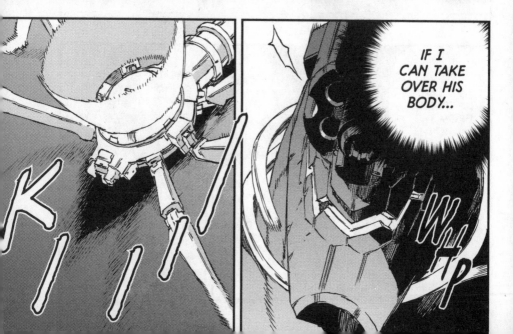

IF I CAN TAKE OVER HIS BODY...

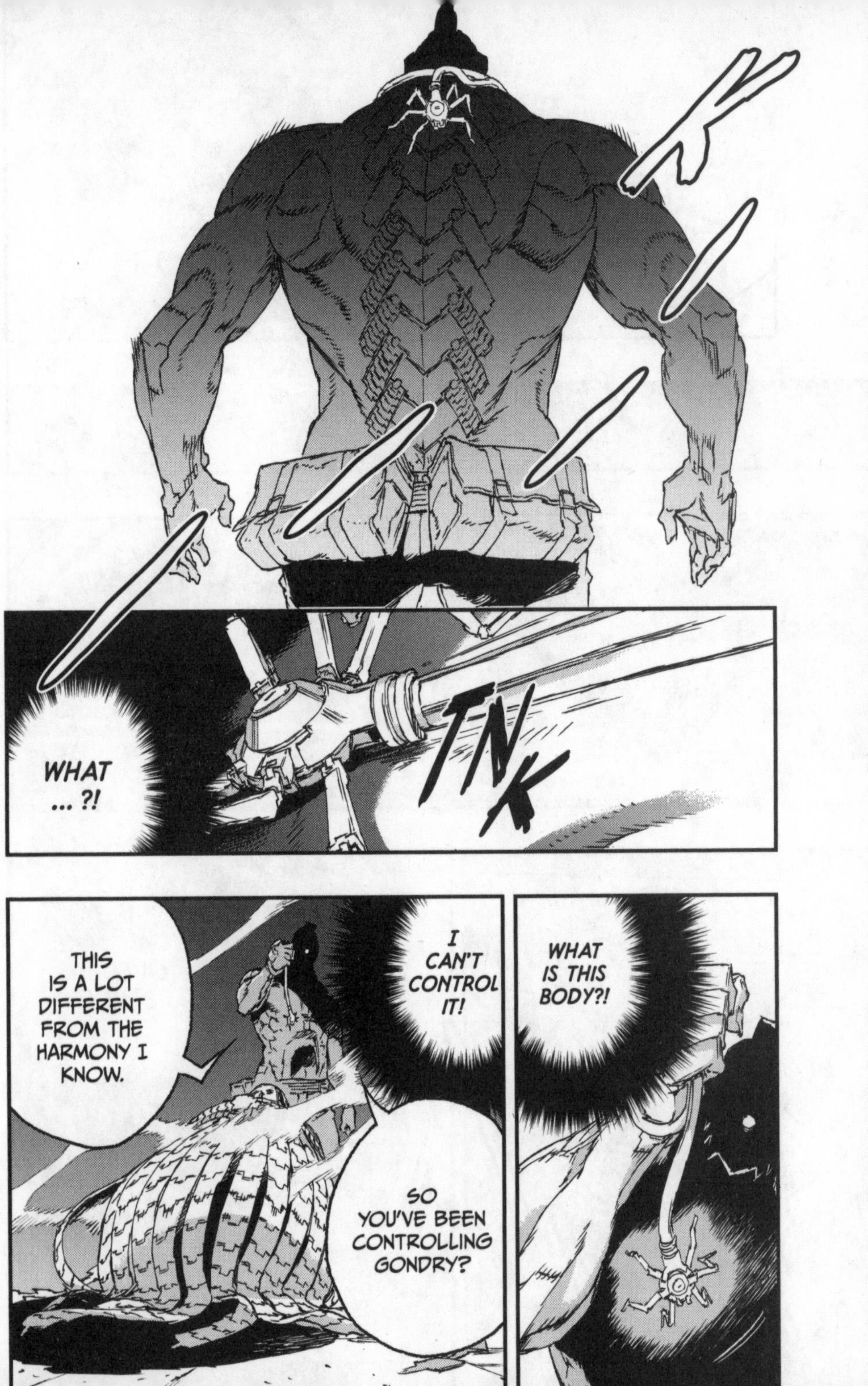
WHAT ...?!
TNK
WHAT IS THIS BODY?!
I CAN'T CONTROL IT!
THIS IS A LOT DIFFERENT FROM THE HARMONY I KNOW.
SO YOU'VE BEEN CONTROLLING GONDRY?

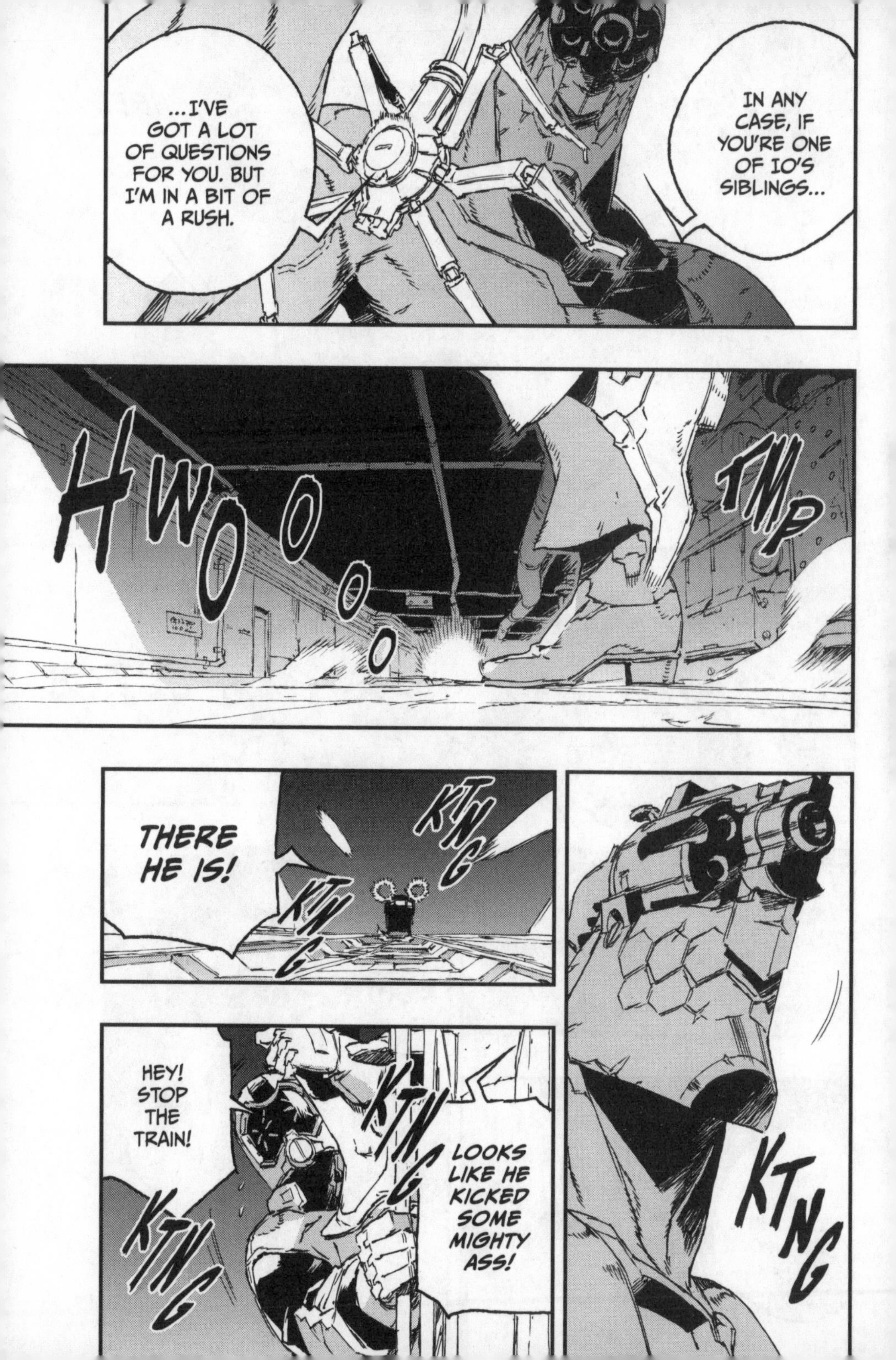
IN ANY CASE, IF YOU'RE ONE OF IO'S SIBLINGS...
...I'VE GOT A LOT OF QUESTIONS FOR YOU. BUT I'M IN A BIT OF A RUSH.
TMP
HWOOOOO
KTNG
KTNG
THERE HE IS!
KTNG
HEY! STOP THE TRAIN!
KTNG
LOOKS LIKE HE KICKED SOME MIGHTY ASS!
KTNG

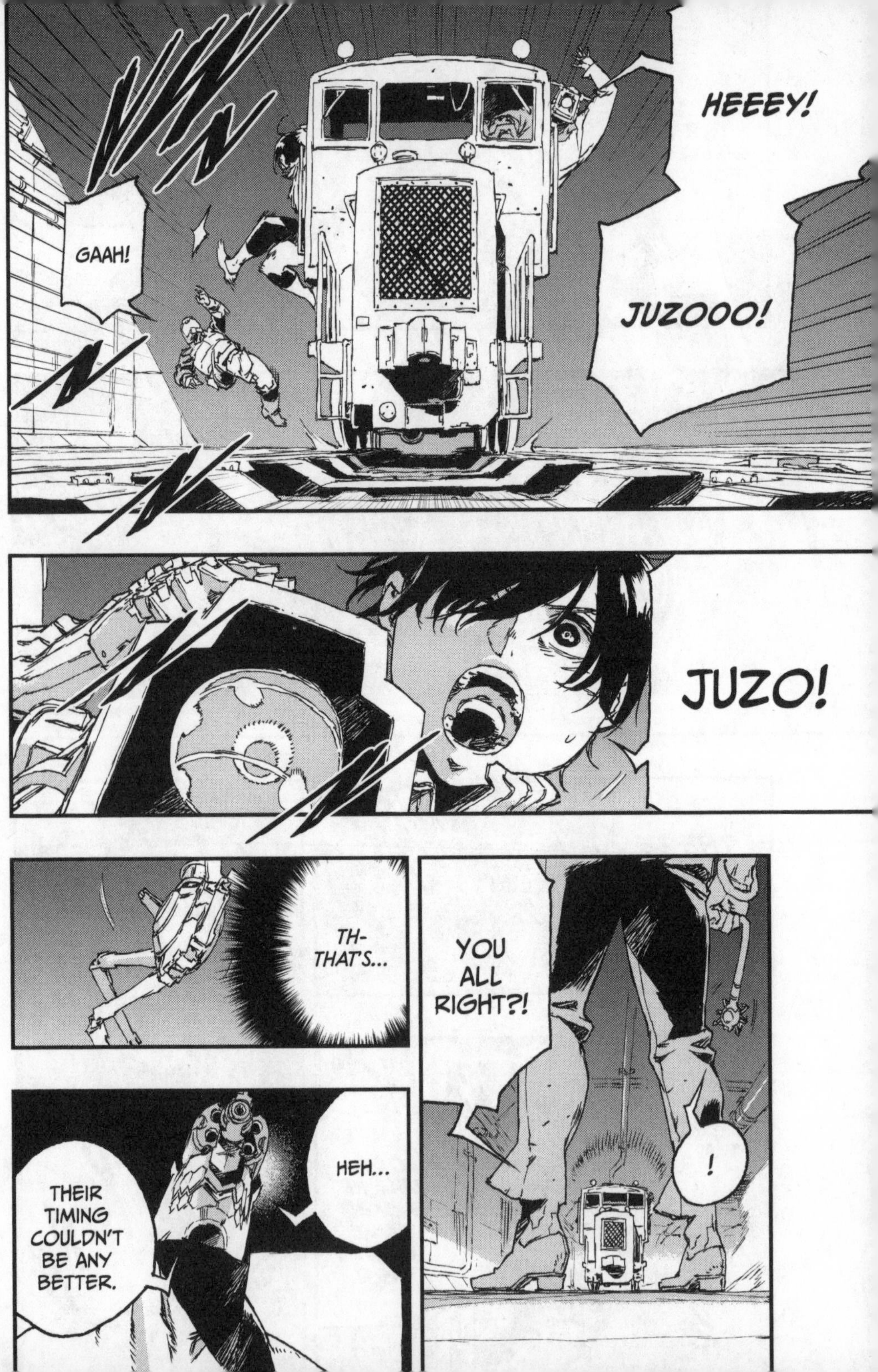
HEEEY! JUZOOO!
GAAH!
JUZO!
YOU ALL RIGHT?!
!
TH- THAT'S...
HEH...
THEIR TIMING COULDN'T BE ANY BETTER.

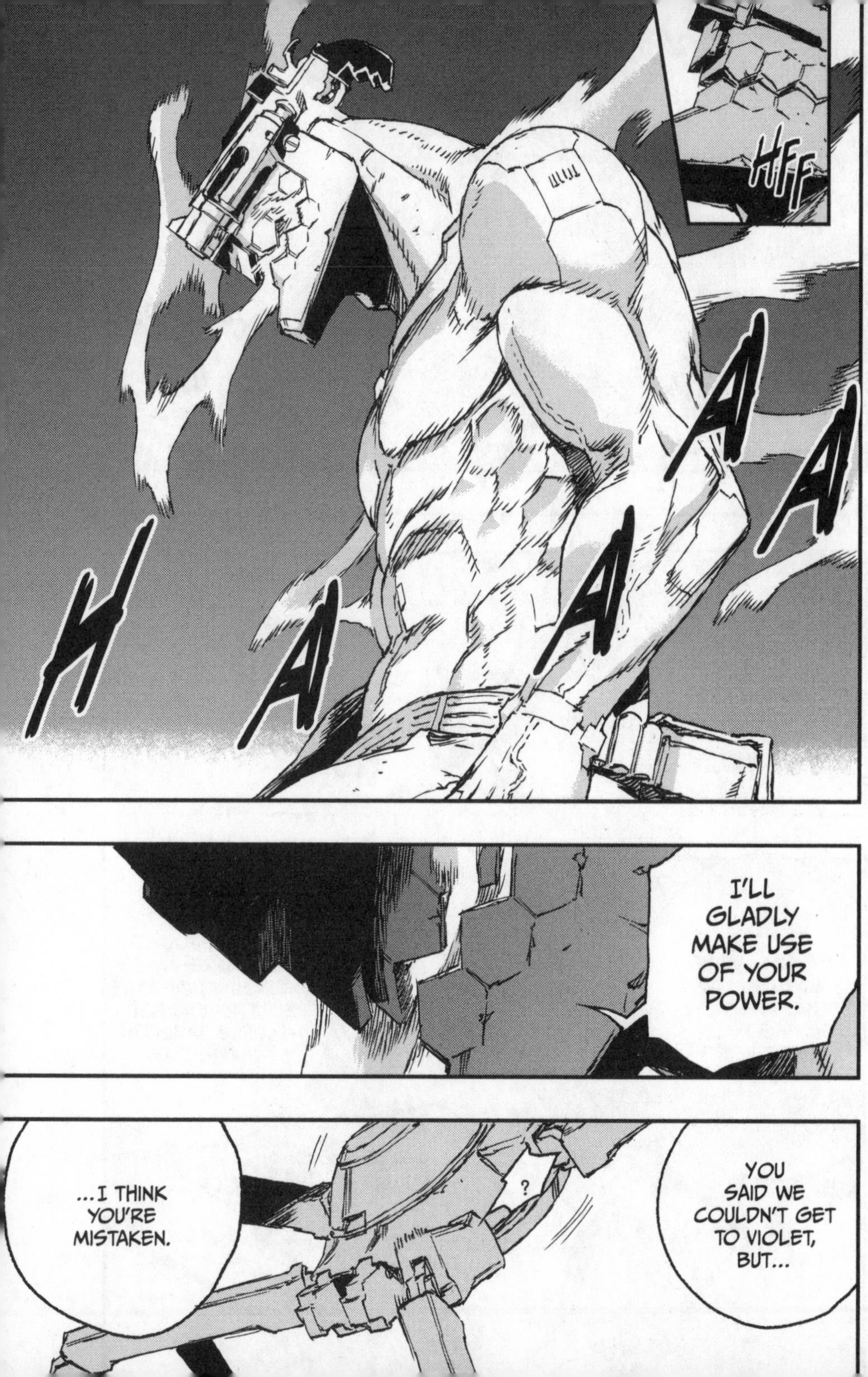
HFF
HAAAAAA
I'LL GLADLY MAKE USE OF YOUR POWER.
YOU SAID WE COULDN'T GET TO VIOLET, BUT...
?
...I THINK YOU'RE MISTAKEN.

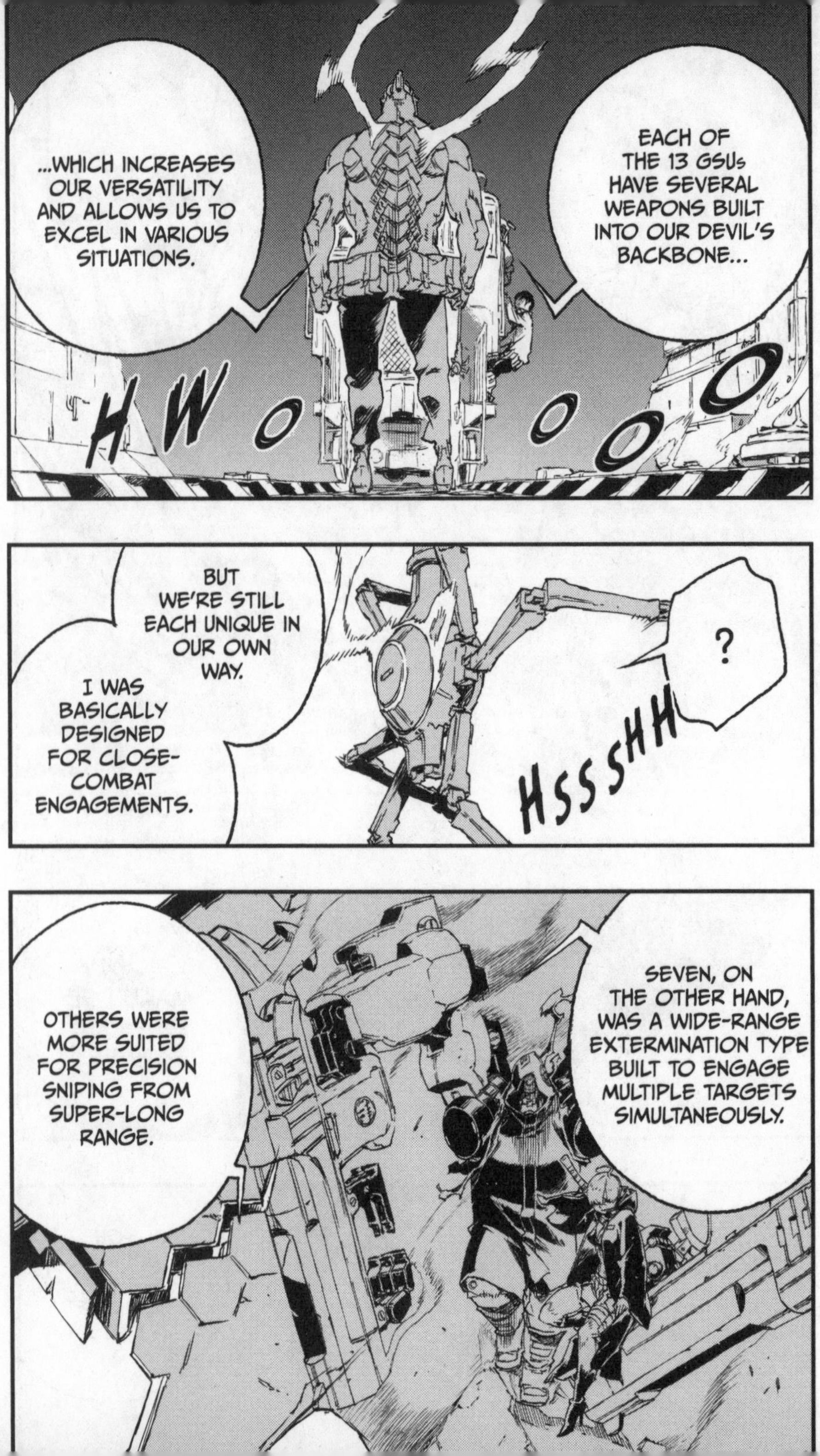
EACH OF THE 13 GSUs HAVE SEVERAL WEAPONS BUILT INTO OUR DEVIL'S BACKBONE...
...WHICH INCREASES OUR VERSATILITY AND ALLOWS US TO EXCEL IN VARIOUS SITUATIONS.
HWOOOOO
?
HSSSHH
BUT WE'RE STILL EACH UNIQUE IN OUR OWN WAY.
I WAS BASICALLY DESIGNED FOR CLOSE-COMBAT ENGAGEMENTS.
SEVEN, ON THE OTHER HAND, WAS A WIDE-RANGE EXTERMINATION TYPE BUILT TO ENGAGE MULTIPLE TARGETS SIMULTANEOUSLY.
OTHERS WERE MORE SUITED FOR PRECISION SNIPING FROM SUPER-LONG RANGE.

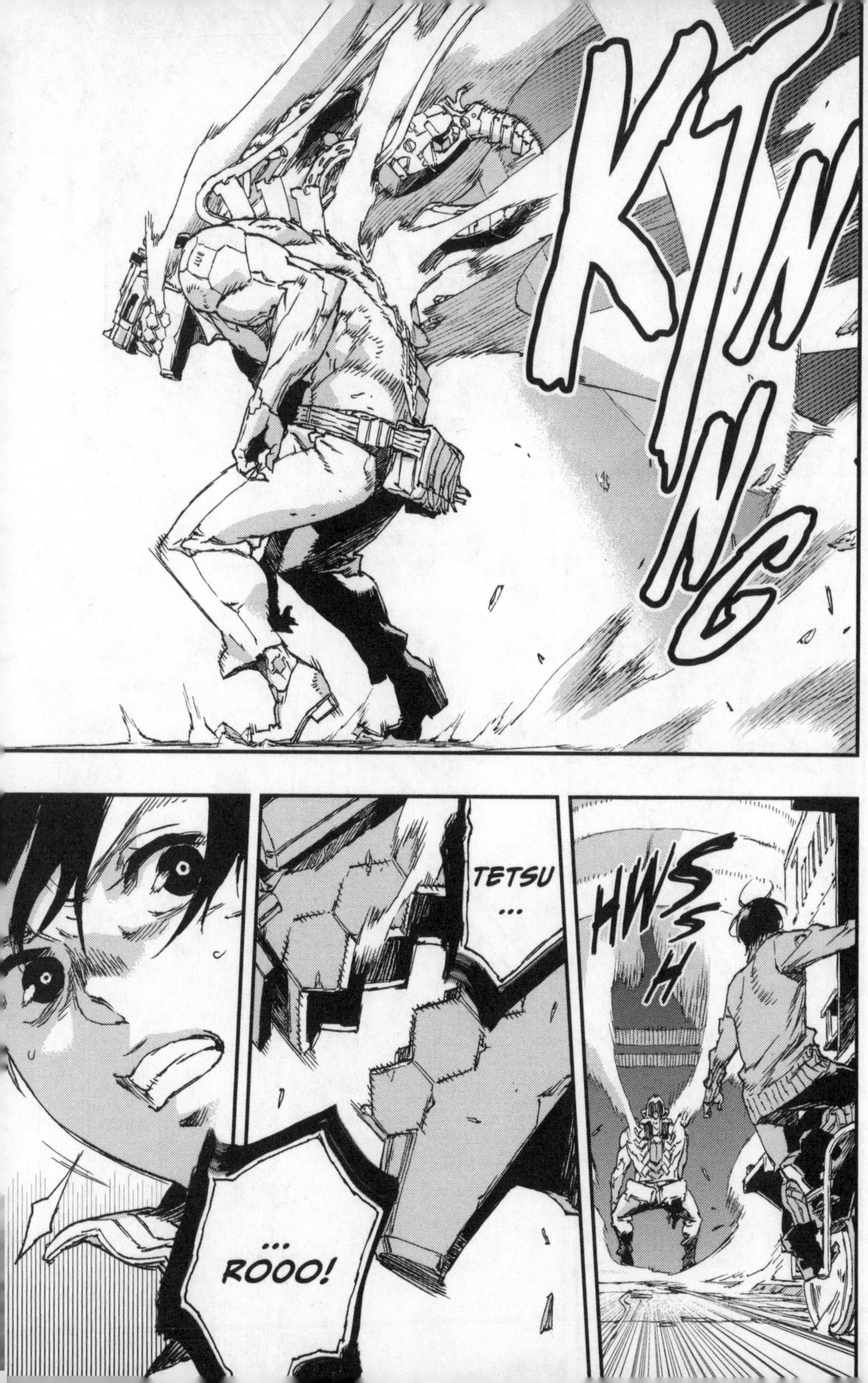
HWSSH
TETSU ...
... ROOO!

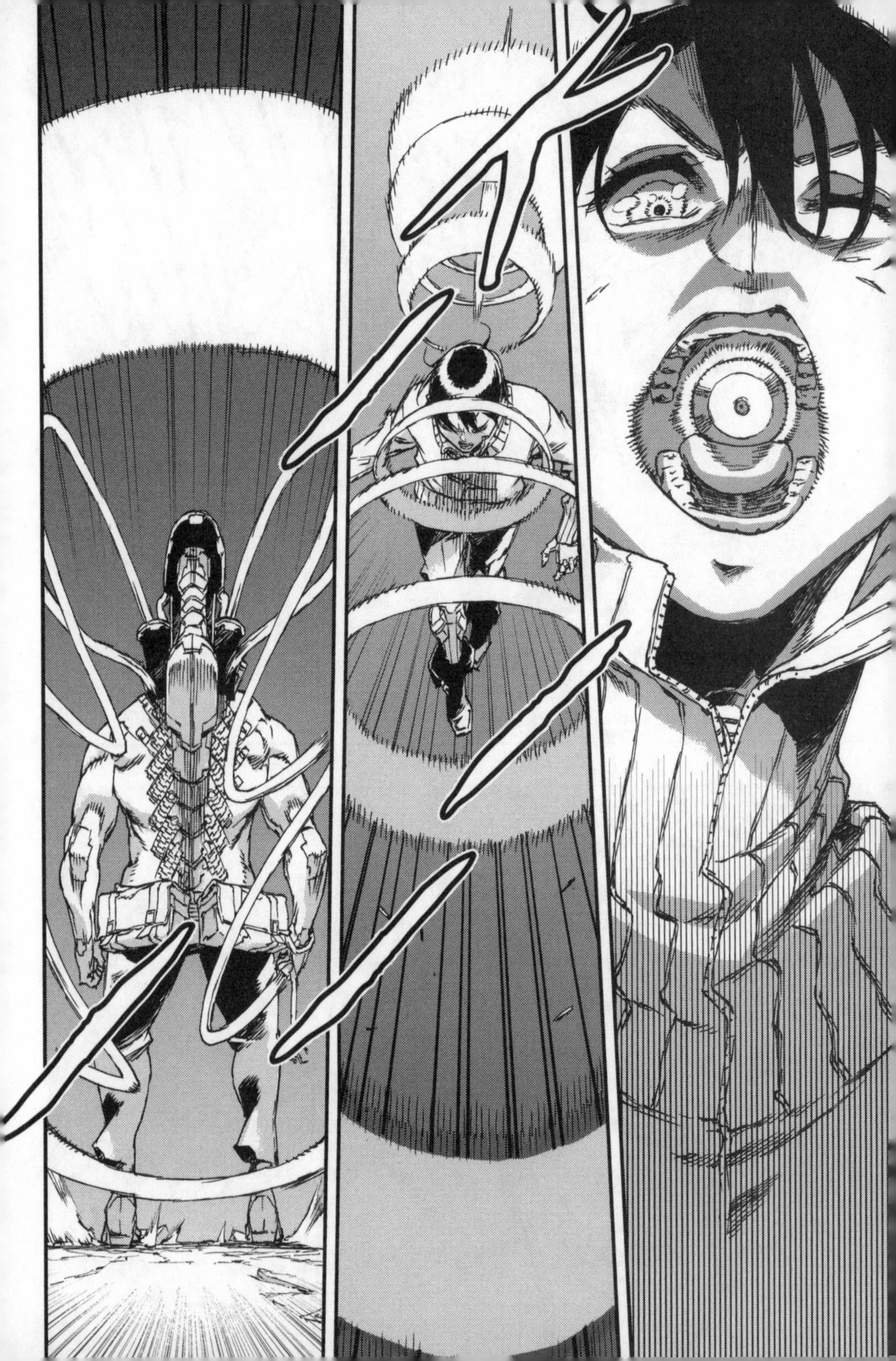

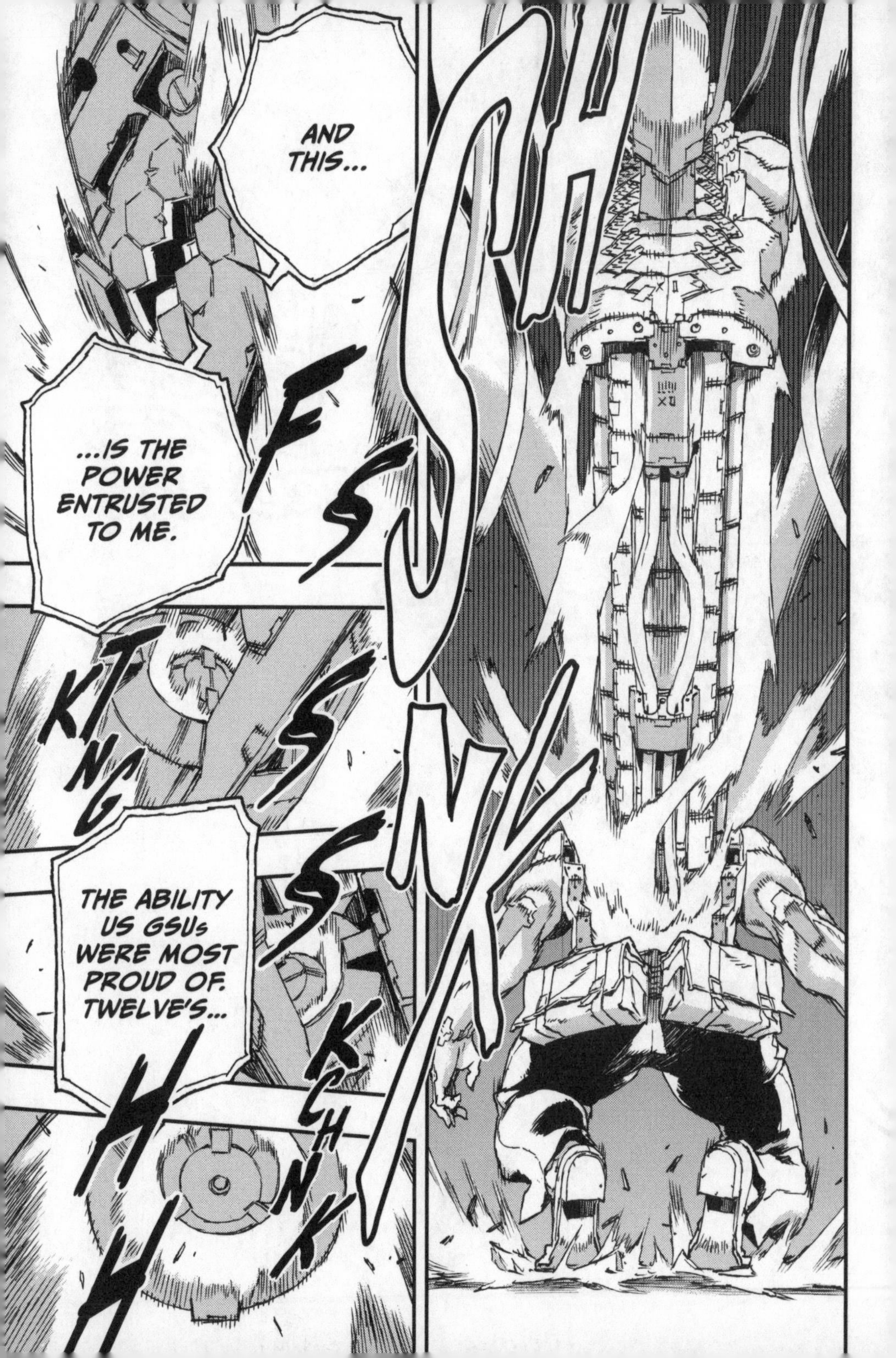
AND THIS...
...IS THE POWER ENTRUSTED TO ME.
FSSS
THE ABILITY US GSUs WERE MOST PROUD OF. TWELVE'S...
KCHNK

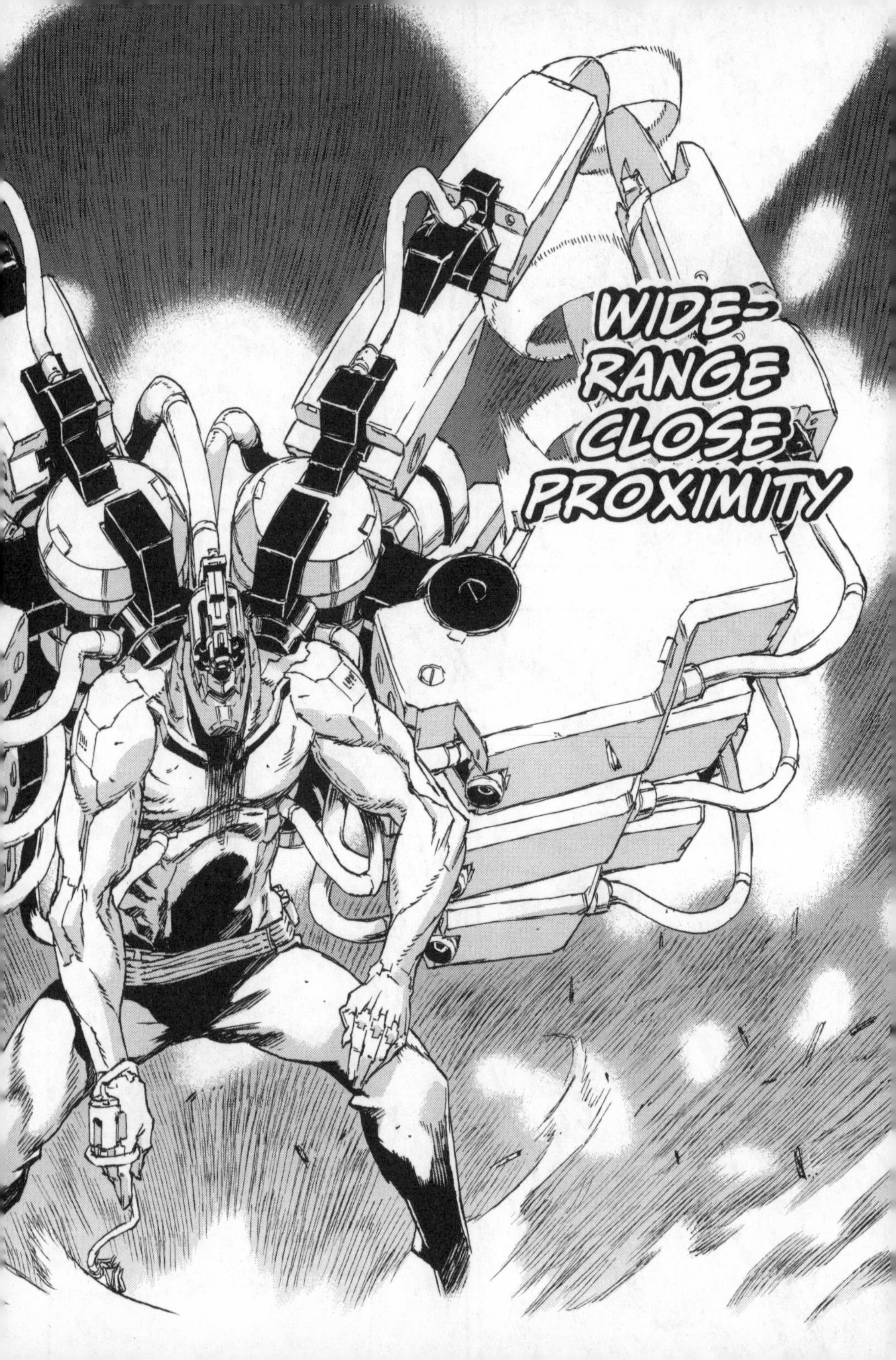
WIDE-RANGE CLOSE PROXIMITY

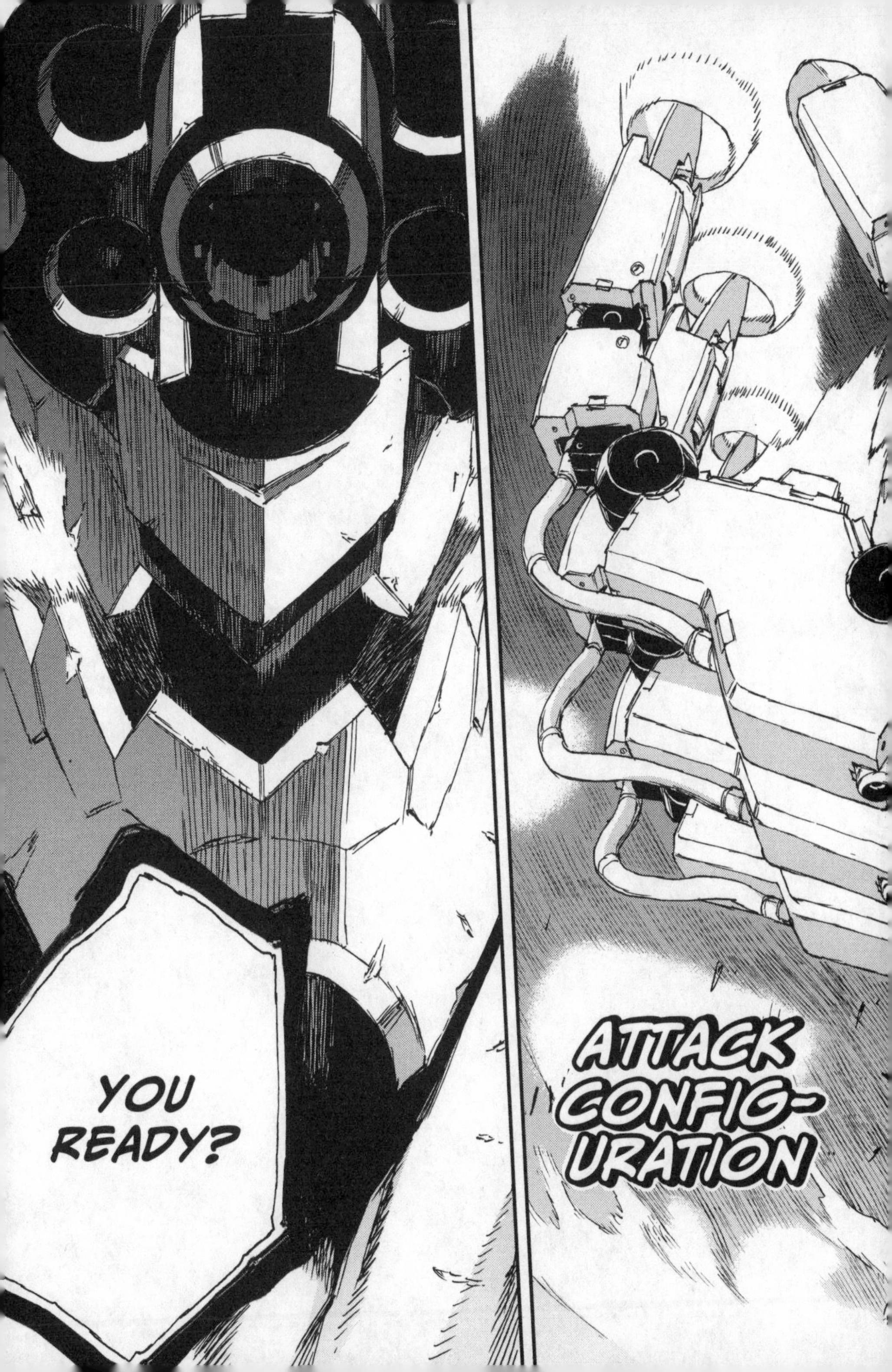
ATTACK CONFIG-URATION
YOU READY?

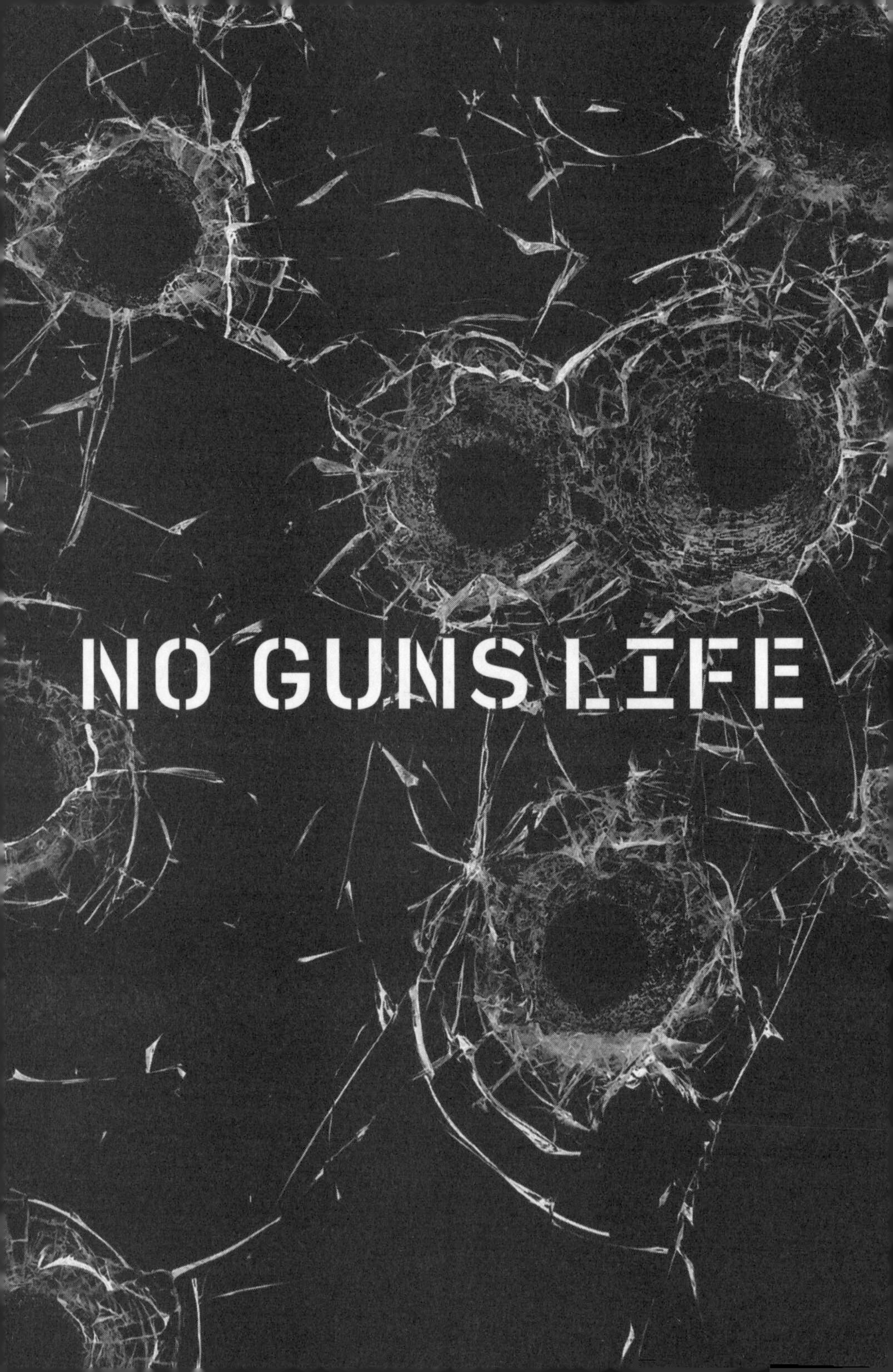
NO GUNS LIFE

Chapter 55
Pursuit

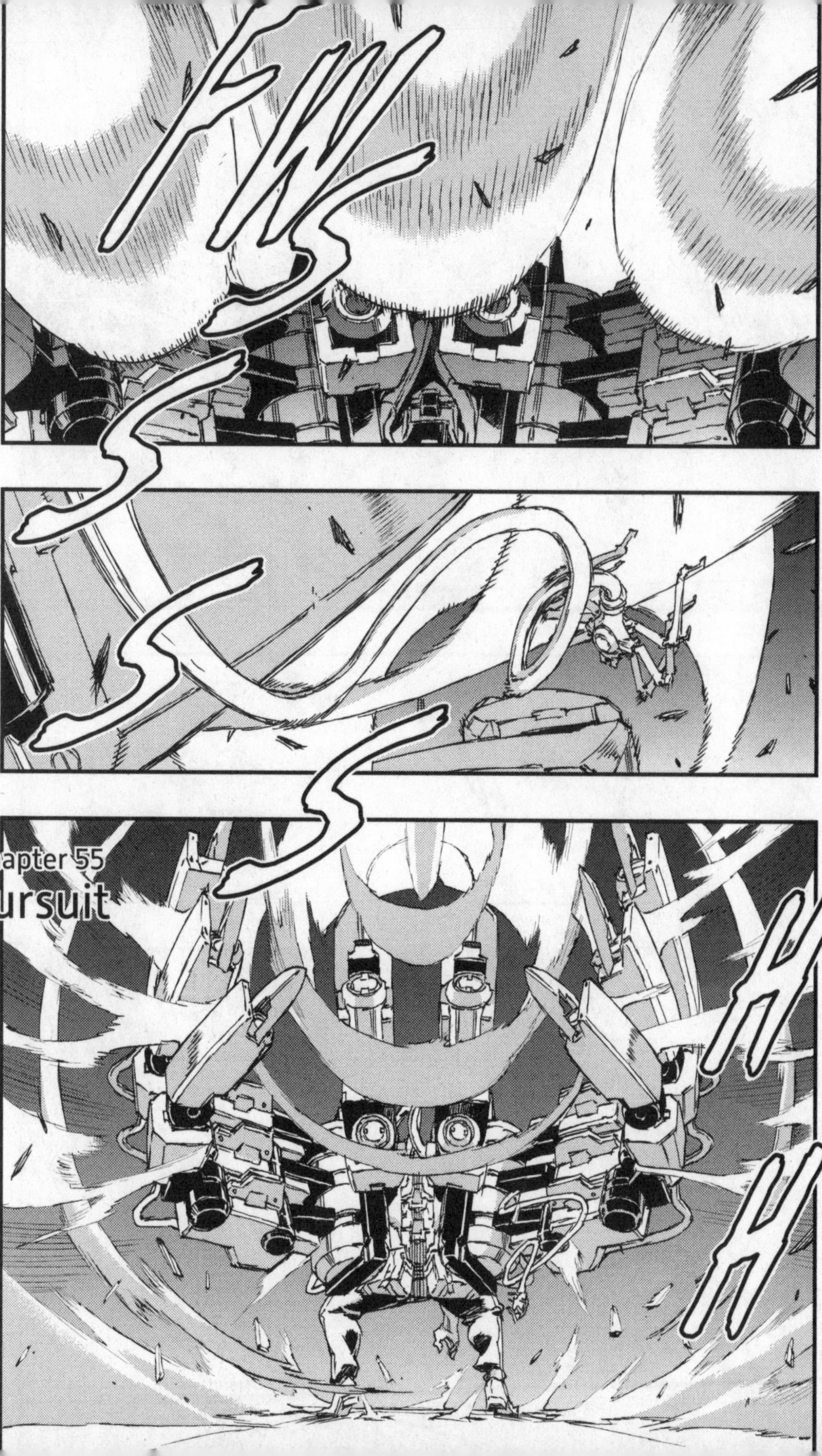
FWSSSS
HHH

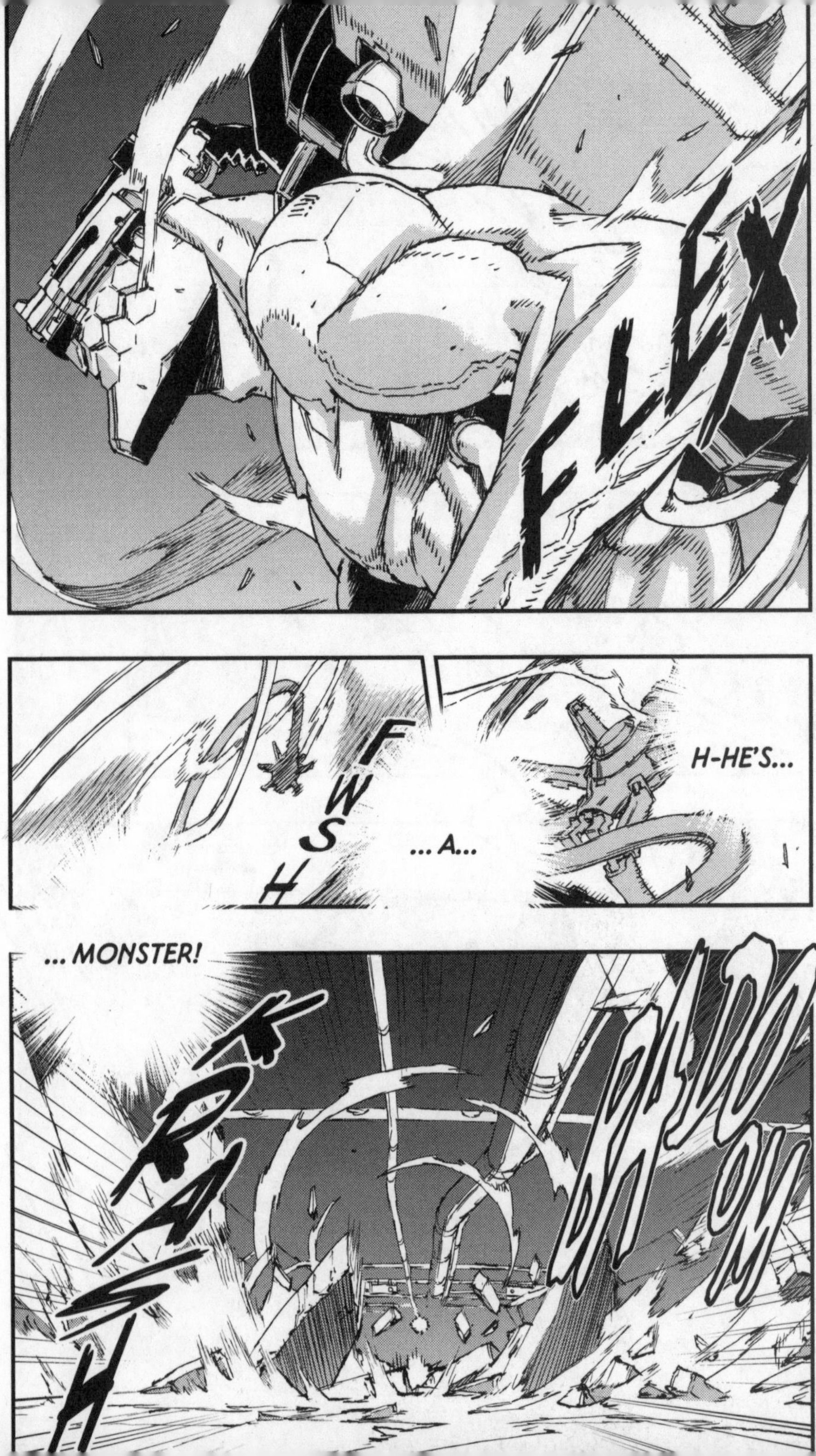
FLEX
H-HE'S...
...A...
FWSH
...MONSTER!

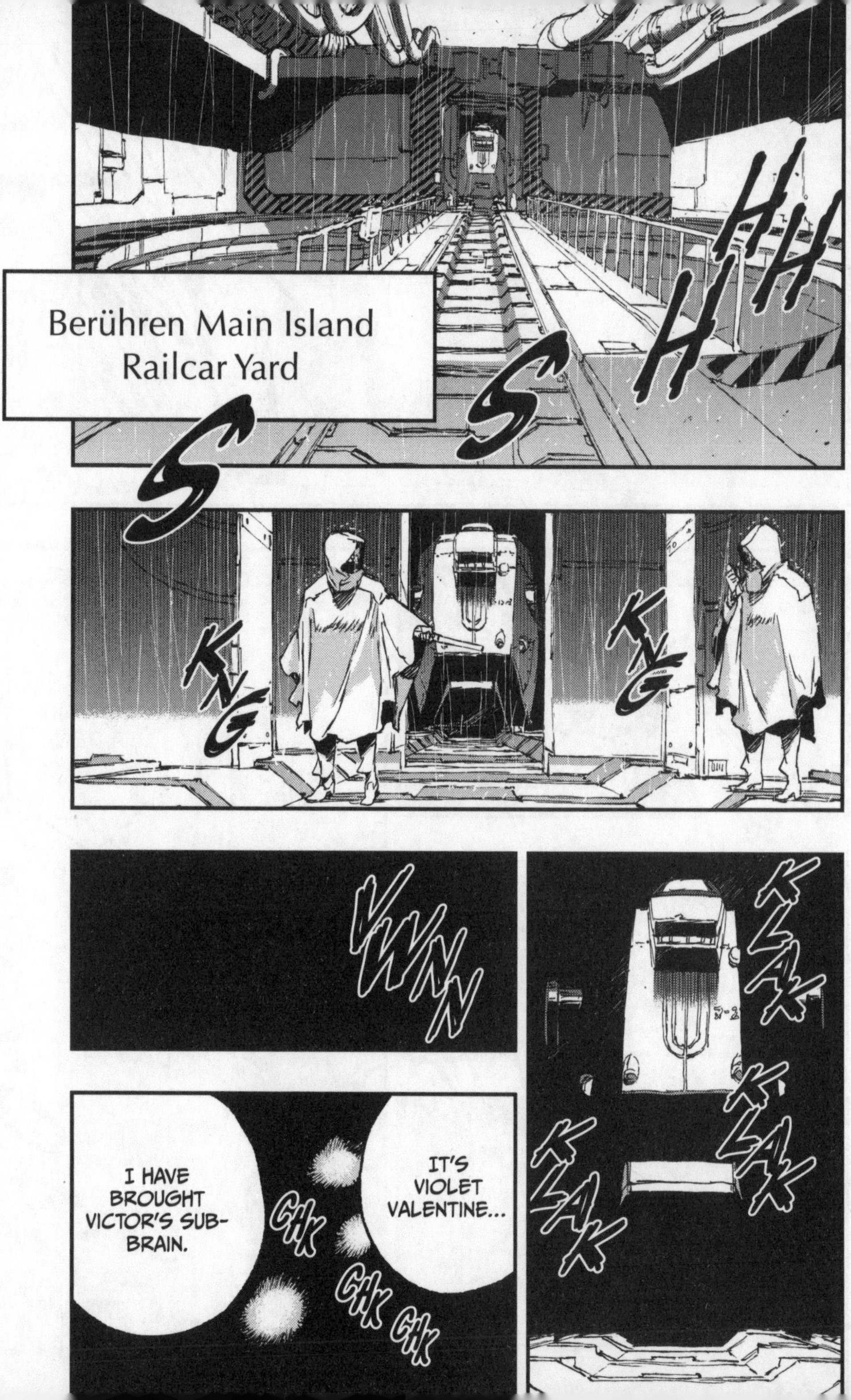

Berühren Main Island Railcar Yard
SSHHHH
KNG
KNG
KLAK
KLAK
KLAK
VWNN
IT'S VIOLET VALENTINE...
I HAVE BROUGHT VICTOR'S SUB-BRAIN.
CHK
CHK
CHK

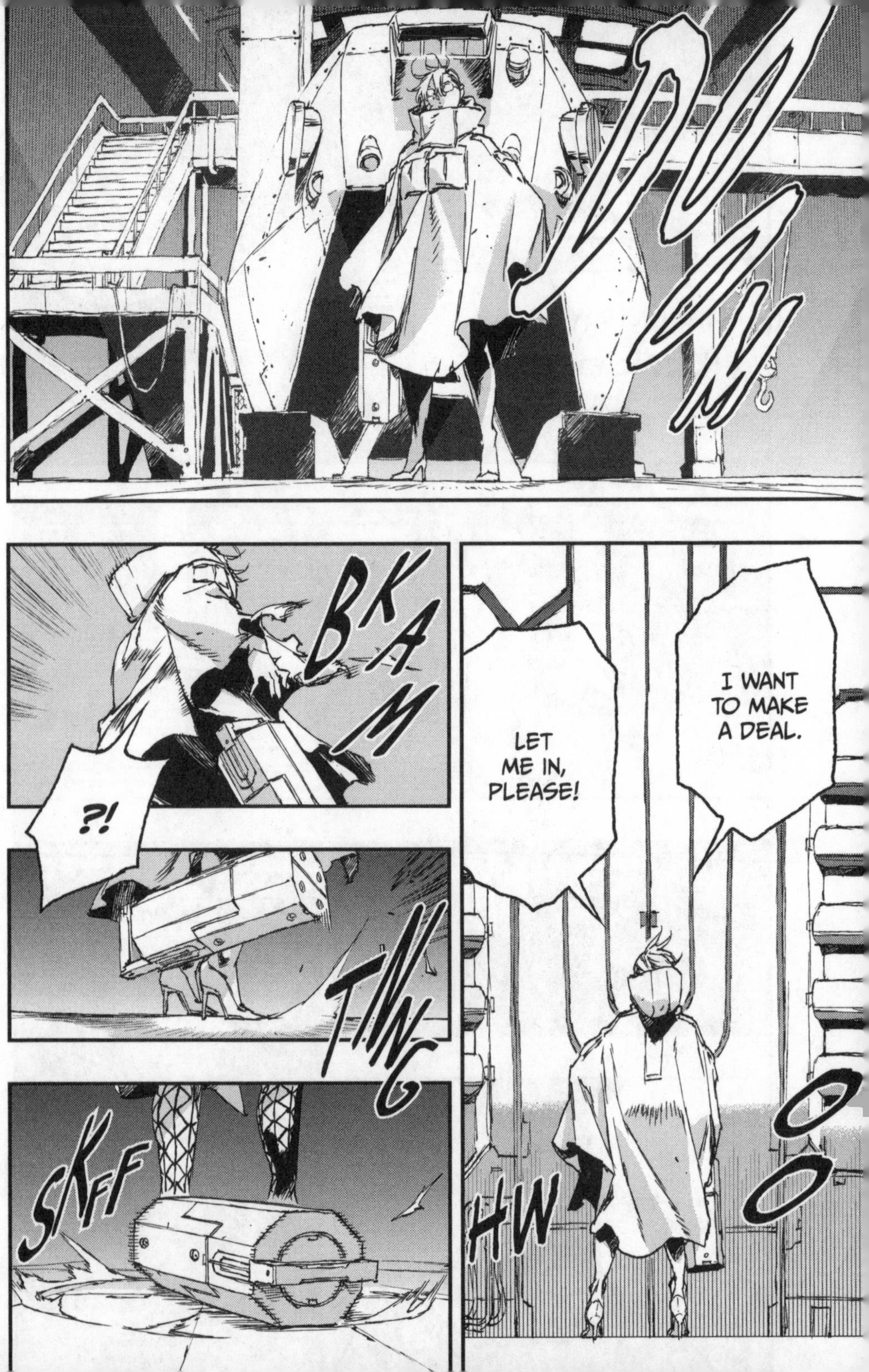
I WANT TO MAKE A DEAL.
LET ME IN, PLEASE!
BKAM
?!
SKFF

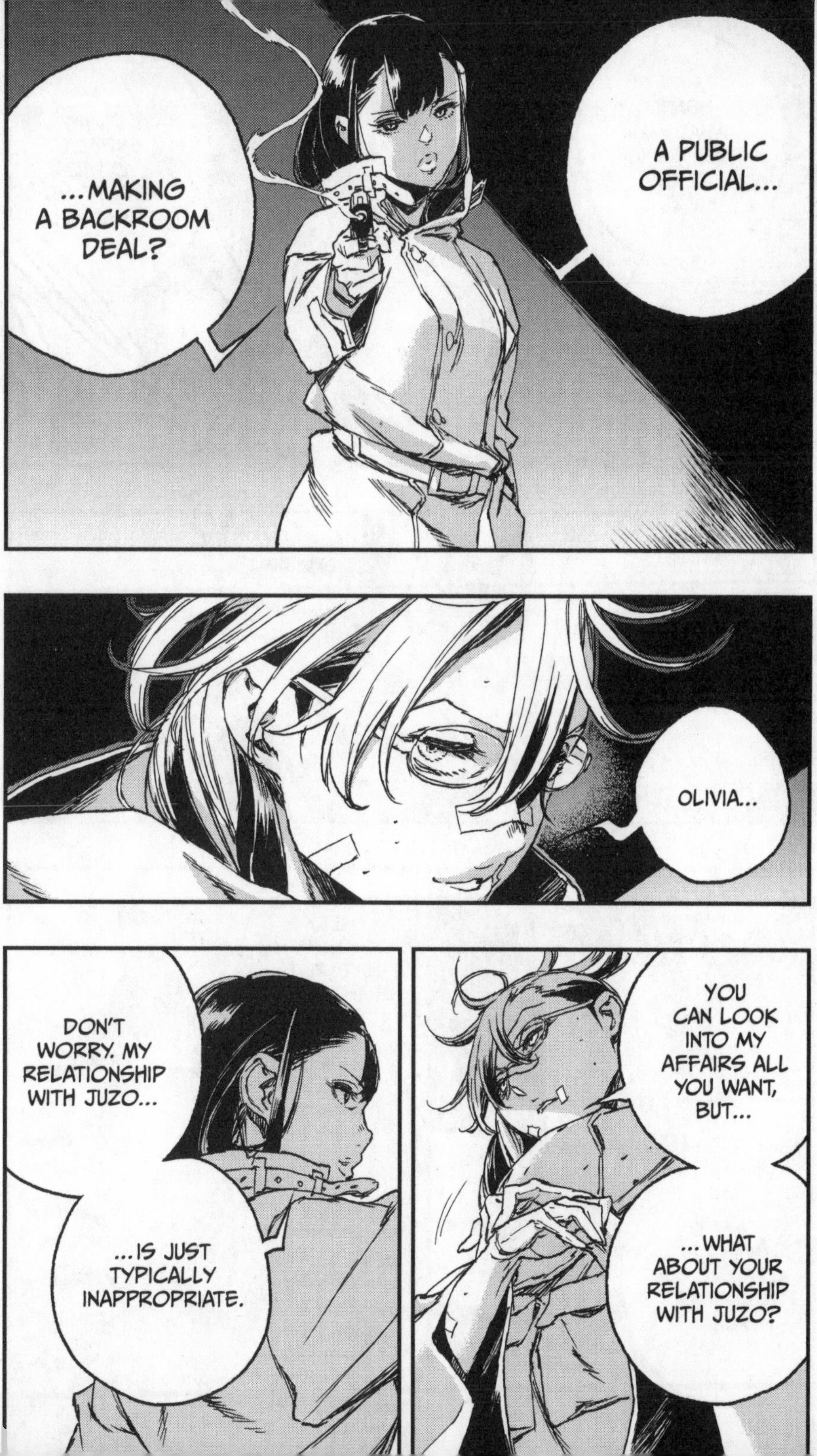
A PUBLIC OFFICIAL...
...MAKING A BACKROOM DEAL?
OLIVIA...
YOU CAN LOOK INTO MY AFFAIRS ALL YOU WANT, BUT...
...WHAT ABOUT YOUR RELATIONSHIP WITH JUZO?
DON'T WORRY. MY RELATIONSHIP WITH JUZO...
...IS JUST TYPICALLY INAPPROPRIATE.

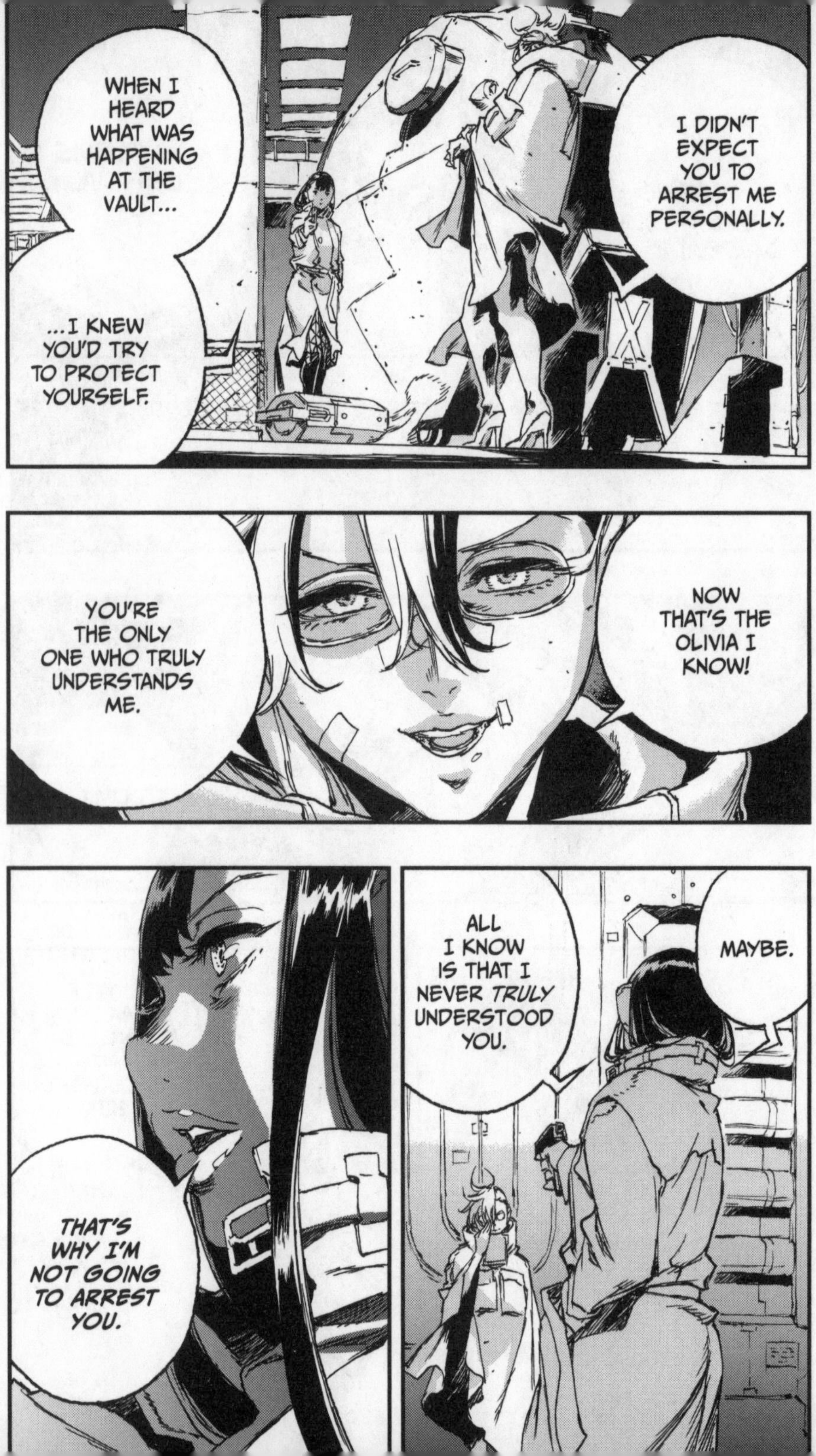
I DIDN'T EXPECT YOU TO ARREST ME PERSONALLY.
WHEN I HEARD WHAT WAS HAPPENING AT THE VAULT...
...I KNEW YOU'D TRY TO PROTECT YOURSELF.
NOW THAT'S THE OLIVIA I KNOW!
YOU'RE THE ONLY ONE WHO TRULY UNDERSTANDS ME.
MAYBE.
ALL I KNOW IS THAT I NEVER *TRULY* UNDERSTOOD YOU.
THAT'S WHY I'M NOT GOING TO ARREST YOU.

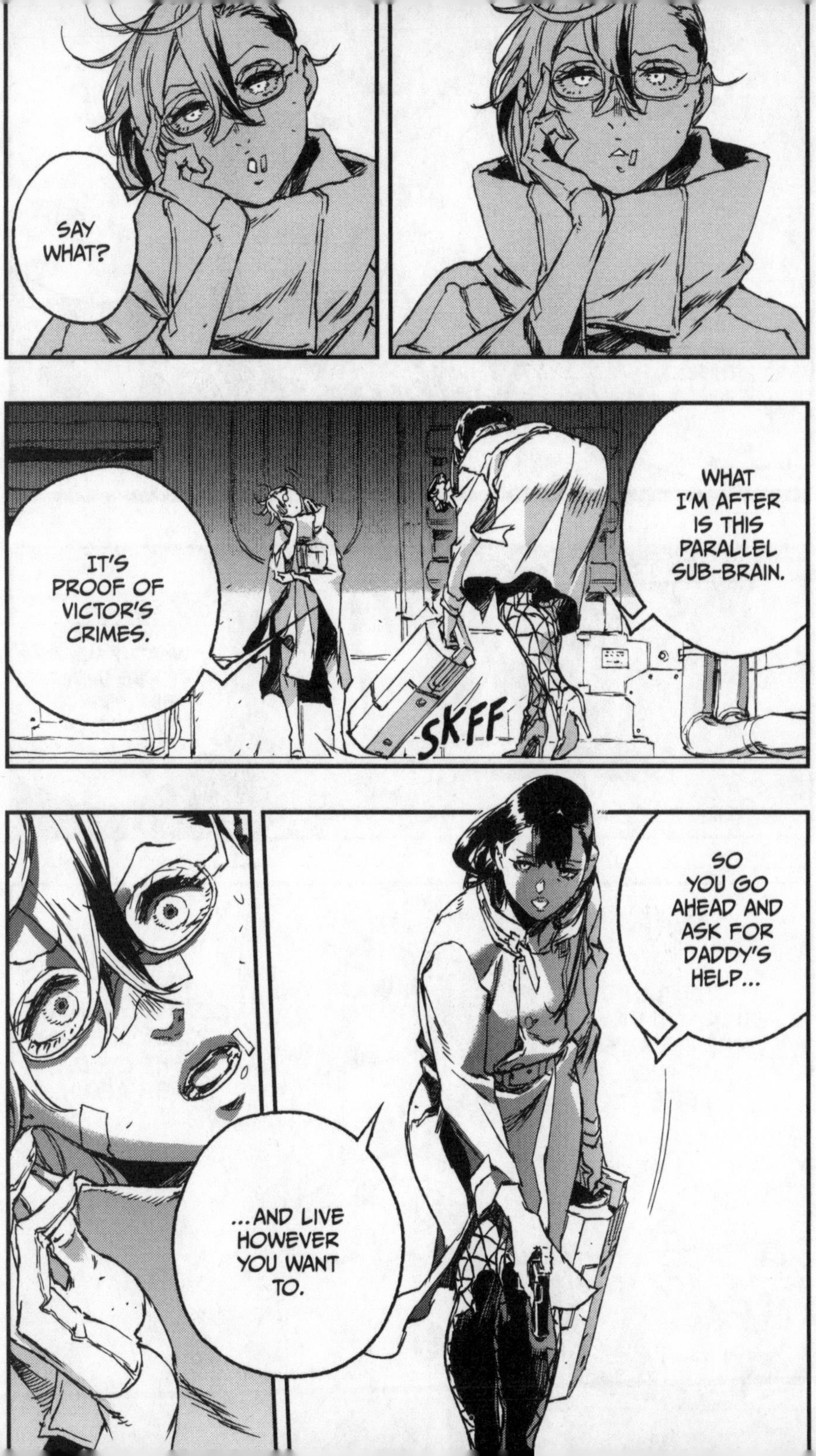
SAY WHAT?
WHAT I'M AFTER IS THIS PARALLEL SUB-BRAIN.
IT'S PROOF OF VICTOR'S CRIMES.
SKFF
SO YOU GO AHEAD AND ASK FOR DADDY'S HELP...
...AND LIVE HOWEVER YOU WANT TO.

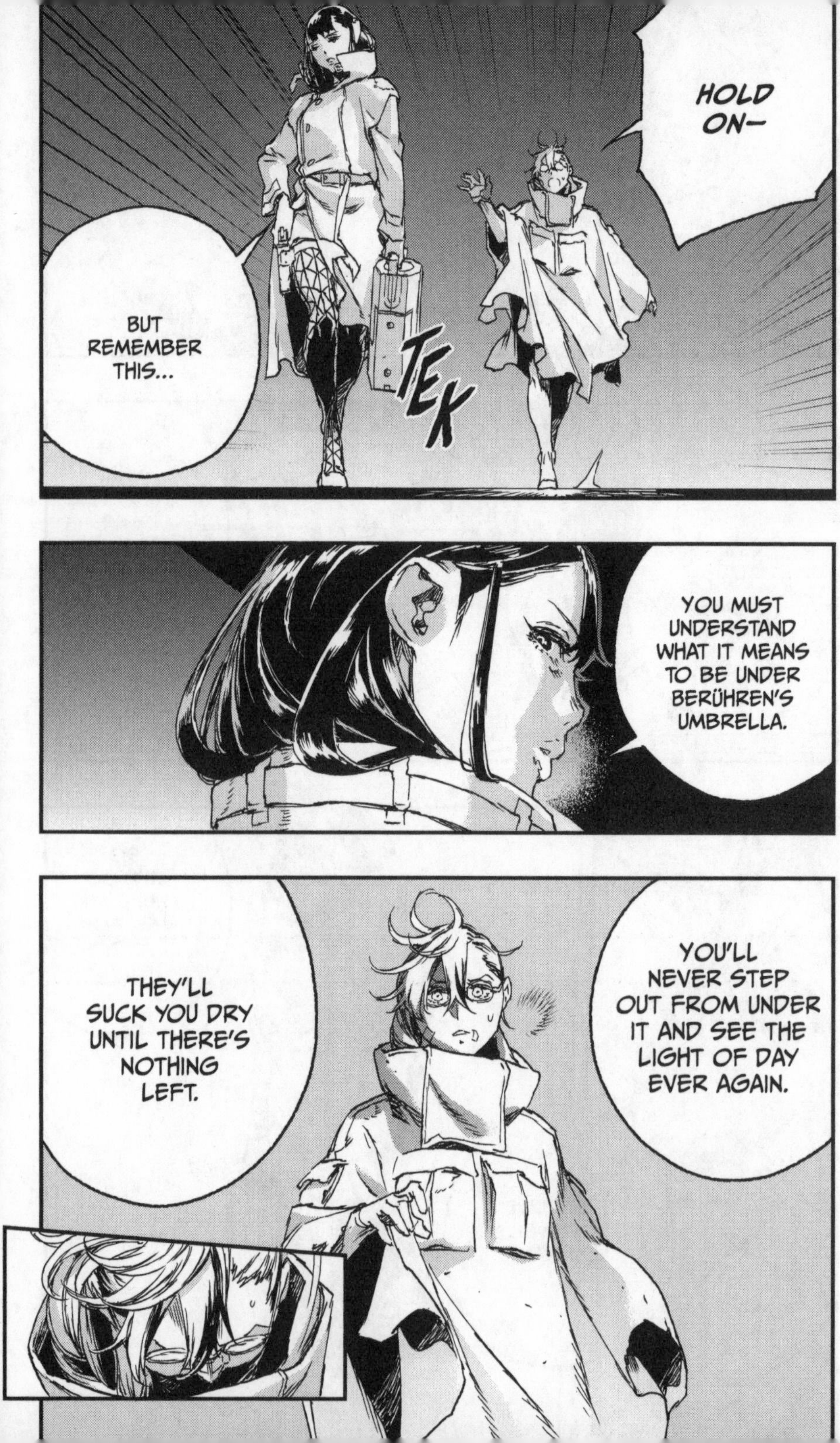
HOLD ON—
TEK
BUT REMEMBER THIS...
YOU MUST UNDERSTAND WHAT IT MEANS TO BE UNDER BERÜHREN'S UMBRELLA.
YOU'LL NEVER STEP OUT FROM UNDER IT AND SEE THE LIGHT OF DAY EVER AGAIN.
THEY'LL SUCK YOU DRY UNTIL THERE'S NOTHING LEFT.

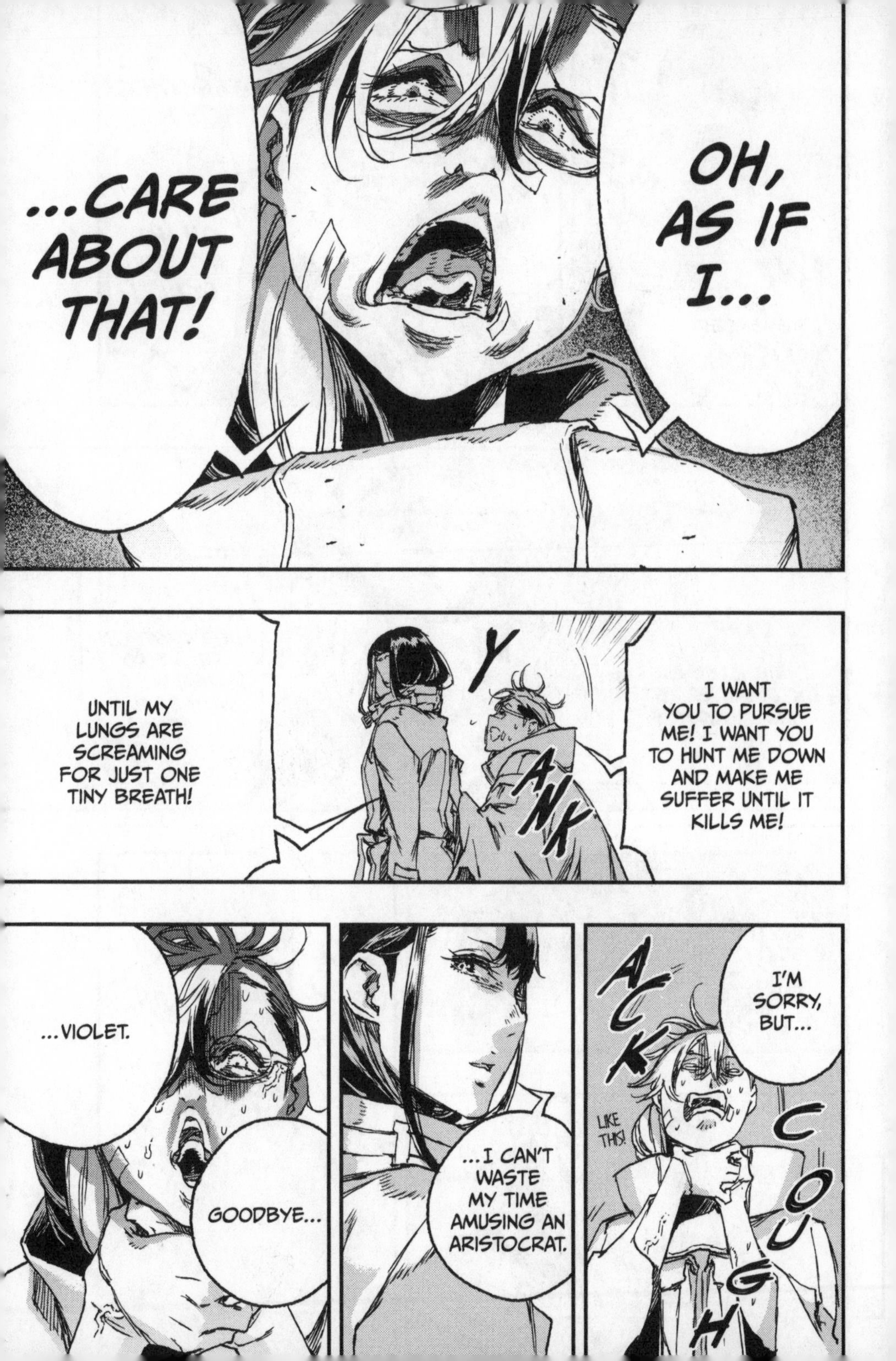
OH, AS IF I...
...CARE ABOUT THAT!
I WANT YOU TO PURSUE ME! I WANT YOU TO HUNT ME DOWN AND MAKE ME SUFFER UNTIL IT KILLS ME!
YANK
UNTIL MY LUNGS ARE SCREAMING FOR JUST ONE TINY BREATH!
I'M SORRY, BUT...
ACK
LIKE THIS!
COUGH
...I CAN'T WASTE MY TIME AMUSING AN ARISTOCRAT.
...VIOLET.
GOODBYE...

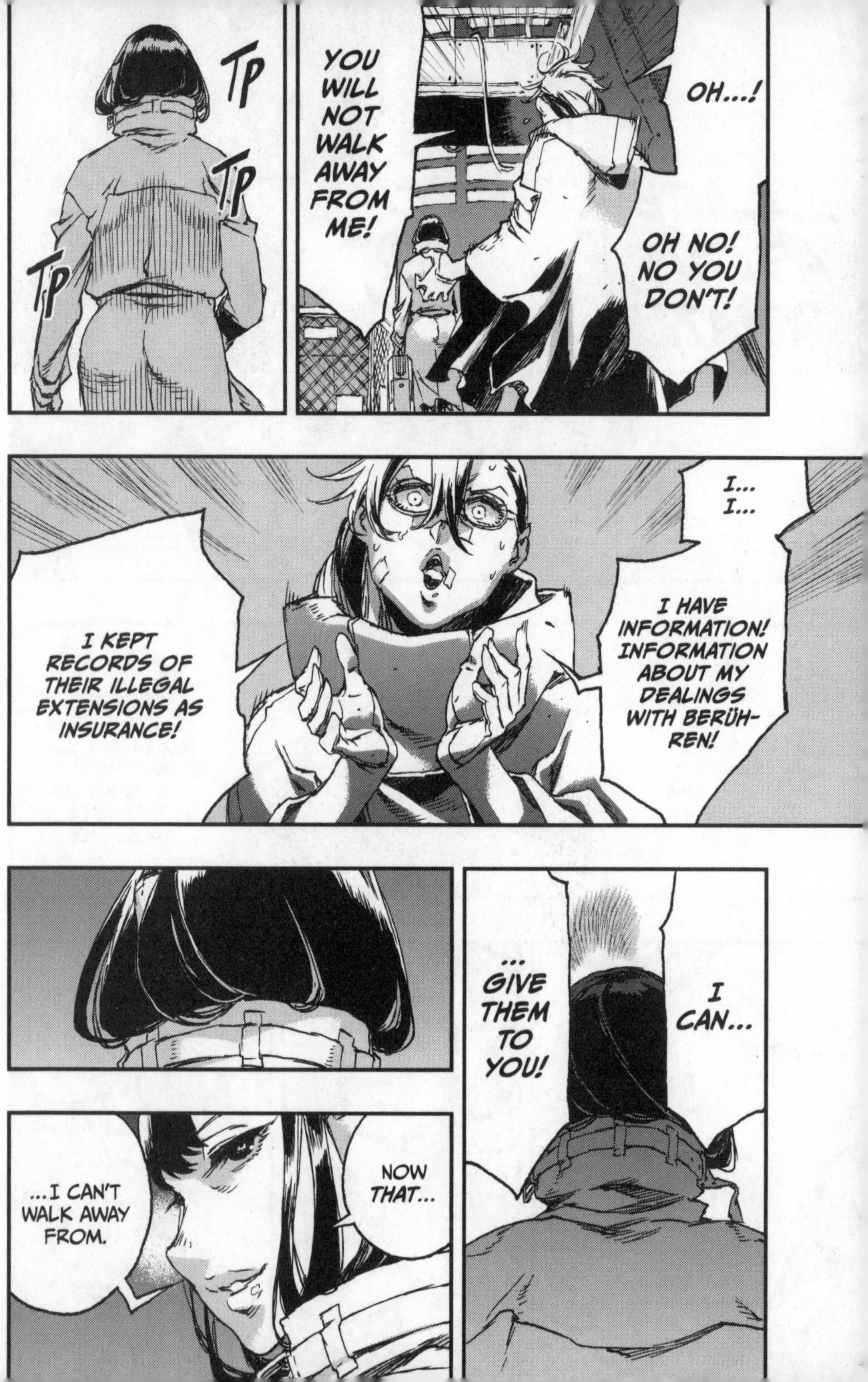
OH...!
YOU WILL NOT WALK AWAY FROM ME!
OH NO! NO YOU DON'T!
TP
TP
TP
I... I...
I HAVE INFORMATION! INFORMATION ABOUT MY DEALINGS WITH BERÜH-REN!
I KEPT RECORDS OF THEIR ILLEGAL EXTENSIONS AS INSURANCE!
I CAN...
...GIVE THEM TO YOU!
NOW THAT...
...I CAN'T WALK AWAY FROM.

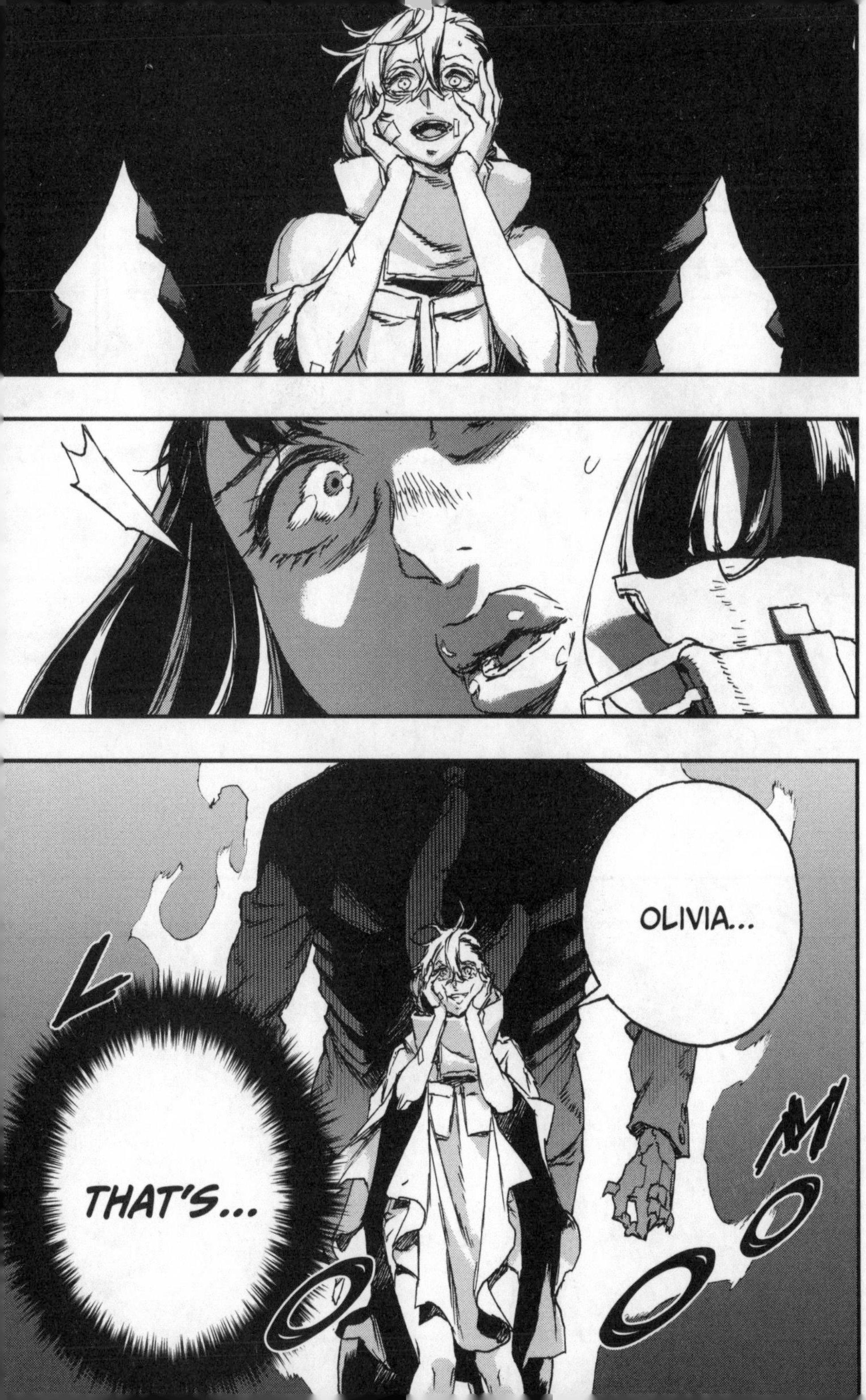
OLIVIA...
THAT'S...

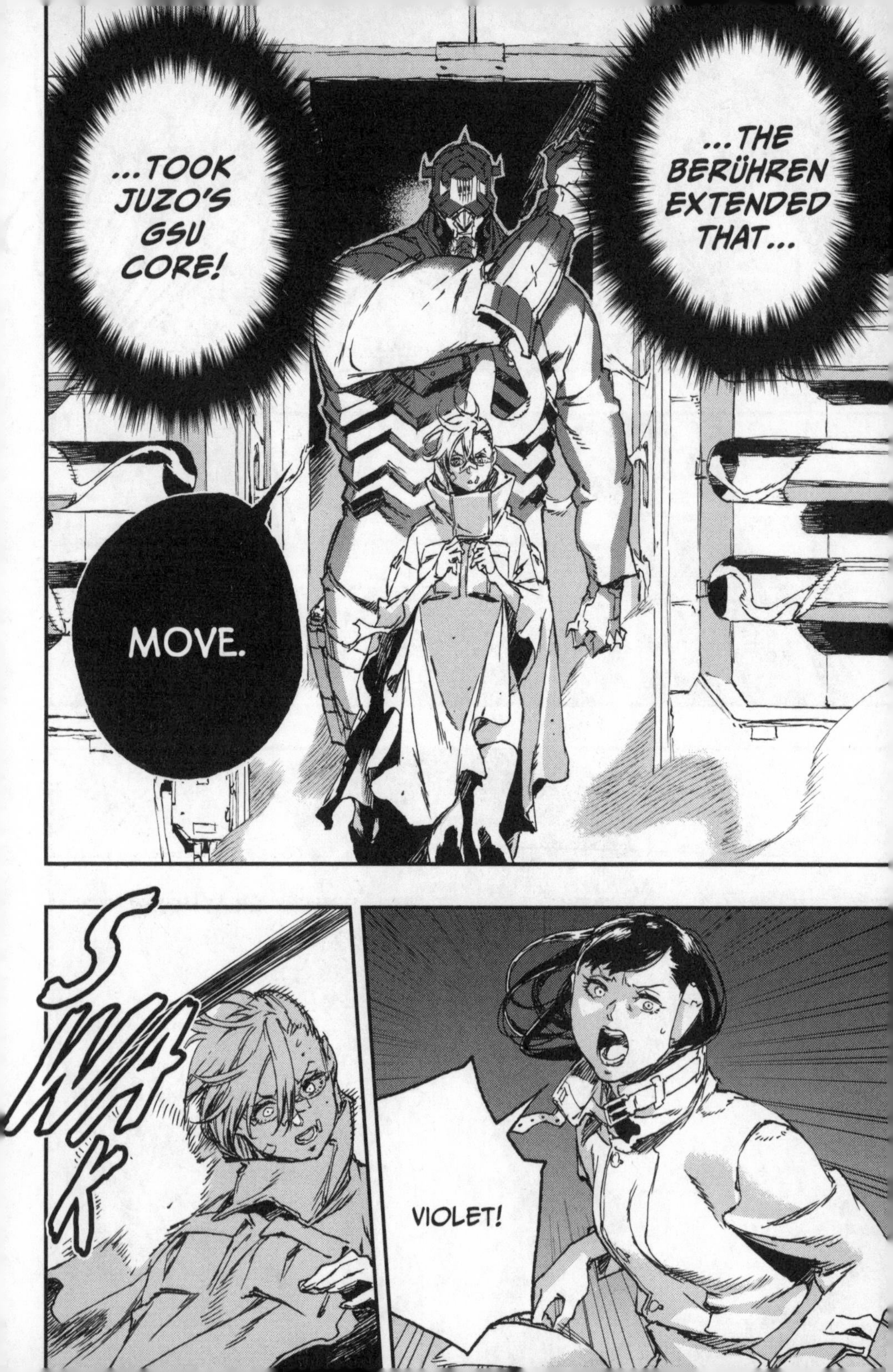
...THE BERÜHREN EXTENDED THAT...
...TOOK JUZO'S GSU CORE!
MOVE.
VIOLET!
SWAK

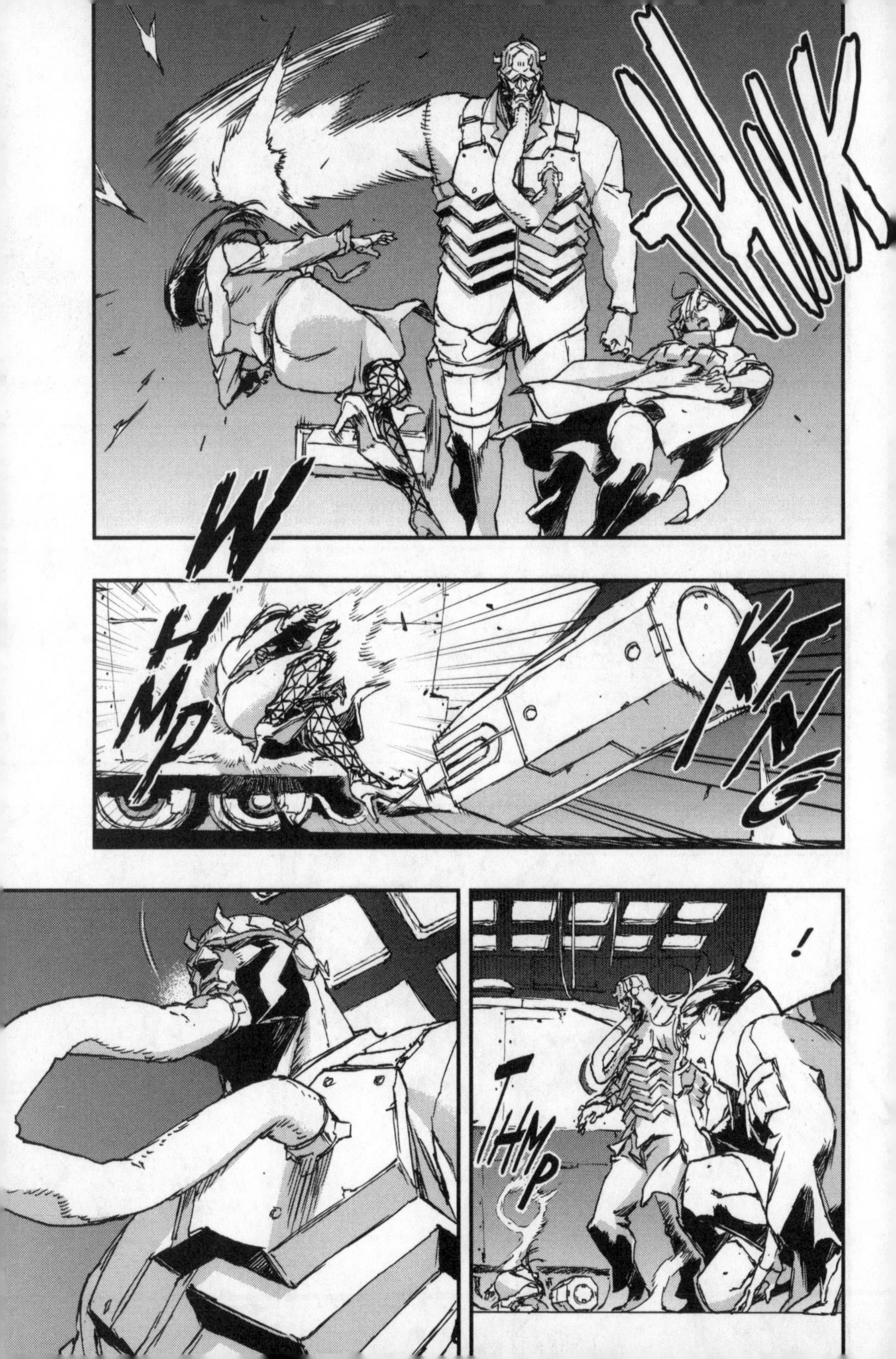
THUNK
WHMP
KTANG
!
THMP

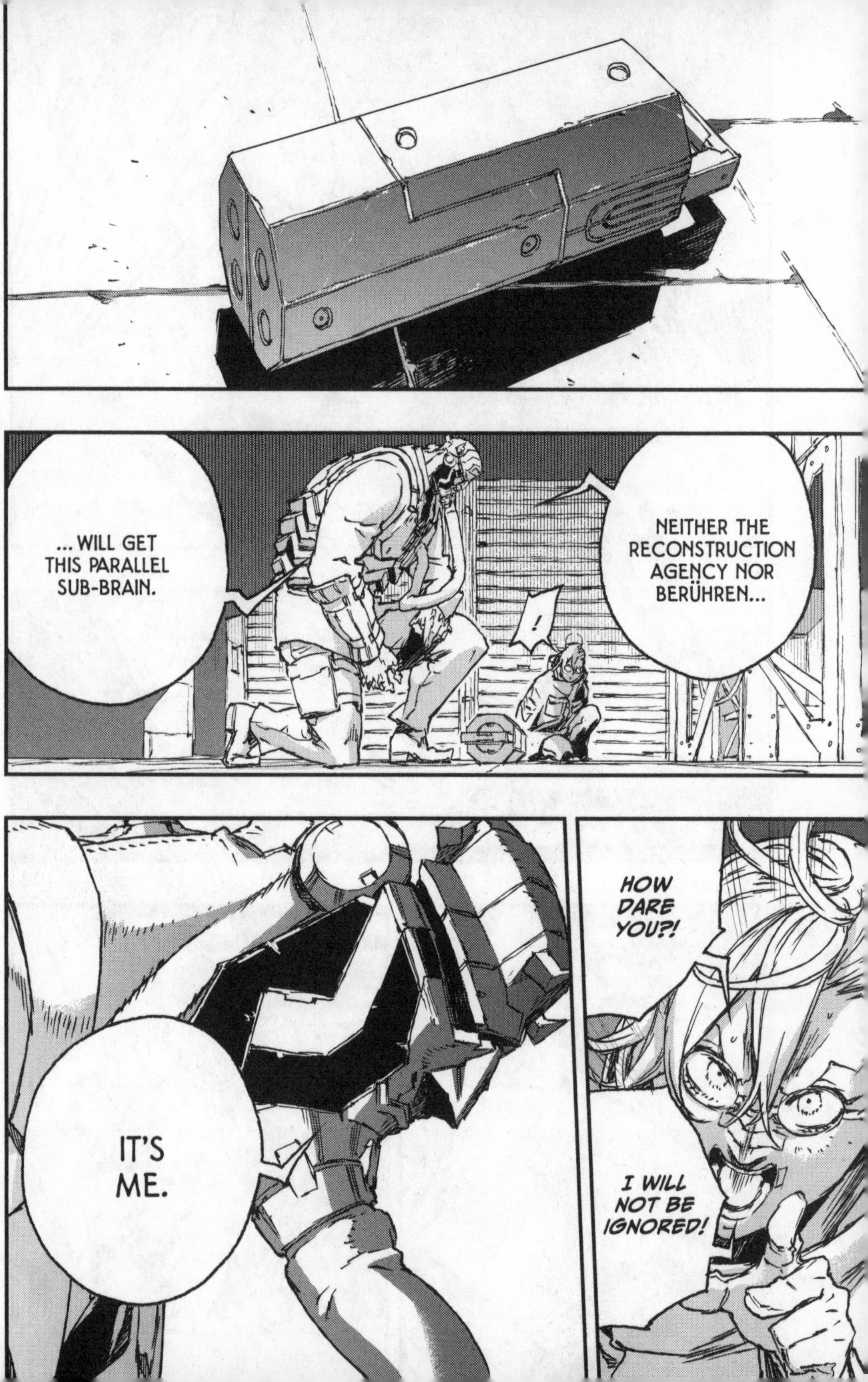

NEITHER THE RECONSTRUCTION AGENCY NOR BERÜHREN...
!
...WILL GET THIS PARALLEL SUB-BRAIN.
HOW DARE YOU?!
I WILL NOT BE IGNORED!
IT'S ME.

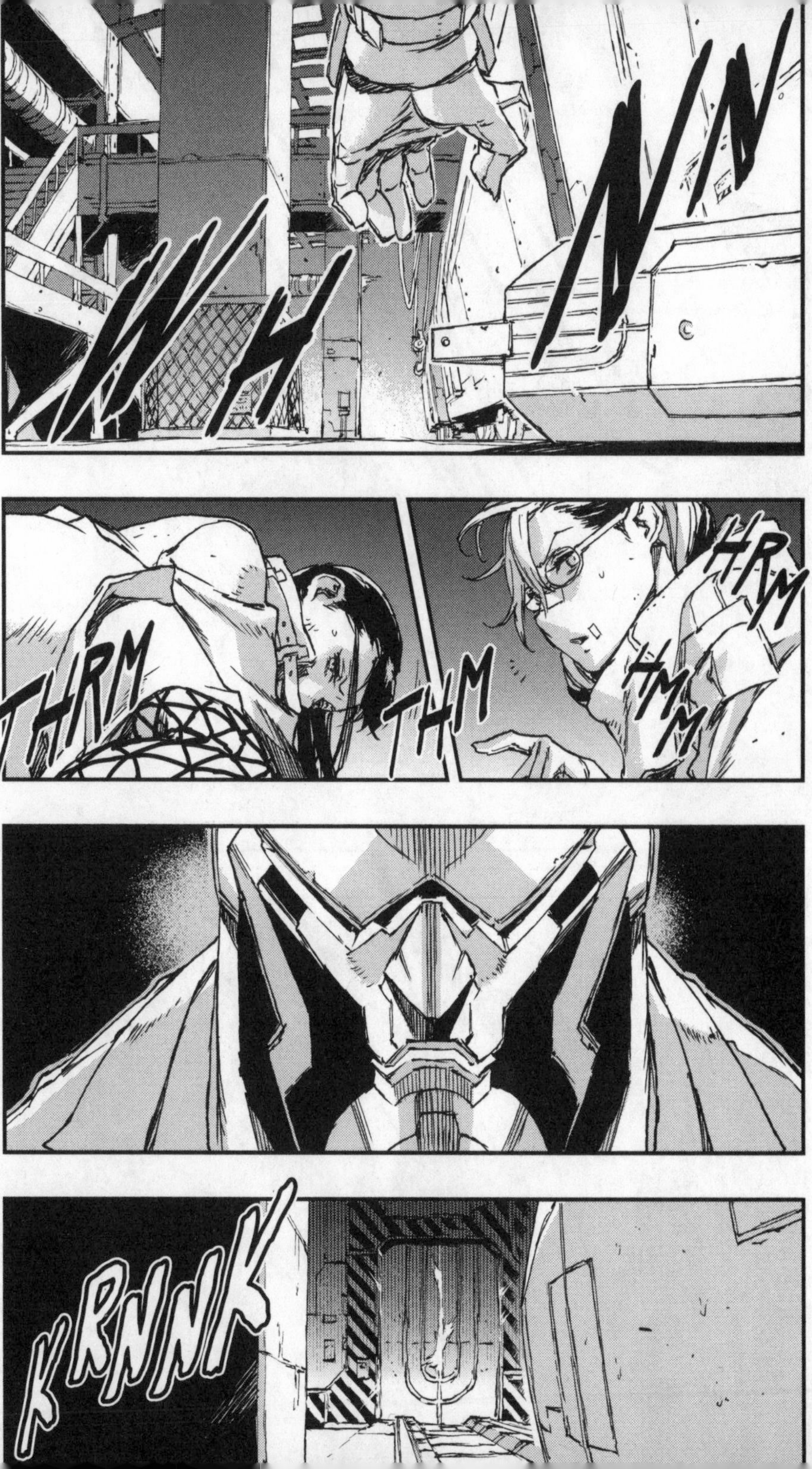
HRM
HMMM
THM
THRM
KRNNK

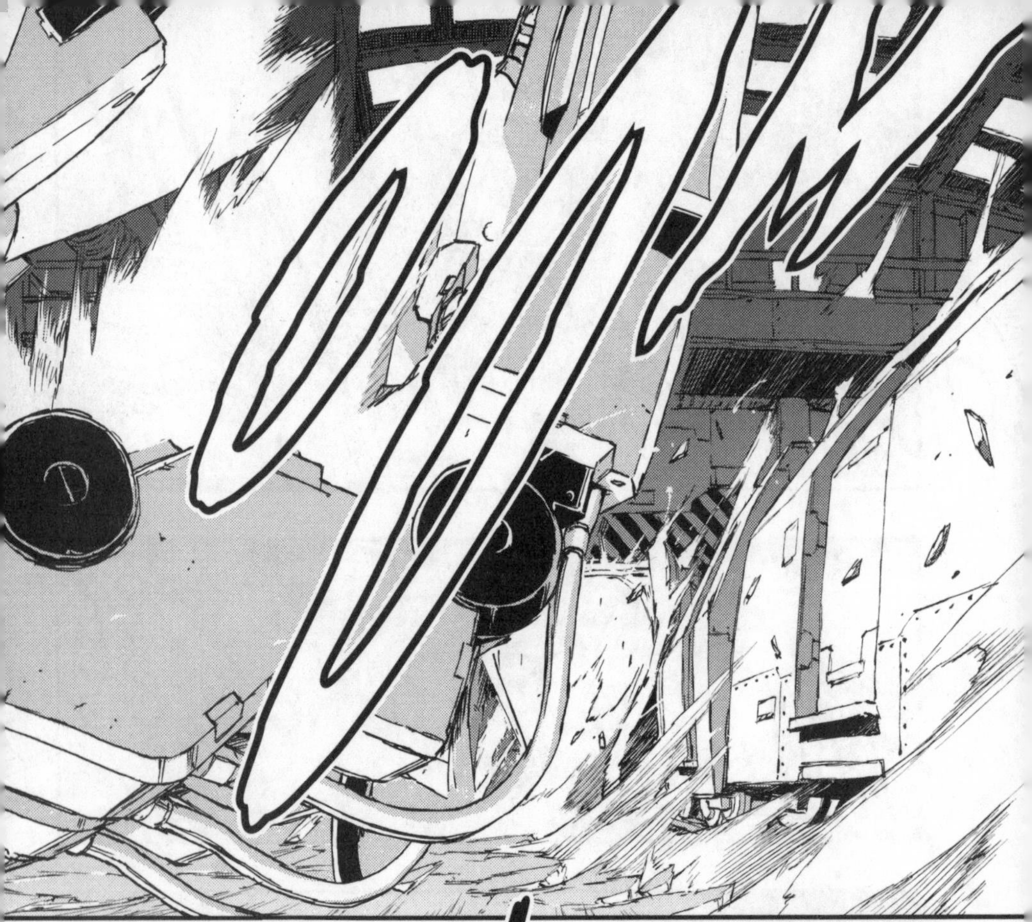
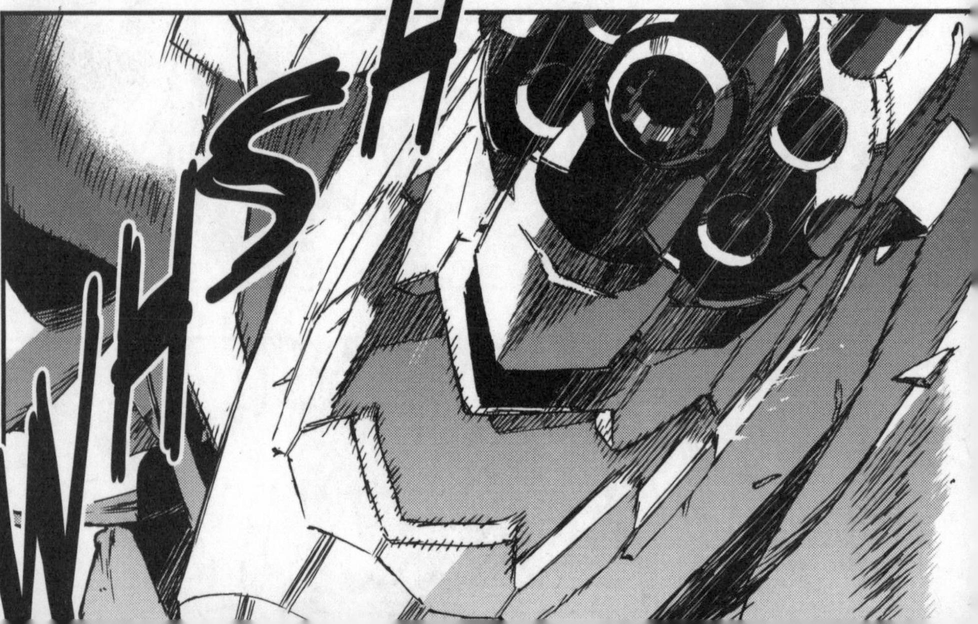
WHSH

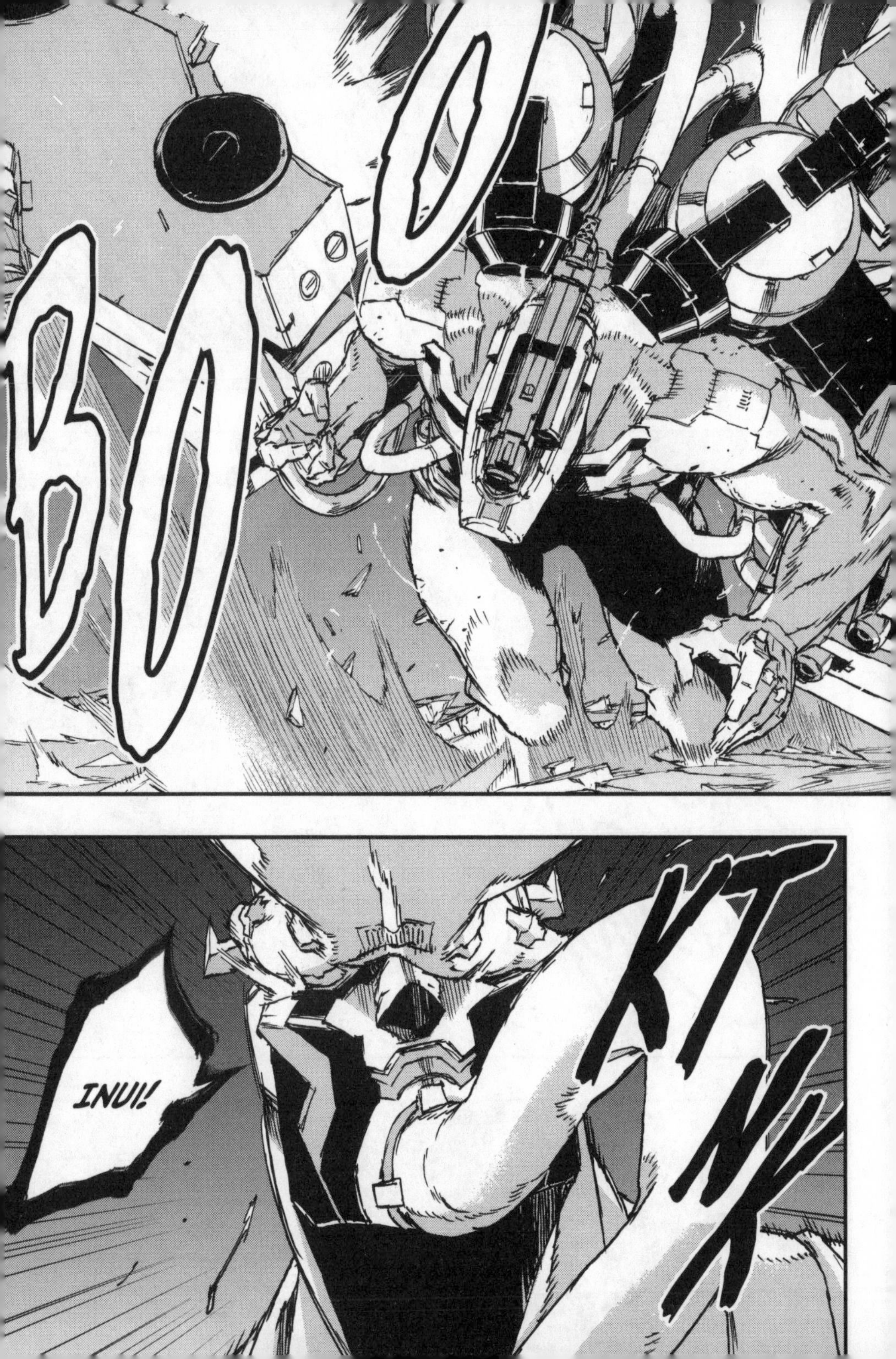
BOO
INUI!
KTNK

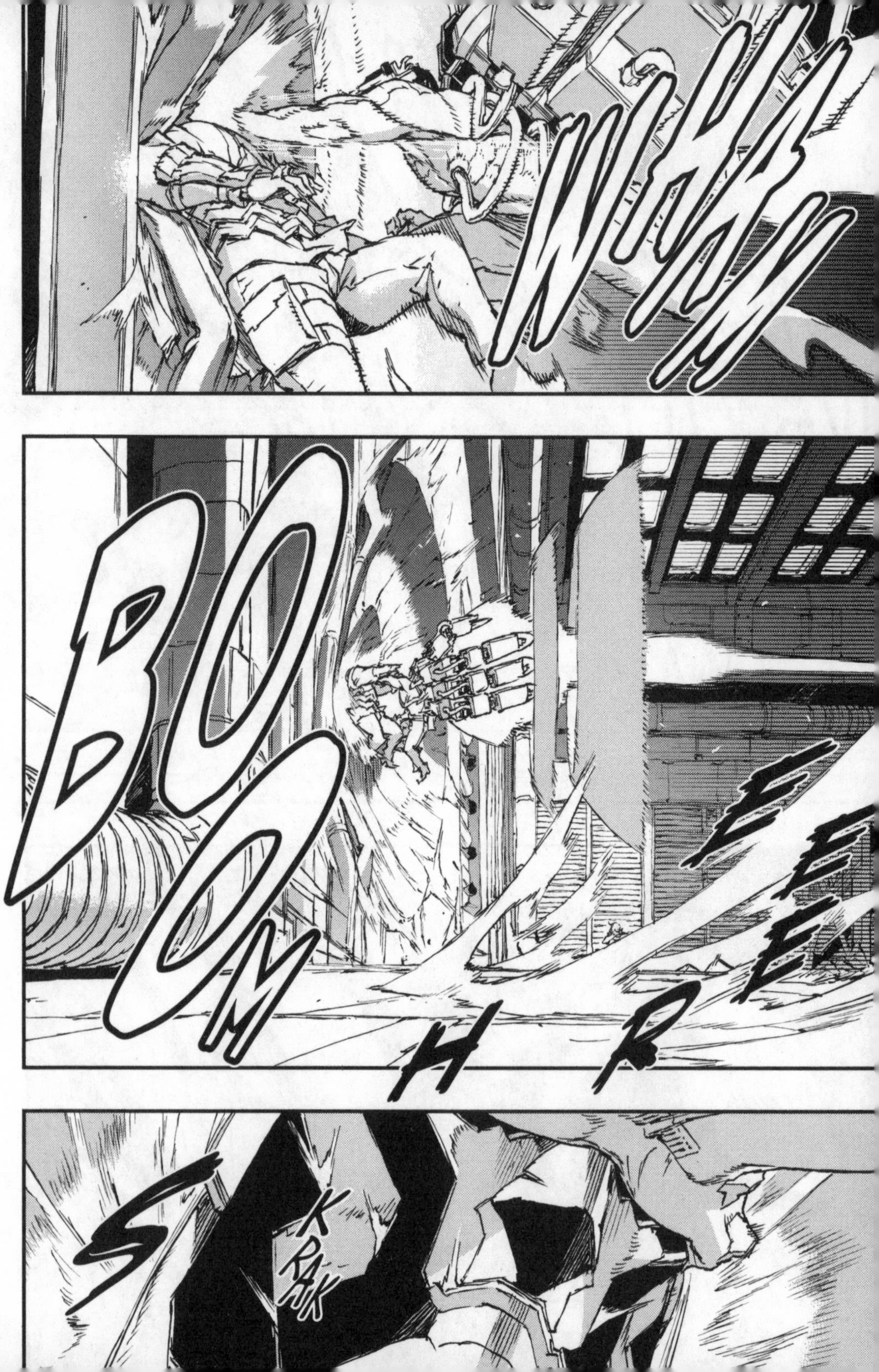
BOOM
KRAK

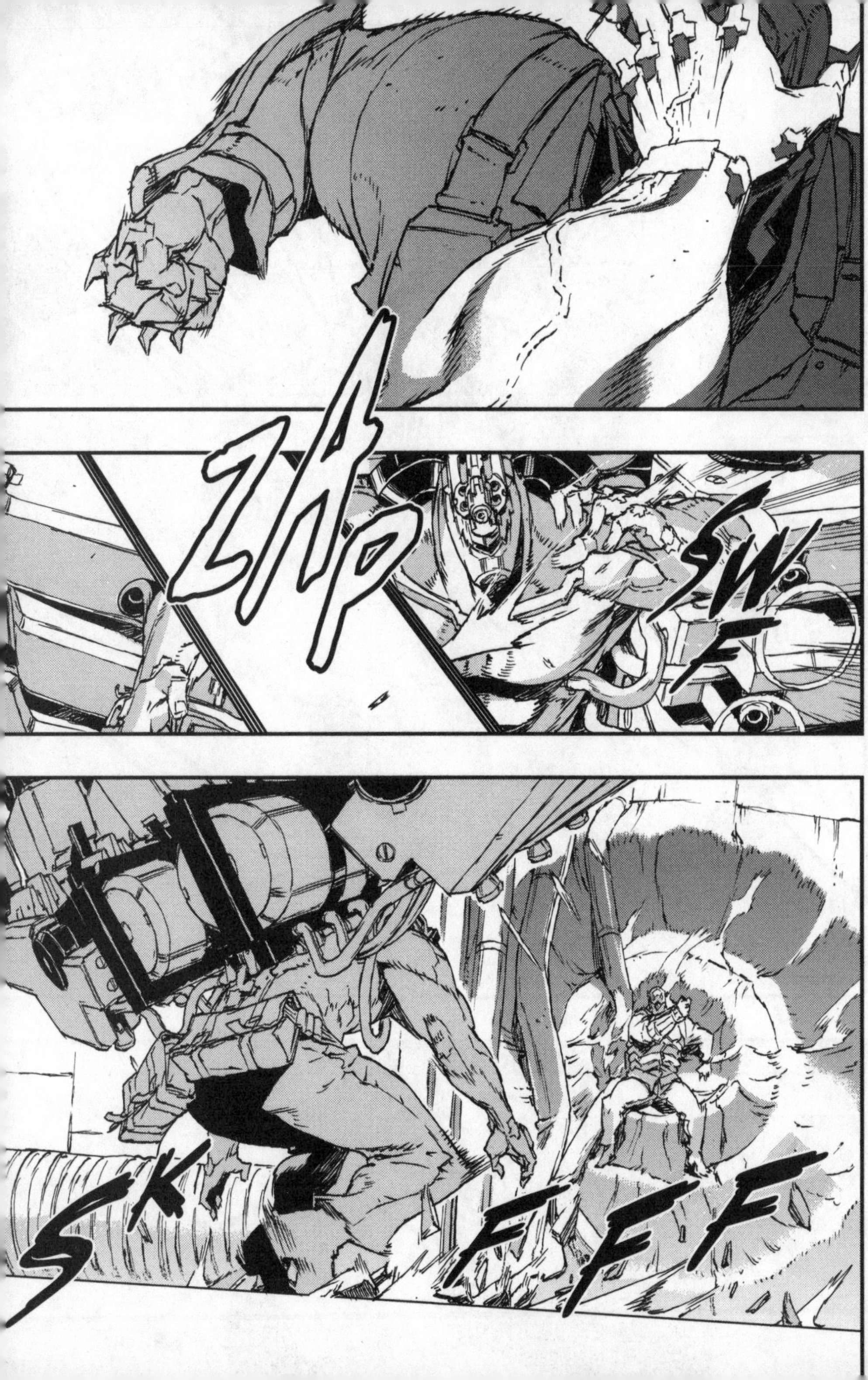
ZIP
SWF
SKFFF

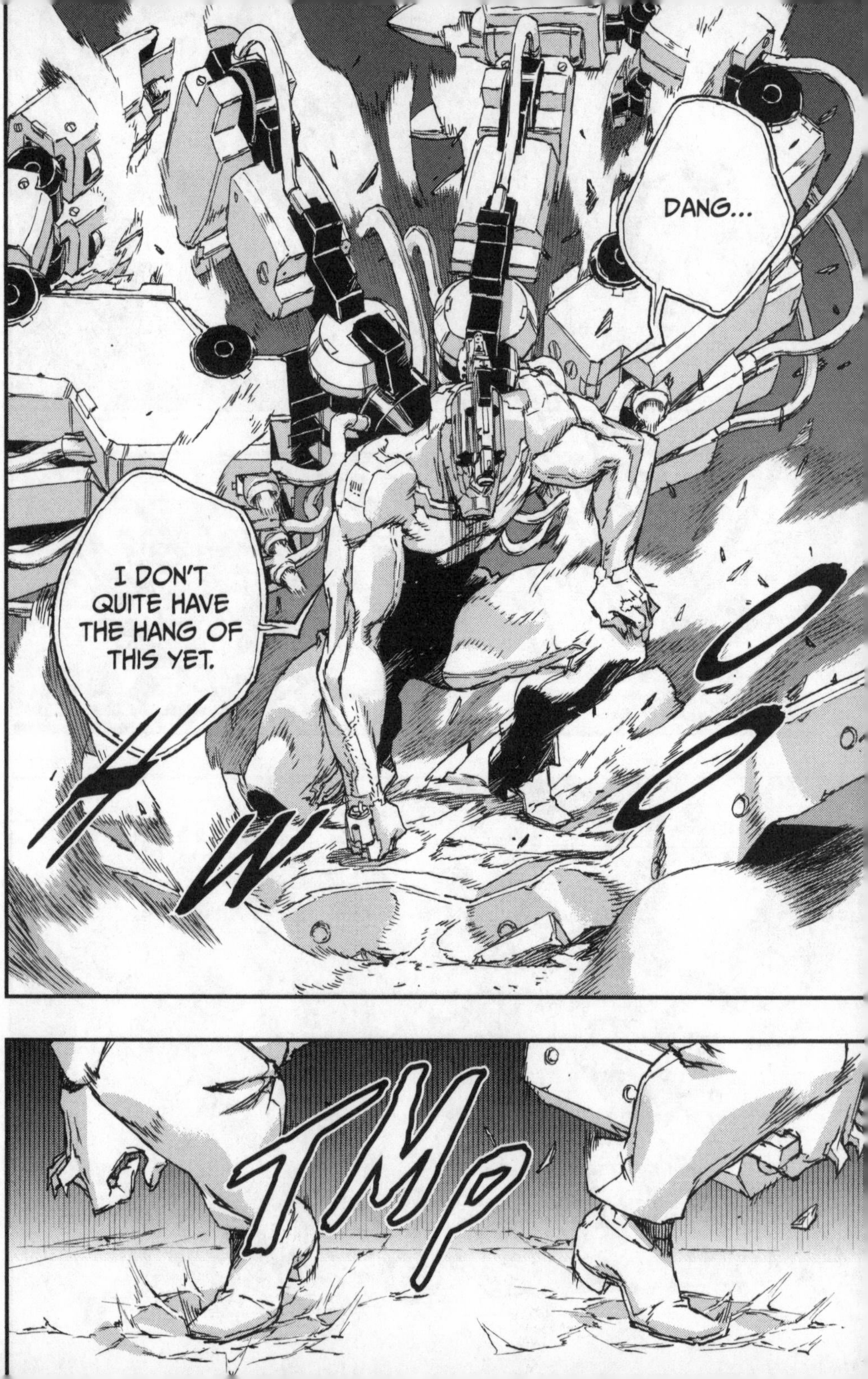
DANG...
I DON'T QUITE HAVE THE HANG OF THIS YET.
HWOOO
TMP

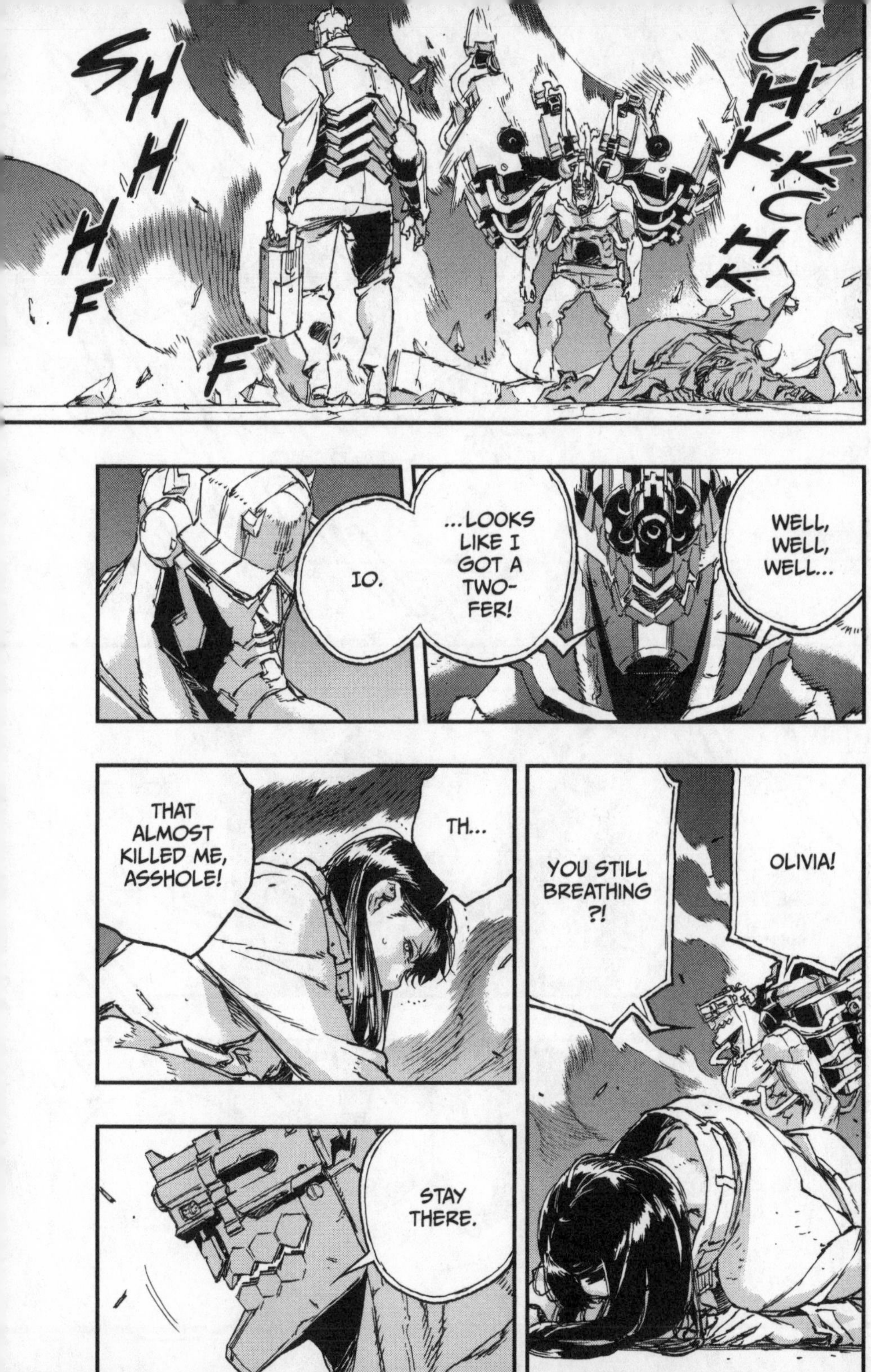
CHKKCHKK
SHHHF
F
WELL, WELL, WELL...
...LOOKS LIKE I GOT A TWO-FER!
IO.
OLIVIA!
YOU STILL BREATHING?!
TH...
THAT ALMOST KILLED ME, ASSHOLE!
....
STAY THERE.

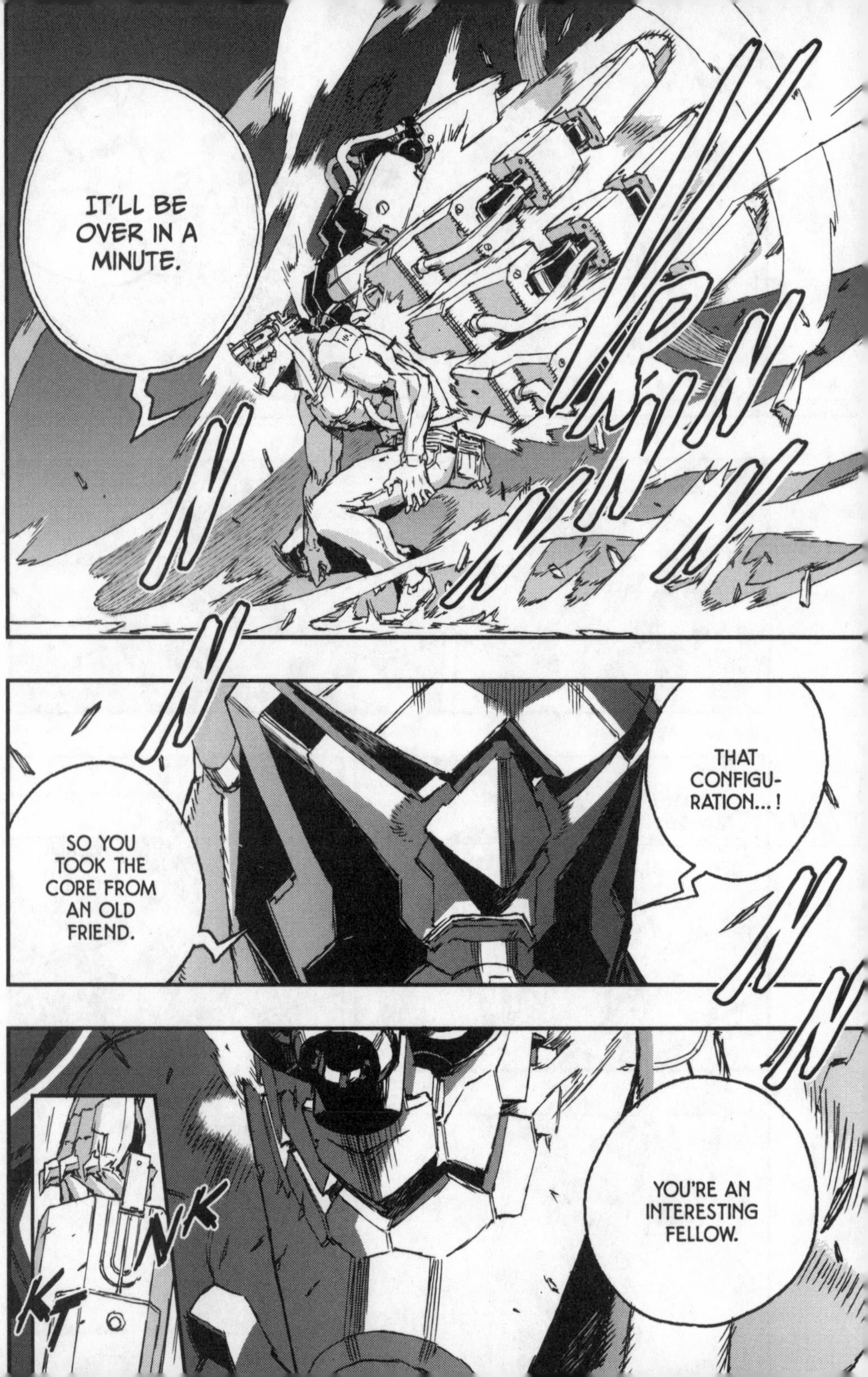
IT'LL BE OVER IN A MINUTE.
VRRN
THAT CONFIGU-RATION...!
SO YOU TOOK THE CORE FROM AN OLD FRIEND.
YOU'RE AN INTERESTING FELLOW.
KTUNK

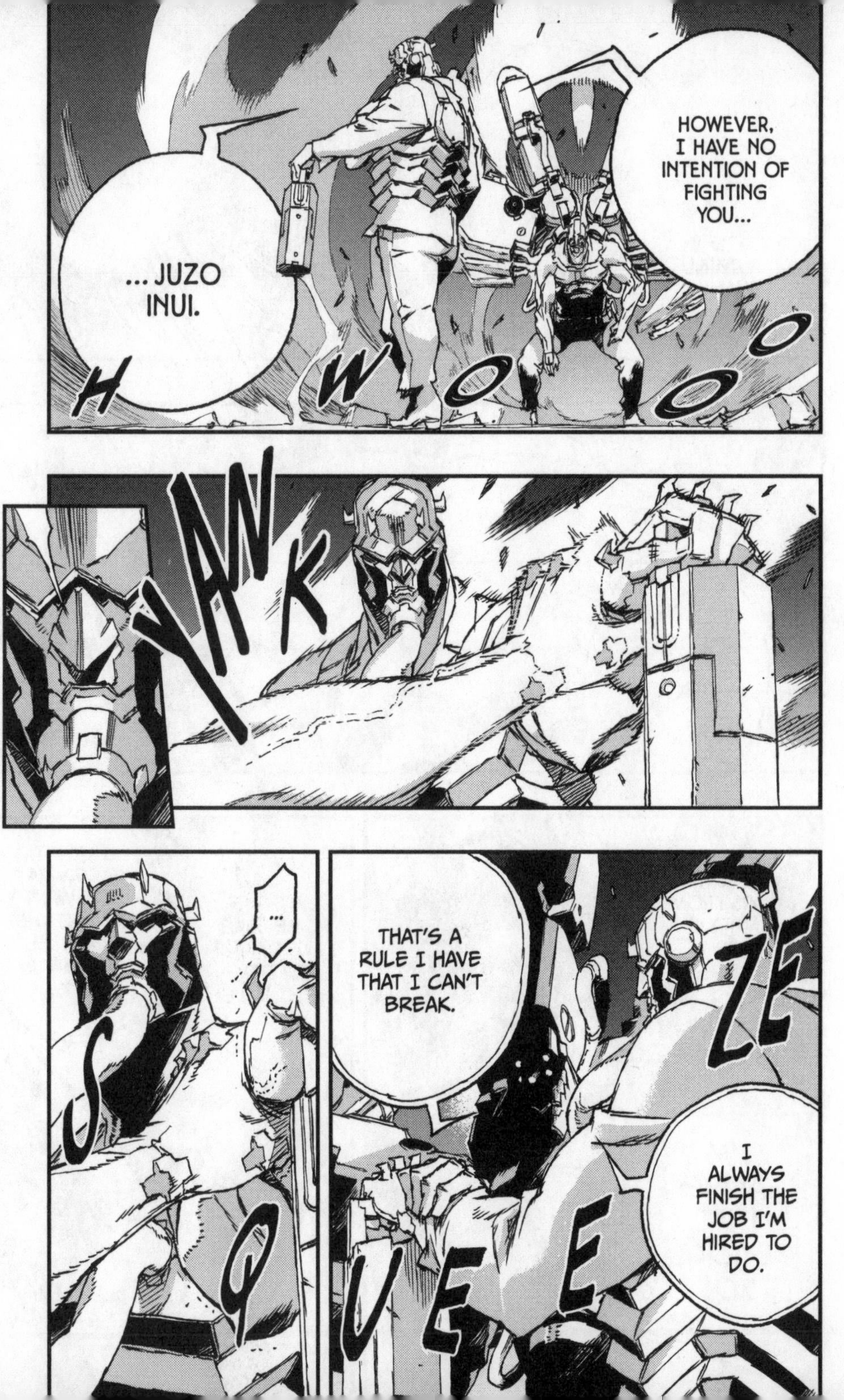
HOWEVER, I HAVE NO INTENTION OF FIGHTING YOU...
... JUZO INUI.
HWOOOOO
YANK
THAT'S A RULE I HAVE THAT I CAN'T BREAK.
I ALWAYS FINISH THE JOB I'M HIRED TO DO.
SQUEEZE
...

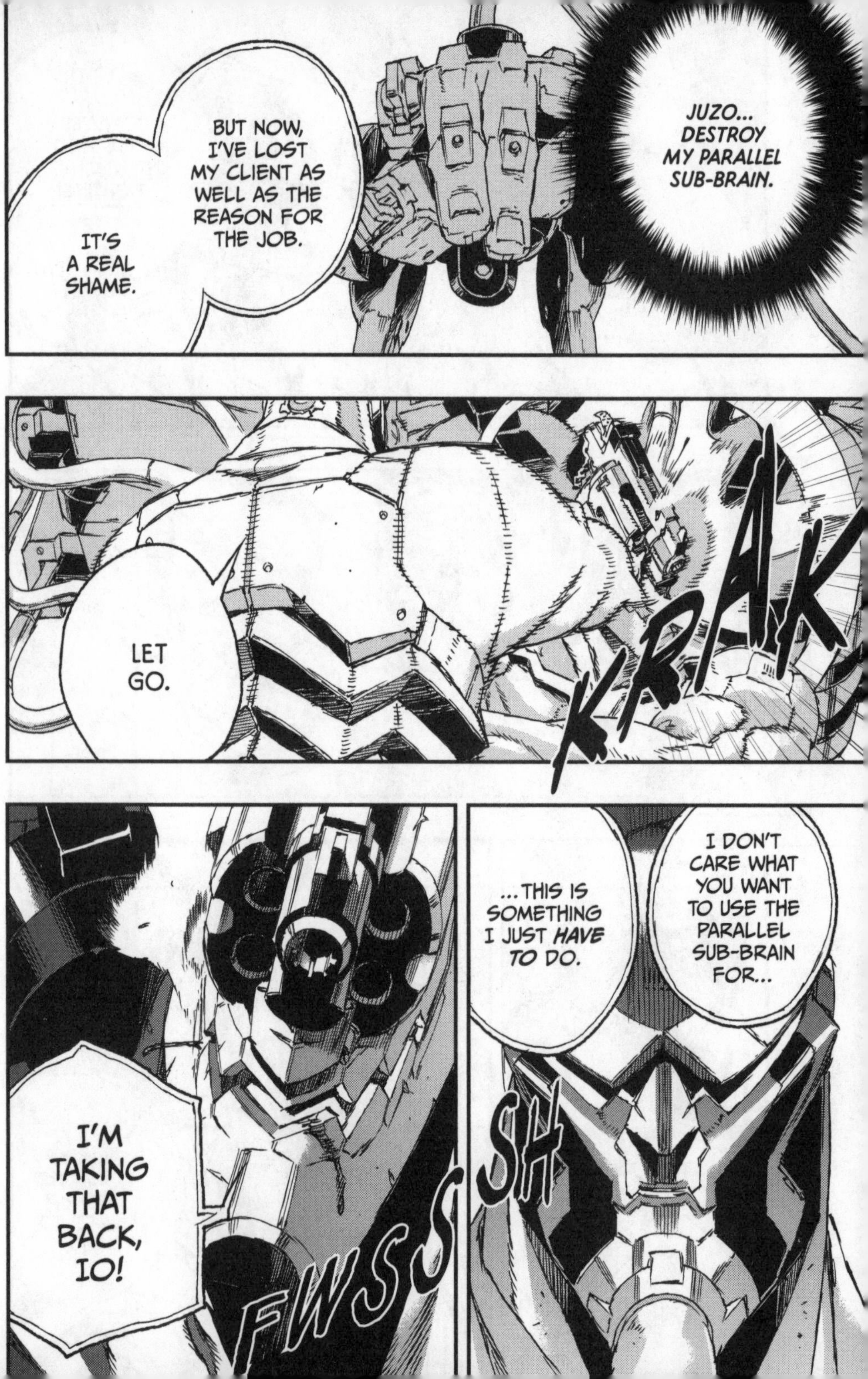
JUZO... DESTROY MY PARALLEL SUB-BRAIN.
BUT NOW, I'VE LOST MY CLIENT AS WELL AS THE REASON FOR THE JOB.
IT'S A REAL SHAME.
KRAK
LET GO.
I DON'T CARE WHAT YOU WANT TO USE THE PARALLEL SUB-BRAIN FOR...
...THIS IS SOMETHING I JUST *HAVE* TO DO.
I'M TAKING THAT BACK, IO!
FWSSSH

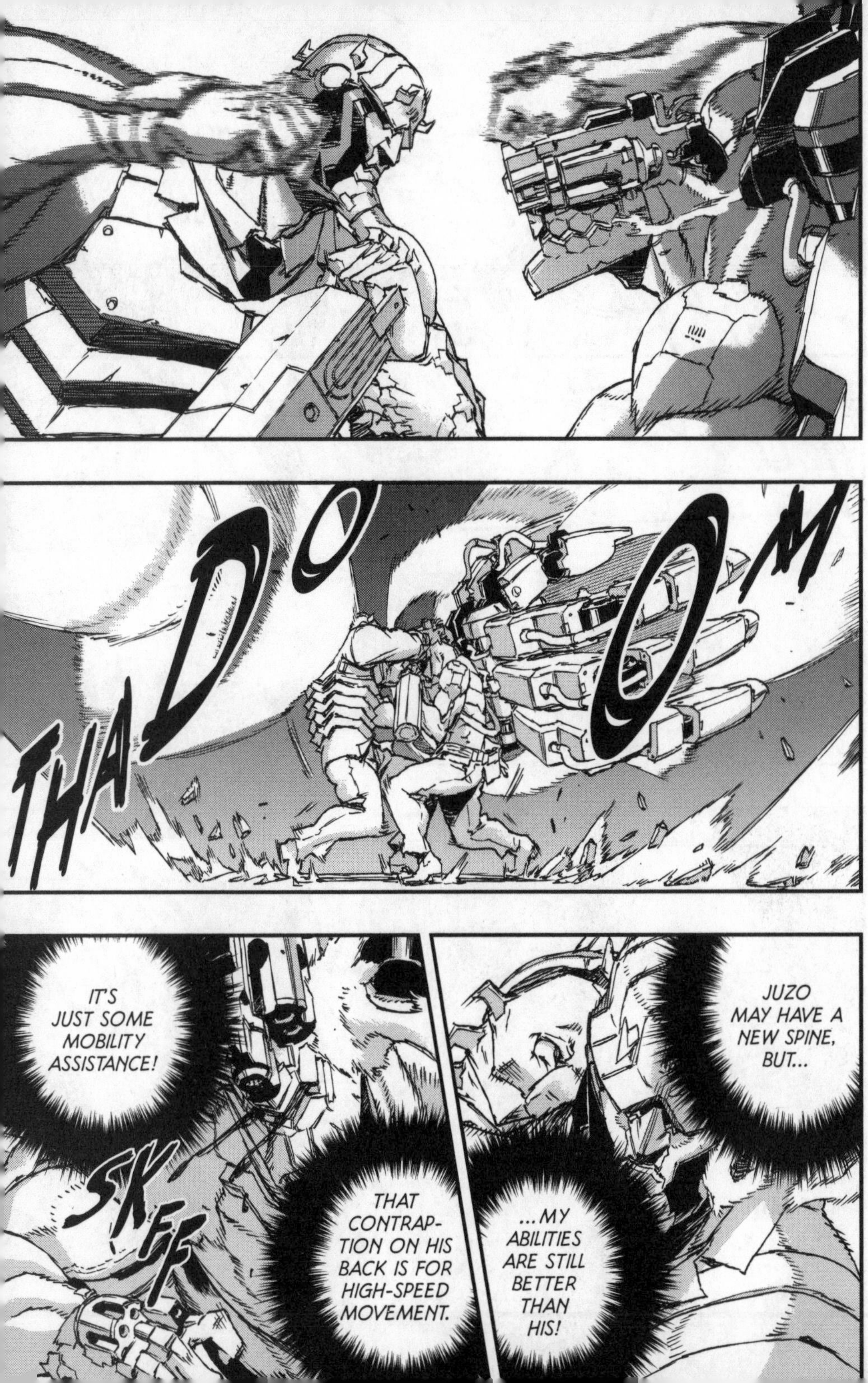
THADOOM
JUZO MAY HAVE A NEW SPINE, BUT...
...MY ABILITIES ARE STILL BETTER THAN HIS!
IT'S JUST SOME MOBILITY ASSISTANCE!
SKFF
THAT CONTRAPTION ON HIS BACK IS FOR HIGH-SPEED MOVEMENT.

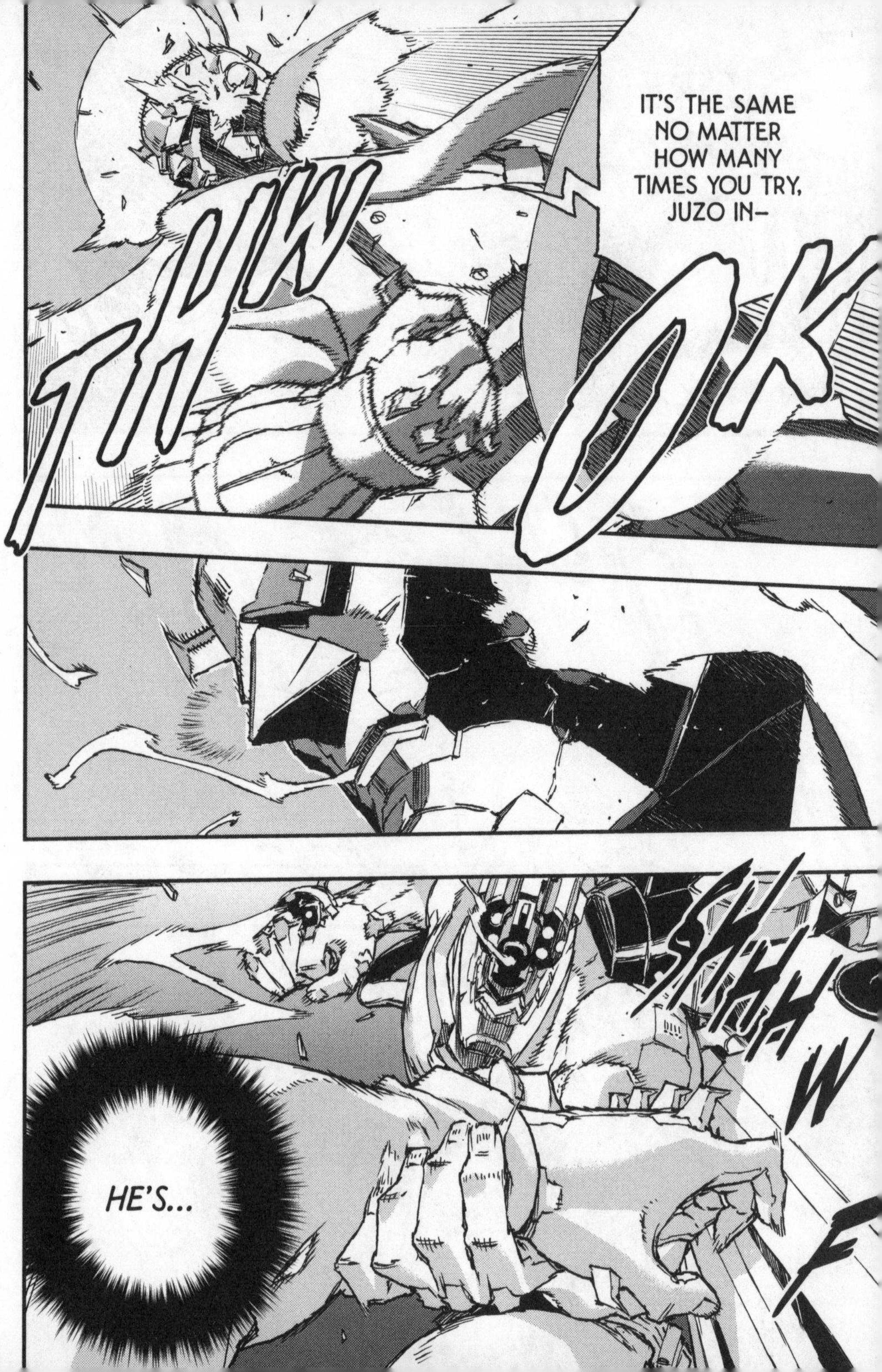
IT'S THE SAME NO MATTER HOW MANY TIMES YOU TRY, JUZO IN–
THWOK
SHHHW
HE'S...

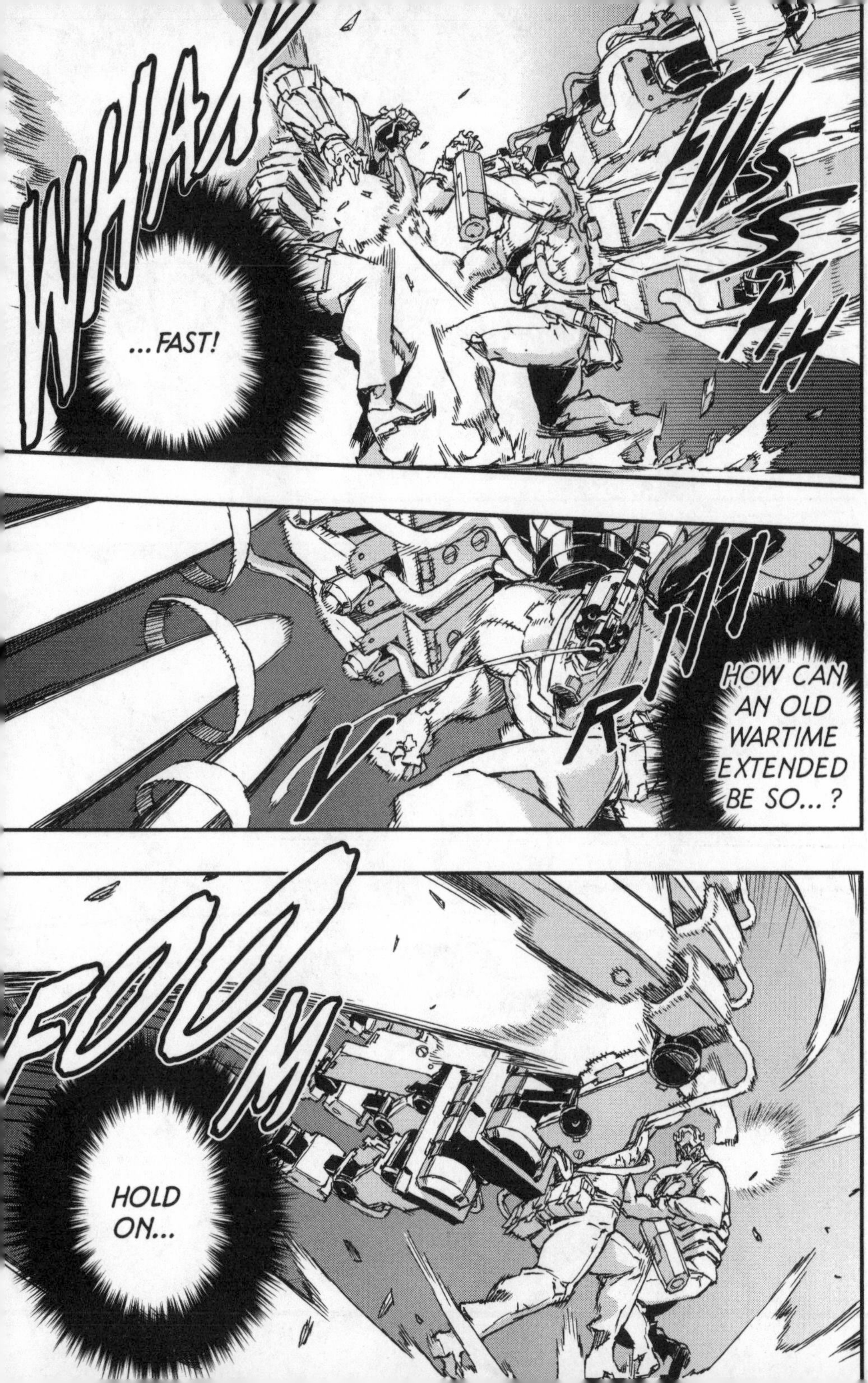
FWSSHH
WHAK
...FAST!
HOW CAN AN OLD WARTIME EXTENDED BE SO...?
VRIII
FOOM
HOLD ON...

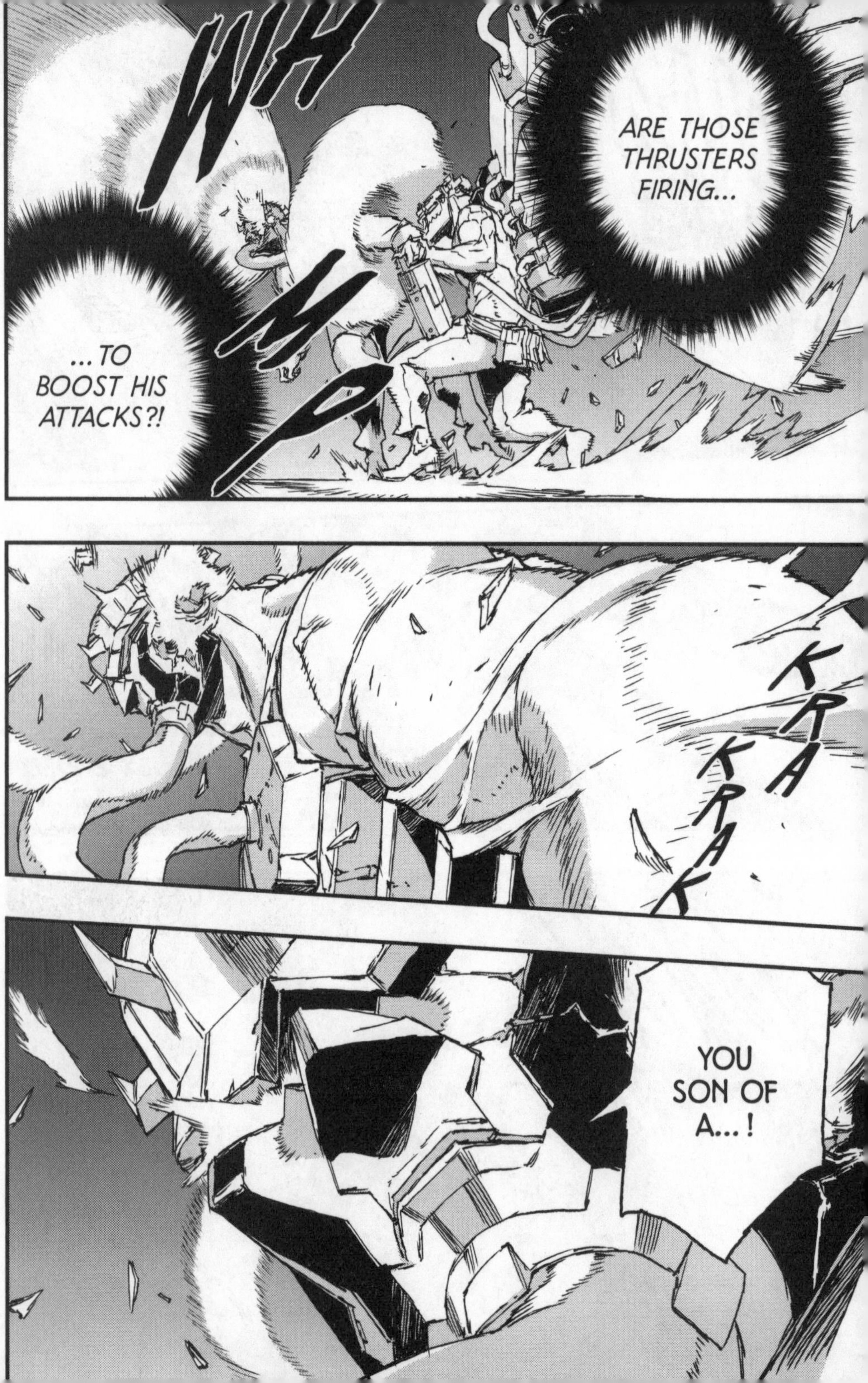
ARE THOSE THRUSTERS FIRING...
...TO BOOST HIS ATTACKS?!
WHMP
KRA KRAK
YOU SON OF A...!

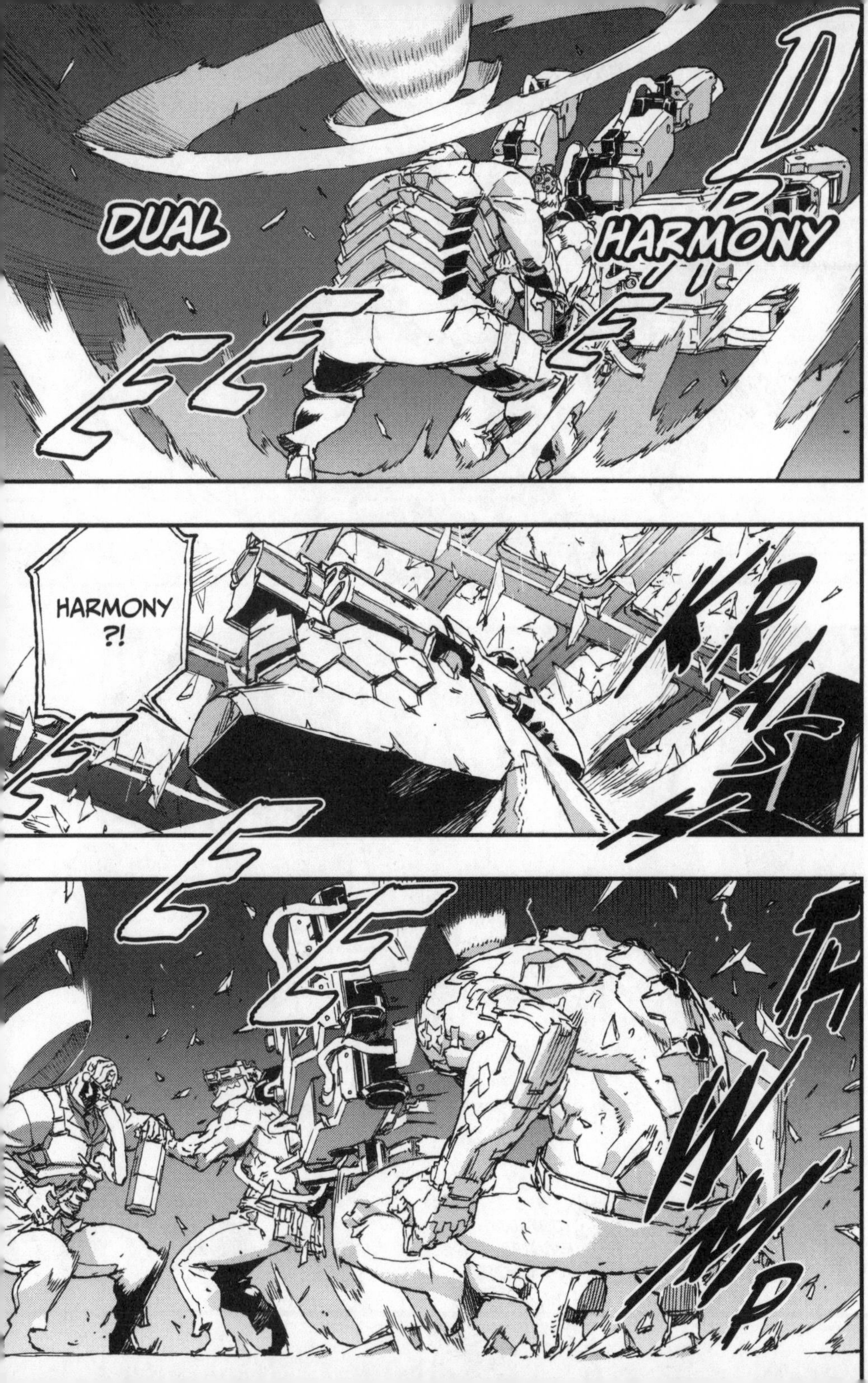
DUAL
HARMONY
KRASH
HARMONY ?!

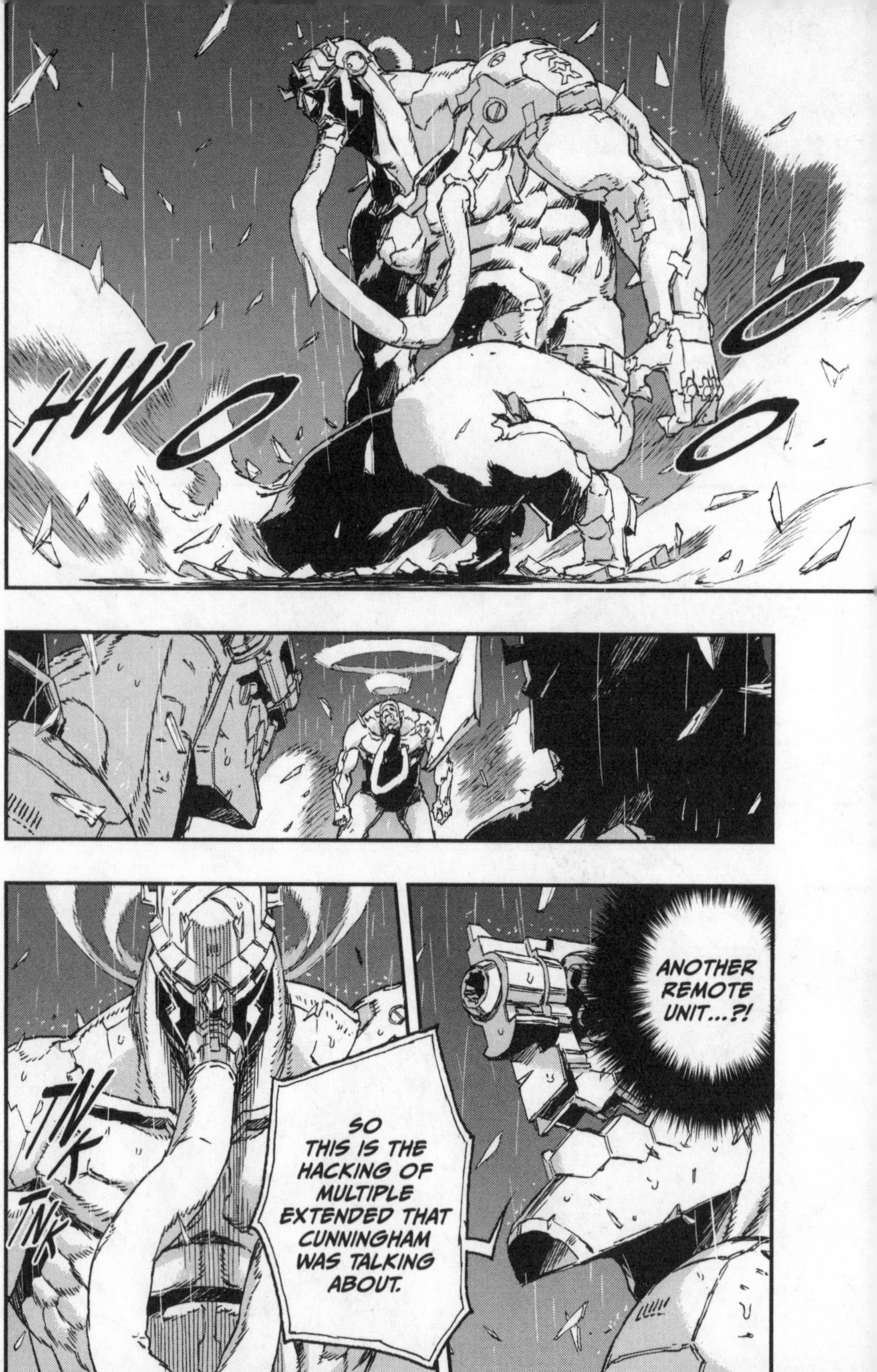
HWOOOO
ANOTHER REMOTE UNIT...?!
SO THIS IS THE HACKING OF MULTIPLE EXTENDED THAT CUNNINGHAM WAS TALKING ABOUT.
TNK TNK

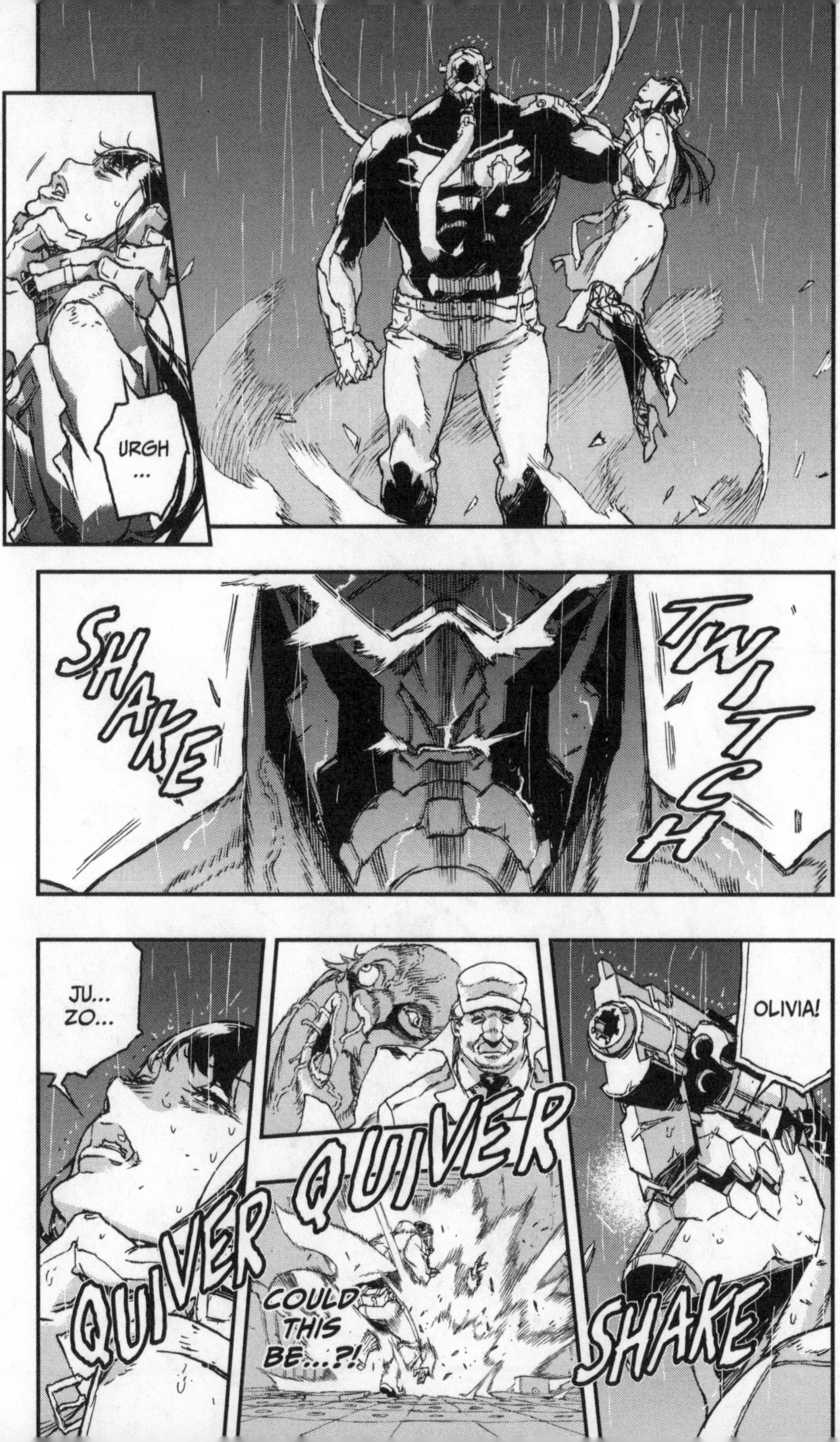
URGH ...
TWITCH
SHAKE
OLIVIA!
SHAKE
QUIVER
COULD THIS BE...?!
JU... ZO...
QUIVER

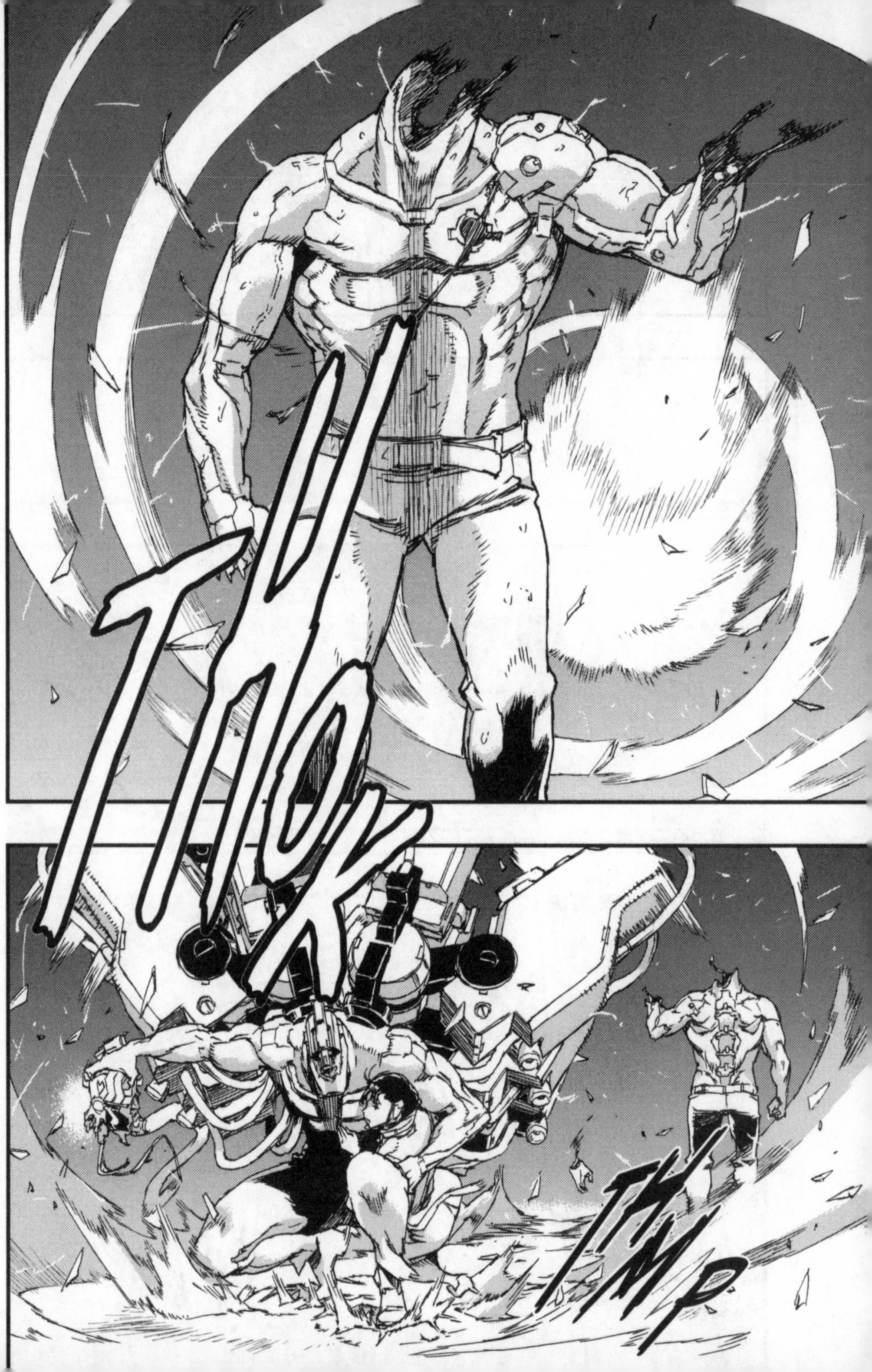
THOK
THMP

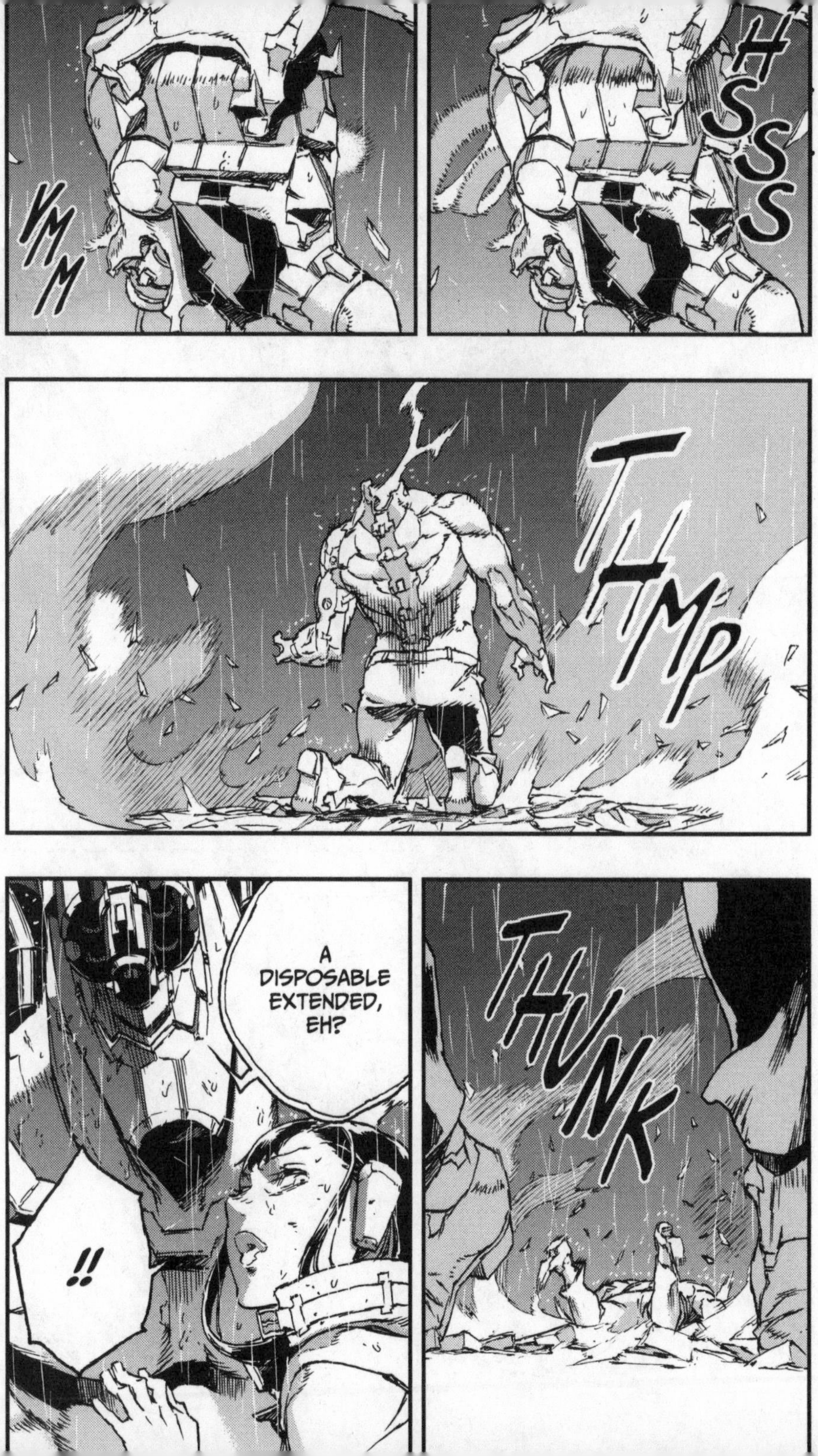
HSSS
VMM
THMP
THUNK
A DISPOSABLE EXTENDED, EH?
!!

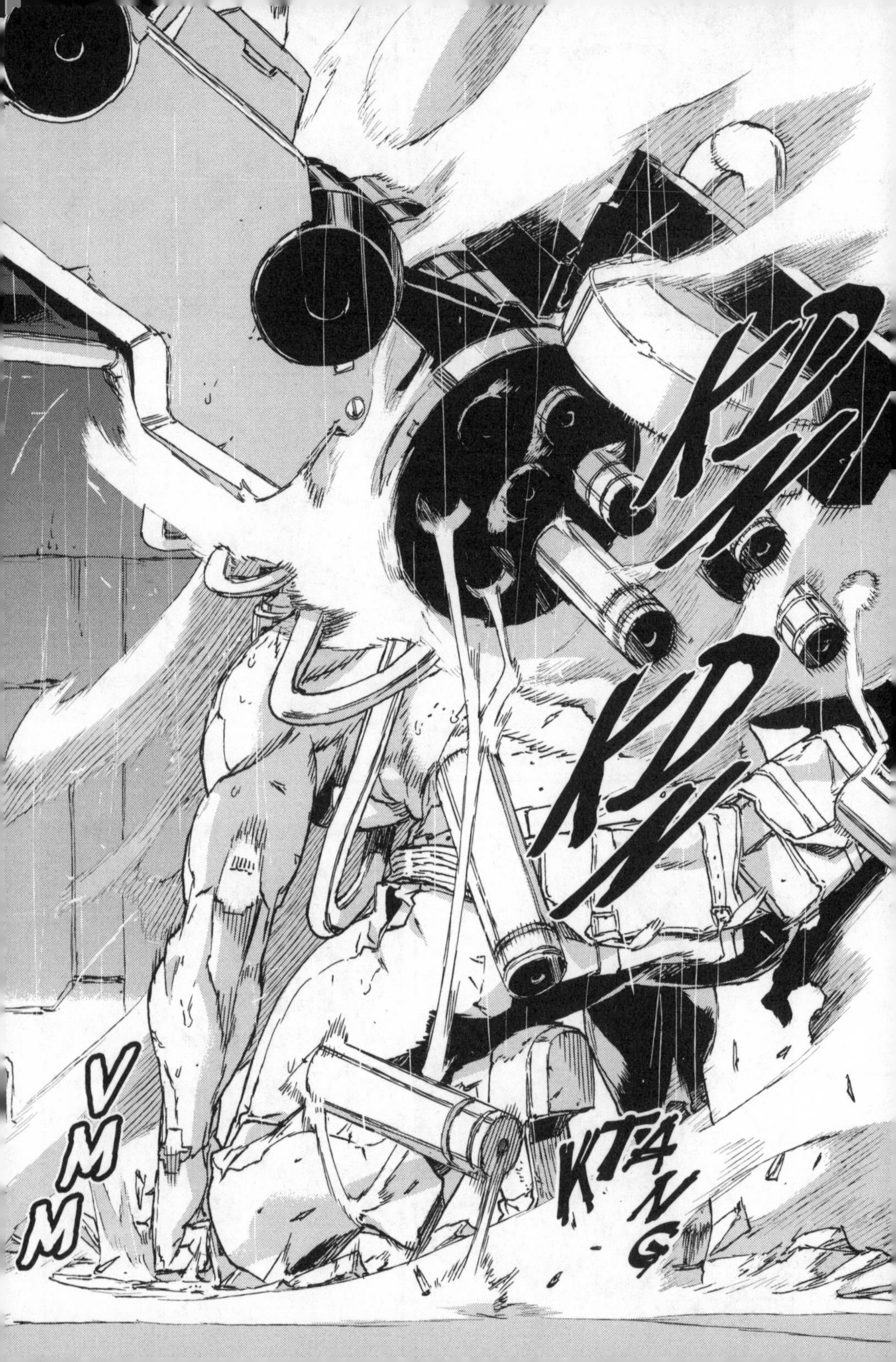
VMM
KTANG

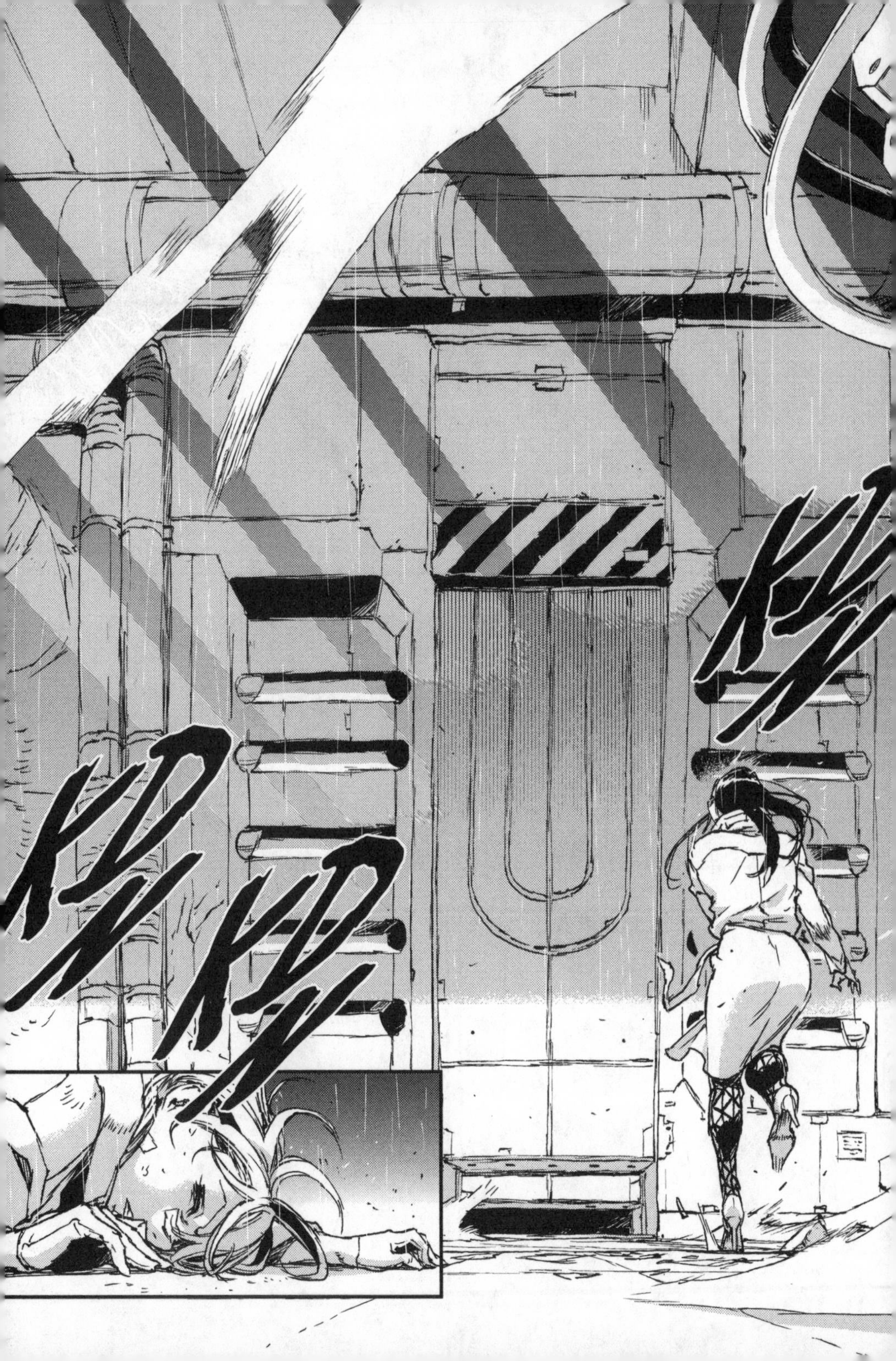

DAMN IT!

...PARALLEL SUB-BRAIN.

WE LOST THE...

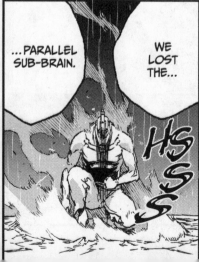

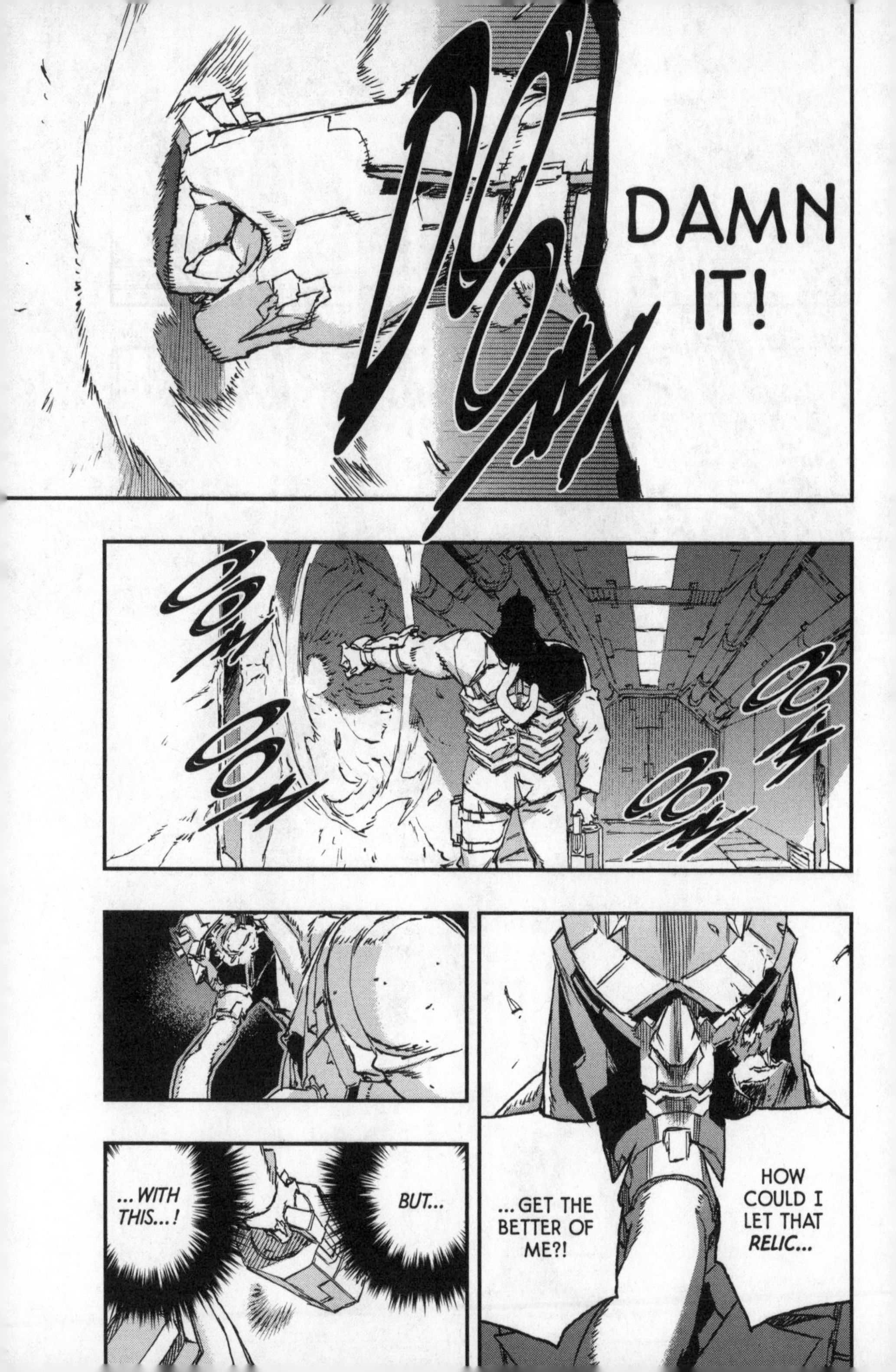
DAMN IT!
HOW COULD I LET THAT *RELIC*...
...GET THE BETTER OF ME?!
BUT...
...WITH THIS...!

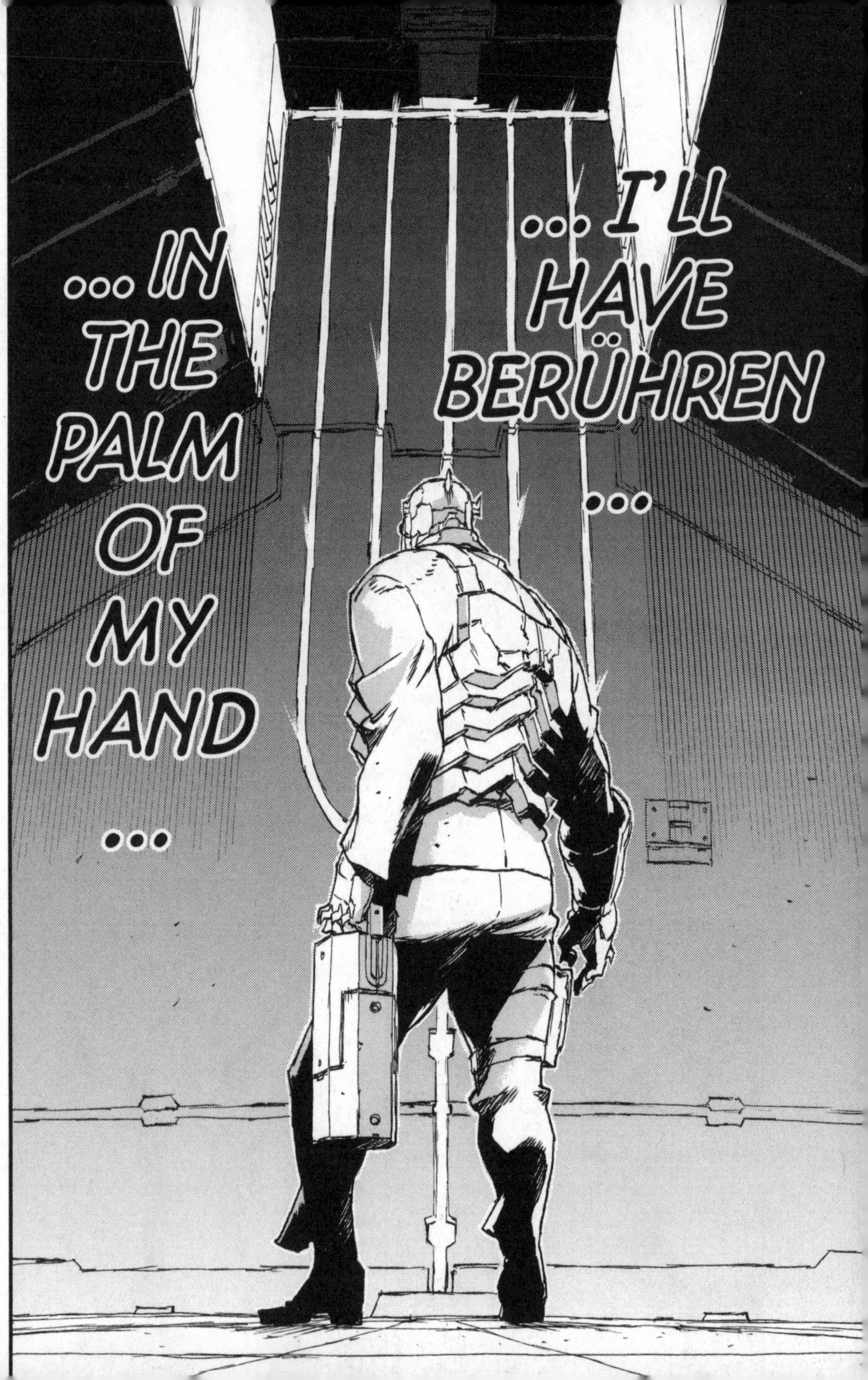
...I'LL HAVE BERÜHREN ...
...IN THE PALM OF MY HAND ...

NO GUNS LIFE

The gunsmoke drifts, the muzzle talks

NO GUNS LIFE

The gunsmoke drifts, the muzzle talks

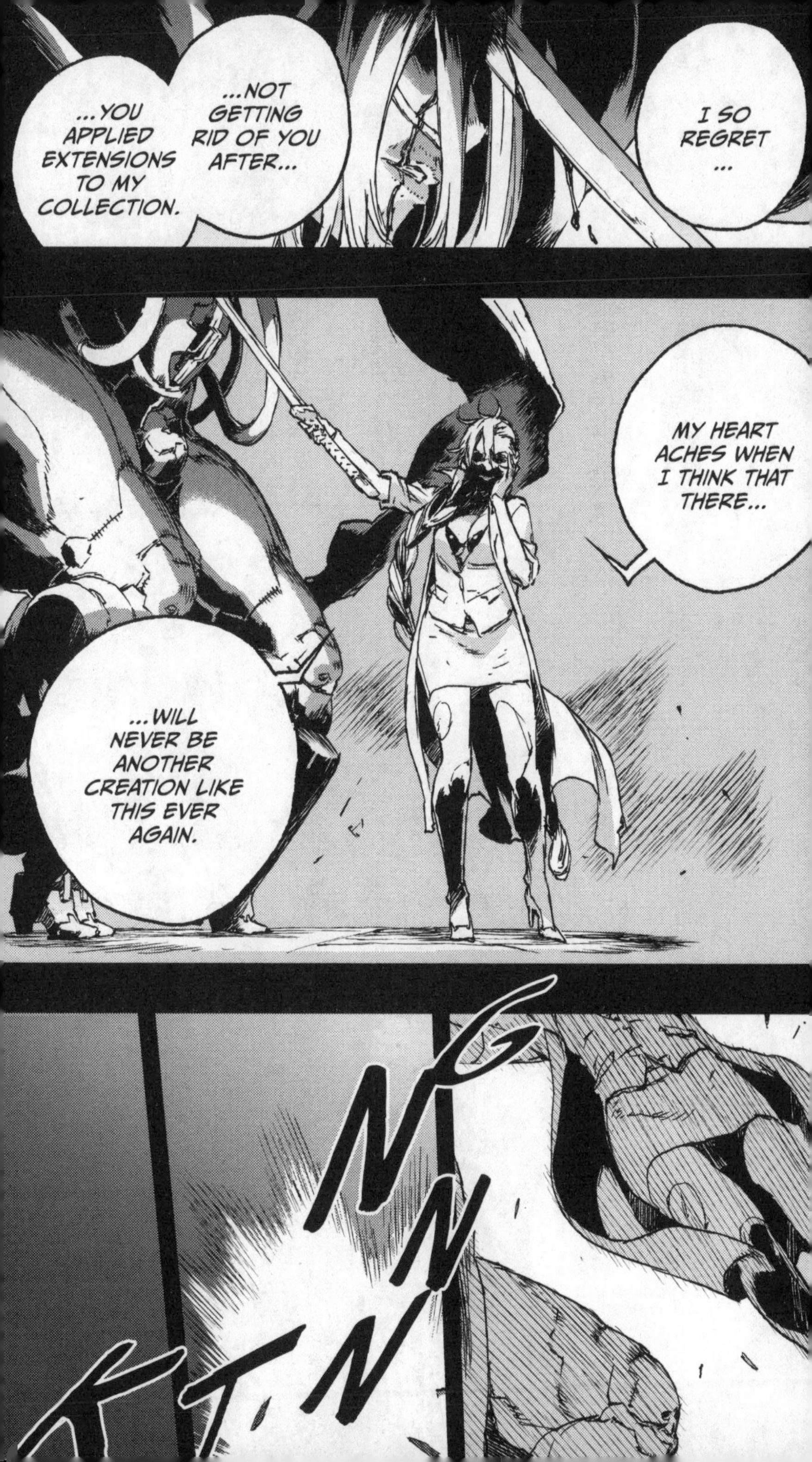
I SO REGRET ...
...NOT GETTING RID OF YOU AFTER...
...YOU APPLIED EXTENSIONS TO MY COLLECTION.
MY HEART ACHES WHEN I THINK THAT THERE...
...WILL NEVER BE ANOTHER CREATION LIKE THIS EVER AGAIN.
KTNNNG

Chapter 56
The Name, The Body

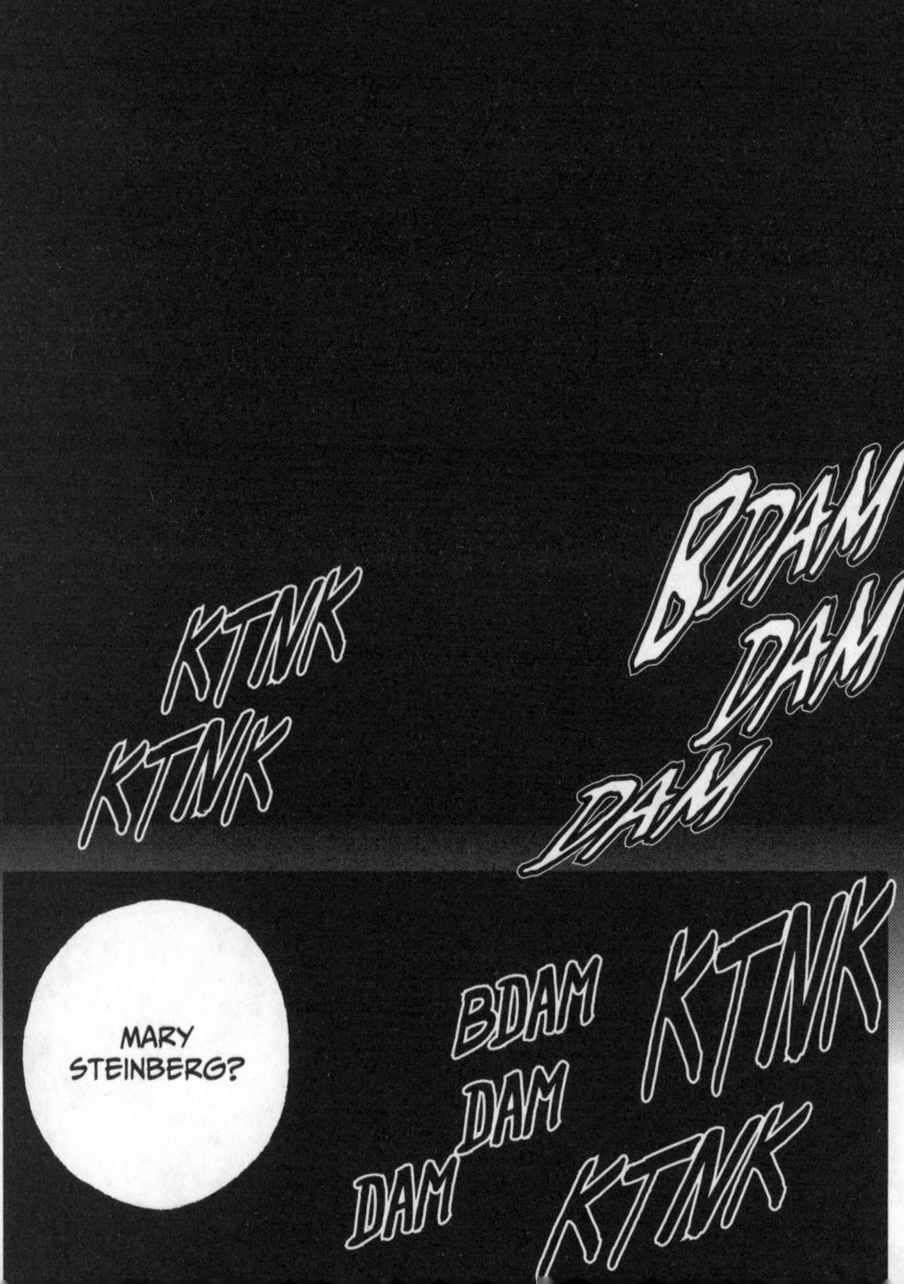
BDAM DAM DAM
KTNK KTNK
KTNK KTNK
BDAM DAM DAM
MARY STEINBERG?

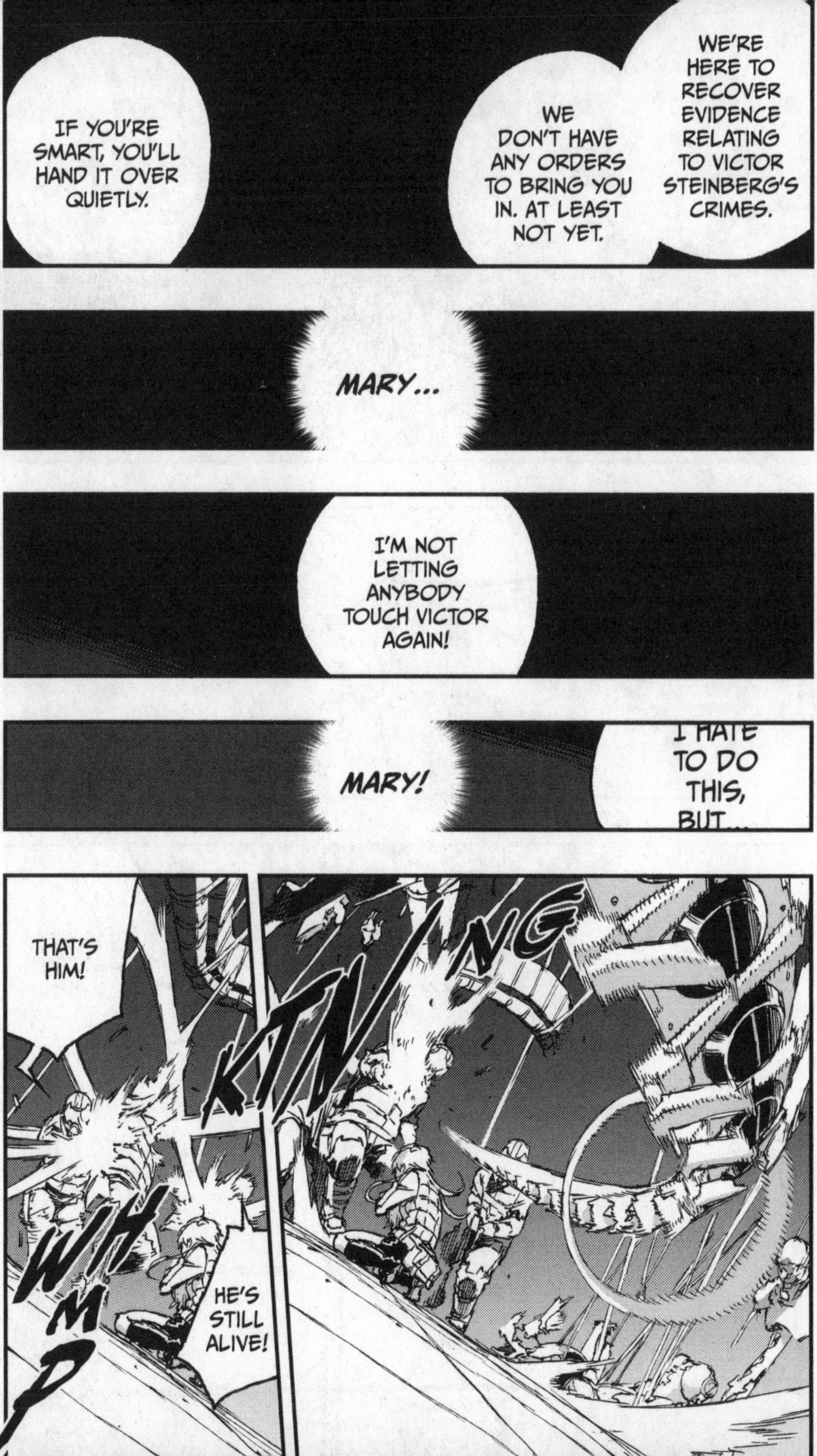

WE'RE HERE TO RECOVER EVIDENCE RELATING TO VICTOR STEINBERG'S CRIMES.
WE DON'T HAVE ANY ORDERS TO BRING YOU IN. AT LEAST NOT YET.
IF YOU'RE SMART, YOU'LL HAND IT OVER QUIETLY.
MARY...
I'M NOT LETTING ANYBODY TOUCH VICTOR AGAIN!
I HATE TO DO THIS, BUT...
MARY!
THAT'S HIM!
HE'S STILL ALIVE!
WHMP

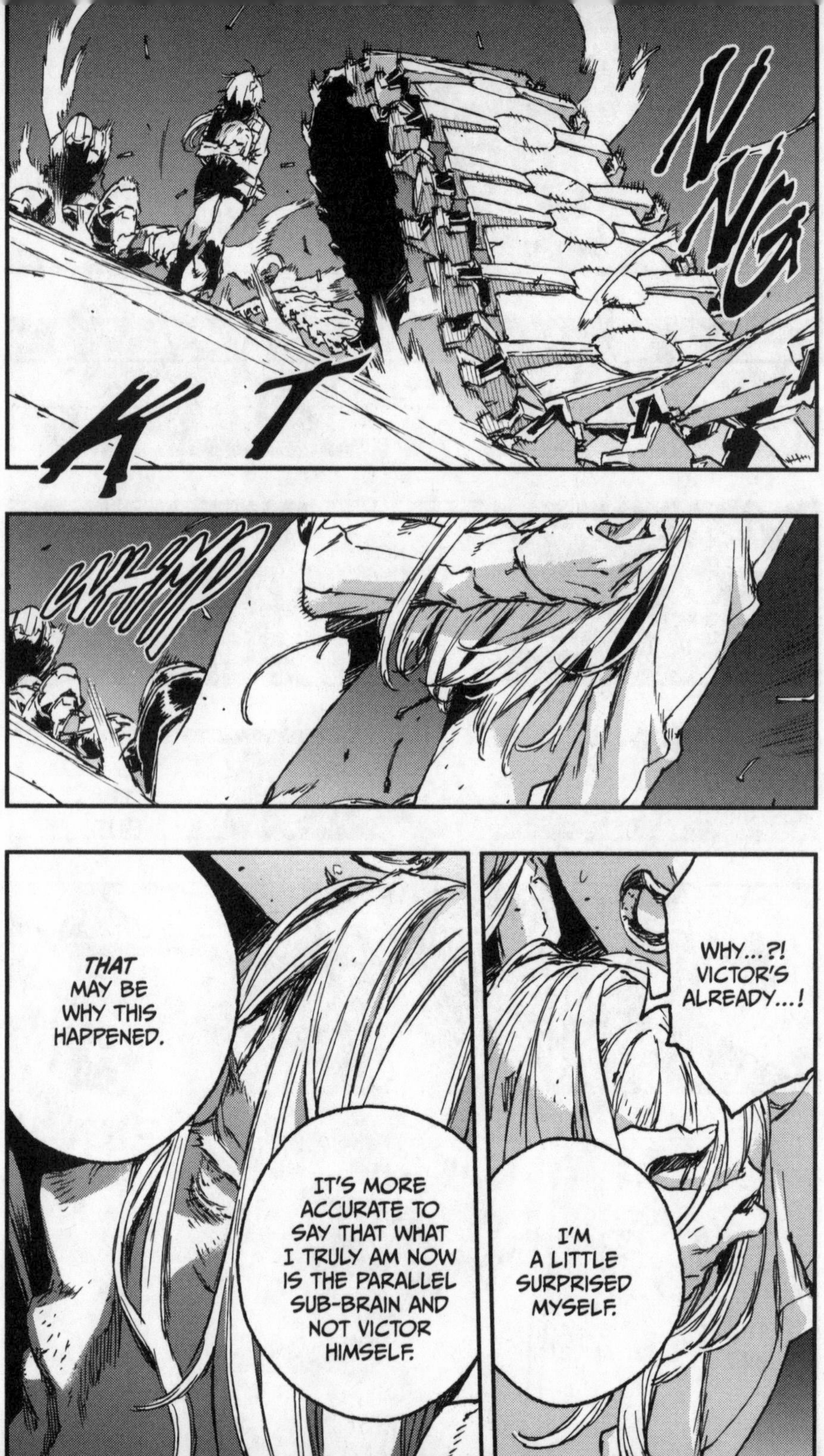
NNG
KT
WHMP
WHY...?! VICTOR'S ALREADY...!
I'M A LITTLE SURPRISED MYSELF.
IT'S MORE ACCURATE TO SAY THAT WHAT I TRULY AM NOW IS THE PARALLEL SUB-BRAIN AND NOT VICTOR HIMSELF.
THAT MAY BE WHY THIS HAPPENED.

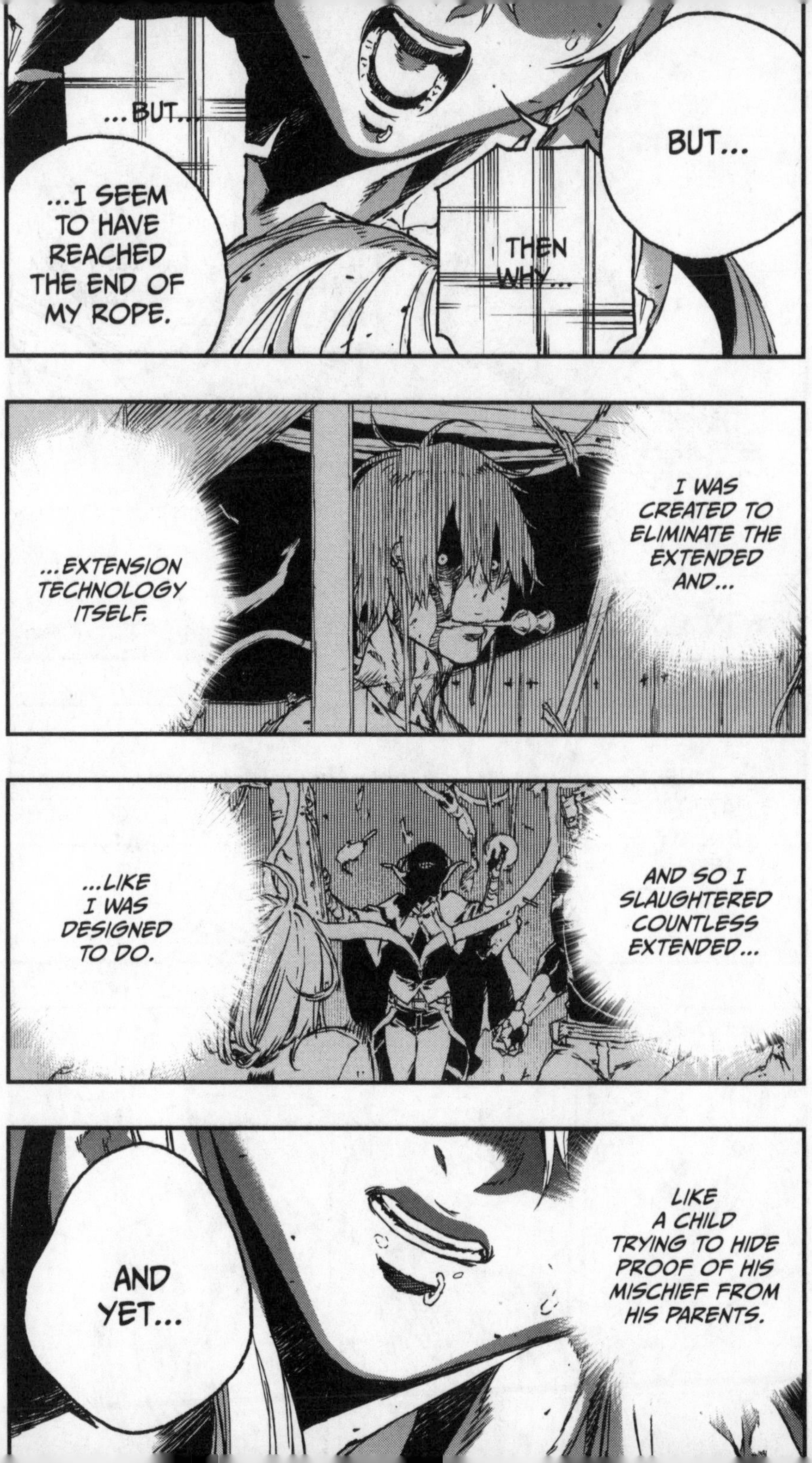
BUT...
THEN WHY...
...BUT...
...I SEEM TO HAVE REACHED THE END OF MY ROPE.
I WAS CREATED TO ELIMINATE THE EXTENDED AND...
...EXTENSION TECHNOLOGY ITSELF.
AND SO I SLAUGHTERED COUNTLESS EXTENDED...
...LIKE I WAS DESIGNED TO DO.
LIKE A CHILD TRYING TO HIDE PROOF OF HIS MISCHIEF FROM HIS PARENTS.
AND YET...

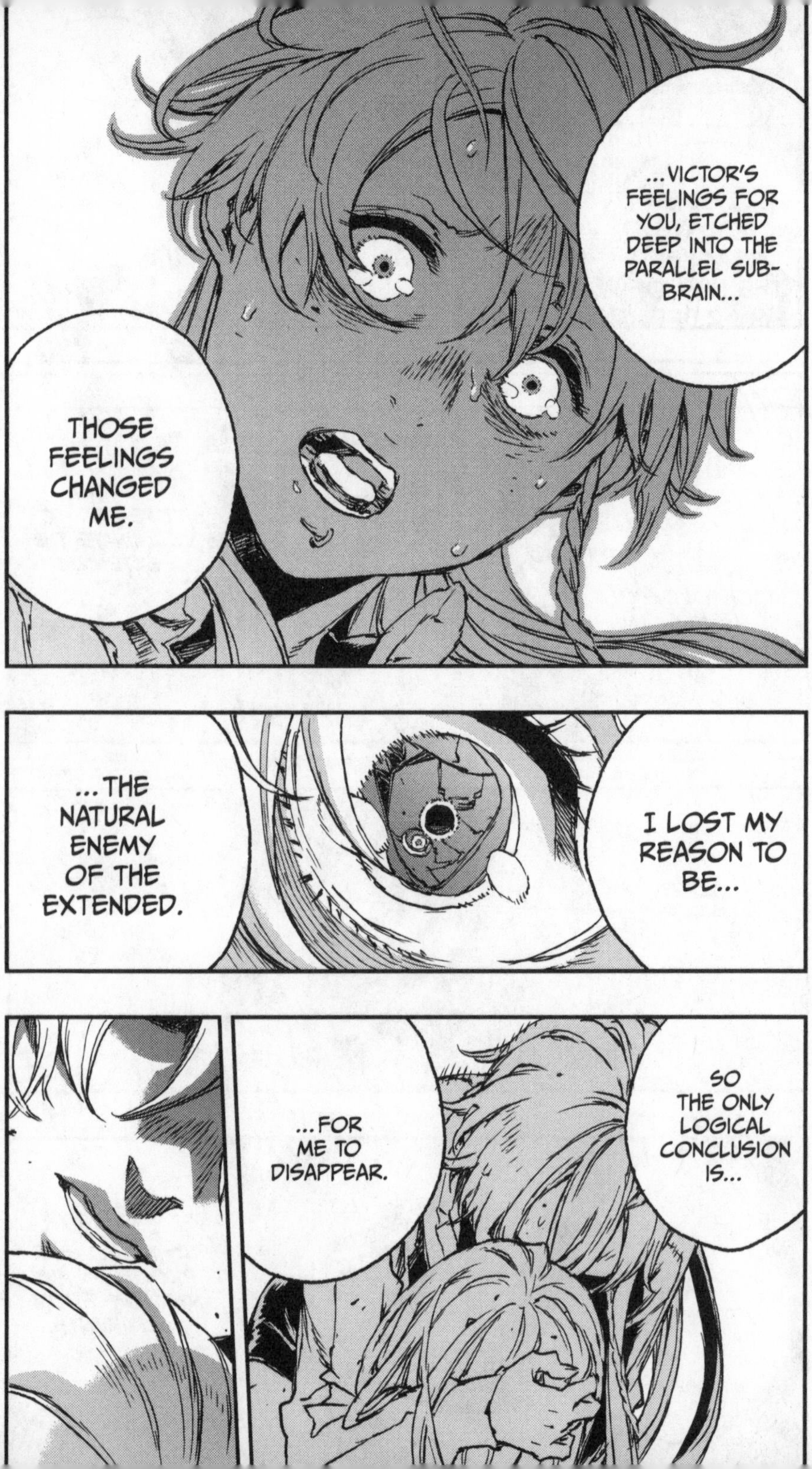
...VICTOR'S FEELINGS FOR YOU, ETCHED DEEP INTO THE PARALLEL SUB-BRAIN...
THOSE FEELINGS CHANGED ME.
I LOST MY REASON TO BE...
...THE NATURAL ENEMY OF THE EXTENDED.
SO THE ONLY LOGICAL CONCLUSION IS...
...FOR ME TO DISAPPEAR.

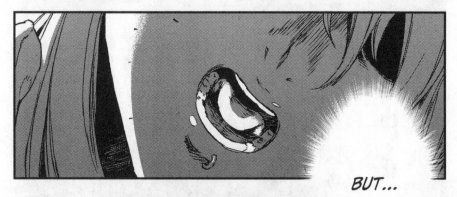

BUT...

...BEFORE
I DO...

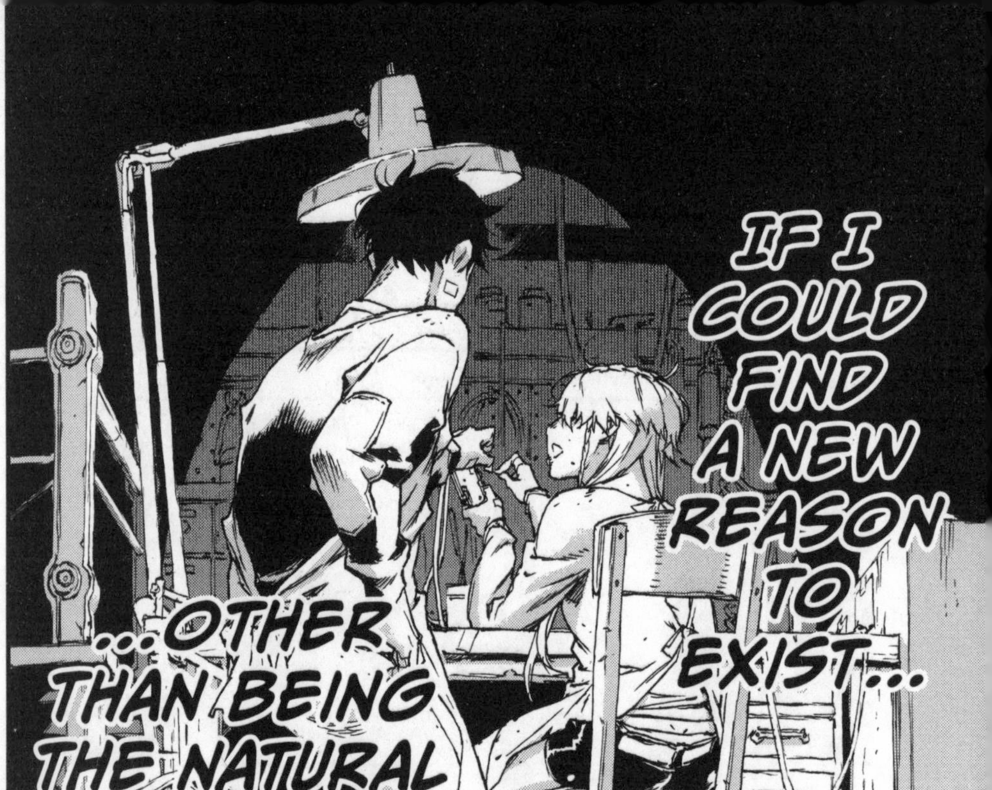
IF I COULD FIND A NEW REASON TO EXIST...
...OTHER THAN BEING THE NATURAL ENEMY OF THE EXTENDED...

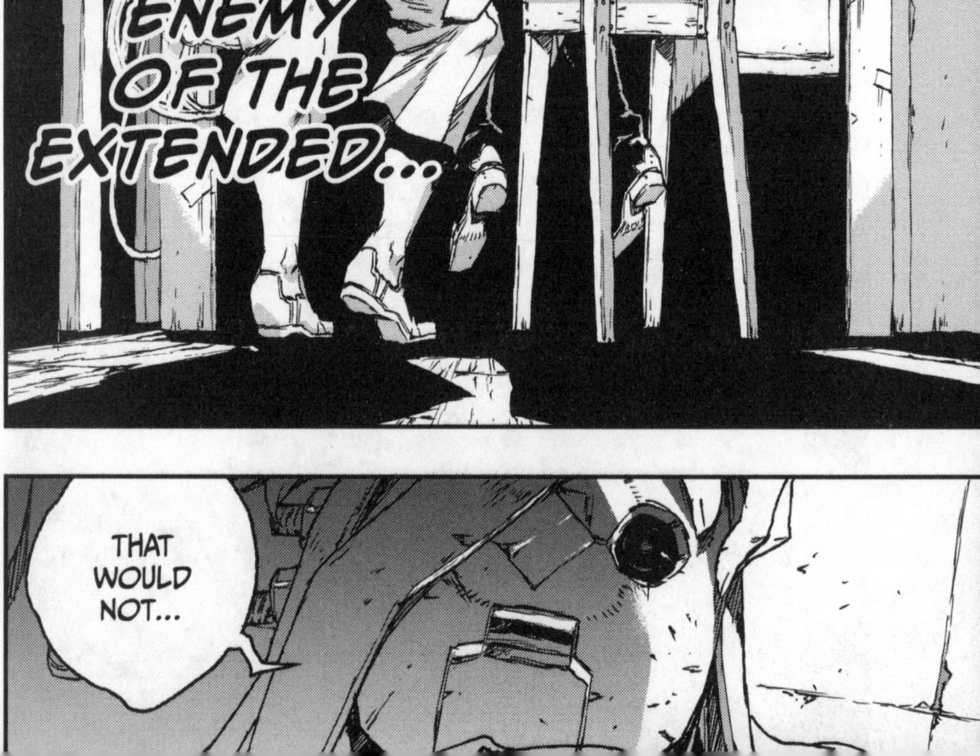
THAT WOULD NOT...

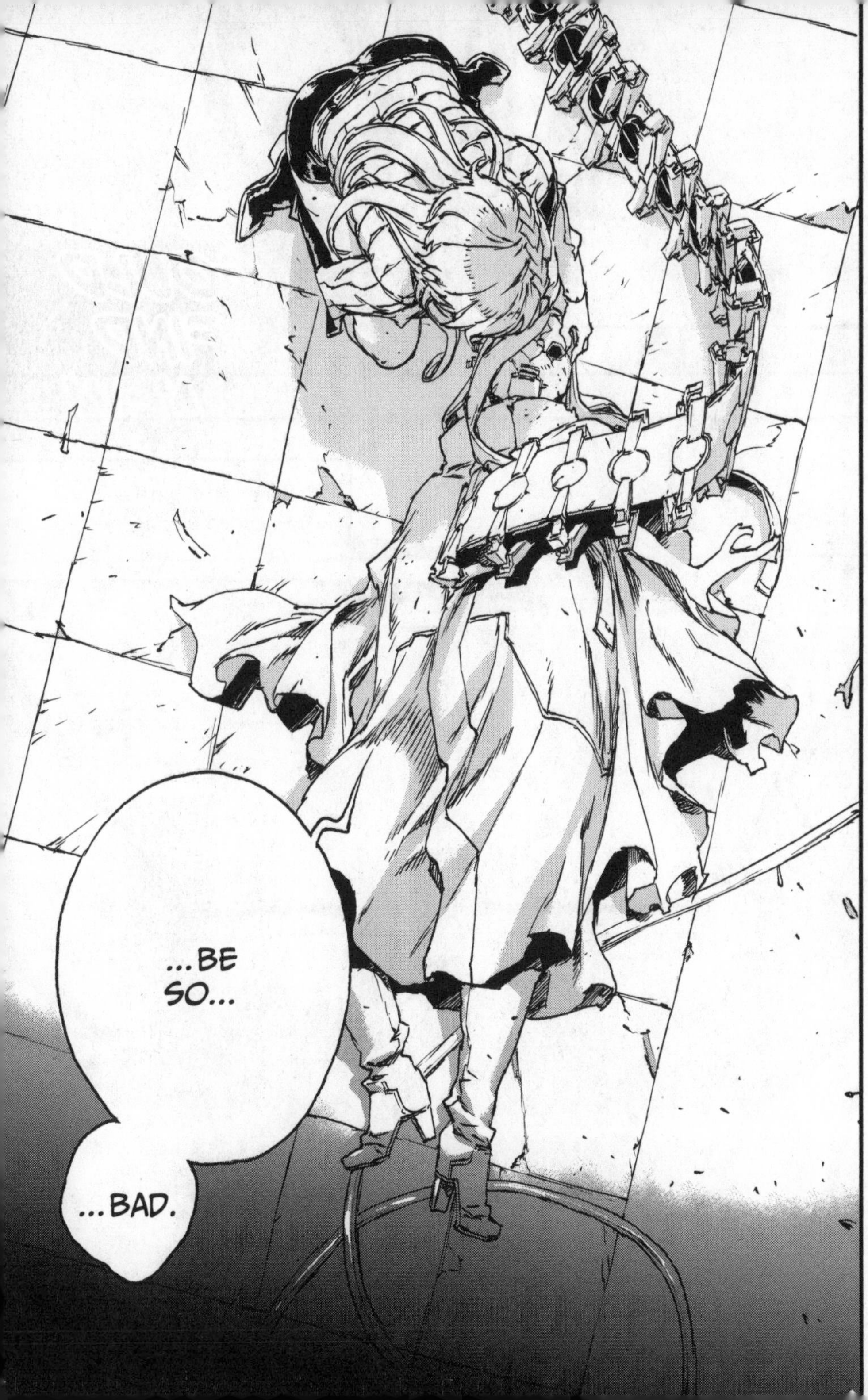
...BE SO...
...BAD.

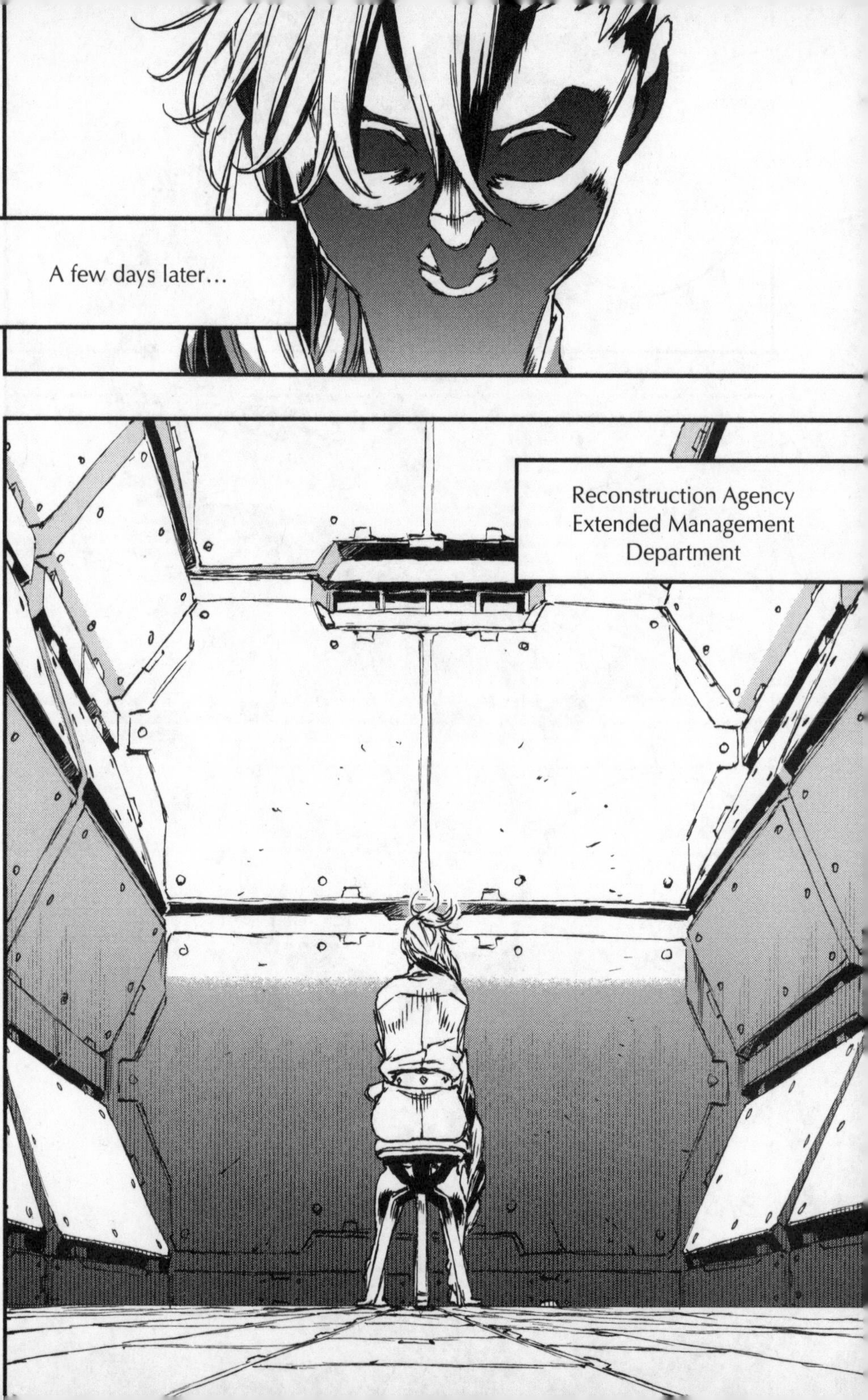
A few days later…
Reconstruction Agency
Extended Management
Department

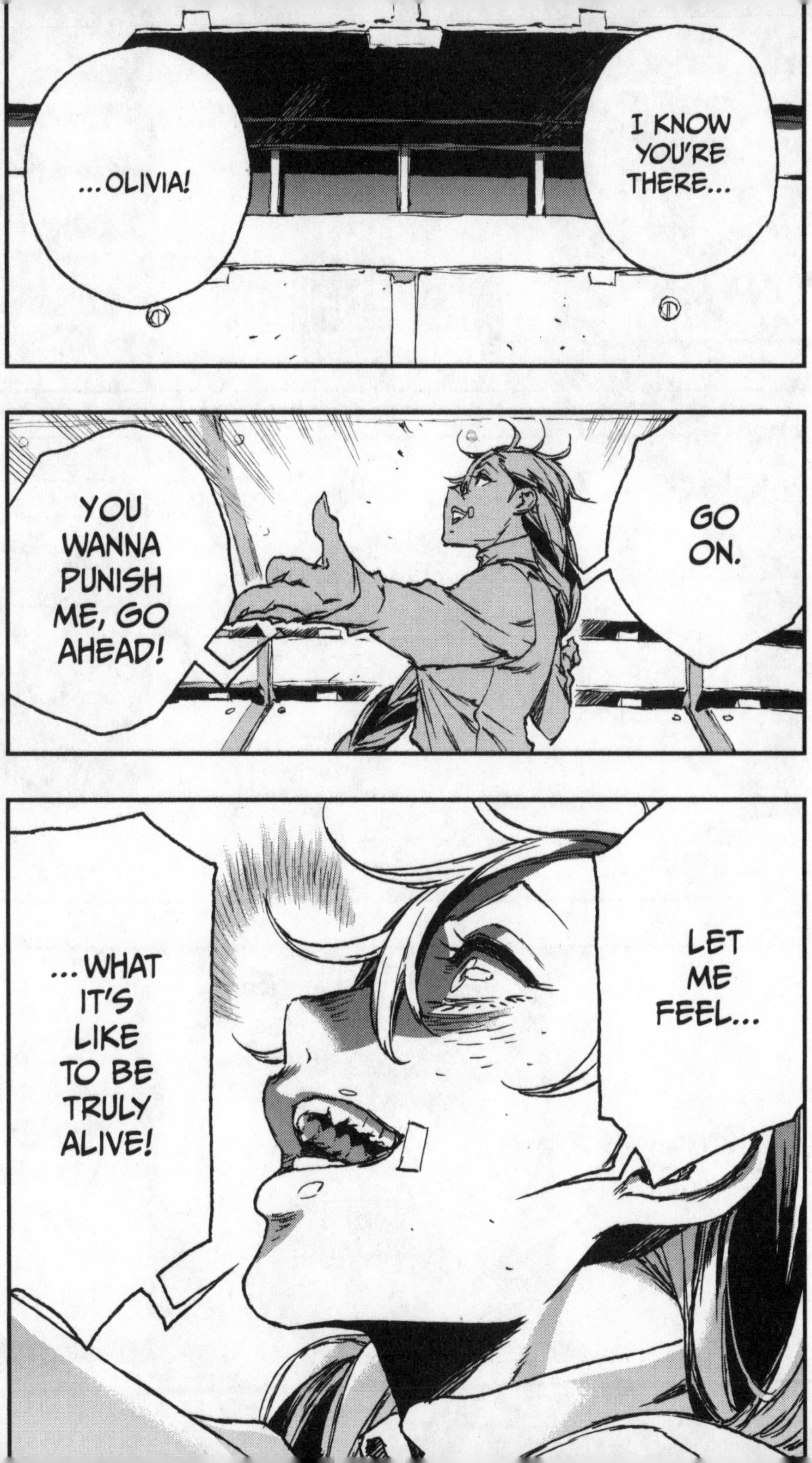
I KNOW YOU'RE THERE...
...OLIVIA!
GO ON.
YOU WANNA PUNISH ME, GO AHEAD!
LET ME FEEL...
...WHAT IT'S LIKE TO BE TRULY ALIVE!

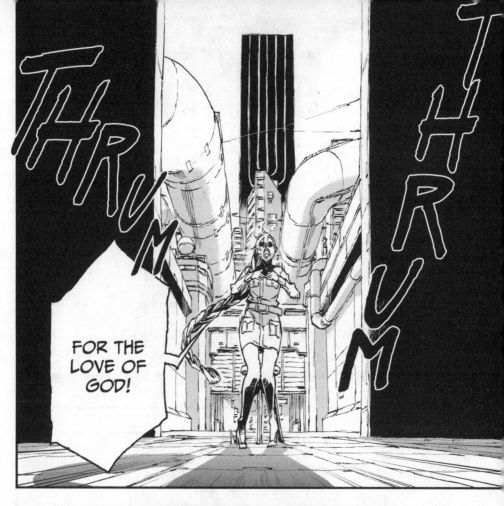

THRUM THRUM

FOR THE LOVE OF GOD!

...IGNORING ME!

DON'T DO ANY- THING AS VULGAR AS...

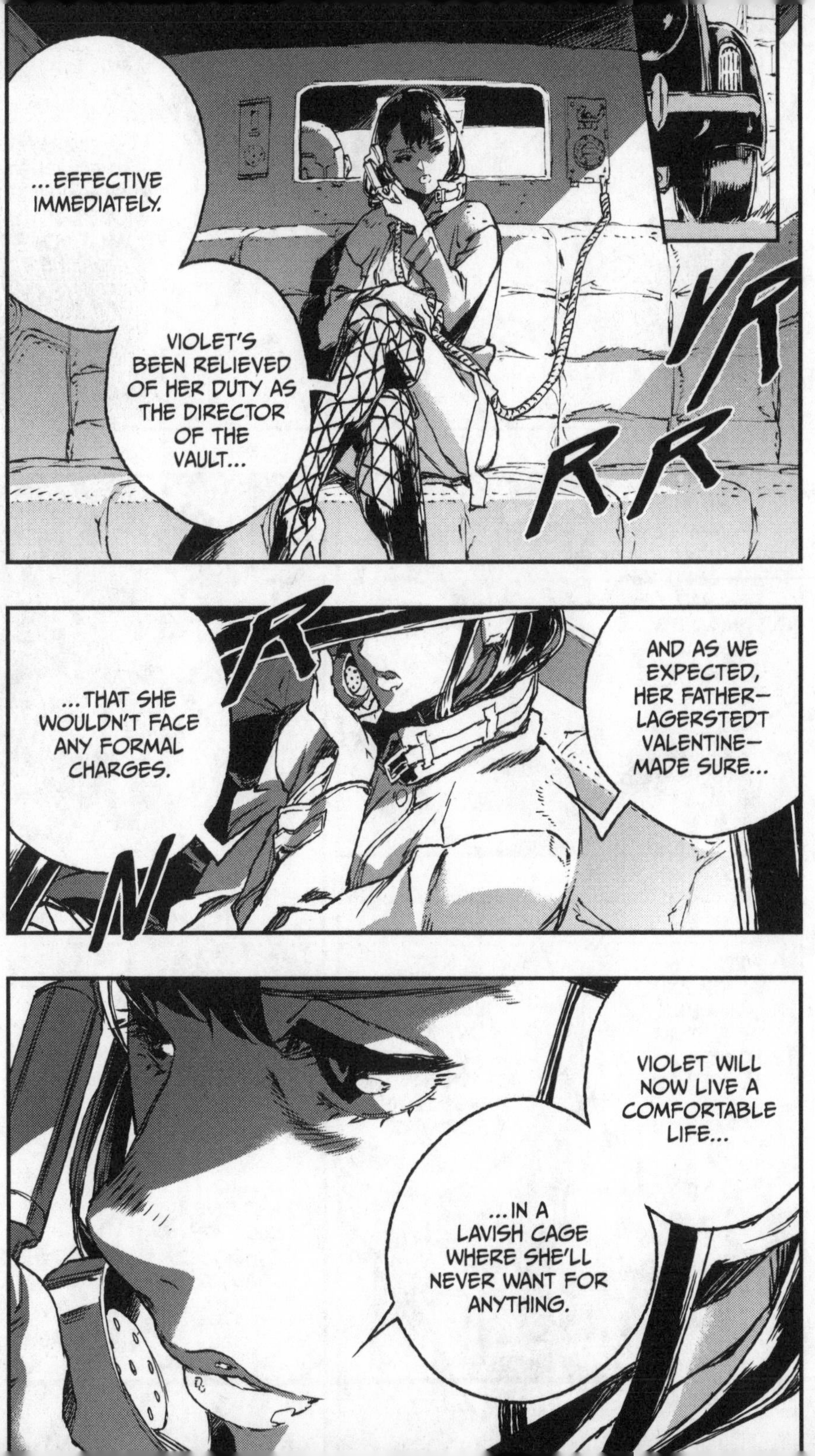
VIOLET'S BEEN RELIEVED OF HER DUTY AS THE DIRECTOR OF THE VAULT...
...EFFECTIVE IMMEDIATELY.
VRRR
AND AS WE EXPECTED, HER FATHER—LAGERSTEDT VALENTINE—MADE SURE...
...THAT SHE WOULDN'T FACE ANY FORMAL CHARGES.
R
N
VIOLET WILL NOW LIVE A COMFORTABLE LIFE...
...IN A LAVISH CAGE WHERE SHE'LL NEVER WANT FOR ANYTHING.

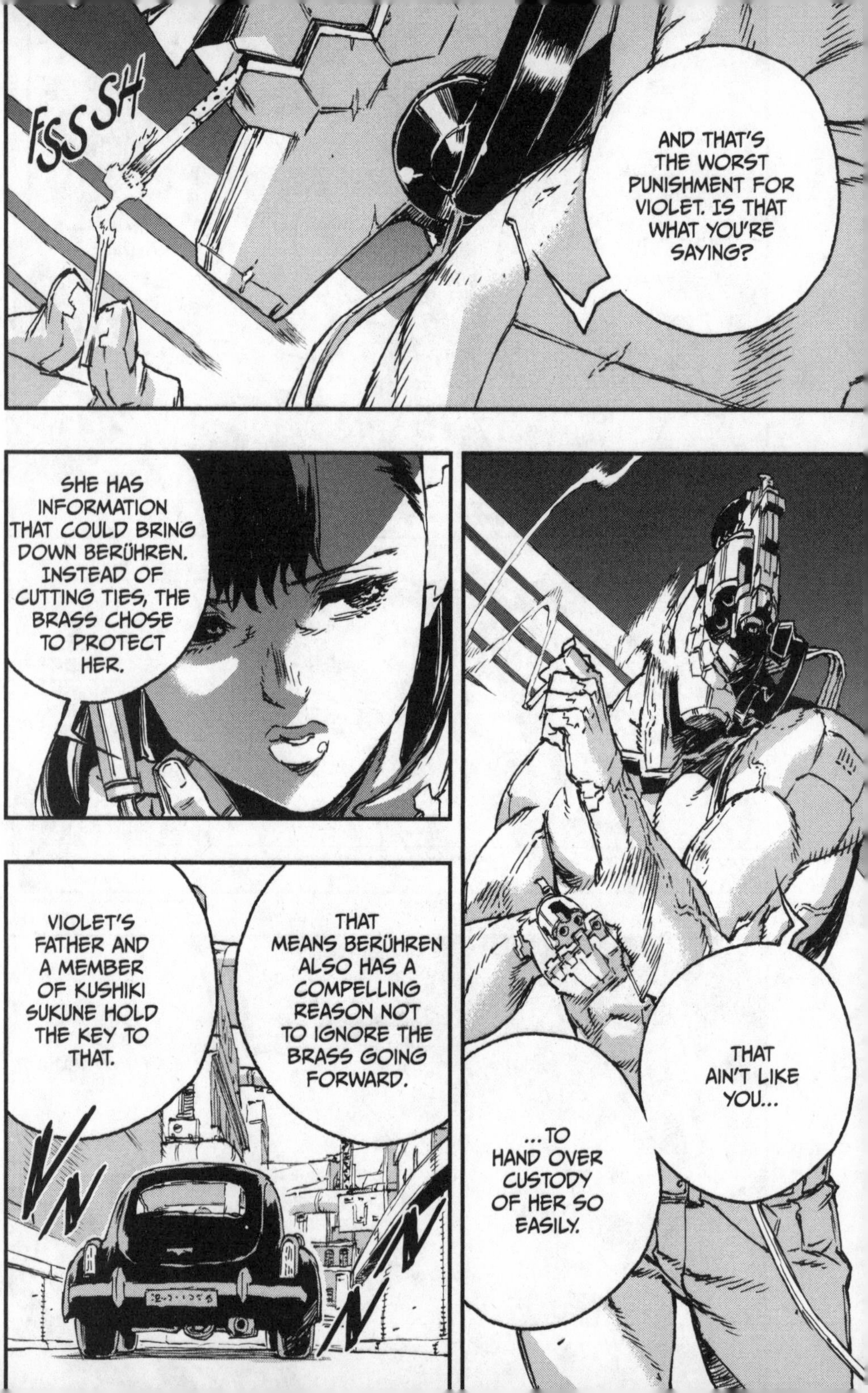
AND THAT'S THE WORST PUNISHMENT FOR VIOLET. IS THAT WHAT YOU'RE SAYING?
FSSSH
THAT AIN'T LIKE YOU...
...TO HAND OVER CUSTODY OF HER SO EASILY.
SHE HAS INFORMATION THAT COULD BRING DOWN BERÜHREN. INSTEAD OF CUTTING TIES, THE BRASS CHOSE TO PROTECT HER.
THAT MEANS BERÜHREN ALSO HAS A COMPELLING REASON NOT TO IGNORE THE BRASS GOING FORWARD.
VIOLET'S FATHER AND A MEMBER OF KUSHIKI SUKUNE HOLD THE KEY TO THAT.

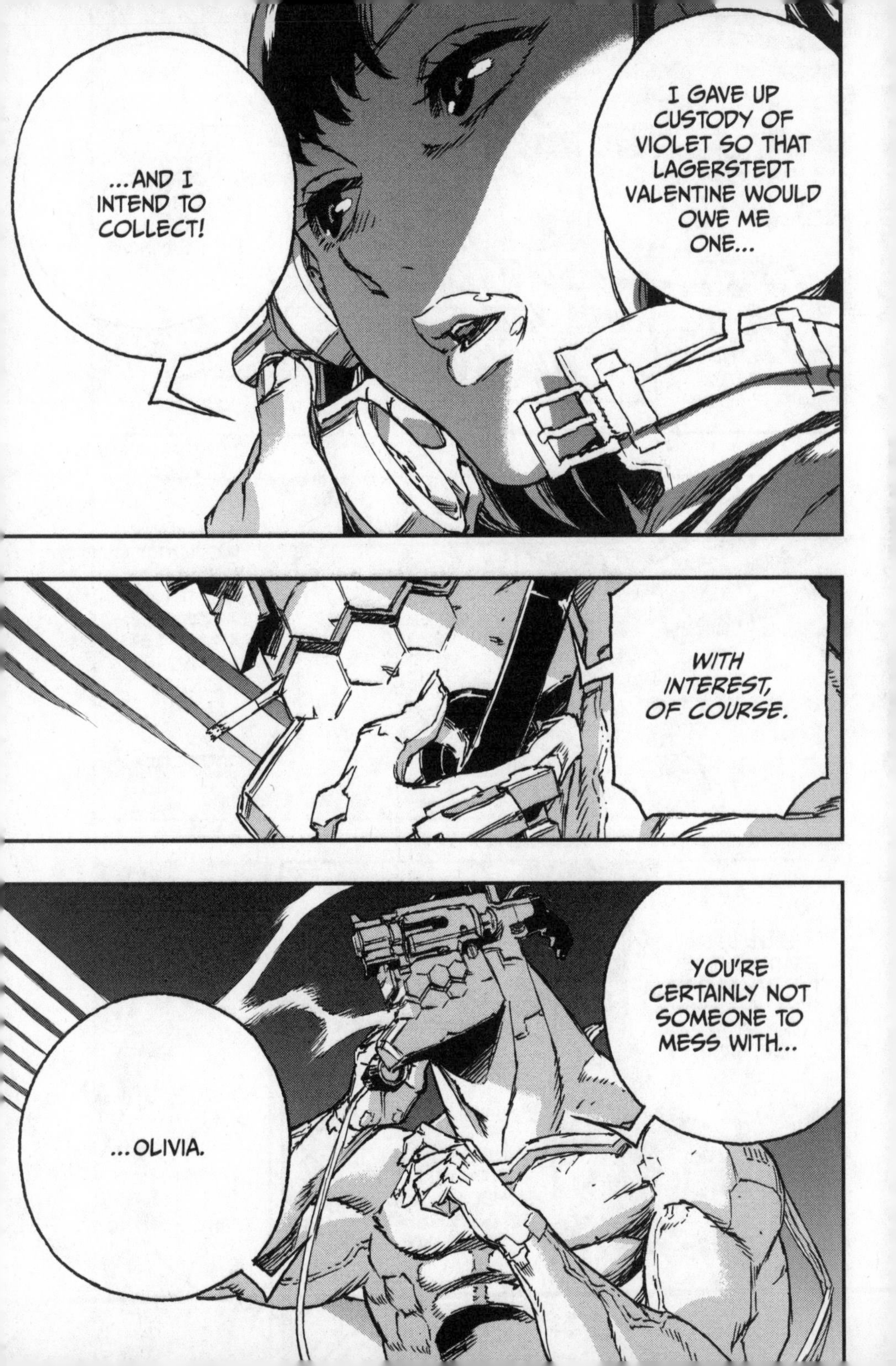
I GAVE UP CUSTODY OF VIOLET SO THAT LAGERSTEDT VALENTINE WOULD OWE ME ONE...
...AND I INTEND TO COLLECT!
WITH INTEREST, OF COURSE.
YOU'RE CERTAINLY NOT SOMEONE TO MESS WITH...
...OLIVIA.

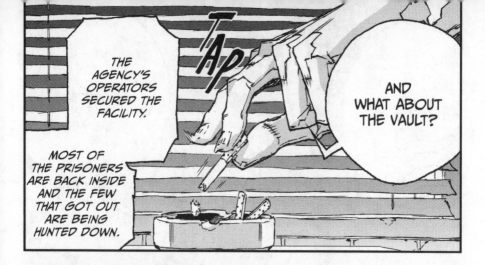

AND WHAT ABOUT THE VAULT?
TAP
THE AGENCY'S OPERATORS SECURED THE FACILITY.
MOST OF THE PRISONERS ARE BACK INSIDE AND THE FEW THAT GOT OUT ARE BEING HUNTED DOWN.
YOU WOULDN'T BELIEVE HOW HARD IT WAS TO CONVINCE MARY TO LET US RECOVER VICTOR'S BODY.
...
OH YEAH...?
WE LOST THE PARALLEL SUB-BRAIN TO BERÜHREN SO WE COULDN'T RETRIEVE ANY VALUABLE INTEL FROM VICTOR'S BODY, BUT...
LUCKILY... WE RECOVERED THE BODY AND SUB-BRAIN OF SOMEONE CLAIMING TO BE BERÜHREN'S SPECIAL ENVOY...
...WHO GAVE US A STATEMENT ON THE BACKROOM DEAL BETWEEN VIOLET AND BERÜHREN.
RRN
VRRR

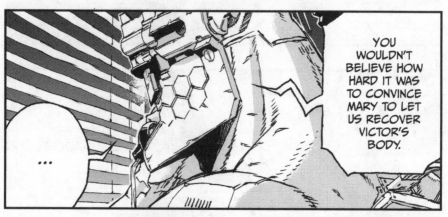

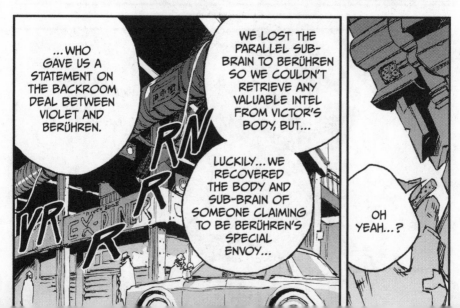

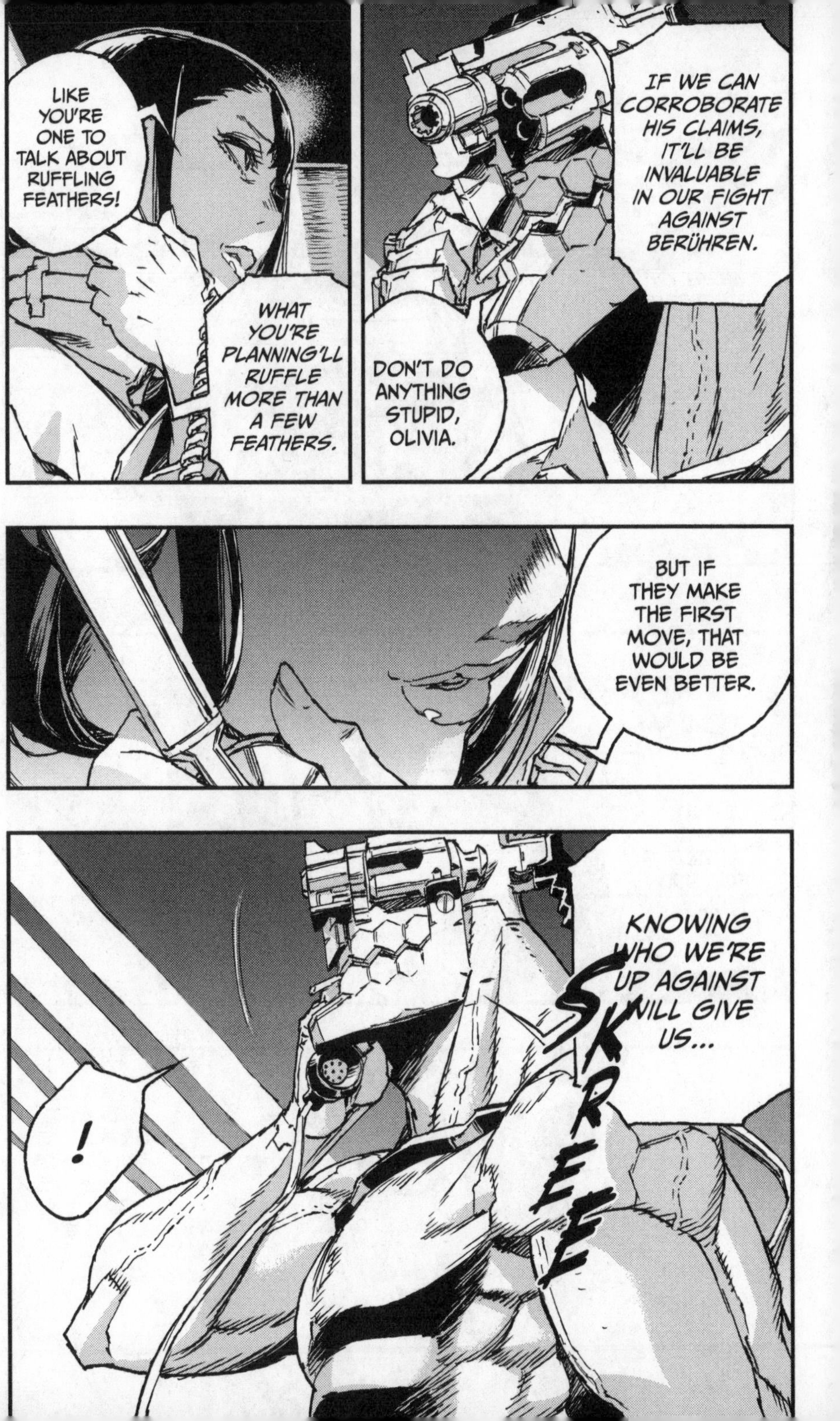
IF WE CAN CORROBORATE HIS CLAIMS, IT'LL BE INVALUABLE IN OUR FIGHT AGAINST BERÜHREN.
DON'T DO ANYTHING STUPID, OLIVIA.
WHAT YOU'RE PLANNING'LL RUFFLE MORE THAN A FEW FEATHERS.
LIKE YOU'RE ONE TO TALK ABOUT RUFFLING FEATHERS!
BUT IF THEY MAKE THE FIRST MOVE, THAT WOULD BE EVEN BETTER.
KNOWING WHO WE'RE UP AGAINST WILL GIVE US...
SKREEEE
!

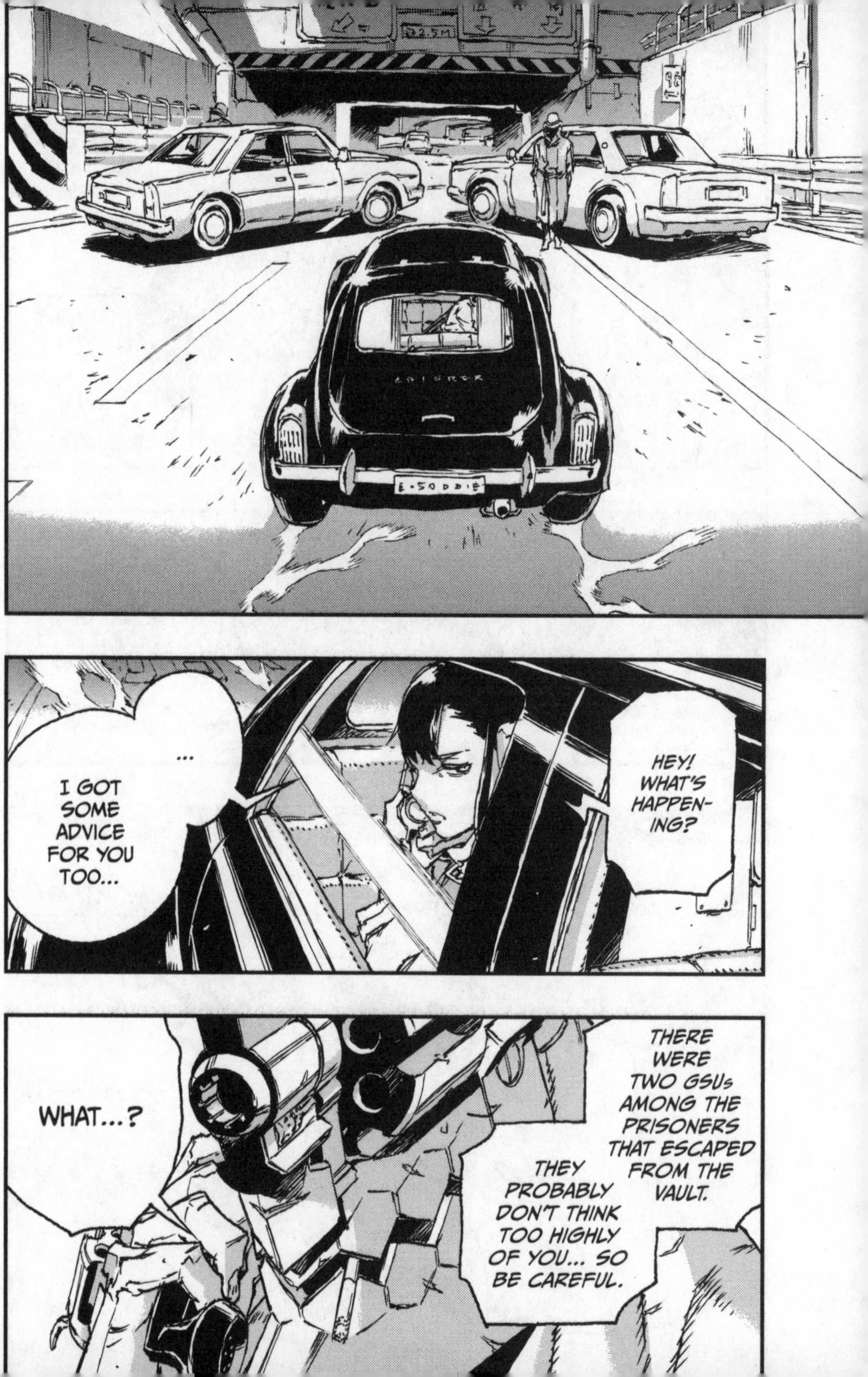
HEY! WHAT'S HAPPENING?
... I GOT SOME ADVICE FOR YOU TOO...
THERE WERE TWO GSUs AMONG THE PRISONERS THAT ESCAPED FROM THE VAULT.
THEY PROBABLY DON'T THINK TOO HIGHLY OF YOU... SO BE CAREFUL.
WHAT...?

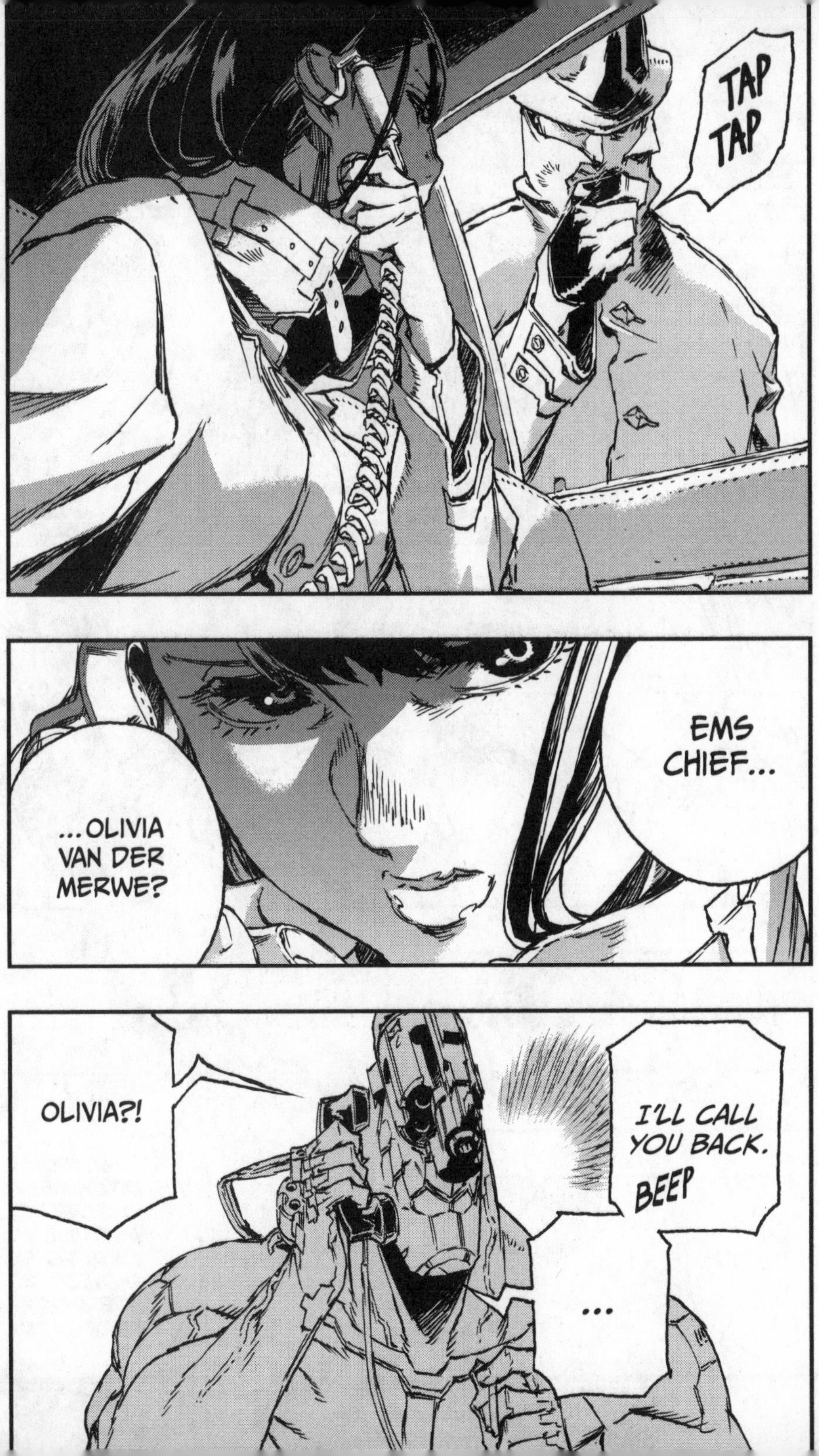
TAP TAP
EMS CHIEF...
...OLIVIA VAN DER MERWE?
I'LL CALL YOU BACK.
BEEP
OLIVIA?!
...

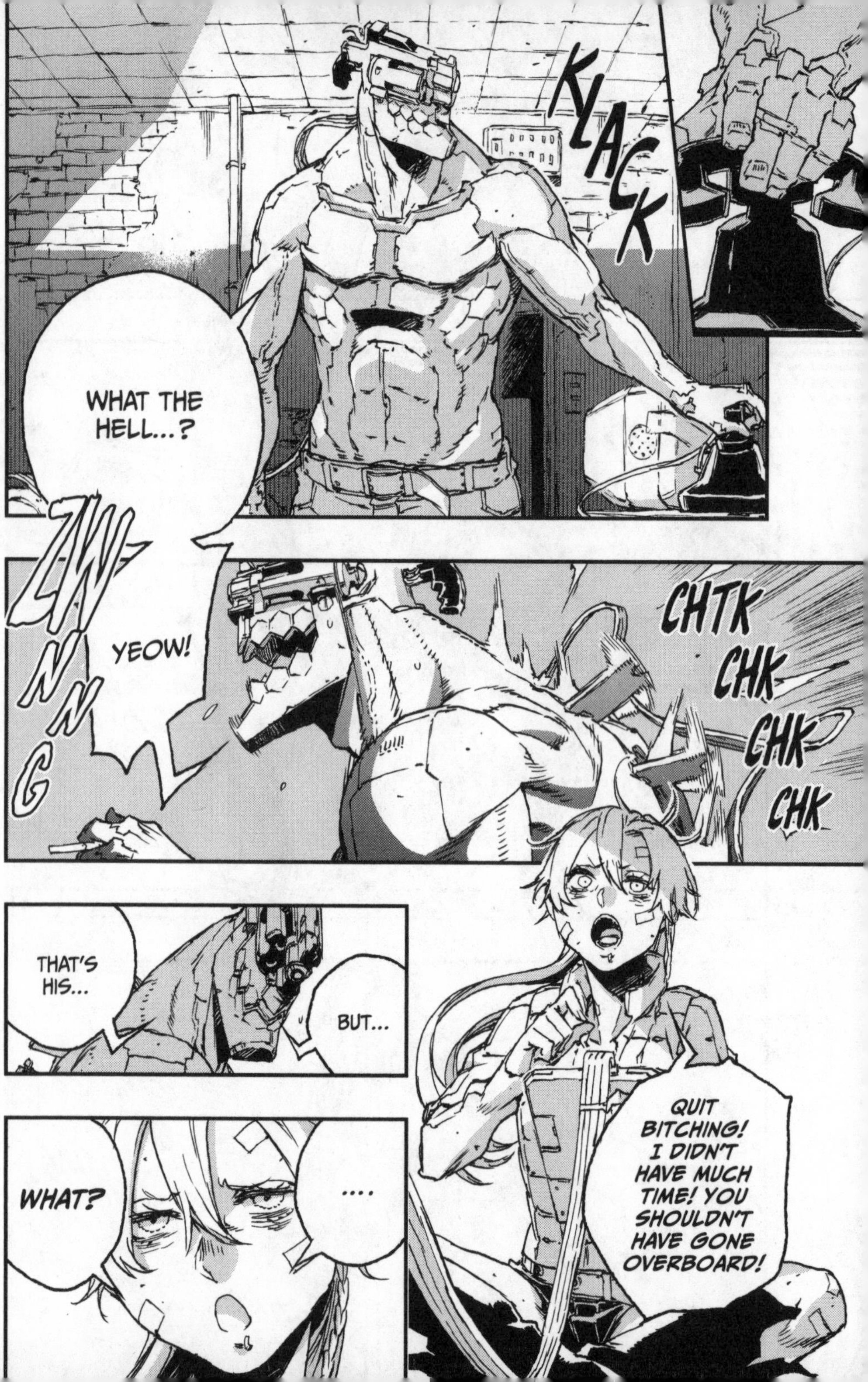
KLACK
WHAT THE HELL...?
CHTK CHK CHK CHK
YEOW!
ZWNNNG
QUIT BITCHING! I DIDN'T HAVE MUCH TIME! YOU SHOULDN'T HAVE GONE OVERBOARD!
THAT'S HIS...
BUT...
....
WHAT?

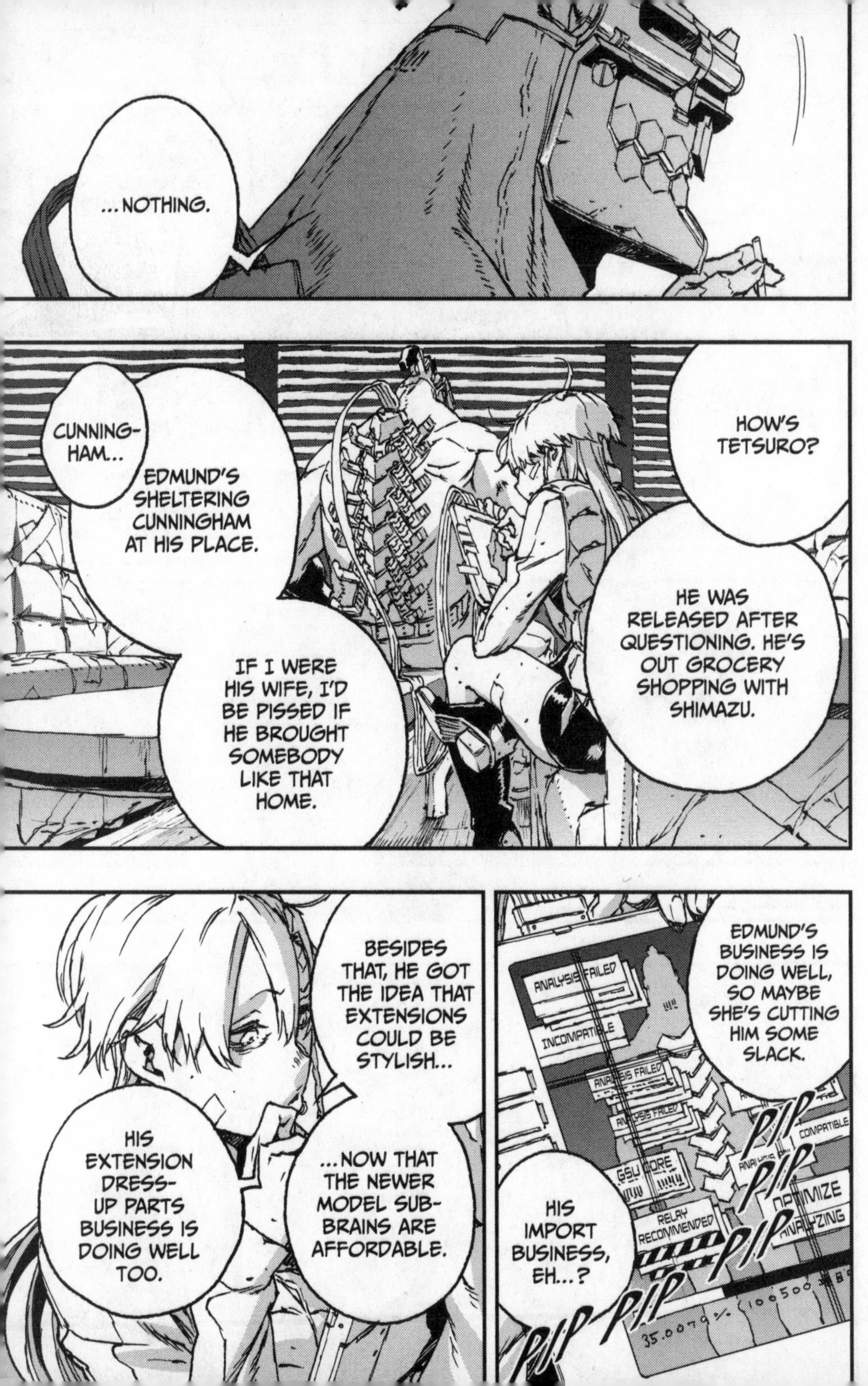
...NOTHING.
HOW'S TETSURO?
HE WAS RELEASED AFTER QUESTIONING. HE'S OUT GROCERY SHOPPING WITH SHIMAZU.
CUNNING-HAM...
EDMUND'S SHELTERING CUNNINGHAM AT HIS PLACE.
IF I WERE HIS WIFE, I'D BE PISSED IF HE BROUGHT SOMEBODY LIKE THAT HOME.
EDMUND'S BUSINESS IS DOING WELL, SO MAYBE SHE'S CUTTING HIM SOME SLACK.
ANALYSIS FAILED
INCOMPATIBLE
ANALYSIS FAILED
ANALYSIS FAILED
COMPATIBLE
GSU CORE
OPTIMIZE
ANALYZING
RELAY RECOMMENDED
PIP PIP PIP PIP PIP PIP PIP
HIS IMPORT BUSINESS, EH...?
BESIDES THAT, HE GOT THE IDEA THAT EXTENSIONS COULD BE STYLISH...
...NOW THAT THE NEWER MODEL SUB-BRAINS ARE AFFORDABLE.
HIS EXTENSION DRESS-UP PARTS BUSINESS IS DOING WELL TOO.

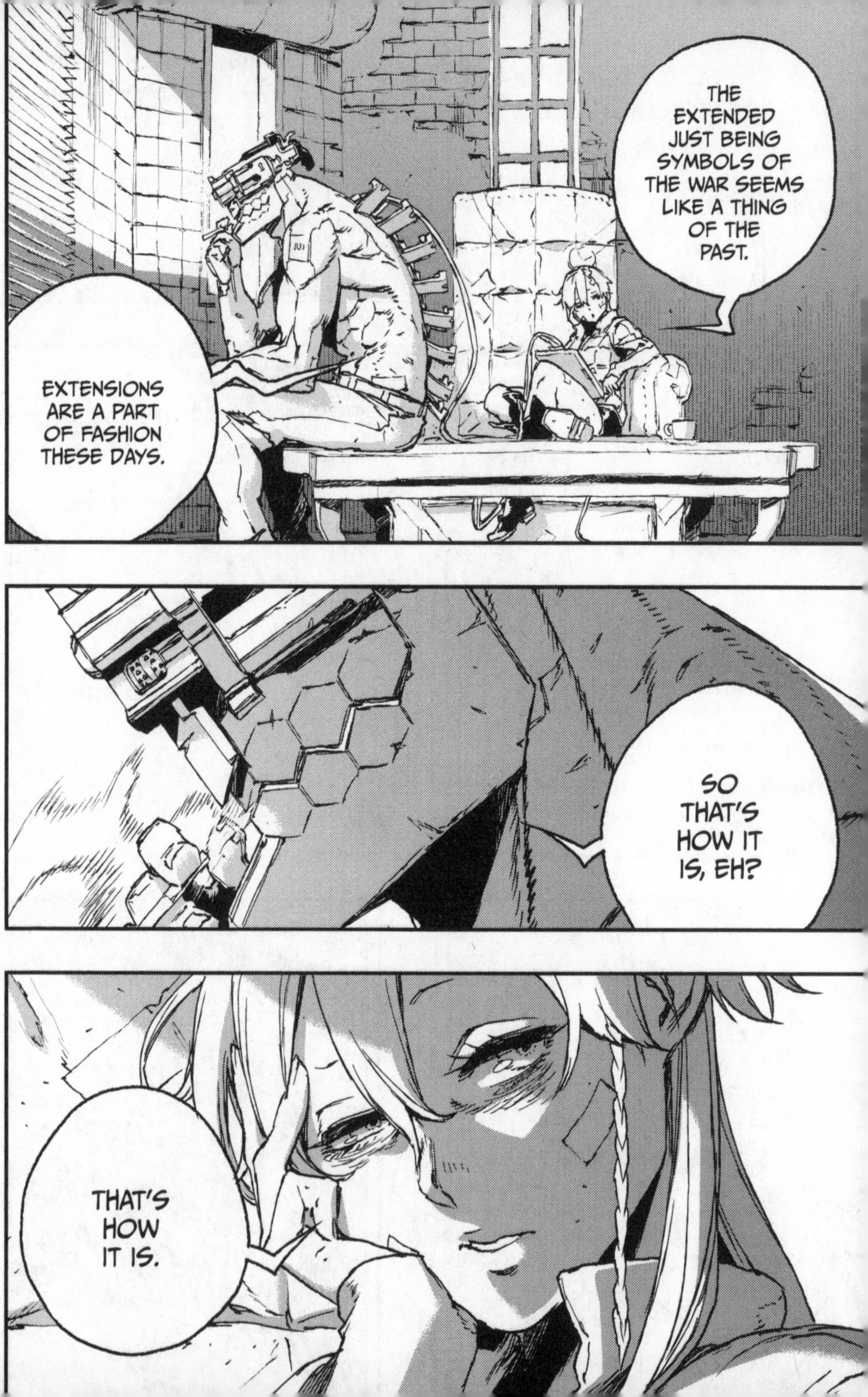
THE EXTENDED JUST BEING SYMBOLS OF THE WAR SEEMS LIKE A THING OF THE PAST.
EXTENSIONS ARE A PART OF FASHION THESE DAYS.
SO THAT'S HOW IT IS, EH?
THAT'S HOW IT IS.

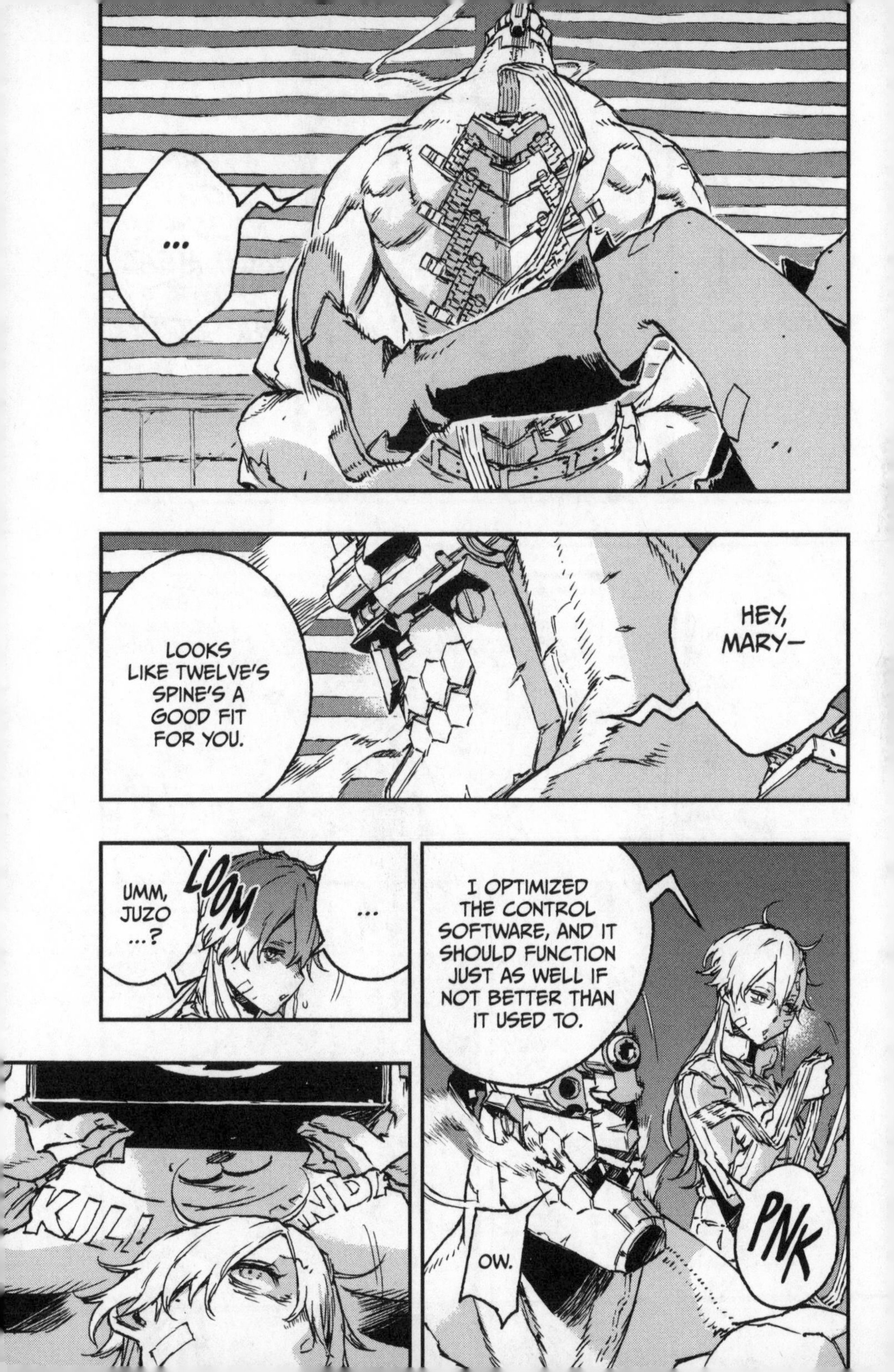
...
HEY, MARY—
LOOKS LIKE TWELVE'S SPINE'S A GOOD FIT FOR YOU.
I OPTIMIZED THE CONTROL SOFTWARE, AND IT SHOULD FUNCTION JUST AS WELL IF NOT BETTER THAN IT USED TO.
PNK
OW.
...
LOOM
UMM, JUZO ...?

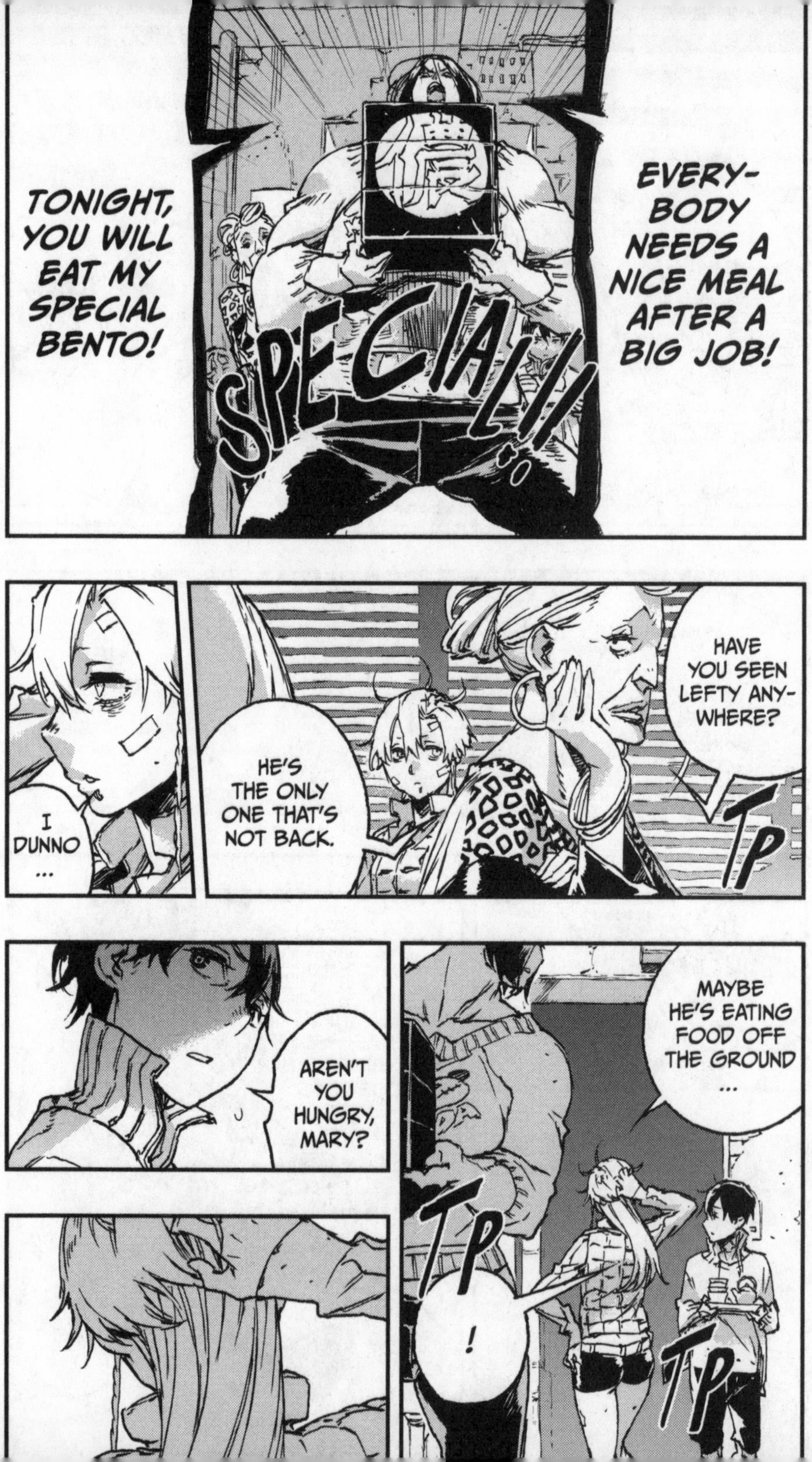
EVERY-BODY NEEDS A NICE MEAL AFTER A BIG JOB!
TONIGHT, YOU WILL EAT MY SPECIAL BENTO!
SPECIAL!!
HAVE YOU SEEN LEFTY ANY-WHERE?
TP
HE'S THE ONLY ONE THAT'S NOT BACK.
I DUNNO ...
MAYBE HE'S EATING FOOD OFF THE GROUND ...
TP
!
TP
AREN'T YOU HUNGRY, MARY?

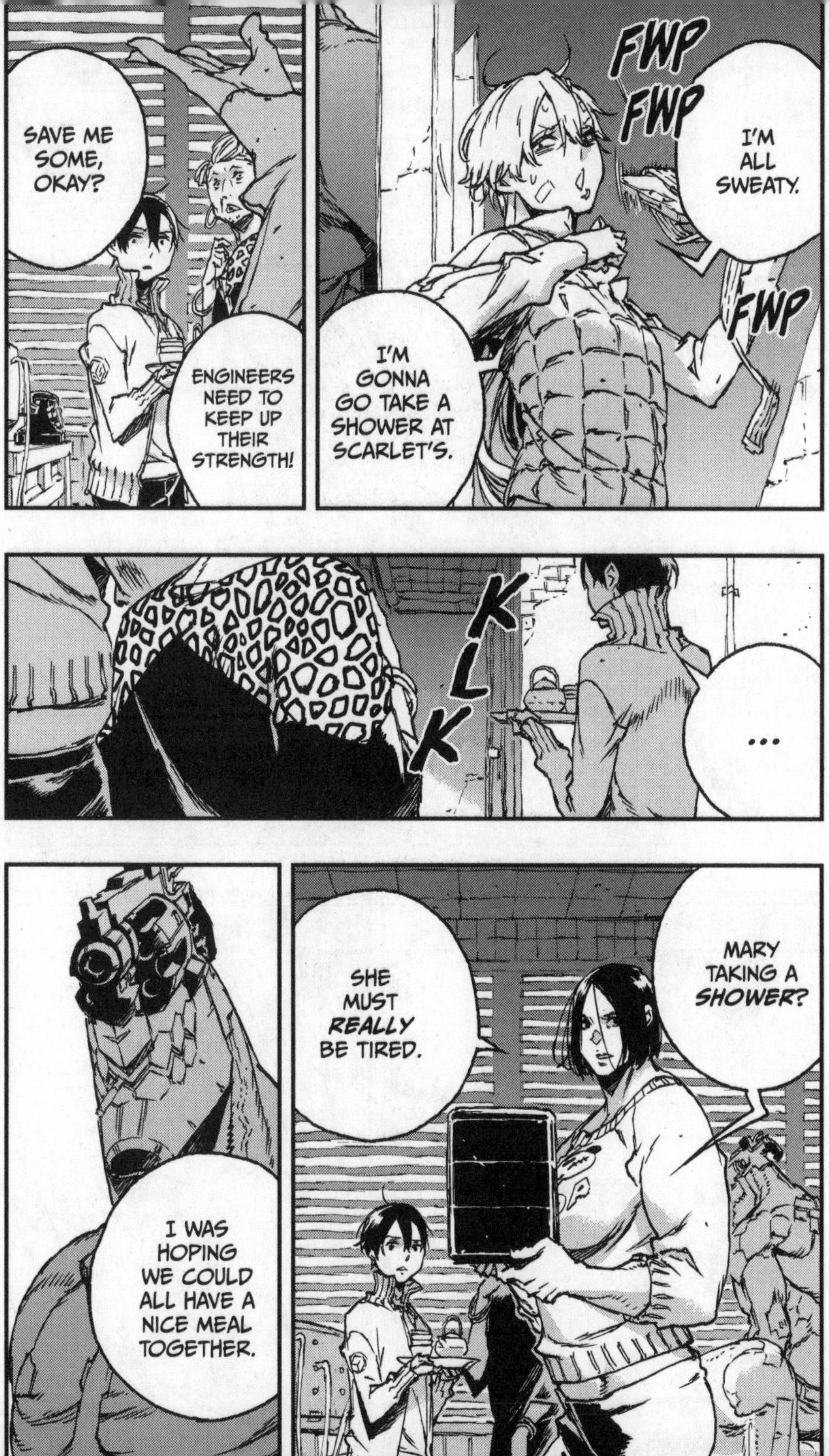
FWP
FWP
I'M ALL SWEATY.
FWP
I'M GONNA GO TAKE A SHOWER AT SCARLET'S.
SAVE ME SOME, OKAY?
ENGINEERS NEED TO KEEP UP THEIR STRENGTH!
KLK
...
MARY TAKING A *SHOWER*?
SHE MUST *REALLY* BE TIRED.
I WAS HOPING WE COULD ALL HAVE A NICE MEAL TOGETHER.

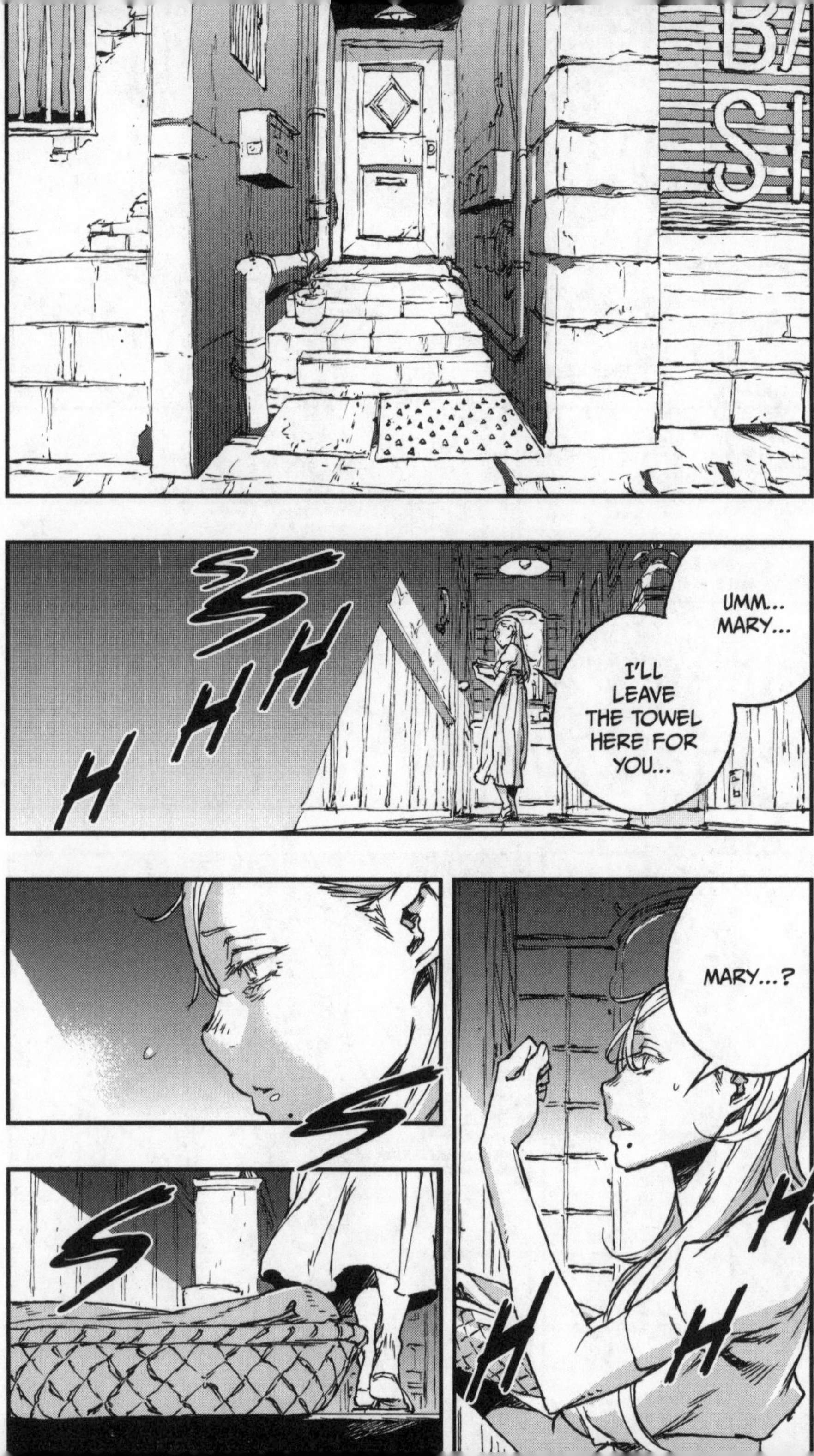
UMM... MARY...
I'LL LEAVE THE TOWEL HERE FOR YOU...
SSHHHH
MARY...?
SHHH
SS

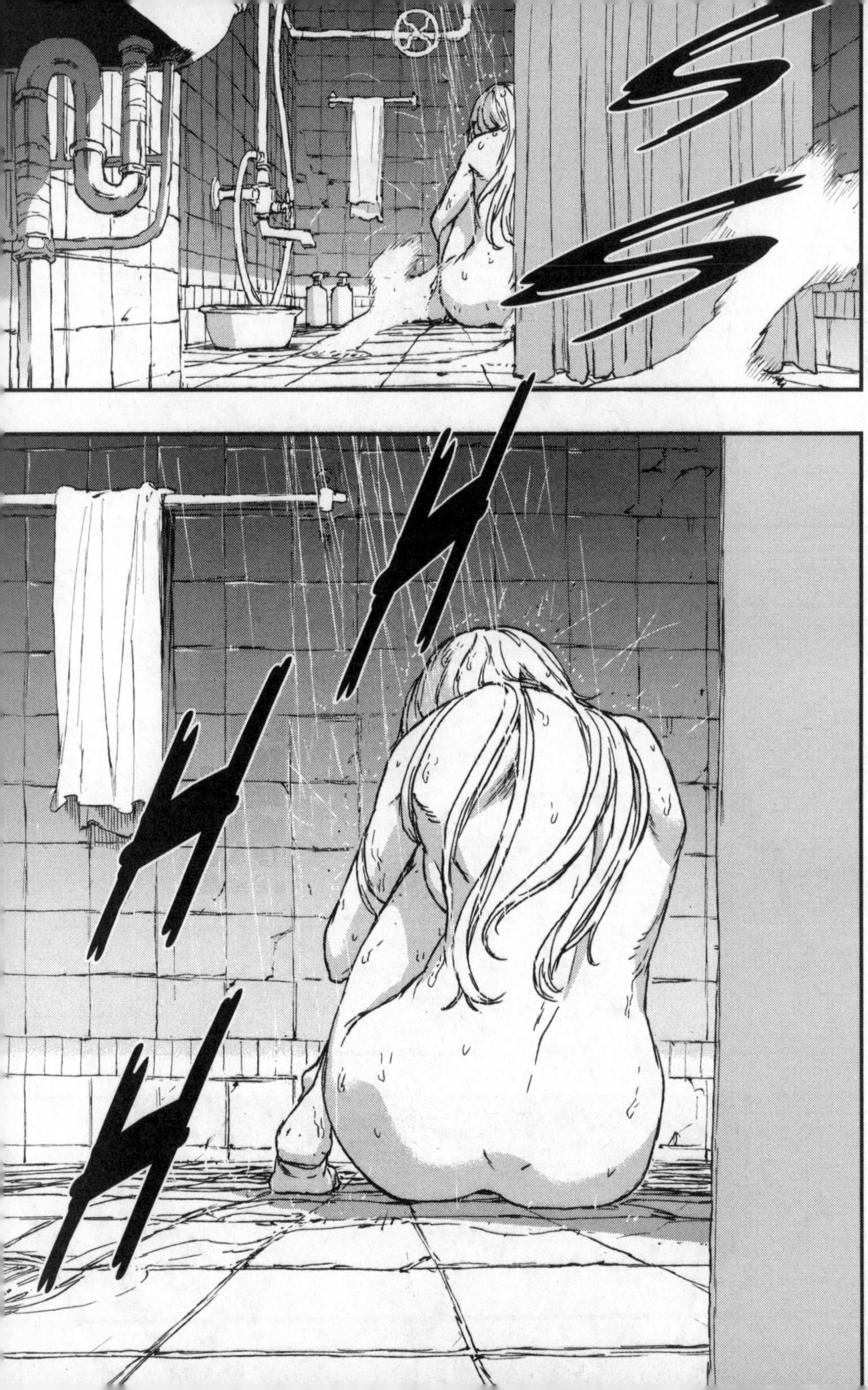
SSHHH

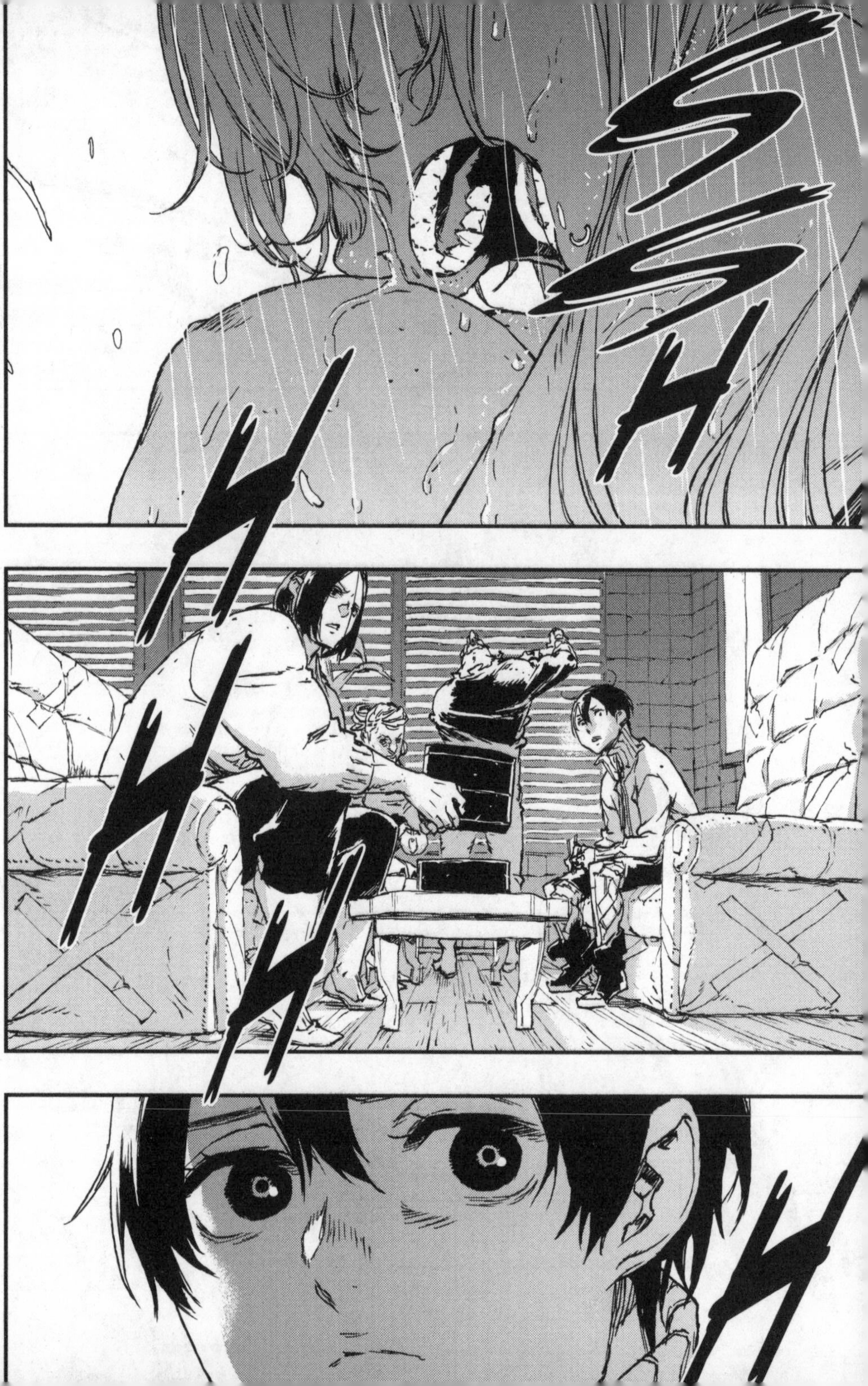
SSHHHHHH

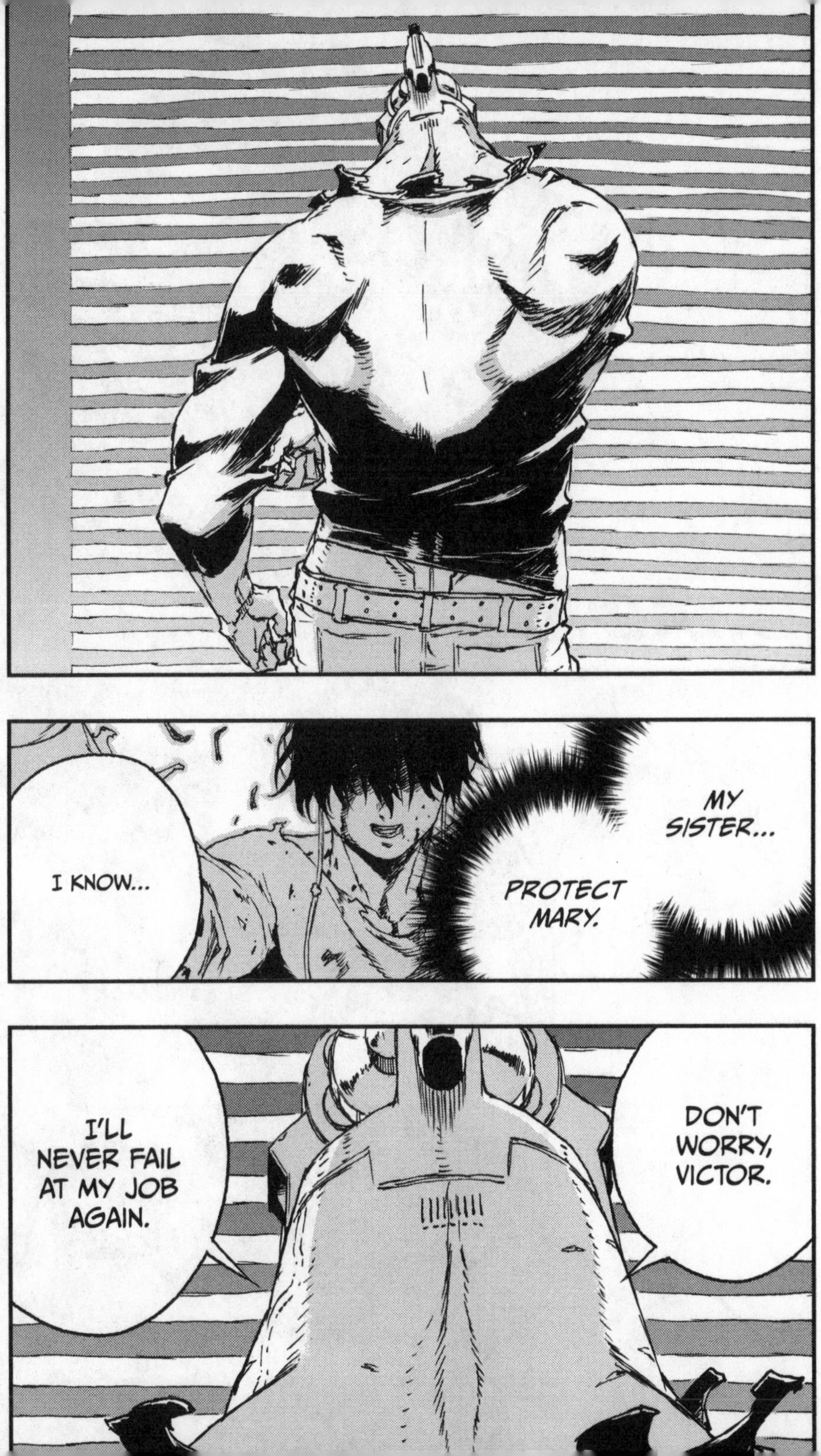
MY SISTER...
PROTECT MARY.
I KNOW...
DON'T WORRY, VICTOR.
I'LL NEVER FAIL AT MY JOB AGAIN.

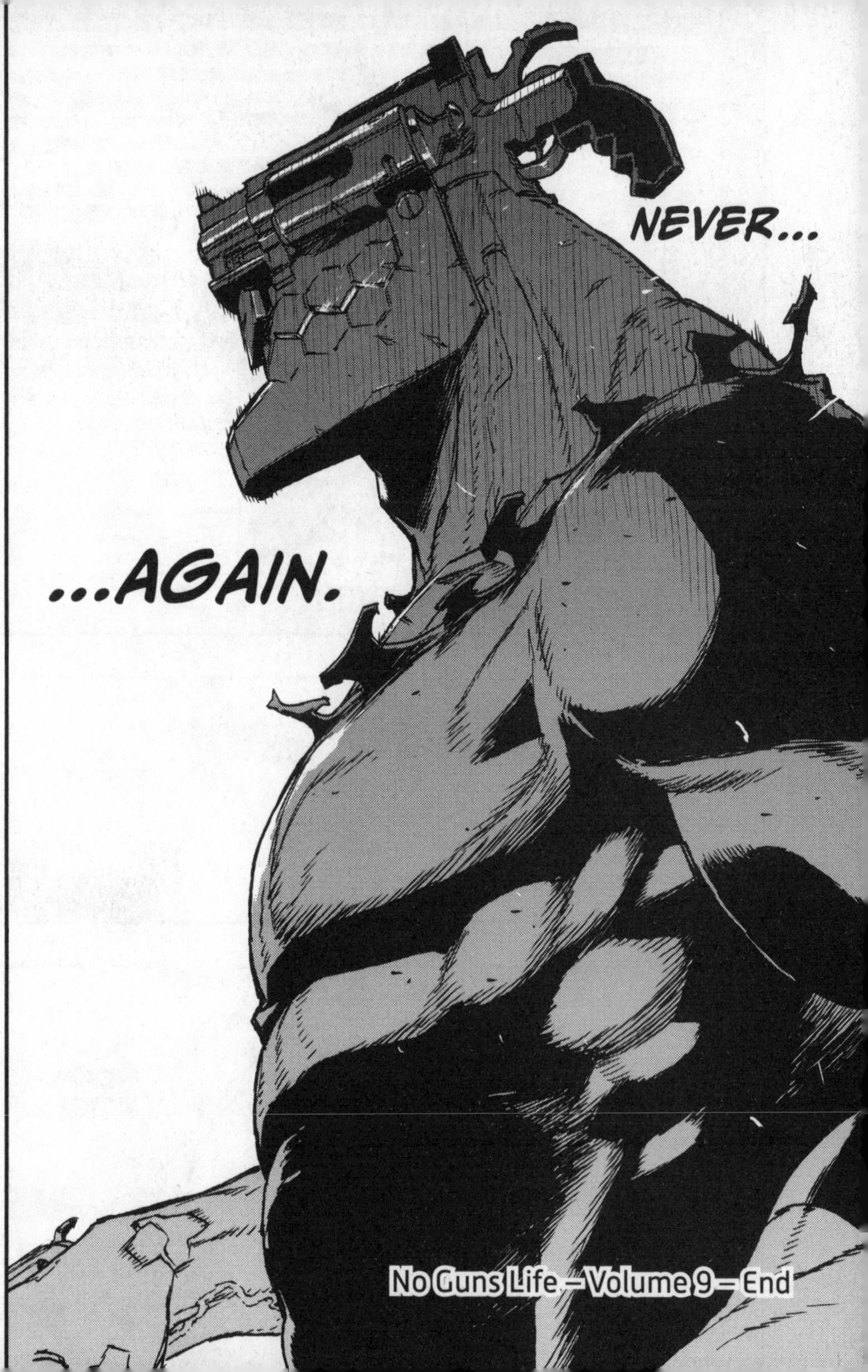
NEVER...
...AGAIN.
No Guns Life —Volume 9— End

NO GUNS
LIFE

Thank you for your time

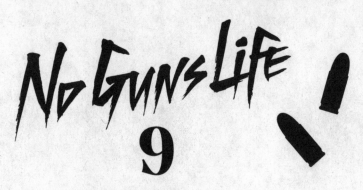

No Guns Life

9

STORY AND ART BY
TASUKU KARASUMA

VIZ SIGNATURE EDITION

TRANSLATION Joe Yamazaki
ENGLISH ADAPTATION Stan!
TOUCH-UP ART & LETTERING Evan Waldinger
DESIGN Shawn Carrico
EDITOR Mike Montesa

NO · GUNS · LIFE © 2014 by Tasuku Karasuma
All rights reserved.
First published in Japan in 2014 by SHUEISHA Inc., Tokyo.
English translation rights arranged by SHUEISHA Inc.

The stories, characters and incidents mentioned
in this publication are entirely fictional.

Printed in Canada

Published by VIZ Media, LLC
P.O. Box 77010
San Francisco, CA 94107

10 9 8 7 6 5 4 3 2 1
First printing, March 2021

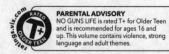

PARENTAL ADVISORY
NO GUNS LIFE is rated T+ for Older Teen
and is recommended for ages 16 and
up. This volume contains violence, strong
language and adult themes.